MW01295039

FINAL ARGUMENT

An inquiry into the torture and murder of Mac and Muff Graham, occurring on Palmyra Island August 1974, perpetrated by Buck Walker and Stephanie Stearns and subsequent murder trial of Stephanie Stearns, revealed in the New York Times best seller, "And the Sea Will Tell," written by Vincent Bugliosi and Bruce Henderson.

Final Argument reviews the questionable trial tactics of renown trial attorney Vincent Bugliosi set forth "And The Sea Will Tell". This examination is supplemented by the court reporter's trial transcript.

COPYRIGHT

ISBN 978-1505721768

IN MEMORIAM
H. WINSTON HATHAWAY,
FRIEND AND MENTOR

(Hathaway, Latimer, Clink, and Robb, circa 1960, Muskegon, Michigan)

If You Can't Dazzle 'em with Brilliance,

Then Baffle 'em With Bullshit!

(Trial Lawyer's Creed)

TABLE OF CONTENTS

INTRODUCTION (p.15)

DRAMATIS PERSONAE (p. 20)

> Malcolm Graham *(Mac)*
> Eleanor Lavern Edington Graham (Muff)
> Stephanie K. Stearns , (aka Jennifer Jenkins, Susan Mallet,
>   Stephanie Allen, and Others)
> Wesley Duane Walker, (aka Wesley Buck Walker,
> Buck Walker, Roy Allen, Sean O' Dougal, Frank Wolf, and
>   Others.)
> Pseudonyms

THE SANDS OF PALMYRA (p.24)

FANNING ISLAND (p. 27)

DAS BOOT — The Ship That Launched a Thousand Lies. (p.29)

> Birth of the Iola (Stearns' Version)
> Other Possibilities
> Stearns Lies about Meeting Walker
> Mehaffy Clarifies
> Elderly and Leaking a Hell of a Lot
> Stearns Pontificates
> Babbling Alway

Fasteners and Things That Go Bump in the Night
Gear
Bilgewater

SEAWORTHINESS OF THE IOLA (p. 60)

Stranded on Palmyra.
Mac Opines From His Watery Grave

PRINCESS STEPHANIE THE NAVIGATOR (p. 66)

Leisure Sailing
Flunking Math
Going to the Dogs
On Again, Off Again, Round Again Finnegan
Experienced Hands
Warped Speed
Blind Leading the Blind
Close But No Cigar

ISLAND LIFE (p. 90)

Arrival of Defendants
Arrival of the Grahams
Edwin and Marilyn Pollock
Curtis Shoemaker
Relationship Between Grahams and Defendants
Other Opinions
Rosencrans and Guildenstern
Crossed Wires

BEATING WINDWARD (p. 122)

   Wheeler Opines
   Gentlemen Never Sail to Windward
   All You Have to Do is Tack
   Leeway
   Steering Error
   Jib Sail Alone
   Two Knot Current

LOG OF THE IOLA (p. 130)

   Daylight Saving Time
   July 1974
   Palmyra Dreaming (and Drooling)
   Shoemaker's Message
   Into the Vortex
   August 23rd
   Battery Charging
   Stearns Misspeaks
   Down the Hatch
   New Math
   Unforced Errors
   Swabbies All
   Sleep Over on the 29th

LOG — AUGUST 30, 1974 (p. 167)

   August 30th

Close By
Up In Smoke
Oops!
Selective Hearing
Time Out of Joint
Stearns Disagrees (With Herself)
Bugliosi Battens Down the Hatch

DEATH OF THE GRAHAMS (p.187)

Murder of Mac Graham
Murder and Torture of Muff Graham

RETURN TO HAWAII (p. 194)

Detention and Arrest of Stearns
Botched C.S.I.

ERRANT SWORDFISH — Differing Accounts (p. 203)

Version One — Book
Version Two — Stearns' Murder Trial Transcript
Version Three — Inter-Island Encounter
Version Four — Suicidal Marlin
Version Five — Walker Pipes Up
Stearns Tutors Enoki
Apple Bobbing Time
Lying Larry Begs to Differ
The One That Got Away

TRIAL OF STEPHANIE K. STEARNS FOR THEFT OF THE SEA WIND (p. 222)

TRIAL OF WESLEY DUANE WALKER FOR THEFT OF THE SEA WIND (p. 223)

SHARON JORDAN DISCOVERS REMAINS OF MUFF GRAHAM (p. 224)

TRIAL OF WESLEY DUANE WALKER FOR MURDER OF MUFF GRAHAM. (p.225)

TRIAL STEPHANIE K. STEARNS FOR THE MURDER OF MUFF GRAHAM. (p. 225)

Vincent Bugliosi
Pretrial Considerations
Calculated Risk

EXPERT WITNESSES (p. 230)

Douglas Uberlaker
Dr. Boyd Stephens
William Tobin, Metallurgist
Dr. Oliver Harris
Ken White

EDWIN AND MARILYN POLLOCK (p. 237)

The Bug Melts Down
Knee-Deep in Water
Ten Dollars To Her Name
You Don't Mess With Popeye
Testimony of Marilyn Pollock
Accusations of Bias

CURTIS SHOEMAKER (p. 282)

Shoemaker Informed Edwin Pollock About His Final
Conversation With Mac Graham on October 30, 1974
Shoemaker Testimony at the Murder Trial of Buck Walker
Shoemaker Testimony at Stearns' Murder Trial
Bugliosi Blunders About the Courtroom
FBI Special Agent Hilton Lui Affirms Shoemaker Testimony
Associated Press Sides with Shoemaker

F.B.I. SPECIAL AGENT CALVIN SHISHIDO. (p. 309)

Shishido's 302 Report (October 29, 1974)
No Golf Today
Lagoon Blues
Stearns the Spinmeister
Shishido Stands His Ground
Where The Zodiac Was Found

BRUCE BENSON — THE MAN WHO WASN'T THERE. (p. 327)

Jail House Rock
Lost in Transmission

Under the Bamboozle Bush
The Benson Stipulation
Unmitigated Disaster

CHARACTER EVIDENCE (p. 340)

Getting Away With Murder
Deborah Noland
Rick Schulz
Leilah Burns
Lawrence Seltzer

FALSUS IN UNO, FALSUS IN OMNIBUS (p. 359)
(False in One, False in All)

Federal Jury Instruction
California Jury Instruction
Hall of Mirrors
You Can't Hide Your Lying Eyes
Sailing In Disguise
High Seas Joy Ride
Bucky Needs Protection
Weasel Words and Wiggle Room
Tangled Webs
Puppet Master
What I Did, I Did For Love
Heir Apparent
Home Coming — Another Version

LOKAHI (p. 389)

    Of One Mind
    Chumped Again

PRINCE OF TIDES (p. 396)

    Slackwater and the Rule of Twelfths
    John Bryden
    Bugliosi Sounds Retreat

JUDGE SAMUEL P. KING (p. 405)

    Judge King has Questions
    Thumb on the Scale

ENOKI SUMMATION (p. 409)

    The Uncertain Trumpet
    Ambuscade
    Leaving Well Enough Alone
    Ignorance Prevails
    *I*nexperience
    Enoki's Conundrum
    Clueless in San Francisco
    Too Little, Too Late
    Mea Culpa

BUGLIOSI SUMMATION (p. 431)

Bugliosi Suborns Perjury

The Bug Melts Down

Bugliosi Erroneously Waives Hearsay Objection

Half-Truth Lie re Seaworthiness of Iola

Half-Truth Lie Supports Stearns' Testimony

Stevens' Testimony Misconstrued

Bugliosi Impeaches Client

Benson Stipulation Slams Prosecution

State of Mind Ruse

Sufficiency of the Evidence

Cause of Death

Forensics on the Sea Wind

Hitching a Ride

Disposal of Muff's Remains

Ballast

We Are All Liars

Waxing Eloquent

Sleight of Hand

The Bookie

Baffle'em With Bull Shit

Bugliosi Concedes A Point

Tattletale

FINAL ARGUMENT (p. 476)

Dinner at Eight

Stearns Asserts Ownership

The Alchemist

For Whom the Diary Was Written

Consciousness of Guilt

One Step Ahead of the Chump
Method Acting
Speculations
Jekyl or Hyde
Bucky the Pirate Man
Taxidermy
Out of His League
Future Prospects
Poison
The Contrivance
Atonement and Absolution

FLOTSAM AND JETSAM (p. 505)

Recovering the Remains of Mac Graham
Just Supposing

CONCLUSION (p. 511)

After   Thoughts

INTRODUCTION

This book is an investigation into the 1974 murder of Mac and Muff Graham occurring on the island of Palmyra located approximately 970 nautical miles south of Hawaii. It is a tale inescapably interwoven with wooden sailing ships and the sea. Found within it's pages is an examination of courtroom tactics of a befuddled prosecutorial team facing an aggressive defense team spearheaded by a determined, yet confused, Vincent Bugliosi.

In 1982 Vincent Bugliosi, (Bugliosi) prosecutor of Charles Manson, now a criminal defense attorney, readied for battle on behalf of his client Stephanie K. Stearns (Stearns) who was accused of murdering Eleanor (Muff) Graham on Palmyra Island in 1974. He was assisted by attorney Leonard Weinglass (Weinglass) of the Chicago Seven fame.

In preparation for the defense of Stearns, Bugliosi observed the trial of her co-defendant Wesley Duane Walker (Buck) which preceded that of Stearns by several months. Walker was successfully prosecuted by Assistant U.S. Attorney Elliot Enoki (Enoki) with Judge Samuel King (King) presiding.) In June of 1985 after two weeks of trial Walker was found guilty of murder in the first degree of Eleanor "Muff" Graham, the jury deliberating approximately one and one half hours. (p. 263)

As thorough as Bugliosi was in his pre-trial preparation he made little effort to understand what it means to sail a small vessel on the dangerous and ever-challenging sea. With the exception of a

15

study of Palmyra tidal flow his knowledge of the sea and sailing was extremely limited as he acknowledges. (p. 355)

Prosecutor Enoki had even less interest in sailing or the traditions and customs recognized and accepted by those that put their lives at risk every time they weigh anchor and hoist the mains'l. This lack of knowledge and failure to include experienced sailors in the inner prosecutorial circle was a significant factor in the failed prosecution of Stearns. Had Enoki taken the time to discuss various aspects of the evidence with experienced sailors, he could have broken through maze of lies issued by Stearns.

The great irony found in Stearns' prosecution is that the evidence of her guilt was present in abundance, but neither side, including witnesses, attorneys, jury and Judge, could comprehend it. So too, the mystery reading public was myopic in failing to notice Stearns' role in the murders after it was detailed in Bugliosi's and Bruce Henderson's book, "And the Sea Will Tell" (ATSWT).

Time and again unable to decipher the clues, Enoki stipulated his case away, failed to notice crucial details, failed to support his witnesses by making timely objections, failed to do his homework. No doubt he was relying on the assistance of Judge Samuel King (King) to further his cause expecting him to "put his thumb" on the scale of justice and intervene as he had done in the prosecution of Walker.

Assistance from Judge King did not materialize. There were several factors at play in the refusal of King to reprise his role and assist Enoki as he had in the prosecution of Walker. King had watched this drama play out before him on several occasions and had been taken in by Stearns' easy manner and appearance of innocence; a pose she had prepared for all her life which was facilitated by her sociopathic personality. The defense was also assisted greatly by

16

Enoki's confusion and his failure to enunciate a plausible narrative. At times during the trial Enoki contradicted himself in the presentation of the evidence, apologized for his lack of preparation, stipulated his case away and failed to explain to the jury Stearns' role in the murder.

The primary source of the information set forth in this inquiry are various original trial transcripts and Bugliosi's and Bruce Henderson's book, "And The Sea Will Tell". (ATSWT) Not available in 1991 are the useful sources Wikipedia and Google wherein the causal reader can visit Palmyra courtesy of Google Maps and the other islands in question and form his or her own opinions about Fanning Island, Palmyra Island and many questions re sailing and ocean phenomena. For those interested in legal issues, there are numerous cases stemming from the actions of Stearns and Walker, which are cited and easily found by use of Google search.

U.S. v. Walker, 575 F.2d 209 (9th cir. 1978); U.S. v. Stearns, 550 F 2d 1167 (9th cir. 1977); U.S. v. Walker and Stearns, 707 F2d 391 (9th cir. 1983); U.S. v. Walker, 802 F. 2d 1106 (9th cir.1986), U.S. v. Stearns, 84-0546-02.

Bugliosi and Henderson's book includes numerous facts for the reader to consider that were not offered to the jury during the trial of Stearns. These facts shed new light on the evidence; e.g., on page 137 Mac's mother thinks Mac took four or five thousand dollars in small bills to use as his cruising funds. (This fact apparently was not available to the jury or known to Edwin Pollock at the time of trial. If Pollock been aware that Mac had substantial cruising funds comprised of many small bills, he might easily have surmised Stearns was flushing Mac's cruising funds down the toilet when she used the bathroom at the yacht club to avoid a conviction for grand theft.)

17

"And the Sea Will Tell" (ATSWT) is an extended presentation of Bugliosi's summation in the trial of the United States v. Stephanie Stearns. (84-0546-02)

"Final Argument" is a rebuttal to Buglioi's summation written by a reasonably experienced sailor and trial lawyer. This book endeavors to take the available evidence and interpret it in a new light — a belated presentation on behalf of the tortured and tormented Mac and Muff Graham that sets the record straight.

From time to time I attempt to pull back the curtain allowing the non-lawyer to have a glimpse of the real world of the trial lawyer, (as does Bugliosi, with astonishing candor). While not always in agreement with his advice re the practice of trial law, nonetheless he frequently gives away hard earned knowledge of trial tactics which few "heavyweights" are willing to do.

Prosecutor Enoki lost a "slam dunk" case. However, his weak performance was not the sole cause of defeat. All the major players in the trial contributed to this result. The hard hitting, battle tested, Vincent Bulgiosi, successful prosecutor of the Manson clan; the gullible, well intended, but biased, Judge King seduced by Stephanie Stearns alter ego, "Little Miss Puffer"; prosecutor Elliot Enoki unable to grasp the essence of his case unprepared and outgunned by Bugliosi; and most formidable, the lying murderess Stephanie K. Stearns who, time and again, changes testimony in mid-air. A liar so facile and prolific the recipient of her lies becomes overwhelmed to the point where the brain becomes numb from the onslaught.

I have included substantial detail about sailing a small boat on the ocean and the dangers inherent in such activity. Some may find this boring, but it is essential information to enable the reader to form an opinion about the seaworthiness of the Iola. *Seaworthiness of the Iola is the single most important factual consideration to be determined.* If the Iola was not seaworthy and Stearns was aware of this fact, then the question arises; what did Stearns and Walker intend sailing a derelict vessel to Palmyra Island, 970 nautical miles south of Hawaii with no possibility of return? There can be only one logical conclusion to this question — she and her partner in crime, Wesley "Buck" Walker, (Walker) sailed south to Palmyra intent on seizing a seaworthy sailboat and murdering her crew.

Above the cacophony and din of battle one hears the voice of Mac Graham. His final words and those of his messenger Curtis Shoemaker (Shoemaker) go unheeded, ignored by the very authorities sworn to seek justice on his behalf and on behalf his horribly brutalized wife Eleanor "Muff" Graham who died an unspeakable death at the hands of Stearns and Walker.

I took the time, trouble and expense to review the original Court Reporter's Transcripts of Stearns murder trial found in the National Archives in San Francisco. Where relevant, I quote verbatim — trial testimony not found in Bugliosi's and Henderson's book. Surprisingly, the court reporter's transcript is often at odds with Bugliosi's best selling account. This clash of transcripts is most evident in Bugliosi's version of the cross-examination of Edwin Pollock (Bernard Leonard) and that of Curt Shoemaker.

Notations from Stearns' original court reporter's trial transcript differ from those referencing excerpts from Bugliosi's book, "And The Sea Will Tell," (ATSWT) Testimony from Stearns murder trial transcript include the volume number and page number. (Vol. __, p. __). Matters quoted from "And The Sea Will Tell" published by Norton, First Edition, 1991, are referenced by page number only. (p. __)

DRAMATIS PERSONAE

Malcolm Graham III   (Mac Graham)

Born into a patrician east coast sailing family, Mac Graham was introduced to the sea at an early age.   He was handy with his hands and had a fascination with machinery. Trained in engineering at General Motors,76 he left, determined to become a "blue water" sailor.   In his early thirties a modest inheritance permitted him to purchase a thirty-eight foot Angelman ketch. The Sea Wind reflected his interest in things mechanical to the point where he installed a small machine shop in the forecastle. He also made numerous other improvements to the boat.   In 1961 he married Eleanor Laverne Edington (Muff) in La Paz, Mexico. Thereafter, they departed on a six year round the world voyage. At age forty-three, the time of his death, he was an experienced blue water sailor and the voyage to Palmyra, after a short stop over in Hawaii, seemingly offered few challenges. (pp. 23-8)

Eleanor Lavern Edington Graham (Muff Graham)

Muffin was a name of endearment given by Mac to his wife and faithful companion. Muff, a dutiful wife and reluctant sailor accompanied her husband around the world as he sailed his 38 foot carvel planked ketch.   At the time of marriage to Mac she was twenty-nine, he thirty.   With no enthusiasm for long distance voyaging, nonetheless she was an expert in the art of provisioning a small sailing vessel for long voyages anticipating what food would be necessary for a pleasant voyage. (p. 26)

She carefully stored each item noting the quantity and location of storage knowing it is one thing to purchase the right stores in the correct amount, but finding and accessing them once brought aboard the ship and packed away was quite another matter. Not one to take the wheel in a blow as keeper of the galley she was a valuable asset. It was her planning and skill in the galley that brought all the comforts of home and the admiration of other sailors when in distant ports. Few sailors had planned their future menus with the care and forethought provided by Muff.

Not much of an adventurer she would have been quite happy to limit her sailing to the pristine waters of the Channel Islands off the Southern California coast with occasional trips to Santa Barbara, Monterey, and San Francisco.   When Mac revealed his plans to sail to Palmyra, a small deserted island a thousand miles south of Hawaii and stay for months she was unhappy with the prospect but agreed to accompany him.

Shortly after the voyage was announced she began having nightmares and premonitions about the voyage. In the past she had felt uncomfortable with the prospect of voyaging, but these feelings and dreams about Palmyra were far more intense and extreme, they foretold doom and death. To combat her distress she obtained a prescription for tranquilizers from her doctor.   Full of anxiety and doubt concerning the upcoming voyage Muff consulted a spiritualist she trusted. The spiritualist advised Muff *"Something terrible will happen"*. (pp. 27-30, 42-6)

Stephanie Stearns (aka Jennifer Jenkins, Susan Mallett, Stephanie Allen, and Others Unknown.)

Stephanie Stearns (Stearns) passed her childhood years in and around the city of New York. Her parents divorced and at age ten her mother moved to the Los Angles area. It is alleged she demonstrated a certain brightness and rebelliousness causing her to drop out of high school. Later she returned to school and allegedly obtained an AA degree from a local junior college claiming to do well in psychology and math. (p. 133) After junior college she drifted about and eventually moved to Hawaii to help her uncle run a small tourist business where she waited tables and helped out wherever needed.

Prior to the theft of the Sea Wind and the murders of Mac and Muff Graham, Stearns had several run-ins with the law; two petty theft convictions (crimes of moral turpitude), a charge relating to use of marijuana and an arrest for possession and sale of MDA. Described by one of her victims, Dannel Peterson, as a hippy with a "foul mouth". Perhaps not someone most would choose as company, however there was nothing in her known background that might portend the horrors she planned and participated in on Palmyra Island concerning the murders of Mac and Muff Graham.

As any reader of "ATSWT" can observe Stearns possesses another talent she exercises nearly every time she opens her mouth....the capacity to tell the most outrageous lies. Anytime a given situation calls for specific explanation no matter the truth, she lies. An admitted perjurer, she lies constantly and compulsively throughout her trial. One cannot without corroboration from a non-biased source believe a single word coming out of her mouth. Need another more convenient version of the facts, no problem, how about this? Having taken position in the past adverse to her current needs so what? Knowing if enough lies are told she can confuse the prosecution and the jury will retreat overwhelmed by the onslaught.

Throughout the book Bugliosi reminds the reader his client is intelligent and resourceful. Yet, she feigns stupidity whenever it is in her best interest; i.e., when ignorance will extricate her from her lies and assist in winning an acquittal.

On reading ATSWT one has an overwhelming suspicion Stearns is a sociopath. A personality disorder manifesting an abnormal lack of empathy combined with strong amoral conduct masked by an ability to appear outwardly normal: a veritable good Dr. Jekyll or depraved Mr. Hyde, depending on the circumstances.

Wesley Duane Walker, (aka Wesley "Buck" Walker, Buck Walker, Roy Allen, Sean O'Dougal, Frank Wolf, and Others)

In 1972 while working for her uncle on the big island of Hawaii Stearns met Buck Walker, a con on the run, who had a five page rap sheet, served time in San Quentin for armed robbery and also a stint in a mental hospital for the criminally insane. (p. 20) Aside from hormonal attractions they shared common interests. Their subconscious minds fit like a well hewn mortise and tenon. Walker since childhood, had a dream of sailing and phantasies of piracy on the high sea: Stearns inner most thoughts reeked of violence, mayhem and murder.

Stearns fascinated with violence and men capable of committing violent acts found in Walker a mate she could dominate and bend to her will. Stearns the brighter of the two fiddled while Walker danced the tune. With overlapping needs they concocted a scheme, aided by friends, to steal a sailboat, murder it's owners and sail off into the blood drenched sunset.

Pseudonyms

(Bugliosi changed the names of certain witnesses who were involved in the trial. FBI Special Agent HILTON LUI is given the name, TOM KILGORE; EDWIN AND MARILYN POLLOCK are given the names BERNARD AND EVELYN LEONARD; RICHARD "DICKIE" MUSICK is given the name RICHARD "DICKIE" TAYLOR and his brother CARLOS MUSICK is given the name CARLOS TAYLOR.)

THE SANDS OF PALMYRA

Palmyra Island, location of the murders of Mac and Muff Graham, is a horseshoe shaped series of sixteen small islands and many more smaller islets surrounded by a vibrant coral reef. It is located approximately 960 nautical miles south, south-west of Hawaii and is part of an island chain that stretches across the Pacific Ocean for thousands of miles formerly known as the Line Islands. This chain has also been known as the Southern Gilbert Islands and most recently as the Republic of Kiribati with capital located on the island of Tarawa. The Kiribati are of Polynesian ancestry and number around one hundred thousand. Palmyra Island is a US possession and is not included in the Republic of Kiribati.

Palmyra was discovered in the late 1700s by Captain Edward Fanning. The island has a history of shipwrecks and failed enterprises. It was used by the US Navy during World War II as a base of operation.

It is estimated the total land mass of the islands comprising Palmyra is approximately two hundred twenty acres with the highest elevation scarcely more than six feet. The islands are connected by narrow land bridges and a causeway built by the Seabees who inhabited the island during WW II. During occupation by the navy numerous concrete structures were built as well as an airstrip. At high tide some sections of the causeway are two feet under water. The West lagoon is approximately 140 feet deep and well protected by the reef and islands surrounding it. Entry to the lagoon is gained by traversing a channel approximately seven hundred yards in length, expanded and dredged by the Seabees during WW II. Like many of the Line Islands, from the deck of a sailboat, it can be seen six to eight miles off. (p. 56)

Palmyra has a large mixed bird population including fairy terns, sooty terns, red footed, blue footed and masked boobies as well as other species numbering in the thousands. There are thousands of coconut trees which grow sixty to ninety feet in height. The lagoon and reefs teem with fish and aggressive black tipped sharks. There is a large population of edible land crabs and coconut crabs. The island was also inhabited by feral rats inadvertently introduced by the navy. The median temperature is 85 Degrees and the island receives on average 175 inches of rainfall each year.

Palmyra was not inhabited by any permanent residents after WW II although adventurous sailors passing by stopped from time to time. Sailing south to Palmyra from Hawaii during the sailing season is an easy voyage with following seas and favorable winds. The return trip mandates a long hard beat to windward and has a reputation for being a difficult passage. Because of the difficulty of the return trip it is not a voyage a prudent sailor undertakes lightly nor ventures without proper preparation. Currently Palmyra is administered by the Cooper family, the Nature Conservancy and the U.S. Department of the Interior. Visiting is restricted.

Palmyra topography plays an important role in exposing Stearns' lies and ascertaining the truth. ATSWT furnishes two different charts enabling the reader to have better understanding of the events that transpired on Palmyra the summer of 1974. On page 72-3 there is a chart that designates various islets and some of the buildings that played a role in the drama. The chart on page 531 shows greater detail specifying locations relevant to the murder of the Grahams.

Using the chart reference guide Buck's camp is approximately three to four-hundred yards distance from where the Iola is tied up to the dolphins and approximately 700 yards from the bathing area. The lagoon was nearly a mile in length and width. A quick search of the internet and Google bring up numerous color photos of Palmyra as well. Google maps of Palmyra clearly show the airstrip and the three small coves also noted on the map page 531.

During her murder trial, Stearns placed a small X where the Iola was secured to the pilings in the water. She also denotes Walker's camp with an X proximate to the most westerly small cove. Measuring this distance using Google technology one ascertains a length of approximately 300 to 400 yards between Walker's camp and the Iola. (One arrives at the same approximate distance using the charts supplied on pages 72-3 and 531 denoting the Iola and Walker's camp.)

If Stearns wished to visit Walker the quickest method would be to row ashore, secure the dinghy, cut through the strip of jungle near the Iola, walk to the air field, then walk in an easterly direction on the air strip to his camp, which is positioned in the jungle halfway between the air field and the lagoon. Another method would be for Stearns to row her dinghy along the shore in an easterly direction until she was adjacent to Walker's camp, secure the dinghy, and proceed on foot approximately fifty yards through the jungle to his tent. (pp. 72-3, 531)

Unfortunately, the prosecution did not insist on a detailed discussion of the layout of various buildings and areas on Cooper Island where many of the activities under discussion occurred. Such an exhibit would have assisted the jury in understanding the evidence and would have been instructive when discussing the supposed activities of defendants on the 30th of August.

FANNING ISLAND

Fanning Island plays a major role in the deception of the Grahams. Discovered by Captain Fanning in 1798, Fanning Island is now part of the Republic of Kiribati, also known as Tabuaeran. It is currently inhabited by less than two thousand Polynesians. In 1974 the island was wretchedly impoverished and still is today. At the time of the murders of Mac and Muff Graham the population was no more than a few hundred inhabitants. Sustenance for the islanders is found in coconuts, fish from the nearby waters, land crab, eggs from the seabirds, and the seabirds themselves. Fruit trees, and the dirt in which they grow, have been imported.

To this day there is no running water or electricity except for a few private generators which meet the needs of outside agencies. There exists no restaurants, bars or public restrooms. Water is drawn from wells and is not always safe for drinking.

Currently there is an on going effort by Norwegian Cruise Lines (NCL) to expand their operations in the South Pacific with a cruise ship which visits Fanning every ten days from Hawaii. It is a two day trip. On arrival of the cruise ship passengers depart in the morning for the island. NCL staff set up umbrellas, lounge chairs and temporary facilities to serve food to the guests. The cruise ship provides a temporary restaurant for passengers during the day on shore. In late afternoon passengers return to the ship which then returns to Hawaii. NCL has paid for the construction of a school house and has built a pier within the lagoon which enables transport boats to taxi back and forth from ship to shore ferrying guests for the day visit on the island.

There are no facilities to enable a cruise ship to dock. The surrounding waters are too deep to anchor, consequently the cruise ship floats off shore drifting with the tide and wind. There is no form of public transportation, but it is possible for guests to rent bicycles for a few hours. Shipboard guests give the island mixed reviews, some enjoy the primitive aspect of the island, while others are vocal in criticizing NCL for bringing them to Fanning and exposing them to the wretched third world poverty of the islanders.

In addition to the island activities relating to NCL, Fanning Island, in the past supported a trans-oceanic cable administered by the Pacific Cable Board. Several homes and shelters were built for those associated with this enterprise which ceased operation in 1963. Thereafter, the Hawaiian Oceanographic Institute used Fanning as a base to study ocean currents.

Entrance to the Fanning lagoon does not require the skill and experience of the Palmyra approach and affords protection from rough seas. However, there was little to be gained by Stearns and Walker sailing to Fanning Island. The diet offered the sailor in 1974, was essentially the same as Palmyra with the exception of fruit trees, perhaps a domestic pig, if money was available for purchase. There is no television, electricity, cell phones, vehicles, or gasoline available unlike the barrels sitting around on Palmyra in 1974 left over from the war era. There are conflicting reports re facilities available presently on Fanning Island depending on the source.

DAS BOOT — The Ship That Launched a Thousand Lies

Birth of the Iola

The Iola, nee Margaret, was a small wooden sail boat, thirty feet in length and nine feet in beam. At time of purchase by defendants the only fair descriptive adjective would be that of "derelict" suffering years of neglect before finally sinking at anchor. How long she sat on the bottom completely submerged is not known although it certainly was for several months. During the salvage operation the mast snapped off. Once ashore she sat "on the hard" for over two years unprotected from the tropical sun and rain before purchase for four hundred dollars by defendants. (p. 18)

According to Stearns the Iola was purchased for the sum of $2,260.00 from an unidentified couple. Allegedly this couple fiberglassed the hull applying 80 gallons of resin. Discouraged with their efforts, Stearns claimed the mystery couple gave up and sold the vessel to Walker. At the time of purchase the Iola did not possess a motor, had no mast, rigging, radio, winches, sails, motor or toilet — nothing necessary for her to safely venture forth on the high seas. (p. 18)

Walker created a ponderously heavy, forty foot, three layered mast from two by six fir planks. He created heavy standing rigging from rusted telephone support cables. Her sailing days long over, the Iola was cursed from the day of her launch. During her second launch she fell off the cradle onto her side, sustaining two large puncture wounds from steel cradle supports which penetrated her hull. As the steel supports of the trailer plunged through her fragile hull, they shattered her thin fiberglass resin coating, splintered old rotted planks, tore loose decayed fastenings, broke and destroyed

29

rotted frames. Moreover, the hull penetrated by two stanchions had to be lifted clear with a crane and reset on her cradle. In this process even more damage was done. Walker made hasty efforts to repair the damage. Knowing little about the application of resin and fiberglass to a wooden hull, he did not do a proper job. Consequently, the hull of the Iola with multiple cracks in her fiberglass covering leaked badly as she heeled under full canvas. (Vol. 10, p. 1573)

Other Possibilities

There is another possibility of the birth of the Iola....one *"more close to the truth"* as Stearns might say. Stearns told FBI special agent Calvin Shishido she met Walker in late April 1974. She also alleged April 1, 1974, was the date the Iola was first launched. Obviously meeting Walker in late April 1974 conflicts with Stearns' alleged launching date since Walker supposedly had worked on the Iola four months before the launch date. (p. 438)

To take the sting out of Stearns' lies Bugliosi calls attention to some of them during his direct examination:

"Jennifer, Mr. Shishido testified that you told him you first joined Roy Allen (Buck Walker) on the Iola is late April of 1974 while the Iola was moored in Keehi Lagoon on the island of Oahu. You testified earlier, however, that you and Buck moved to the island of Maui in October of 1973 and Buck bought the Iola there that same month. And the boat, which you and Buck lived on, was moored in Maalaea Harbor in Maui. Do you recall that?" (p. 438)

Responding to this question Stearns admits she lied about meeting Walker for the first time on April 1, 1974. Her admission to lying is followed by the excuse that she lied to protect Walker. Of note is her claim she and Walker moved to Maalaea Harbor on Maui in October of 1973. She alleges Walker bought the Iola the same month. (p. 438)

Stearns' testimony is contradicted by her friend Larry Seibert, (Seibert) who stated he assisted Walker in raising the mast of the Iola in *September of 1973* at Maalaea Harbor located on the island of Maui.

"Prosecutor Schroeder: *'You knew the defendant Buck Walker at Ala Wai, didn't you, from September of '73 through March of '74?*

Seibert: *"Something like that."*

Schroeder: *"He was working on the Iola during that time, wasn't he?"*

Seibert: *"Yes."*

Schroeder: *"In fact you helped him with the Iola?"*

Seibert: *"Not really helped him. I raised the mast."*

Seibert: *"Yes."*

(Volume 8, pages 14-15, transcript from the 1985 murder trial of Buck Walker) 1974.)

Seibert's testimony wreaks havoc with Stearns timeline concerning the repair of the Iola. Initially the ATSWT reader is informed *"they'd bought the boat four months before"* the supposed launch date of April 1, 1974, inferring the Iola was purchased in December of 1973. However, this leaves the months of September, October and November of 1973 unaccounted for since Seibert testified he met defendants in September 1973, and helped Walker with the Iola at that time. (pp. 17-18)

The testimony of Dannell Peterson, a dentist, further complicates matters. Nearly a year after seizure of the Sea Wind and arrest of Stearns for theft of the vessel the FBI searched the Sea Wind. Peterson's wallet with his credit cards were found aboard.

During Stearns' murder trial in 1986 Peterson testified one evening in December of 1973, he visited the defendants aboard the Iola located in a boat slip at Maalaea Harbor Marina. After the visit Peterson departed only to discover his wallet was missing. Immediately he returned to the boat to retrieve it. Defendants would not permit him aboard. Making a cursory search they informed him the wallet with credit cards and $200.00 in cash was not to be found. Convinced defendants were lying Peterson went to the Maui police who came to the Marina and made inquiry. Satisfied the wallet was not aboard the vessel the police departed after making a report about the incident. It is significant the visit of Petersen occurred aboard the Iola when she was in the marina and not in the boat yard; i.e., she was in the water and not "on the hard" under going repair and that she was in tact at that time.

Years later, shortly before the murder trial of Stearns when interviewed by the FBI, Peterson was asked if he could identify the couple who had taken his wallet. He stated they had *"three dogs, the vessel was run down, the woman worked in a sailor's bar in Wailuku and had a "foul mouth".* When showed a photo lineup Peterson picked out Stearns and Walker as the people whose boat he was aboard in December of 1973. (pp. 298-9)

Because of the Maui police records one can be certain Peterson was aboard the Iola, which was *berthed in a boat slip* at Maalaea Harbor in December 1973. This fact is at odds with Stearns assertion Walker was at work rebuilding the Iola at Tuna Packers boat yard from December 1973 to April 1, 1974. Obviously, if the boat was in the water in December of 1973, it could not at the same time have been in the boat yard under-going repair. Peterson described the Iola as a run-down boat but did not suggest she had no mast.

The above information leaves one pursuing two different launch dates. Because of the testimony of Dannell Peterson and the Maui police records we can be certain the Iola was in the water at the marina in Maalaea Harbor in early December 1973 and that the defendants were living aboard. From these facts one can reasonably infer that at an un-named date prior to December 1973, the Iola was launched after storage on land for two years, following her salvage.

Mehaffy Clarifies

Frank Mehaffy's testimony during the Stearns' murder trial throws a different light on the issue of the launch date, purchase of Iola and subsequent work purportedly performed by previous unnamed owners. Frank Mehaffy, a college teacher and experienced sailor, spent several years in Hawaii aboard a small sail boat with his wife. He entertained defendants on board his sailboat in Nawiliwili harbor, on the island of Kauai, October 13, 1974. (pp. 235, 354-55) Defendants anchored near his boat the previous day, and appeared the evening of October 13 with a bottle of (Muff's) wine. Invited aboard, they talked for about three hours.

Mehaffy, on direct-examination by prosecutor Schroeder:

"Did she (Stearns) mention where they started out from when they went to Palmyra?"

"Yes. From Maalaea Harbor on the island of Lanai."
Responds Mehaffy.

The Court: "What island?"

"I'm sorry. On .....Maui." Corrects Mehaffy.

33

"And did she say anything about....any occurrence with respect to their boat at Maalaea?"

Mehaffy: *"Yes. She mentioned that.....the boat had been a wooden hull boat, and they had hauled out during the summer, and when they hauled out — the boat had been out of the water for quite some time."*

"And when they put it back in, the wood had shrunken, and the boat tried to sink. And either — maybe even did sink. They had a lot of trouble pumping the water out." (Vol. 5, pp. 853-4)

During this meeting Stearns told Mehaffy the Iola had been hauled out during *the summer (of 1973).* Stearns states the boat had been out of the water for *"quite some time" and the planks had shrunk:* (i.e., the Iola had been out of the water, sitting on shore for two years before Walker purchased her). At the time of first launch one can infer the Iola did not have a fiberglass covering, and as a consequence either sank, or almost sank after launch because the wooden planks had shrunk.

In all probability, there were two launchings of the Iola.   The first occurred in the fall of 1973. It was shortly before the September launch that Larry Seibert assisted Walker in raising the mast of the Iola.   It was at this launch a photo of Seibert was taken showing him on the deck of the Iola with a bottle of champaign in hand.

At the time of the September launch one can deduce the Iola was not encapsulated with a covering of fiberglass.   Stearns tells us on the occasion   of her first launch the Iola was a *"wooden hulled boat"* and had been out of the water *"for quite some time"* — so long that her planks had shrunk.   Stearns comments reference the fact that the Iola had been sitting in dry dock for nearly two years before her purchase by the defendants.   There was no mysterious couple that wasted a several thousand dollars applying 80 gallons of fiberglass to her hull as Stearns alleged during her murder trial.

Numerous implications arise from these facts. Since the hull of the Iola is nothing but "bare wood," and Walker had purchased her after she had been *"out of the water for quite some time,"* it appears defendants, the summer of 1973, bought the Iola directly from the party who owned the boat at the time she sank at anchor. Rather than paying $2,260.00 as Stearns alleged it is reasonable to believe it was they and not the mystery couple that paid a trifling $400.00 for the vessel. Even that sum was more than she was worth — absent mast, engine, batteries, radio, standing rigging, main sheet and jib sheet, halyard winches, toilet, life lines, stanchions, ground tackle and almost all gear necessary for blue water sailing; i.e., she was a rotting, useless derelict. (p. 18)

At the first launch, in September 1973, defendants had problems keeping the Iola afloat. She had been on land for so long her planks had shrunk and seams opened. Inexperienced and untrained in wood, Walker probably applied seam compound without reaming and re-caulking the seams. He then slapped a coat of paint on her bottom, and expected the boat to float. On launching he had a crisis on his hands as sea water poured through the seams engulfing the Iola.

Mehaffy recalls defendants had *"a lot of trouble pumping the water out,"* speculating that the Iola did sink at that time or nearly sunk. (Vol. 5, pp. 853-4)

Schroeder enquires further of Mehaffy:

"Now did she mention the boat sinking or occurring — or incurring any difficulty at any other point?"

"Well, there was a mention at another time about the boat needing to be — having a leak, and needing to be pumped, yes."

35

This was probably at the time of the first launch when Stearns raced off to the Coast Guard to borrow a pump to keep the Iola afloat. (Vol. 5, pp. 853-4)

Enoki inquiring of Stearns about a launch (the first launch in September 1973) of the Iola at Maalaea Harbor:

"Do you recall Mr. Mehaffy testifying about some problem about when you launched the boat in Maalaea?"

Stearns: *"Yes. We had a problem." (Vol. 12, p. 1805)*

"Did it take on water or — you said it did not sink. So did it take on a lot of water; is that what —"

Stearns, not waiting for Enoki to finish his question, interrupts:

"Well, there were two problems. The first problem was when we were putting her in the water the first time (inadvertently admitting there was a second launch) *she wasn't secure on the trailer tightly enough. And on the way going down the ramp into the water she shifted (indicating). And....the trailer penetrated her — ribs and caused substantial damage."*

(In all probability, the launch where the supports penetrated the hull of the Iola, occurred during the second launch in late March or early April of 1974, and not the first, which probably took place in September of 1973.)

"Okay. That was the first. What's the other problem?" Queries Enoki.

Stearns responds:

"The other problem is after we then brought her back up, and Buck fixed all of that damage, when we put her in the water and — finally did put her in the water and launch her, Buck had neglected to

36

— well, I don't know if he had neglected. There was a shaft that goes through the boat."

"And when she was the Margaret she used to have an inboard motor. And so there's that shaft hole that goes through, and it hadn't been stopped up."

Rather than admit Walker failed to caulk the exposed wooden seams properly, Stearns blames the sinking or near sinking at time of first launch on an obvious and easily detected hole in the hull left by the absence of the propeller shaft. A defect so patent that even Walker might notice the defect with a cursory glance.

Stearns continues:

"So when we first put her in the water, she picked up a lot of water. And I ran up to the Coast Guard Station, and they came down with their...bilge pumps, because I was afraid that she might sink. But Buck then found the problem, and stopped up the — the open end, and she was okay." (Vol. 12, pp. 1805-6)

To be sure, an unstopped propeller shaft hole would admit large quantities of water sufficient to sink the Iola in a short time. But how believable is it that Walker is such a total incompetent he leaves an obvious deficit uncorrected? With defendants and others checking the boat before launch the jury is to believe no one observed a short-coming as obvious an open propeller shaft hole?

Mehaffy's account of the near sinking, or actual sinking of the Iola at the time of first launch is confirmed by Stearns. The amount of water entering the Iola overwhelmed the manual bilge pump. Realizing this Stearns rushed over to the Coast Guard station and borrowed a high volume gas powered water pump which saved the day. The following day as the planks slowly expanded the influx

37

slowed down to the point where they did not need the gas powered pump to keep the Iola afloat.

Defendants probably made a decision to keep the Iola in the water hoping the planks would eventually swell sufficiently to permit them to sail to Palmyra the summer of 1974. After a few months at the marina in Maalaea Harbor the Iola was still taking on too much water. In December of 1973 after the visit from Dannel Peterson, at which time she and Walker stole his wallet, they decided to haul out the Iola once again. This time the plan was to stanch the influx of water by the addition of a thin fiberglass coating hoping it would succeed sufficiently to allow them safe passage to Palmyra.

For next few months Walker inexpertly applied fiberglass to the hull of the Iola. After applying a few layers of resin and woven-roving the Iola was relaunched in April of 1974. While not a complete fix in that the Iola still leaked excessively they were willing to gamble their lives and risk the voyage to Palmyra secure in the knowledge they would chance on a better vessel kill her crew and claim it for themselves.

One might ask what Stearns hoped to gain from the lies she promulgated surrounding the birth of the Iola? Most probably what she sought was to confuse the jury about the fiberglass work performed on the Iola. By suggesting a phantom couple applied 80 gallons of fiberglass to the hull of the Iola Stearns was hoping to hide the fact it was Walker who applied the resin. Had the jury known this fact, they would assume the work was substandard. (p. 18)

Suggesting defendants paid over two thousand dollars for Margaret, causes one to believe there was substantial value added to the moribund hull by the couple. If the jury knew defendants paid a trifling $400.00 for the Iola they would know defendants purchased a derelict that should never have put to sea. More importantly, one might deduce the purpose in voyaging to Palmyra was for the purpose of piracy, mayhem and murder, and not to grow marijuana. (p. 18)

Bugliosi, wisely did not cross-examine Mehaffy concerning his recollection of events detailed by Stearns. (Why Enoki failed to examine Stearns re the identity of the phantom couple who owned the Margaret, is a question left unanswered.)

Elderly and Leaking a Hell of a Lot

The Iola was *"elderly and often repaired"* and *"leaked a hell of a lot".* (p. 52) She rolled excessively to the point where Walker was seasick for nearly a week at the commencement of the voyage to Palmyra Island. *The forward hatch leaked badly and everything in the bow was wet during the entire voyage.* Stearns, herself admits, *"in optimum conditions they could not go more than fifty or sixty miles in twenty-four hours."* Unable to employ the mainsail in combination with the jib, defendants were forced to rely solely upon the jib sail. (Use of the jib without the main sail, while sailing downwind would cause the boat to wallow and roll excessively.)

Arriving at Palmyra, she told Edwin Pollock at times, during the voyage, they were *"knee deep"* in water. Stearns "bilged" every day to keep the water level down to prevent the boat from sinking. The leaking was so bad that it took a toll and began *"to wear on"* the defendants. (pp. 47-8, 52-3, 55)

Don Stevens, a naval architect, visited Stearns aboard the Iola in August of 1974. *He observed "cracks in the fiberglass 'between the wooden planks' indicating water leakage."* and mentions *"he would never have purchased Iola."* (pp. 332-3)

(Ominously, the cracks in the fiberglass coating paralleled the lines of the rotted underlying planks indicating movement of the planks sufficient to crack the fiberglass through and through.)

Stevens stated:

"Jennifer told him the Iola had leaked during the trip down from Hawaii, necessitating constant pumping." (Stearns describes the action of manually pumping out the bilge during the voyage south to Palmyra.)

On the least stressful point of sail with only a jib sail in use, the Iola still required *"constant pumping".* (pp. 332-3)

Stearns Pontificates

Stearns, a sailing ignoramus, alleges *"80 gallons of fiberglass"* was applied to the hull of the Iola. Whatever the amount of resin and fiberglass applied to the hull, Walker's efforts failed. The planks were cupped as observed by both Pollock and Briggs. (Vol. 11, p. 30, transcript from Walker murder trial.) Beneath the layer of fiberglass the planks continued to move as the boat sailed to Palmyra, consequently the seams between the planks opened up and cracks appeared in the fragile fiberglass covering admitting sea water.

Stearns acknowledges this as Enoki cross-examines:

"And did you attribute the necessity for the increased bilging to the trip from Hawaii down to Palmyra?"

"Yeah. It — It's common knowledge that when you fiberglass — when you buy a plank — hulled boat and you fiberglass over it,

the wood — the planks work. And this causes cracks to occur. But
that is just the way it is. This is....common." (Vol. 11, p.1632)

Stearns is completely off-base with this remark. Planks do
not work independently in a properly fiberglassed wooden hull,
planks and hull become one. Appearance of cracks is *"not the way it*
is." As usual, Stearns is lying about a subject which she knows
nothing in an effort to draw the jury's attention away from the fact
that Walker was the one who glassed the hull and did a poor job.

Stearns pontificates on direct examination by Bugliosi:

What's the significance of many, many layers?"

"Well, the more layers you have it means that you could have
a crack that was on the outside — well, on some of the outside layers,
without it necessarily going all the way through."

"So Tom Wolfe I think testified that he saw a crack. He could
have seen a crack that was outside. It may or may not have caused a
leak." (Vol. 11, p. 1633)

Once again Stearns is wide of the mark. She advocates a
thick layer of fiberglass can have a crack outside that would not
penetrate into the interior of the hull. However, by Stearns
admission, the cracks appearing in the hull were a result of the
underlying planks working independent of the fiberglass coating.
The cracks were radiating from the wooden hull outward and not a
result of some external force radiating inward. They penetrated the
hull through and through which is why the cracks ran parallel with
the planking of the hull.

Enoki, in the dark, continues to quiz Stearns about the leaky
condition of the Iola:

41

"So neither of those problems had to do with a ...deficiency in the fiberglassing, or ....cracking, — or leaks in the...in the construction of the boat?"

"That's correct." Opines, Stearns.

"Was the fiberglass cracked when the Iola was on Palmyra?" Queries Enoki.

Stearns fictionalizes:

"The people who had the boat prior to us, we were told, had put eighty gallons of fiberglass resin on the boat, which...is a considerable amount, as far as I know." We thought that she was, if anything —"

Enoki interrupts:

"Well, I'm sorry. I don't believe you're answering my question —"

Stearns: "I'm sorry."

Enoki: " — I'm just asking you if the fiberglass was in fact cracked when the Iola was on Palmyra?"

Stearns:

"I never went into the water and looked underwater to see if she was cracked below the waterline. I know that the tendency of wooden planks to warp and crack — cause cracks in the fiberglass is...known to happen when you fiberglass over a wooden boat."

Enoki: "That's what —".

Stearns: "This was — ".

Enoki: "I'm sorry."

Stearns: " — expected, and she did pick up water. And this was undoubtably how the water got in was through cracks in the fiberglass."

(Finally, Stearns, admits that the Iola is taking on water through the cracks in her hull.)

Enoki: *"That was — you're in agreement with Mr. Pollock then about the fact that a wood plank boat does leak?"*

Stearns: *"All wooden boats leak, whether they're fiberglassed over or not."*

(Again, another statement without foundation — all wooden boats do not leak. Those that are not maintained and not cared for do leak, but a properly maintained wooden boat does not leak. The purpose in fiberglassing a wooden boat is to stop the ingress of water. If a wooden vessel leaks after the application of fiberglass, the shipwright has not done his job. Stearns, as usual is completely off base. But the prosecution does not call her to account.)

Enoki continues: *"Okay. But — Well, you're in agreement that a fiberglass — a wood planked boat with fiberglass over it is — is more likely to leak that just a wood plank boat?"*

Stearns: *"It's my understanding that all wooden planked boats, and all boats that are fiberglassed over, leak. But to answer you question, the answer is: Yes, the Iola did leak."*

Enoki: *"I believe that was two questions ago. But...you said you didn't go underwater, or anything, to see — if there were any cracks or leaks for yourself; is that — is that right?"*

Stearns: *"That's correct."*

Enoki: *"And did you -- did you see any leaks above the waterline in Palmyra?"*

The Court: *"Leaks or cracks?"*

"Cracks. I'm sorry." Replies Enoki.

Stearns begins discussing Wolfe's testimony that he saw a crack on the hull of the Iola. She locates the crack high up on the hull in an area she labels a gunnel.

"I was trying to remember when Tom Wolfe was testifying about the crack along the side. I...seem to remember it." (Vol. 12, pp. 1805-10)

She admits water might come in the crack, but only if the boat was severely heeled over and then makes it clear that is not the kind of sailing she enjoys.

Enoki continues: *"Okay, and in your anticipated trip to Fanning Island, likewise you would — you would not have expected that leak to cause — I'm sorry, that crack to cause you any problems?"*

Stearns: "That's correct." (Vol. 12, p.1810)

"I think it — it was going to be fixed, though. I'm not saying that I would ignore a crack, any crack like that. Buck had resin. And I'm sure Buck would — well, I'm sure Buck did fiberglass over what ever damage he saw."

"Did you recall Mr. Stevens saying that plugging fiberglass would cause the same — would result in the same leaks if you went to sea?" Quizzes, Enoki.

(Stevens, a naval architect, opined that plugging the cracks with underwater epoxy would not stanch the leaking once the Iola put to sea and was subject to the stress of on-coming waves during her supposed voyage to Fanning Island.)

Suddenly, faced with a real expert, Stearns fearing impeachment by Stevens, backs away from her role as an expert, admitting she knows nothing about the application of fiberglass and resin to a cracked hull.

"Well, I didn't — I don't know a lot about that type of thing. Buck handled all the boat maintenance, and he seemed to be pretty good at it."

Enoki: "You don't have any — you don't dispute that at this point."

"I have no knowledge of that." Replied Stearns. (Vol. 12, p. 1811)

After all the blather from Stearns about wooden boats that were, or were not fiberglassed, and their supposed propensity to leak, she does an about-face, admitting she has no knowledge of what she has been talking about.

Babbling Away

Bugliosi attempts damage control in an effort to minimize the impact of Pollock's testimony that Stearns told him, while en route to Palmyra from Hawaii, several times she was "knee-deep" in water on the Iola.

"Incidentally, Mr. Pollock testified that you told him that somewhere en route to Palmyra — he did not know where — you were knee-deep in water on the Iola."

"Did you tell him this?"

Stearns does not deny making the statement to Pollock, but suggests he was confused,   offers the   following   ridiculous explanation:

"I think that what he remembers is what happened on the first leg of our voyage, when we went from Maui to Oahu. Buck had taken out the through-hull fittings on the boat and he had neglected to cap them. And so in

45

between Maui and Oahu, we picked a lot of water, and it was sloshing over the floorboard. But certainly, knee-deep is an exaggeration." *(Vol. 10, p. 1600)*

Stearns admits telling Pollock during the voyage they were in trouble with the Iola leaking badly, water was coming in faster then they could bail it out. As a result, it rose above the floorboards, and it was *sloshing* around in the main cabin.

Attempting to explain away the crisis, not knowing what she is talking about, she makes matters worse suggesting the reason the water was above the floorboards "sloshing" around in the cabin was because Walker had taken out the *"through-hull fittings"* and failed to cap the holes. (If this were true the Iola would have gone to the bottom immediately — no amount of bailing or bilging would have saved them.)

Through-hull openings are easily observable and inexpensively capped. There would be no reason to remove a through-hull fitting that supports a valve or cap. (Stearns ignorantly claims that not only were the through hull openings not capped, but that the fittings themselves had been removed.)

If Walker did not have the money to purchase ball valves he could have capped off the through-hull openings with inexpensive zinc plated iron caps. Had our would be pirates put to sea with through hull openings that were not capped off the deficit would have been immediately apparent — the interior would have flooded as soon as the boat was in the water. Without immediate correction of the deficit the Iola would have sunk in less than a minute.

What makes Stearns' lie even more absurd is her allegation that Walker had *"taken out the through-hull fittings*." Meaning there was not so much as a bronze nipple to attach a cap to. Stearns not having the slightest idea of what she is talking about, informs the jury they put to sea with all of the through-hull openings nothing but bare wood holes — nothing to support a cap or valve. All this is zany beyond comprehension. In this instance Stearns is not speaking of only one opening but apparently all the through-hull openings in the hull. (Approximately seven in number on a vessel the size of the Iola if one were to include the cockpit scupper drains.) Just another example of Stearns' ignorance and ridiculous lying, yet without opposing expert opinion no one in the courtroom is the wiser.

Fasteners and Things that Go Bump in the Night

An important seaworthiness consideration in a wooden boat is condition of the fasteners securing the planks of the hull to the frames. It is not uncommon for an older wooden vessel sailing windward under the stress of on coming seas to *"spring a plank"*. This can occur when the fasteners have deteriorated and no longer function effectively. When this happens there is little that can be done but to save oneself. Bilge pumps are overwhelmed in an instant and the vessel sent to the bottom.

A recent example of an older wooden boat breaking up is found during the 1998 Sydney to Hobart race wherein a large, well-kept, wooden sailing vessel, the Sir Winston Churchill, (in far better shape than the Iola) broke up with the loss of six crew.

Fasteners (what the landlubber would call screws, or nails) come in many varieties, wood, iron, stainless steel, copper, or bronze. Silicone bronze is favored in quality construction although zinc coated iron fasteners are common. While inferior to silicone bronze they are less expensive and probably used to fasten the planks of the Iola.

Electrolysis is the curse of all vessels that course the seas. It is aided by the presence of salt water. Electrons flow from one metal part to another. Boat owners purchase *"sacrificial zincs"* by the basketful to protect the more noble metals exposed to the salt water environment such as propellers, propeller shafts, bronze through hull fittings and the like. The theory being that the sacrificial zinc, being less noble, will decay leaving the more noble metal to which it is attached in tact. Fastenings exposed to salt water decay because of galvanic action which is why with any proper survey several screws located in the under part of the hull, are extracted and examined to ascertain their condition. In a well cared for wooden vessel one can expect silicone bronze fasteners to last twenty years or more before replacing. Zinc coated iron fasteners may not last as long.

Because of the age of the Iola, her poor maintenance, rotted condition, sinking at anchor, and the fact that she was undoubtably "iron fastened", one can be certain that the fasteners were in extremely poor condition, had rusted in place and were no longer capable of securing the planks to the frames.

Aside from the loss of holding power, as iron fasteners decay rust sets up a particularly pernicious rot in the wood adjacent to it. Above the water line in older zinc coated iron fastened vessels one frequently notices rust spots as decaying fasteners bleed through the paint.

For the Iola there were no viable options left she had deteriorated past the point of return. It was too late for the application of fiberglass and resin — she should have been broken up or used as a decoration at a seafood restaurant.

Gear

Normally on a vessel the size of the Iola, one would expect an internal engine with alternator capable of charging her 12 volt battery system.   The primary function of the deep-cycle marine batteries would be to start the engine, supply power to the running lights, binnacle light, interior lights, service the automatic 12 volt bilge pump and power a 12 volt VHF radio, power the auto-pilot, and etc.

After reviewing the testimony one can conclude it is likely the Iola did not possess any of the above devices.   Every reference to the bilge pump by defendants and other experts, such as Wheeler, indicate the presence of a manual bilge pump on the Iola and not an electrical pump.   Stevens, contrary to what Bugliosi suggests, withheld his "seaworthy" seal of approval because of the inadequacies of the bilge pumping system. (Vol. 2, p. 92.)

Stearns ignorantly testifies they were *"leisure sailors"* meaning they did not sail during the hours of darkness. (Vol. 12, p. 1910) Thus, there is no reason to light the binnacle...if it had a light. This leaves only interior and running lights in need of 12 volt power. The interior could be lighted by a kerosene lamp. As for running lights mandatory in the vicinity of Hawaii, but out in the vast reaches of the Pacific relatively unimportant.   There was no engine to start, no electric bilge pump dependent on 12 volt power and no 12 volt VHF radio, so why waste money on expensive batteries?

Within a few months of their arrival they expected to steal a properly equipped boat at the expense of an unfortunate sailing couple.   The Iola was unseaworthy in the extreme.   Once they murdered an unsuspecting crew and had stolen their boat the Iola would be sent to the bottom along with the unfortunate crew members, so why spend the money?

Down to their last ten dollars defendants could not afford to purchase a used, inexpensive, VHF radio that would permit contact with other vessels within a twenty mile range. Unable to afford a fixed unit they could have purchased a handheld unit capable of broadcasting up to five miles.

A clear example of the value of a VHF radio can be found when the Iola ran aground in the shark infested channel while attempting to enter the lagoon at Palmyra. With no manner of signaling their plight to sailors in the lagoon defendants were forced to wait until someone happened by. Moreover, with a VHF radio on board information from knowledgeable seamen in the lagoon could have been transmitted advising them of the best time to enter the channel and the hazards that would confront them. Likely someone in the lagoon would have sped out in their dinghy and towed them inside to safety had the request been made.

It is unclear whether or not the Iola possessed the most rudimentary signaling devices such as flares, a bell, horn, or life jackets as mandated by Coast Guard regulations pertaining to small craft. In all probability they did not purchase these items because of the expense involved.

An AM/FM radio is referenced as being aboard. Stearns claims to use this device for calculating the exact time for purposes of navigation. This assertion is questionable as a small, cheap radio, thousands of miles from the transmitting base would have difficulty picking up a signal. (pp. 27, 55)

Missing were basic electronics one would expect on any vessel contemplating blue water sailing. There was no knot meter — a device that measures the vessel's speed through the water. It usually is combined with a log, measuring the distance in nautical miles. The log is cumulative, much like an auto speedometer. This permits a skipper to proximate the distance traveled during a 24 hour period as well as the cumulative distance and is useful in plotting a Line of Position, (LOP) which is critical for proper navigation.

Another important navigational instrument missing is a depth sounder. An instrument that informs the helmsman the depth of the water under the keel.   There are non-electric means of sounding depths by use of a weighted, measured, line. There is no indication that either was available for use. It is an important item that could well mean the difference between life and death, shipwreck and safe harbor.

The galley probably consisted of a one or two burner alcohol stove with no oven. Any baking of bread (or cake) would have to be done in a pot sitting atop the stove, a most primitive arrangement. Stearns alleged the galley possessed a two burner stove, with oven, fueled by butane. This assertion is most likely a fiction created by Stearns in that butane is usually associated with small camper stoves. Unlike propane, butane in any sizable container in 1974 was not readily available. In addition to carbon monoxide butane gives off a toxic gas when burned.   Furthermore butane gas is much more expensive than propane. Another fact arguing against the existence of a proper two burner stove with oven aboard the Iola is the cost.   In the mid 1970s a three burner propane stove with oven, would cost close to a thousand dollars. (Unlike natural gas propane is heavier than air and requires a sophisticated installation of safety valves and proper hoses. Should the device leak and the gas subject to a point of ignition the boat could explode.)

The Iola, thirty feet in length with a beam of nine feet, was probably built in the late 1940s when design considerations did not give the sailor the spacious options found on current 30 footers. She had interior headroom clearance of no more than five and a half feet whereas modern thirty footers frequently offer clearance of over six feet and a beam around ten feet. Fiberglass vessels of today offer all the conveniences one might expect in a small condominium as well as a reliable diesel engine with alternator, fully equipped head with shower, burner propane stove with oven, VHF radio, proper internal lighting, automatic bilge pump, manual bilge pump, automatic pilot, roller furling headsail, GPS, radar, depth sounder, canvas dodger, bimini, speed indicator, log, pressure hot and cold water, and etc. The list goes on and on. Not all these devices are necessary to insure seaworthiness, but they make life aboard much more pleasant.

Traditional designs tend to heel at a sharper angle, broad beamed modern craft resist this tendency. Weight aloft is a challenge for any boat designer. These days masts commonly are made of aluminum or more exotic materials such as carbon fiber. The heavy, forty foot, three ply, two by six fir mast constructed by Buck would cause considerable weight aloft and tend to de-stabilize the Iola, making her unsafe in strong winds.

On deck there are other notable deficiencies. Astonishingly, the Iola did not posses winches to assist in raising the main or jib sheets. Without winches to assist in handling the main and jib sheets it would be exceedingly difficult to control the sails while underway. This burden would be multiplied by a considerable factor during the hours of darkness or in strong winds. (Vol. 2, p. 205)

Bilgewater

Stearns does not understand the relationship between the bilge pump, battery and gas powered generator which defendants had on board the Iola.

At a minimum one would expect to find two functional bilge pumps aboard a boat the size of the Iola; one manual and the other an automatic 12 volt The manual pump, accessible from the cockpit, could be used in the event the 12 volt automatic pump failed to function or became overwhelmed.   A manual bilge pump normally relies on a bladder to suck water from the bilge with one stroke and with the return, expel it.   They work fairly efficiently providing the bladder does not rupture or the intake, located deep in the bilge, does not become clogged.   The downside of a manual bilge pump is that after a short time operating the pump, one becomes fatigued.   It requires crew to cause it to function unlike a 12 volt automatic bilge pump which cycles on or off anytime water reaches a designated level in the bilge and operates so long as supplied with 12 volt power from the ship's batteries.

Bugliosi, in an aside, suggests the existence of a 12 volt bilge pump aboard the Iola when he reviews the difficulty the Iola had once she set out on the voyage to Palmyra.   However the evidence weighs heavily against this proposition.

"Everything looked fine while the Iola sat in the harbor, but in the ocean sailing, wooden planks tend to work back and forth, causing the Iola's fiberglass to crack immediately. This exposed the old leaks and allowed seawater to soak through the hull."

".....the cabin's forward hatch let in water, even though they kept it shut tightly as possible. Everything in the bow stayed soaked. Because of all the leaking they had to start the generator and run the pump daily to keep down the water level in the bilge." (p. 52)

This is Bugliosi speculating and not Stearns testimony. Like Stearns he does not understand the relationship between the generator, battery and automatic bilge pump. All references to de-watering the Iola found in Stearns murder trial testimony employ terms indicating the use of a manual bilge pump and not one that is 12 volt driven.

If the Iola possessed a 12 volt automatic bilge pump it would be properly powered by a deep cycle, 12 volt marine battery of approximately 100 amp hour reserve capacity. An automatic 12 volt bilge pump is triggered into action whenever the water level in the bilge reaches a preselected height depending upon the placement of the water level sensing device which is connected to, or an integral part of the pump itself.

A 12 volt bilge pump functions so long as the wire connections to the battery are not corroded nor the water intake blocked by debris. In turn, the marine battery which powers the pump is dependent upon an outside source of power to recharge it. When the vessel has an internal engine this source is the alternator or generator attached to the engine. When the engine is in operation the alternator recharges the battery. Because the Iola had no internal engine the defendants allegedly employed a portable gas powered generator that could generate 120 volt alternating current. A portable generator may have possessed a twelve volt, direct current charging mechanism to recharge the battery. If the generator did not have an internal battery charger, the defendants could have used an inexpensive external charger much as one uses to charge the battery of an automobile that has run down.

However, it is unlikely the Iola possessed a twelve volt automatic bilge pump. While no small sailing vessel should go to sea without such a device, because defendants were without funds, it is probable the Iola did not have this essential item on board. There are many facts that indicate this to be true. When Stearns speaks of the bilge pump she always speaks in terms of *bilging* (meaning a manual activity). When she alleges the intrusion of a swordfish on return of the Sea Wind to Hawaii, unfamiliar with 12 volt automatic bilge pumps, she incorrectly explains how the water was expelled.

Stearns allegedly on discovering water at sufficient level to wet the fur of her dog (i.e., it is above the floor-boards) states Walker started the bilge pump—meaning he turned on a switch. Had she the slightest understanding of an electronic bilge pump, she would know that it automatically cycles on whenever the water in the bilge reaches the pre-selected level. It is not necessary to turn on, or flip a switch. The automatic bilge pump starts and stops itself.

Bugliosi's comment that the gas powered generator allegedly was in *operation daily* is revealing. If true, it signifies the automatic bilge pump was placing an exceedingly heavy electrical demand on the battery. Because of this demand, it was necessary to run the generator and recharge the battery every day. It is unusual for an automatic bilge pump to run constantly, if this assertion were true, it indicates the Iola suffered from catastrophic leaks.

On arriving at Palmyra, Stearns made several definitive statements about the problems she encountered during her voyage from Hawaii. On direct examination by prosecutor Schroeder, during the murder trial of Stearns, Edwin Pollock testified:

"She (Stearns) said that at times during the trip she was knee-deep in water down below."

Schroeder inquires:

"Did you have occasion to talk to Jennifer Jenkins (Stearns) about how they would manage to leave Palmyra?"

"She said she wasn't going to leave the island on that boat." Replied Pollock. (p. 317)

There are several implications that flow from the above statement. If true, the Iola was severely leaking because it was necessary for the bilge pump to run every day. Another indicator the pump must have been running throughout the day because there was substantial draw-down of the battery to the point where it was necessary to "start the generator" and run it everyday to keep them sufficiently charged.

To the contrary there was persuasive testimony from various witnesses suggesting the Iola did not possess a 12 automatic bilge pump. The most damning testimony comes from Stearns herself during direct-examination by Bugliosi:

"You heard Mr. Wheeler testify that you were bilging the Iola every day while he was there. You heard that testimony?"

"Yes."

"Is that true?"

"When we first came in, it probably is true. We had just completed a long sea voyage. And Buck wanted to get the bilge totally dry to see if we had sustained any damage when we had bonked ourselves on the coral heads."

"So we bilged, and then — not at all, because you can only bilge so long. (Meaning the operator becomes fatigued and runs out of energy.) *So for several days we probably were bilging the first few days."*

A few questions later, Bugliosi asks:

"With respect to the bilging, what did you have to bilge the Iola with?"

Stearns responds: *"We had several bilge pumps. I don't remember exactly right now. We either had...two manual pumps and one or two electric pumps. Something like that. Two — we had three or four."*

"After the initial bilging; that is when you first arrived and had to bilge quite a bit, thereafter how often did you bilge the Iola on Palmyra?"

56

*"I would bilge....probably a couple of times a week. Just —
not because that she was picking up so much water, but when the
water stood in the bilge it threw off a musky order."*

*"So I would bilge two, maybe even three times. Whenever it
started to not smell right, I....would clean it out."*

*"Did you bilge more on Palmyra than you did prior to the trip
from Hawaii to Palmyra?"*

*"Yes. Yes. She — she had picked — she was picking up more
water in Palmyra than she was in Hawaii. In Hawaii I bilged maybe
once every two or maybe even three weeks."*

*"And did you attribute the necessity for the increased bilging
to the trip from Hawaii down to Palmyra?"*

*Stearns replies: Yeah.   It — it's common knowledge that
when you fiberglass — when you buy a plank-hulled boat and you
fiberglass over it, the wood — the planks work. And this causes some
cracks to occur.*

But there is just the way it is.   This is...common."   (Vol. 1,
pp. 1631-2)

There is much that can be gleaned from the above colloquy.
Stearns misdirects the jury with the notion that bilging will dry out
the bilge.   All bilge pumps whether they are electronic or manual
will lower the water to a given level.   Depending on the type strainer
there will always be a small amount of water in the bilge with any
type of pump, manual or electric.

With the use of a manual bilge pump even with the most
effective device there will remain in the bilge a quarter to half an
inch of water due to the intake attachment. Normally there is a filter
attached to the intake hose. The only method to completely dry out

the bilge would be to remove the remaining water by use of a towel or sponge.

Although Stearns existence   at sea depends on a properly functioning bilge pump, in her confusion and ignorance, she displays a cavalier attitude towards the bilge pumps on board.   She does not know how many pumps are on board, nor how they function.   She supposedly had "three or four".

It is Stearns' testimony that establishes, beyond a reasonable doubt,   the Iola did not possess a single functioning 12 volt bilge pump.   It is found in the testimony of Stearns every time she addresses the issue of pumping the bilge.   She always speaks in terms of "bilging" when removing water from the bilge.   To bilge, is a verb.   It is the physical act of operating a manual bilge pump. When a 12 volt automatic bilge pump is in use one might state the "bilge pump was running," or perhaps the bilge pump was in "operation."   They are quiet and   independent to the point where many prudent skippers employ an alarm which sounds when the pump is functioning advising it is in operation. Cautious boat owners frequently add a manual over-ride switch to cycle the pump on without the stimulus of the water-level sensing device.

Stearns points out a downside of the use of a manual bilge pump...it tends to tire the user after a short period of time.   She testifies:

"So   we bilged, and then — not all of it, because you can only bilge for so long."   (Vol. 11,   p. 1631)   (Meaning both defendants working in tandem, had to stop and rest, due to exertion from manually pumping the water out of the Iola.) "....but when we got into the lagoon, Buck bilged out the water so that the bilge was totally dry..." (Vol. 10, p. 1584)

Wheeler reinforces Stearns' testimony regarding the use of a manual bilge pump under cross-examination by defense attorney, Weinglass:

"Now, later on, you testified yesterday you heard sounds emanating from the Iola which was next to you on the dolphins side. Could you describe those sounds for us?" (Weinglass, unknowingly asks a question that reinforces the case against Stearns.)

"You can hear things through the water real good. And, I could tell there was a pump in operation." Replied Wheeler.

Weinglass: *"A pump. In other words, you're indicating with your arm now a motion kind of thing?"* (Wheeler is moving his arm in the manner a sailor might do if he were engaging a manual bilge pump.)

"I'm sure it was a manual type of pump of which I never saw, of course.

"You never saw the pump?"

"(Shakes head negatively.)"

"But you heard the sound and you think that (the sound) *was the pump."*

"Um — hum. Yes sir." (Vol. 2, p. 189)

It is obvious from her testimony Stearns has no idea of how an automatic bilge pump functions. In relating her lies about the supposed swordfish attack while aboard the Sea Wind returning to Hawaii, Stearns on discovering the bilge of the Sea Wind allegedly was "full to over-flowing", comments:

"And Buck picked up the floorboards of the bilge and the bilge was full to overflowing. It was filled with water."

"So Buck got the pump started, and we started searching, and we had our heads down on the side of the boat and we could hear,

kind of hear, a trickling sound of water running." (Vol. 11, p. 1696)

In closing argument during the murder trial of Walker, Enoki summarizes the testimony of Larry Briggs, skipper of the Caroline, who assisted Wheeler in pulling the Iola off the coral reef and into the lagoon after she had run aground:

> *"Mr. Briggs testified the boat leaked. It had to be pumped diligently and manually by hand; and, Mr. Briggs testified that it was not unusual for a vessel of that size to take on that much water."* (Volume 11, page 30, Court Reporter's Transcript from murder trial of Walker.)

Briggs, during the murder trial of Walker, testified that the bilge pump of the Iola was a manual device. The Iola had to be pumped by hand. He also employs the word "diligently" meaning vigorously.

SEAWORTHINESS OF THE IOLA

Seaworthiness of the Iola is one of the fundamental issues in the trial of Stearns. Resolving this issue is a crucial element in determining the guilt or innocence of Stearns. If the Iola was not seaworthy, and Stearns knew it, then all the talk about sailing to Fanning Island is a fraud and deception, a mere ploy to cause the Grahams to lower their guard thus facilitating their murders and theft of the Sea Wind. Moreover, if the Iola were unseaworthy Stearns could not safely return to Hawaii aboard her. If the Iola could not return safely to Hawaii one might infer defendants only purpose in sailing her to Palmyra was one of theft, mayhem, and murder.

Iola's numerous deficiencies were observable to defendants the first time she was exposed to the water. Anyone who has sailed the islands comprising the state of Hawaii has experienced the strong winds and rough seas that flow around them. The planks of the Iola started working from the time the first wave swept under her hull. No doubt on discovering the deficiencies of Iola there was a discussion about the wisdom of sailing to Palmyra Island. After experimenting sailing down wind, using the headsail alone, defendants forged ahead knowing a change of vessel would be made at the expense of some unfortunate crew once they arrived at Palmyra.

Stearns asserted visible cracks in the hull did not mean water was penetrating the hull *"because there were many layers"*. (p. 411) Naively, Stearns believed an outer layer of resin could crack while a layer underneath would resist cracking. One sailor observed the cupping of the planks was visible under the thin layer of fiberglass. As the underlying planks worked, the fiberglass layer covering the planks cracked, in turn these cracks would then radiate to the surface of the hull. (It would not be possible for the covered planks to work causing cracks to appear at the surface without first appearing at the point of stress.)

During the murder trial of Stearns, the prosecution called several eyewitnesses to the summer events of 1974, among them: Larry Briggs, Jack Wheeler, Edwin and Marilyn Pollock, Donald Stevens and Thomas Wolfe. Testimony from these witnesses had a common theme; defendants were "running out of food" and the Iola was "unseaworthy". (p. 228)

Larry Briggs, charter boat captain of the Caroline, helped tow the Iola into the lagoon on June 27, 1974, and was of the opinion that *"according to his standards"* the Iola was not a *"seaworthy"* boat. It was very *"run down"*. He stated that the sail from Hawaii to Palmyra is *"known as an easy sail."* And that the reverse would be a *"rough trip in any boat."* He would not have attempted a trip to Hawaii from Palmyra on board the Iola unless he *"had no choice."* (p. 227)

Tom Wolfe, another experienced sailor, testified that the Iola *"did not appear to be seaworthy"* and he would not have taken a long voyage on her. (p. 333) When advised defendants were thinking about sailing to Fanning Island Wolfe informed them they would *"....take a hell of a pounding against the wind."* He did not tell Stearns his private thoughts; that *"he would not have sailed anywhere on the rickety-looking Iola."* Wolfe observed that the rigging was *"rusted telephone cable";* *the mast was inexpertly homemade and likely to snap in a bad storm; the spars were spindly; and, the boat while sitting at anchor in the lagoon, leaked badly.* (p. 113, 117)

Criticism concerning the seaworthiness of the Iola comes from defendant herself. On page 121 she writes in her supposed log,

"August 24, Made further strides in getting the boat seaworthy, tho hardly looks it at a cursory glance." Stearns writes *"further strides in getting the boat seaworthy."* (In other words, by her own admission, the Iola was not seaworthy on August 24 almost two months after it arrived at Palmyra and just a few days before her alleged voyage to Fanning Island, the implication being that the Iola was not seaworthy when it sailed from Hawaii.)

Stearns' assertion that she made *"further strides in getting the boat seaworthy"* is suspect given the fact she did not have skills to repair the boat,nor resin or catalyst to make fiberglass repairs. *"Swabbing the deck"* hardly qualifies as an activity that would promote seaworthiness in a leaky, run down vessel. Swabbing may be a quaint term, but is seldom used by the sailing community to describe washing down the deck of a sailboat. Its use in the log of the Iola is a misplaced effort by a novice to appear experienced.

The extraordinary length of time it took to make the voyage from Hawaii to Palmyra speaks volumes about the seaworthiness of the vessel and the capabilities of the crew. We are told the forward hatch leaked badly and the outboard motor seized to the point that even a sailor with the skills and knowledge of Mac Graham declared it finished. (p. 407)

An another alarming deficit was lack of a life raft or inflatable, dinghy which would serve this purpose. If the bilge pump became clogged or overwhelmed the Iola would go to the bottom leaving Stearns and Walker adrift in a tiny wooden rowboat with no positive floatation, no VHF radio, no water and no escape from the tropical sun. There would be little chance of survival and death would come quickly.

Stranded on Palmyra

An astonishing and damning notation is made by Bugliosi re the issue of seaworthiness. He references a Motion to Suppress hearing that occurred in Honolulu on January 24, 1975, several months before Stearns trial for theft of the Sea Wind. It was brought on behalf of Stearns with the intent of obtaining a ruling dismissing the charge of grand theft in stealing the Sea Wind. (p. 442)

A part of the Motion to Suppress included her sworn testimony:

"She informed the court she had "no alternative" and had to take Mac's boat, the Sea Wind, because she was stranded". (p. 442)

This statement made under oath would be viewed by most as an admission by Stearns that the Iola was an unseaworthy vessel and could not make the return trip to Hawaii. No doubt Stearns hoped to avoid the charge of theft by pointing out to the court she had no other choice but to take the Sea Wind if she was ever to safely leave Palmyra, implying her death at sea was certain to occur if she departed on the Iola because the vessel was not seaworthy.

Bugliosi characterized Stearns' admission that she was "stranded" on Palmyra as "devastating" and rightly so, for not only does the statement point out Iola was unseaworthy, but it reveals that Stearns recognized this fact. Bugliosi discovered Stearns' damning testimony in a transcript given to him by prosecutor Enoki. (The prosecution is required by law to furnish underlying documents to defense counsel.)

In discussion with Bugliosi,   Stearns excuses her sworn testimony that she was *"stranded"* informing him it was a lie to accompany her lie that the Iola ran aground when they were attempting to return to Hawaii with the Iola in tow.   Stearns admission to perjury and her excuse attending this admission satisfied Bugliosi. (p. 442)

At the time of the Motion to Suppress hearing in January 1975, Stearns thought she had gotten away with the murder of the Grahams. There was no one to contradict her version of the alleged facts. There were suspicious circumstances, but Muff's remains had not been discovered — Stearns thought she was home free. Feeling safe she testified honestly secure in the belief her crime would never be discovered.

Bugliosi chose not to bring Stearns' admission to the attention of Enoki, gambling Enoki had over looked the comment.   His judgment proved correct. Enoki unaware of Stearns' sworn testimony implying the Iola was not seaworthy, never questioned her about the statement and in failing to do so lost an opportunity, once and for all, to settle the issue of seaworthiness.

Mac Opines From His Watery Grave

Mac speaks of seaworthiness from his watery grave. Mac's friend Curtis Shoemaker testified at the theft trial of Stearns June 25, 1975, in Honolulu. Bugliosi on cross-examination at the murder trial of Stearns reads into evidence part of Shoemaker's testimony given years before at Stearns theft trial.

Bugliosi reading to the jury from the theft trial transcript:

"What was the nature of your last conversation with Mac Graham? What was the nature of that communication with you?"

"Well, he (Mac) had spoken about this prior to this. I think one of the dogs of the other two people had almost attacked his wife. So there seemed to be a problem. It was a boat that had gone down there that was — according to him he said it was unseaworthy and leaking badly, and the people on the boat were having a hard time, apparently, running out of food, and these were the ones with the dogs."

"That conversation was on the 28th of August?"

"That was on the 28th, the last time I heard from them."

"Did you have another contact with him after that?"

"No. That was the last time I heard from him and he (Mac) said the other boat was leaving the next day." (p. 353)

(The "next day", was Thursday, August 29, 1974.)

The above testimony, given by Curtis Shoemaker, about his last conversation with Mac less than a year after the murder of the Grahams established Mac thought the Iola was not seaworthy. Moreover, it demonstrates Mac had bought into defendant's ruse and believed defendants were departing for Fanning Island the next day, Thursday, August 29, 1974.

PRINCESS STEPHANIE THE NAVIGATOR

Another of the great hoaxes promulgated by the defense during the trial was Stearns' supposed navigational skills which, for all intents, were non-existent.

Stearns attempting to explain her navigation process to the jury testified:

"The way I navigated was I took sights. I saw where I was, and knew where I was going, and took a compass heading that would take me in that direction." (p. 449)

At this point her mythical navigation skills could have been exposed had the prosecution demanded a demonstration. She should have been handed her $25.00 plastic sextant and a chart with a request for a demonstration. It can be said for certain she was not using celestial navigation techniques as they are difficult to compute and require various tables, a knowledge of the navigational stars, and much practice. Moreover, she does not properly explain her system of navigating by "noon sights" which mandate more than an accurate fix, although it is doubtful she is even capable of this.

Stearns does not explain in any comprehensible manner the process of plotting a LOP (Line of Position). In truth she does not know the difference between GHA (Greenwich Hour Angle) and LHA (Local Hour Angle), nor their navigational significance. She does not delineate the numerous steps necessary to obtain an accurate fix, nor what publications are necessary to assist in this process such as the Nautical Almanac and H.O. 249. The idea that Stearns taught herself navigation while on her way to Palmyra is a complete fraud.

It is one of the many ironies of her murder trial Stearns, a novice and inexperienced sailor, was never properly questioned on any issue of seamanship or navigation. Unchallenged, she ends up the "expert". The jury has no choice but to rely upon her exaggerations and absurd account of her navigational skills during the voyage to Palmyra.

Not only do we have Stearns strange and chaotic log remarks upon her approach to Palmyra, there is the unexplained painfully slow return from Palmyra to Hawaii aboard the Sea Wind. (Stearns' admits the stolen Sea Wind left Palmyra Island on September 11, 1974 and arrived at Nawiliwili, Kuai on October 12, 1974, a return voyage totaling 31 days.) (pp. 133, 415)

On the return voyage to Hawaii our intrepid sailors have no excuses. After murdering the Grahams defendants stole a well designed and equipped Angelman ketch nearly thirty-eight feet in length. On board they had the results of years of planning by an experienced sailor including the luxury of an autopilot.

The presence of an autopilot aboard the Sea Wind meant defendants need not stand watch tedious hour after bone numbing hour. It relieves the crew of constant attention to the wheel and for the most part excels in keeping the vessel on course nearly eliminating "pilot error". Once the desired compass heading is fed to the autopilot, it does the rest. It is also probable that defendants had no knowledge about how to use most of the devices aboard the Sea Wind that assisted in sailing. (Vol. 2, p. 205)

The only deficit the Sea Wind manifests on the return voyage is the bullet hole in the hull resulting from the discharge of Muff's derringer as she struggled for her life against Stearns. No doubt it leaked somewhat after Walker effected a crude patch, but it was nothing that would threaten the vessel on the return voyage.

Given the superb condition of the Sea Wind how does Stearns explain the long delay in returning to Hawaii — a total of thirty-one days? The winds were either south easterlies or north easterlies; in any event excessive tacking would not be necessary. One wonders what happened? Knowing little about sailing and navigation did they get lost? Unfortunately none of the attorneys on either side were reasonably well informed re the sea and sailing and there was no effective cross-examination exposing or resolving these issues.

In all probability on the return to Hawaii, Stearns observing her chart selected a compass setting that she hoped would take them to Hawaii and did nothing more expecting to sight the high peaks of Hawaii from a great distance, essentially the same system of navigation she used while meandering south to Palmyra.

As an untried sailor Stearns could not be certain of her navigation skills. When a navigator first observes a small atoll through binoculars it appears as a gray line on the far horizon. Identifying the grey smudge on the horizon as the goal one is attempting to reach with exactitude mandates the helmsman cautiously approach within a mile or two — sufficient proximity to identify the shape of the island and channel of entry, yet distant enough to avoid ripping the bottom out of the boat on an uncharted reef. Without close examination there can be no certainty the goal has been achieved... even in this day of GPS. From the distance of six to eight miles most low lying islands look the same. A cry of "land ho" from a crew member, when a grey wisp on the horizon is first observed, is not really the same "land ho" as in now we have arrived at the desired destination.

Exaggerations of her navigational skill lend credibility to Stearns claim to have mastered the sextant and navigation by sun sights, but are misleading and unrealistic. Bugliosi finds marvelous accuracy in the mathematical fumblings of Stearns. At one point she states Iola is only 120 miles from Palmyra as if the assessment is a certainty. Until the Stearns sailed within a few miles distant and circled the island while studying the shoreline with binoculars comparing observations with her chart could she be reasonably sure their goal had been attained. The grey streak on the horizon could have been Washington or Fanning or any one of the thousands of islands found in the South Pacific. Only a close examination would deliver the final verdict.

The reader is blissfully unaware of the unease and apprehension gripping the mariner drifting about at night, in pitch black darkness in a small frail boat not knowing one's location with the ever present danger of running aground on a hidden reef. The problem is compounded by the fact that the Iola did not have a functioning depth gage. (A serious hazard facing defendants on the journey south was the presence of Kingman Reef, a hidden, 16 kilometer long submerged coral reef, guarding the approach to Palmyra from the North.)

Ascertaining latitude in the northern hemisphere is a relatively simple matter so long as one can locate Polaris. Finding longitude is quite another matter. In days of old many sea captains would sail to the desired latitude knowing their vessel to be well east or west of their destination. On arriving at the chosen latitude they would head east or west until the destination was achieved. (Referring to the imaginary latitudinal line as an "easting" or "westing" as the case may be.) Using this method of navigation added considerable time and distance to a voyage in that the vessel is not sailing a direct course towards its goal but traveling two legs of a right triangle rather than traversing the hypotenuse — however it did insure arriving at one's destination.

It is likely defendants on departure from Hawaii simply headed the Iola due south relying on the fact that the island would be visible with the use of binoculars from seven to ten miles distant. This makes the target considerably larger since the island would be visible seven miles distant passing to either side, assuming daylight conditions. (Should they have stumble upon Palmyra at night it is possible they might sail right on by never knowing it was there.) All in all, bumbling about the South Pacific with thousands of submerged reefs and small atolls is a risky enterprise. No matter what system was used, luck was on their side when Palmyra came within sight.

The return trip to Hawaii aboard the Sea Wind would have been a simple matter requiring few navigational skills. The mountains tower above the clouds, visible for well over one hundred miles. The islands themselves stretch out for hundreds of square miles. Even the most inept mariner could bump into them eventually. (All else failing, the oblivious skipper might observe the numerous contrail markings of the jets flying in and out of Hawaii.)

The long beat back to Hawaii might have been uncomfortable for the crew, but would not present a major challenge for a boat the likes of the Sea Wind. The logical explanation for the exceedingly slow return voyage of the Sea Wind was due to the fact that neither Stearns nor Walker had any appreciable navigational skills. They merely blundered about the Pacific until they finally spotted Hawaii, much the same as they did on the voyage to Palmyra.

Leisure Sailing

Stearns felt hard pressed to explain the extraordinary length of time it took for the Iola to arrive at Palmyra. However nothing is more zany than her invention of a new lie and rationale to explain her extremely slow passage. The term she employs is *"leisure sailing."*

Bugliosi, with no understanding of sailing and the sea, foolishly accepted her absolutely goofy rationalizations in an effort to explain and excuse the miserably slow progress of the Iola as she bumbled towards Palmyra. Reviewing the original court reporter's transcript from Stearns' murder trial we find the following bizarre colloquy (wisely not included in ATSWT) between a naive Bugliosi and an ignorant, yet clever and manipulative client. Bugliosi is put up to the following idiotic inquiry:

Bugliosi questions Stearns during her murder trial:

".........you classify you and Buck as being leisure sailors or did you try to travel as much as you could everyday?"

Stearns responds:

"No we were leisure sailors."

"Did you sail at night?"

"No, we didn't." Replies, Stearns.

"Bugliosi: *Many on the sea do that?"*

"Yes."

"One sleeps and the other stays awake; is that correct?"

"That's right." *(Vol. 12, p. 1910)*

Stearns informed the jury she and Walker did not sail during the hours of darkness. The prosecution does not comprehend the unbelievable stupidity of her testimony and fails to examine Stearns demanding she expand on what she claims was her practice of not sailing at night during the voyage to Palmyra.

Of all the inanities sold to the jury none can compare with the above quoted dialogue. Bugliosi was obviously conned by Stearns into asking the above questions. Is one to suppose defendants took down the sails every evening just before sunset and drifted with

71

wind, wave, and current during the hours of darkness with no one at the helm? (With no canvas flying what purpose would there be in controlling the helm?)

While it is true that a fatigued sailor particularly if he is sailing single handed will from time to time throw out a "sea anchor" and rest as needed. (The prudent do this during the day and presumably well away from shipping lanes.) If a sea anchor is used then it is necessary to strike the sails and secure them. There are also various means of adjusting main and jib to prevent forward motion of the vessel and discourage excessive rolling. Lacking knowledge neither one of the above methods were employed by these meat-heads.

No sailor in his right mind would choose to drift about the ocean every night while on a voyage. With modest wind and/or current, a sailing vessel such as the Iola could drift twenty or thirty miles or more off course. Charting would be extremely difficult — the Line of Position would snake about in the most unimaginable manner. The entire idea is laughable. Selecting an "Assumed Position" from which to commence calculations the following morning would be a crap-shoot. Not only does Stearns have the gaul to pass this nonsense off to the jury as proper navigation, but in so doing makes a fool of Bugliosi by convincing him it is a common practice to engage in navigation in such a rudimentary and careless manner. Drifting about during the hours of darkness would wreak havoc with navigation. One would wake up every morning with not a clue as to where the vessel might be.

Not only does the above testimony from Stearns expose her as an incompetent navigator, but again, the reader is exposed to her pathological and compulsive lying.

Flunking Math

The Iola allegedly departed Port Allen, Kauai, on June 1, 1974 bound for Palmyra. Defendants were traveling with three dogs, a small mixed female belonging to Stearns known as Puffer, and two dogs belonging to Walker, a female lab and an aggressive pit bull. (p. 47)

Allegedly they had a thousand dollars worth of provisions. The galley at best had a two burner alcohol or kerosene stove without an oven (although Stearns argues to the contrary) and a small sink. They carried a mere thirty gallons of fresh water for themselves and the three dogs. In the early part of the voyage Walker slipped and struck his head on a stanchion. On another occasion he ran a fish hook through his thumb. (pp. 47-9, 53, 57) A week out of Hawaii they had lost their way. At one point she thought they had traveled seven hundred miles east. Another day they she alleges they had traveled three hundred miles south. After reviewing an instruction booklet she claims to have understood her errors and could properly navigate using the sextant and sun sights. (p. 55)

On the June 11, 1974 the tenth day of the voyage, Stearns believed the Iola had completed half the distance to Palmyra, approximately 480 nautical miles. Just three days later on June 14, she claimed to be 120 nautical miles from Palmyra Island. Her log states Palmyra Island was sighted off the port side at 4:15 P. M. on the 19th. (pp. 56, 59, 60)

The claim is suspect for many reasons. The figures do not add up. Supposedly, the first ten days of the voyage the Iola, at best averages 48 miles a day, approximately two miles an hour. Without explanation, for the next three days the Iola more than doubles her speed covering 120 miles a day, averaging an unheard of speed (for the defendants) of five knots. (p. 55)

Stearns testified it took the Iola four and a half days to cover the remaining one hundred twenty miles with the Iola covering less that 30 miles a day. This snail-like pace averages out to be just slightly over one knot per hour. (p. 55) In all likelihood these figures are another figment of Stearns imagination. Not possessing the requisite skill or materials to navigate by sextant, on leaving Port Allen, June 1, 1974, she simply headed due south flying just a jib sail. In all probability, rather than taking eighteen days to sight Palmyra as Stearns alleges, it took the full twenty-six days. All the hide and seek with the island outlined in the so-called log is a sham. They finally found Palmyra only to run aground in the channel as they attempted to enter the lagoon. They did not flounder on the reef because of a drop in the south-east trades as alleged in the book, but due to poor seamanship. (p. 61)

Contrary to the allegations of Bugliosi and Henderson, Stearns murder trial transcript reveals Walker ran aground because they were "shoaling" the entrance on approach to the lagoon and not because the wind suddenly died as Stearns claims in ATSWT. (Vol. 10, p. 1583)

Reviewing the trial transcript other unmentioned facts are brought to light testimony not found in ATSWT. Stearns admits to Stevens they did *not* employ the main sail during their trip southward to Palmyra. They only used the small jib sail. This would account for the extremely slow speed of the vessel. It would also account for the excessive rolling experienced while underway. (Vol. 12, p. 1820)

Enoki cross-examines Stearns:

74

"You heard Mr. Stevens testify that he told — I am sorry — that you told him that you were afraid to raise the mainsail because you, meaning —meaning you and Walker — could not handle that."

"Do you recall Mr. Stevens testifying to that?"

(Enoki quizzes Stearns about Steven's testimony wherein she told him that neither of the defendants could handle the mainsail, working solely, or together. This would be expected because they did not know how to sail and the Iola did not have winches to assist in controlling the main and jib sheets, or the main halyard. Raising or lowering the main sail without a halyard winch could present serious challenges particularly if it was nighttime or there was substantial wind.)

Stearns disagrees with Stevens testimony, responding:

"No, I believe I told him that I didn't raise the mainsail because I, personally, could not handle it. Buck was below and very seasick and not getting up. If Buck got up, he could do it."

Enoki in his usual softball style having pinned down Stearns gives her a way out by following with a question suggesting that Stevens, who testified neither Stearns nor Walker could raise the mainsail was mistaken:

"So if Mr. Stevens thought that you had said that the two of you couldn't handle it, he would be mistaken about what you were talking about then?"

Stearns, sees her opening and heads for the exit:

Right, I was just talking about me handling it by myself." (Vol. 12, p. 1820)

Going to the Dogs

75

Sharing the space of a small wet cabin and cockpit with three dogs urinating and defecating, along with two unwashed humans, must have been an unusual olfactory experience. Who was assigned the cleaning detail and what disinfectants and detergents were employed? A small matter perhaps, but just one more thing to add another layer of discomfort to a cursed and forbidding voyage. Creatures of land, canines must be trained to accept shipboard life. When confined to a small boat they get confused and often identify the ship as their den and have a difficult time taking care of bodily functions in a spot designated for such activities. Then too there is the problem of cost and space for storage of dog food as well as sufficient water for the animals — three dogs could consume as much water as defendants, particularly in tropical climes.

On Again, Off Again, Round Again Finnegan

Stearns testified during her murder trial she kept a diary/log of her time spent on the Iola. She states it started out as a ships log written by Walker. Around the 16th of June she alleges treating it more like a daily journal and would *"make entries each day"*. It was her custom to make these entries in the *"late afternoon, before dark, and after some things had already transpired during the day."* Stearns explains she made her entries during the "daylight hours" in late afternoon because it was difficult to *"write after dark."* (Vol. 10, pp. 1586-7.)

The morning of June 19, 1974 Stearns claimed according to her calculations the Iola is twenty miles away from Palmyra Island. She predicts they will see the island around three p.m. *"off the port bow"*. (p. 59)

As the Iola approached Palmyra *"they altered course to come around well west of the island to a narrow channel indicated on the chart."* They were so close Stearns claimed she could observe the surf line by use of binoculars. (Meaning they are only a mile of two distant.) (p. 60)

"June 19. LAND HO! At 4:15 p.m. we spotted Palmyra off our port side. Wind very light--unable to make landfall before dark. Headed east. Strong winds all night. Then becalmed." (p. 60)

The island allegedly is sighted east of the Sea Wind and observed to the port (left) side of the boat. Passing the island Stearns changes her southerly course and heads east. Approaching Palmyra from the north one wonders why our intrepid sailors did not sail directly towards it? Knowing the entry channel to lagoon is located on the southern shore why not sail over to the shallows and drop anchor? Had they done so, with three hours to spare before darkness, it would have been a small matter to avoid coral heads and drop the hook in fifty feet of water and await the next day. Her decision to sail away from the island makes no sense.

"June 20. Spotted Palmyra again this morning, dead west. Winds very light. Very frustrating—rain squalls and enough wind to get us just about where we were yesterday at this time. But then the wind ceased. So near and yet so far!"

On June 20, 1974 Stearns purportedly observes Palmyra Island *"dead west"* which would locate the Iola due east of Palmyra. The reader is not informed as to the distance off during the morning sighting, obviously close enough to clearly see the island — one would imagine somewhere between two and six miles. This being so why did she not sail directly to Palmyra? She supposedly saw the island in the morning and had all day with a favorable two knot current to drift over to it. Why sail on by south of Palmyra heading

77

in a westerly direction and return to the *"same place"* they were the day before between the hours of four and six p.m. ?   If they could traverse that distance during daylight hours why could they not sail into anchor range and drop their hook? Why sail on by? (p. 60)

"June 21. Though winds are light last night and brisk today, we are having trouble relocating our island."

Stearns claims she is capable of navigation by the use of the sextant. If she truly has these skills why is she unable to utilize them and relocate the island?   Why is she lost? With the island no longer visible her vaunted navigational skills have vanished. Now Stearns alleges she has drifted to the west (and perhaps somewhat south) and cannot locate Palmyra Island. (p. 61)

All this hide and seek with the island is a bit difficult accept. We are to believe our peerless navigator with all her supposed skills, nearly obtains her goal, the island is within sight and she is unable to traverse the last couple of miles.   In the course of a few days this problem occurs on several occasions. The proposition does not make sense. It would have been great sport to examine Stearns in detail concerning the allegations in her so-called log.   A well informed prosecutor would demand she diagram on a chart the peregrinations of the Iola as Stearns bumbles about looking for Palmyra.

The explanation for all this nonsense is that Stearns navigational skills and log entries, are for the most part a fiction, a subterfuge to explain away the slow pace of the ailing Iola as she makes her way south to Palmyra. If the time required to complete the voyage was approximately 26 days, departing on the 1st of June and running aground on the 27th in the channel, the average speed of the Iola was a shockingly slow 1.6 knots per hour.   No wonder Walker thought if he fell into the sea, it would be a simple matter to catch up with the Iola and climb aboard. (p. 70)

"June 22. Couldn't find her. Lowered all sails last night--no wind thru today. Reading. Took sights."

Our intrepid navigator is again befuddled and cannot find the island. Stearns claims no wind blew that day. She *"took sights"* but is uncertain as to the location of Palmyra. Another incomprehensible entry. Since she is such a supposed expert in navigation and can locate Palmyra at a distance of 120 miles with exactitude why is it that she cannot locate the island when close by? Why is she unable to plot a Line of Position? (pp. 60-61)

"June 23. Fair trade winds. Hoisted all sails and went in pursuit of our island. Re-LAND HO at 12:30, giving us plenty of time to gain anchorage. For entry, we're hoping for a SE wind. We are off SW shore. Saw a light on the island at night. Possibly another boat."

Stearns allegedly finds Palmyra once again around 12:30 (presumably p.m.) on the 23rd. She believes the position of the vessel is off the southwest shore placing the island to the northeast. If true a southeast wind would make an easy starboard reach back to the island up the channel and into the lagoon.

Oddly in this notation there is no mention of dropping anchor. After a long voyage, with the goal obtained, it is always a notable event when the "hook" goes down and the vessel secured, yet there is no mention of this activity.

June 24. So nice to wake up and have the island right there in front of us.

June 25. Another day of reading. Strong NE winds continue.

June 26. Buck caught two big fish this morning. Soaked them in brine and hung them out to dry. Will use for bait. A family of manta rays came scouting for their dinner. Still NE trades. Still waiting and reading.

Another entry that has every appearance of being filler.

June 27. A strong SE wind was blowing. Stearns claims the winds had shifted. Defendants *"tumbled out of bed,"* hoisted sail and got underway. Desiring a southeast wind, Stearns claims to have waited nearly three and a half days, (presumably at anchor off the island) before attempting entry.

Finally on the 27th of June with *"southeast trades"* blowing defendants decide to attempt entry to the Palmyra lagoon only to run aground, not because the wind died (as alleged in the book) but because of faulty navigation as Stearns admits during her murder trial.

Bugliosi writes: *"...as Buck took the wheel and tried to do so, the wind suddenly died and the Iola came to a halt, subject now to the outflowing current. Minutes later, as the Iola drifted backward, there was a sudden bump followed by a harsh scrunching sound from beneath the boat. The fragile Iola had gone aground on a coral head."* (p. 61)

However, Stearns testimony at her murder trial *impeaches* Bugliosi's book concerning the reason why the Iola ran aground attempting entry to the lagoon. Her trial transcript contradicts the text of ATSWT and lays the blame for the grounding on poor seamanship.

Enoki cross-examining Stearns:

" I thought you sailed in under southeast wind."

Stearns replies:

"That is an advantageous wind to go to the northeast."

"But you wound up on the reef?" Inquires Enoki.

Stearns:

"That wasn't so much the wind's fault. I believe that we approached the island too close so that, in approaching the two

(channel) markers that we had to line up to come in, if we were further out, we wouldn't have bonked ourselves on those coral heads, but we were approaching from too close to the island." (Vol. 12, p.1829)

Stearns explains to the jury the cause of the grounding was due to the fact they were *"shoaling"* the entrance to the channel and not the capricious wind.

The only certainty in this alleged series of events, is that the Iola departed Hawaii on June 1, 1974, and ran hard aground in the channel as defendants were attempting to enter Palmyra lagoon on June 27, 1974. The deficiencies and inconsistencies in the above log entries cause one to suspect the above log entries are lies designed to cover the inadequacies of Stearns as a navigator and the wretched condition of the Iola as a sailing vessel. (pp. 47, 61)

Experienced Hands

Sufficient food to meet the needs of the crew on a small sailboat is an important aspect of cruising, but an adequate supply of drinking water is a far greater concern. One can go without food for several weeks, but without drinking water the human body has trouble functioning more than a few days. Water for drinking is far more precious than food aboard a small boat. The Iola, a small cramped vessel with three dogs and two crew had little room for water storage. Water for bathing would be limited to that which the rain provided. The drinking water supply was sufficient for two crew and three dogs for a few weeks and then only if everyone was extremely careful. (The reader is informed that defendants had only 30 gallons of drinking water aboard the Iola for crew and dogs.) (p. 49)

81

Lacking knowledge of the sea defendant (and Bugliosi) proudly proclaim they used "bottled water" to wash their dishes, as if this act bestowed on defendants an aura of sailor like care and knowledge when it demonstrates exactly the opposite. (p. 49)

Even the most inexperienced landlubber would have sense enough to preserve the small amount of precious drinking water by washing and rinsing dishes in salt water which is a common practice among sailors with restricted access to fresh water.   Why waste precious drinking water to wash or rinse dishes when access to fresh water, during a voyage of uncertain duration, may spell the difference between life and death?   Once the water was gone they would have to rely on rainfall as a source of fresh water assuming our erstwhile sailors had   fashioned   some kind of water collecting system (the existence of which, there is no mention).

Warped Speed

Why did the Iola sail so slowly? Why average slightly better than two miles an hour under the most favorable conditions with following wind and seas?   Why did they not proceed at a more reasonable 3 to 4 knots, arriving at Palmyra in twelve to thirteen days given Iola's theoretical hull speed in excess of five knots? What are the implications of the alleged hide and seek game with Palmyra Island upon purported arrival?

A part of the navigation puzzle is missing. The Iola had a theoretical hull speed between five and six knots.   (Roughly calculated to be 1.3 times the square root of the waterline.) Why did the Iola scarcely achieve more than two knots per hour heading almost directly downwind with following seas? (p. 55)

The answer to this question is found in the fact defendants relied entirely on their small jib sail as the means of propulsion during the voyage to Palmyra. There was danger of sinking if defendants sailed with the normal combination of main and jib. While it is true this combination is the norm for a sloop, it is also true employing the main in combination with the jib caused the Iola to heel. As the Iola heeled under pressure of wind and sail more cracks in the hull were submerged causing sea water to find it's way into the boat. (The smallest crack can admit enormous quantities of water as defendants no doubt discovered during their inter-island trips before departure from Hawaii.)

Walker's attempt at fiberglassing the hull was not successful. As the underlying planks worked, the thin layer of fiberglass cracked admitting water. (p. 52) The weight aloft from the heavy mast and the pressure of the wind on both main and jib required skills beyond defendant's capability. The manual bilge pump could keep ahead of the influx of water so long as there was not excessive angle of heel for a prolonged period. With both main and jib flying the angle of heel increased to the point where the manual bilge pump was overwhelmed by incoming sea water. The only solution to this problem was reliance solely upon the jib. Admittedly, use of jib sail alone caused excessive rolling, but did not submerge the numerous cracks in the hull for long periods of time. Defendants were sailing "under-canvassed" for a very good reason....their survival.

Stearns attempts to gloss over and obscure the absurdly slow speed of Iola, well below what one would expect of her design. The question arises; why was it so important to fabricate a false log of Iola? Why create the ridiculous hide and seek version of the approach to Palmyra? First you see it then you don't. Now dead ahead, now off to the west then off to the east. Even the most

83

inexperienced crew would have the common sense to observe the chart, find a suitable location in the shallows, and drop the anchor while waiting for south-easterly wind.

Bugliosi, while admitting many deficiencies of the Iola, portrayed Stearns as a competent navigator. On sighting Palmyra inexplicably her expertise vanishes and the reader is entertained with an alleged seven day pursuit as Palmyra appears, disappears, and reappears.

This ludicrous episode of hide and seek with the island is an effort by Stearns to obscure the fact it actually took twenty-six days to reach Palmyra and not eighteen. The purpose of the hide and seek was to conceal the obvious fact the Iola was not seaworthy and incapable of returning defendants safely to Hawaii.

Arriving at this conclusion the question arises: what was defendant's purpose in sailing to Palmyra with no possibility of return to Hawaii aboard the Iola? A cockeyed scheme to get rich by growing and harvesting marijuana, or, the darker purpose of boat theft and murder?

The leitmotif of this drama, which reoccurs throughout ATSWT, is one of a ship of doom. When the Iola, nee Margaret, sank in Hawaii in 1971, she was finished despite Walker's amateurish efforts to rehabilitate her. Dr. Sanders, Tom Wolfe, and the Pollocks, appreciated this fact and after a short exposure to the bizarre couple wisely fled lest they be drawn into Stearns nightmare of lies, torture and death.

All one can know for certain regarding the Iola's voyage from Hawaii to Palmyra Island is that she departed Hawaii on June 1, 1974 and while attempting to sail into the Palmyra lagoon on June 27, 1974 ran hard aground in the channel because of Walker's poor seamanship. (Vol. 12, p. 1829)

Even if one were to accept an interpretation most favorable to Stearns with the Iola achieving two or two and one half knots per hour, because of adverse wind and current the voyage to Fanning could never have been completed and would have ended in defendants death at sea.

It was necessary for Stearns to promote the fiction of seaworthiness to obscure her darker purpose of mayhem and murder. To this end the reader is regaled with various distractions such as the asinine marijuana grow-op; the supposed aid from her fellow conspirators who promise a turkey for Thanksgiving; and the purposeless voyage to impoverished Fanning Island with Mac's fifty dollars in her pocket to purchase food.

Blind Leading the Blind

Enoki, cross-examining Stearns during her murder trial demonstrates her (and his) spectacular ignorance pertaining to wooden sailboats that are glassed over:

Stearns offers her "expert" opinion: *"All wooden boats leak, whether they'r fiberglassed over or not."*

Her comment as usual is wide of the mark. (The purpose in fiber-glassing the hull of a wooden boat is to stop the leaking and preserve the integrity of the hull.) Stearns' ignorance is surpassed by Enoki who erroneously believes a wooden hulled vessel that has been properly covered over with fiberglass, is more likely to leak than it was, prior to fiberglassing.

Enoki:

"Okay. But—well, you're in agreement that fiberglass — a wood planked boat with fiberglass over it is — is more likely to leak than just a wood plank boat?"

Stearns:

"It's my understanding that all wooden planked boats, and all boats that are fiberglassed over, leak. But to answer your question, the answer is: yes, the Iola did leak."

Enoki:

"I believe that was two questions ago. But...you said you didn't go underwater, or anything, to see any — if there were any cracks or leaks for yourself; is that — is that right?"

"That's correct."

"And did you — did you see any leaks above the waterline in Palmyra?"

The court: *"leaks" or "cracks"?*

Enoki: *"Cracks. I'm sorry."*

Stearns:

"I was trying to remember when Tom Wolfe was testifying about the crack along the side. I...seem to remember it."

"...irrespective of whatever the testimony was, where do you seem to remember it was?" Queries, Enoki.

"I thought that it was up around the gunnel." Responds Stearns.

"Okay. And for people who don't know where a gunnel is, is where?"

" The very top part trim around the top part of the boat. It kind of comes up from the deck."

"And...that would not be into the water?"

"No, that would be far above the water. But, if you were— well heeled over in the water, she could ship water through it."

"And do you recall whether that—that area that you're thinking of is fore or aft—or was fore or aft?"

"I believe it was on the starboard side."

"That's the right side...starboard is right?" Enoki corrects Stearns.

Stearns: *"Right. I'm sorry. I think it was on the port (left) side."* (Vol. 12, pp. 1801- 9)

Stearns evades Enoki's question as to the location of the crack. Then she demonstrates her ignorance of sea terms and literally does not know port from starboard. Enoki informs her of the meaning of the term starboard whereupon she changes her testimony indicating the crack was on the left (port) side of the vessel but fails to indicate whether it was fore or aft.

There are several pertinent observations pertaining to the above quoted testimony: "all" wooden vessels do not leak. Whether or not a planked vessel leaks depends on it's age, care in construction and maintenance. Throughout the trial Stearns repeatedly misinforms the jury regarding the effect and purpose of fiberglassing over a wooden hulled vessel. If a crack was in the gunnel there is little possibility sea water would be admitted to the interior of the boat because the gunnel normally sits atop the deck. Thus a crack would admit water to the deck which would then flow back into the sea and not penetrate the interior.

Enoki continues:

"Okay, would you have expected that area to be under water if the vessel were to go to sea?"

"No, not with me aboard."

"What...what do you mean by not with you aboard?" Asks Enoki.

Stearns: *"I didn't like it when the ship heeled over a lot. My two favorite sayings at sea were: 'reef the main, and head her up'."*

Enoki: "Well, irrespective of what you liked about the — about the voyages that you took, would you have expected that vessel

— or that portion of the vessel to be underwater, if you went into heavy seas?"

Stearns: *"Only if you were a racer, and you were trying to get as much speed out of the boat as possible, and so you had her heeling over all the way. I wasn't comfortable in that position. And so — when you are at sea you can really control that type of thing by the angle that you go into the wind and how much sail you have."*

Enoki: *"Would it be fair to say that that — that in your opinion that crack ...was — would not have caused a leak in your opinion?"*

Stearns: *"If somebody liked going very fast in the water..."*

Enoki: *"No, as it — as it sat in Palmyra."*

Stearns: *"Oh, it wouldn't in Palmyra, no"*

Enoki: *"Okay. And in your anticipated trip to Fanning Island, likewise you would — you would not have expected that leak to cause — I'm sorry, that crack to cause you any problems."*

"That's correct."   Stearns. agrees.   (Vol. 12,   pp. 1808 -10.)

(One would have to look far and wide for an example of cross-examination as substandard and amateurish as that found above. Soft-ball questions — telegraphing answers favorable to the defense.)

Close But No Cigar

Bugliosi argues the Iola must have been seaworthy because it delivered defendants to their destination. (p. 491) This assertion is incorrect. Against the odds the Iola almost completed her mission. Attempting to enter the Palmyra lagoon she ran hard aground because of the poor seamanship of Stearns and Walker.   Defendants fell short of their goal.   (p. 61)

Alert sailors within the lagoon (Wheeler and Briggs) seeing their plight rushed to rescue pulling the Iola off the coral reef and into the security of the lagoon.   (Without the assistance of other sailors, hard aground, the Iola would have been smashed to pieces on the coral as soon as the wind picked up.)

Defendants had many troubles during the voyage south to Palmyra. Stearns greatest test, which easily could have ended in disaster, was the alleged dangerous meandering near the island of Palmyra once they supposedly arrived.   Time and again Stearns claimed they had the island in view but because of poor seamanship was unable to sail to their destination.   Stumbling about in pitch darkness in the proximity of a reef such as Kingman or those of surrounding Palmyra, not knowing one's location, is an extremely dangerous pastime.   Stearns admits several times during this period she was lost. If true any night could haver spelled disaster for the Iola and defendants.

Had the Iola a functioning engine it would have been a simple matter of starting the motor, close with the island and motor up the channel. It was mere chance and the assistance of other sailors that permitted the Iola entrance into the security of the lagoon.

The test of seaworthiness is not the ability of a boat to complete a voyage under optimum conditions. (Our feckless sailors voyaged to Palmyra sailing under the most favorable conditions with fair winds and a following seas.)   Seaworthiness of a vessel is tested as conditions turn foul, wind and seas rising, adverse currents and darkness at noon. How then would the Iola fare? The answer is obvious; her fragile rotting hull would give way and with her defective bilge pump completely overwhelmed, she would quickly go to the bottom along with all hands.

The proposition the Iola must be seaworthy because she delivered her murderous crew to Palmyra is erroneous. Moreover, a resupply mission to Fanning Island or a return voyage to Hawaii facing adverse winds and seas would be out of the question.

ISLAND LIFE

Arrival of Defendants

Defendants were short on supplies and money on arriving at Palmyra, June 27, 1974. Within a day or two of arrival Stearns had to resort to begging for staples such as sugar and flour. Fortunately there were abundant coconuts, crab, fish, and fresh water. They had plenty to eat, but the diet was woefully lacking in variety. Stearns made bread and baked a few cakes before her flour and sugar ran out. Whether this was done from a pot on a burner or using the oven on shore was not clarified. (Apparently there was an outdoor oven available on shore for use. Although primitive, use of the oven would make sense as few sailors would want the heat of an oven in the confines of a small boat cabin in the tropics.) (p. 413)

On arrival defendants commenced contact with their co-conspirators, the Musick brothers via mail and Wheeler's radio. Ostensibly for the purpose of obtaining food, supplies, and repair materials. (p. 315) At the same time in an effort to draw attention away from their devious purpose and impoverished condition Stearns began making inquiries about the feasibility of voyaging to Fanning Island for resupply knowing full well the Musick brothers had no intent to follow through with their promises.

Jack Wheeler, (Wheeler) spent many months on the Palmyra and fashioned himself the "mayor". He and his son helped in the rescue of the Iola after she had run aground. He showed Stearns an icebox which defendants were able to employ using the 120 volt power produced by their gas powered generator. Gasoline was abundant on Palmyra in that there was a plentiful supply left over by prior island occupants. (p. 78)

When approached by Stearns, Wheeler a veteran of Micronesia, advised against attempting a voyage to Fanning Island because it was against the prevailing southeast trade winds. They would also be fighting a two knot current. He suggested it would be easier to sail to Samoa, over a thousand miles to the southwest, because of favorable winds and current. (p. 100)

Arrival of the Grahams

July 2, 1974 a few days after the arrival of the Iola, the answer to defendant's dreams sailed into Palmyra lagoon in the guise of the Sea Wind, a sea-proven thirty-eight foot Angelman ketch. Just the right size, easily crewed by two, extremely well stocked with food, and exceedingly well equipped . Moreover there were only two crew to contend with; Mac Graham and his wife Muff.

The Sea Wind was everything defendants desired as a vessel. The Grahams planned to stay for a lengthly period allowing Stearns time to observe her prey and formulate a plan of murder.

To prevail over the Grahams there was one major problem to overcome; Mac was well armed. He was disciplined and knew how to use his weapons. He seldom went anywhere on the island without his .357 magnum on his hip, or the .38 derringer in has pocket.

91

Attacking Mac with Buck's small .22 caliber pistol was out of the question.

Mac was wary of defendants, but did not fear them. Muff disliked them and was fearful of both of them to the point where she would never trust or befriend either. Nor was she inclined to invite either of them aboard her home, the Sea Wind.

Less than a *month before* her torture and execution Muff's attitude towards defendants is set forth in a letter written to friends July 30, 1974.

"The hippie couple Jennifer and Roy, have been busy trying to get their garden going........I sure wish we hadn't picked a time to come here and stay just when they did. I'd just rather their type weren't here. They are supposed to have some friends (two guys) coming down on a boat to bring them supplies, as they are nearly out of everything. Jennifer, (an alias for Stearns, Bugliosi employed in his book "And the Sea Will Tell") *has been after the boats that come in for extra food. It really makes me mad — their mooching. They came down here to live off the land so why don't they do it and stop asking for things?"* (pp. 103-4)

Muff expresses anger with Stearns who was constantly pestering her for basic food such as sugar, cooking oil, and flour.

Mac's opinion of defendants is found in a letter of July 30, 1974, he pens to his sister Kit McIntosh:

"I have told you about the other couple, Roy and Jennifer, who arrived a week before us to 'their' deserted island to live the 'survival life' indefinitely. I am not really upset at other people being on the island, but Muff is. (Walker assumed the alias of Roy Allen on arrival at the island), *Roy and Jennifer are not really our type, but to dissect them would take another letter."* *(p. 103)*

92

The two couples did interact from time to time. Mac frequently gave them fish as neither Stearns or Walker were good fishermen. Mac purportedly played chess with Walker and Stearns from time to time. The Grahams allegedly attended Stearns birthday party at which time Mac presented Stearns with the anchor she left in the channel during the failed attempt at entry into the lagoon. Frequently Walker would come over to Mac's workplace hunting for any discarded cigarette butts he might find lying about. On one occasion Mac made a minor repair to the generator belonging to defendants. Ironically it was during this contact Stearns began to formulate her murder scheme. (pp. 119, 407)

It is probable when the Grahams first met defendants they offered modest acceptance. As the summer wore on the Grahams, observing the antics of defendants and their dogs, became less and less accepting of their behavior. The rejection of Walker and Stearns heightened with each passing day until it had deteriorated to the point where Tom Wolfe, a passing sailor, characterized it as *"almost total war"* when he left aboard the Toloa on the 17th of August bound for Australia. (p. 118)

Edwin and Marilyn Pollock

Bugliosi chose to change the names of some of the witnesses to the events pertaining to the murder of the Grahams. Such is the case with EDWIN and MARILYN POLLOCK, two crucial witnesses to the events leading up to the murder of the Grahams on Palmyra Island and the subsequent arrest of the defendants in Hawaii. (In the book "And The Sea Will Tell" EDWIN POLLOCK is given the name BERNARD LEONARD and his wife, MARILYN is called EVELYN LEONARD. They were both school teachers in Hawaii at

93

the time of the events herein described. Their yacht, TEMPEST, a Calkins 50, was called VOYAGER by Bugliosi in his book.)

The Sea Wind dropped anchor in the Palmyra lagoon July 2, 1974. A few hours later Edwin and Marilyn Pollock arrived aboard Tempest, a fifty foot Calkins, cutter rigged, sloop. The Pollocks became good friends with the Grahams frequently getting together for dinner. The Pollock's intent was to stay for the summer. They tied up to dolphins within 50 feet of the Iola. (p. 90)

Walker cutting down coconut trees with a chain saw and acting in a threatening manner created tension on the island. Stearns was a constant nuisance scurrying about begging for food under the guise of bartering when she was not disseminating her cover stories alleging assistance by the Musicks, or speaking of a voyage to Fanning Island to replenish her stores.

Uncomfortable with the presence of the defendants and their bizarre behavior, fearing for their own safety, the Pollocks cut short their planned vacation and returned to Hawaii July 16, 1974. Before departing they warned the Grahams about defendants, urging them to leave.

On departure of the Pollocks, Muff was in tears wanting to leave with them, but Mac feeling secure in his competence and weaponry refused to heed their advice.   The Pollocks, bearing no grudge, gave Stearns a departing gift of flour and cooking oil. Prudently, they felt the better course was to vacate the island believing defendants were a constant source of trouble, dangerous and were totally unpredictable. (p. 94)

Marilyn Pollock testified during Stearns' murder trial that Stearns told her she would not return to Hawaii aboard the Iola:

"......There's no way I'll leave on the Iola......She was very definite about that." (p. 326)

94

She found Walker to be a *"eerily frightening figure,"* testifying:

"I would be scrubbing the decks or doing something topside and he would row past our boat. I would speak to him but he would never acknowledge me. Never speak back. He'd just watch what I was doing, making me uncomfortable." (p. 326)

She stated this happened at least *"ten times"*.

Prosecutor Schroeder continues:

"Was it your intention to stay on Palmyra for two weeks?"

"No, we had planned on spending the summer there."

"For some reason you decided to leave early?"

"I felt uncomfortable. I felt threatened. I suggested to my husband that we leave."

Marilyn Pollock described her last conversation with Muff:

"I was...I was quite...This is so hard......I was fairly anxious about the situation. And I knew Muff was very anxious. I asked her if she couldn't try to leave...try to persuade Mac to leave Palmyra."

"Did you tell her to leave?"

"Yes, I said this is not a safe place to be. It would be wise if they would leave."

"Do you recall how she responded when you told her this?"

"She was crying. She would have liked to have left, she said. But Mac was not interested in leaving."

"And did she say anything else?"

"She was afraid for her life. She said she knew she would not leave the island alive." (pp. 326-7)

Curtis Shoemaker

Curtis Shoemaker (Shoemaker) was an experienced blue water sailor who built his own fifty-seven foot sailboat, (Sivada) resided in Hawaii, and was employed by the phone company as an engineer. He was active in ham radio operations and was well-known throughout the South Pacific. Before leaving Hawaii, Mac became friends with Shoemaker arranging to speak with him over ham radio, bi-weekly on Mondays and Wednesdays at 7:00 p.m. (ATSWT erroneously implies the conversations between Shoemaker and Mac occurred only once a week on Wednesday evening.)

Bugliosi, cross-examining Shoemaker:

"And you told Mr. Lui — You told Mr. Lui about your twice weekly radio contacts with Mac Graham, did you not?" (The writers of ATSWT renamed FBI Special Agent HILTON LUI, calling him TOM KILGORE.)

Shoemaker: *"Yes."* (Vol. 5, p. 770.)

Shortly thereafter Bugliosi read to the jury Shoemaker's testimony given during Stearns' theft trial in June 1975, (less than a year after the murder of the Grahams and long before any murder charges were laid against the defendants.) wherein Shoemaker mentions his last conversation with Mac of Wednesday, August 28, 1974.

"Question: Did you have contact with him (Mac) after that?"

"Answer: No. That was the — that's the last time I heard from him was he said that the other boat, (the Iola) *as he referred to, was leaving the next day."* (Mac thought the Iola was departing for Fanning Island the next day, Thursday, August 29, 1974.)

"Question: What did you do next after that point in time? After the last conversation that you said you had no other contact with him. Did you do anything with respect to contacting him?"

"Answer: Well, this was, I believe, a Wednesday night, so the next scheduled contact would have been the following Monday. And he didn't — there was no, you know, communications from him." (Vol. 5, pp. 776-7.)

During these radio sessions they would exchange news about the island and family matters. Shoemaker also acted as a relay for those in Hawaii that might have news for others on Palmyra. On one occasion Shoemaker relayed a message from Richard Musick to Stearns (via Mac) wherein he stated his intent to voyage to Palmyra with a boat load of food and repair materials.

Shoemaker played a pivotal role as a witness to the events as they unfolded on the island that summer. He was the last person, aside from the defendants, to speak with Mac before he was executed by Walker aboard the Iola on Thursday morning, August 29, 1974.

His first appearance as a witness was made during the June 1975 trial of Stearns for theft of the Sea Wind. Several months after the theft trial of Stearns, Shoemaker was again called as a witness when Walker was tried for his role in the theft of the Sea Wind. The third occasion Shoemaker was called to testify was during the 1985 trial of Walker for the murder of Muff Graham. His forth and final appearance came during the 1986 trial of Stearns for the murder of Muff Graham.

Because Shoemaker was in bi-weekly contact with Mac Graham via ham radio during the summer of 1974 he was witness to the events unfolding the Wednesday evening of August 28th. His testimony revealed the Grahams invited defendants to a bon voyage dinner that evening. Contrary to the testimony of Stearns, it also established the Grahams believed defendants intended to depart Palmyra Island for Fanning Island the following morning Thursday,

97

August 29, 1974 and not on Saturday, August 31st as Stearns suggested in her murder trial testimony.   (pp. 350-53)

His role as the messenger of Mac's final words was a function he never quite understood. Stearns had cleverly covered her tracks. Moreover, one could hardly expect a person not experienced in law to comprehend the facts surrounding the murder of the Grahams. (Not only was Shoemaker unaware of the significance of his last conversation with Mac, but those supposedly "in the know", i.e., the Coast Guard, the FBI and counsel for both sides, did not comprehend its significance.)   (pp. 105-6)

Relationship Between the Grahams and Defendants

Mac sets forth his opinion of defendants in the letter of July 30, 1974, to his sister, Kit Graham, less than a month before his murder:

"I am not really upset at other people being on the island, but Muff is. Roy and Jennifer are really not our type, but to dissect them would take another letter." (p. 103)

Muff expressed her attitude in a letter to her friends, the Jamiesons, August 1, 1974.

"They are supposed to have some friends (two guys) coming down on a boat to bring them supplies, as they are nearly out of everything. Jennifer has been after the boats that come in for extra food. It makes me mad — their
mooching. They came down here to live off the land so why don't they do it and stop asking for things." (p. 104)

(The reader can glean from the above excerpt Muff bought into Stearns' ploy that the Musick brothers were going to come to Stearns' rescue.)

In another letter August 16, 1974, less than two weeks before her death, Muff wrote to her mother:

"I just wish that couple would leave with their damn dogs. They've attacked two people. Now I don't walk around without a big stick...." (p. 119)

Walker was a scruffy looking dropout, running around Palmyra shirtless, in dirty shorts, front teeth missing, flip-flops, and a chain saw cutting down palm trees. to obtain coconuts. With Stearns constant begging for food it is easy to see why Muff would be unhappy in their presence and avoid them whenever possible. She was virtually a prisoner of the defendants under house arrest. The only place she felt safe was in the presence of Mac or on the Sea Wind where she had immediate access to her .38 derringer pistol.

Mac did not share Muff's fears. He was a man of action and foolishly felt secure in his weapons and the ability to defend himself. He brought with him two pistols, a .38 derringer for Muff and a .357 Magnum which he carried on his person. In addition to these weapons he kept a high powered 30.06 rifle aboard the Sea Wind. (p. 87)

We find Mac somewhat above the fray with a false sense of security in himself and his weaponry. His love for Muff would never permit him to take any act adverse to her interests such as inviting either the defendants aboard the Sea Wind without her express permission. Muff had a strong dislike of the defendants and knew in her heart they were the dark instruments of her death. With the exception of the evening of August 28th, neither of these foul mouthed, scruffy, would-be sailors, were ever allowed aboard Muff's boat.

There were also issues of class and upbringing. Walker and Stearns were crude and ill mannered. Several witnesses noted

Stearns had a *"foul mouth"*. (pp. 95 298-9) Bugliosi informs even
in the 1980s, during the period he was defending her, she used
"latrine language" . (p. 334) (One can be certain she received a
strong lecture from Bugliosi about the use of this kind of language in
the presence of the judge or jury).

Defendants arrived on Palmyra with virtually nothing. Their
boat was a derelict unable to transport them off the island. They had
little or no food other than that which they could scavenge from the
island and were reduced to relying on coconuts, fish, to some extent
crab, as their primary sources of food.   They were not going to
starve, but it was a monotonous diet.   The absence of flour, meat,
fruit, sugar, or spices, and cooking oil, for months on end could not
have been a happy prospect.

Shortly after arrival of the Pollocks, Stearns offered them the
last ten dollars she possessed in exchange for supplies. Ominously
she also offered to barter the ship's compass and an inexpensive
transistor radio allegedly used for navigational purposes.

Schroeder examines Edwin Pollock:

*"Did you ever have an occasion to talk to Stephanie about
the state of their food provisions?"*

"Yes."

"What did she say in that regard?"

*"One of the first times, she said they were low on food. They
would like to barter. They had a compass and a radio and a few
other boat pieces of equipment that they would like to barter for
some food. They also had $10.00."*

"So she offered to barter some equipment; is that it?"

"True."

"And $10.00 in cash?"

"Right."

"Now did either you or your wife ever give Stephanie and Roy (Walker) *any food?"*

"My wife was in charge of stores, so she had to check that out, and she gave Stephanie a few things as we left -- not very much."

"Did you ever —."

The court: *"Did you say as we left?"*

The witness: *"As we left Palmyra."*

Prosecutor Schroeder: *" Getting back to the question about bartering, did you ever barter with her?"*

"No."

"Did you ever accept her offer to barter?"

"No."   (Vol. 2, pp. 257-8)

(At one point Stearns requested permission to board the Tempest — this request was wisely denied by Evelyn Pollock.)

Given a dearth of variety in food Stearns was reduced to begging in one form or another. Every time she approached a sailor for food a difficult social dynamic arose. She attempted to disguise her begging behind the pretense of a swap or trade; however each party to the trading transaction knew full well what is going on. Stearns was begging for food.   Most without hesitation would give food to a starving person, but Stearns and Walker were not starving. To the contrary they had all the food they could eat, but were bored with their diet. Compromising one's personal comfort and possible future well-being because an ill prepared stranger is starving is one matter; to do so because that person is bored with his or her diet is quite another.

Each encounter caused a negative dynamic to build. If Muff refused to barter or give in to Stearns' begging she felt guilty. If she gave away a portion of her limited supplies she resented the fact that she felt morally forced to do so — as if she had been manipulated or conned.   For Stearns, with each act of begging a resentment built against her beneficiary no matter how generous. The mere fact that she was reduced to begging was foreign to her. She hated every act, every plea, and hated her donor even more.   With each passing day her anger and resentment grew towards the Grahams who had so much when defendants had so little.

The Grahams may have had more and a greater variety of food, but there was no super market on Palmyra. Sooner or later they would run out of provisions and have to return to Hawaii to replenish.   Every sailor knows giving away vital supplies be it fuel, water, or food to another who ventured out on the sea ill-prepared, may have dire consequences for the giver and his crew at a later time. At best it may be a mere inconvenience wherein because of their charity the Grahams are forced to terminate their stay and return to port a thousand miles distant for resupply.   At worst one never knows what emergency is just around the corner.

In the end as Stearns moved in to torture and kill Muff with the assistance of Walker, she was a seething caldron of rage over the manner she thought she had been "mistreated" by the Grahams. Her ire focused on Muff who thought she was "better" than Stearns.   For both defendants the spleen within building up over a lifetime of supposed slights was soon to be vented on Muff the target of their frustration. This rage, along with the sociopathy of Stearns, was one of the factors accounting for the unusual viciousness and ferocity of the attack on her.

Walker on first sighting the Sea Wind decided this was the boat he wanted and was eager to kill the Grahams at the earliest opportunity. Planning was left up to Stearns. He hated the Grahams because they thought they were above him, and because of the daily humiliation he endured while scrounging around for cigarette butts Mac discarded in his shop area. Secure in the knowledge the Grahams planned on staying for several months defendants had the summer to observe their prey, plot their revenge, and wait for the other sailors to depart in the fall, which they knew was certain to occur.

Other Opinions

On the date of his departure aboard the Toloa, August 17, 1974, Tom Wolfe observed the two camps were nearly at war. Wolfe's observations are found in a letter he had written to a friend shortly after the Toloa departed Palmyra.

"We sailed 1,000 miles to a tropical island named Palmyra,".....It has plenty of room, an abundant supply of water and coconuts and good fishing.
It's really a beautiful setting, right out of a South Pacific movie, with a lagoon, palm trees, beaches, coral reefs. But living there are two couples who are close to war. It's amazing. I mean, we came to paradise and found resentment and distrust. Isn't that a sad commentary on the world we live in?" (p. 118)

These are the observations of a sailor, not partial to either side, written to a friend in California, *just twelve days before* the murder of the Grahams.

August 16, 1974, less than two weeks before her torture and execution, Muff wrote to her mother and Mac's sister. In these letters she describes defendants as, "hippies" who dropped by fish — indicating the Grahams had a certain modest degree of trust towards them. She writes; *"August 12, 1974, Buck requested Mac's help to repair his Sears portable generator. Mac went with him and made the necessary repairs."* Muff wishes they would sail away and has bought into the Stearns' ploy that the Musicks were actually sailing down with supplies. In a letter to "Kit" McIntosh, sister of Mac, Muff wishes defendants would leave Palmyra with their "damn dogs." (p. 119)

A few days before, Walker's dog attacked Muff on her way to the shower. There was a nasty confrontation and Mac threatened to kill the pit bull if he ever repeated his behavior. While tensions were building between the couples, still there was an outward civility. Mac forwarded messages from Stearns to the Musicks via radio and his friend Shoemaker as late as August 21, 1974. (pp. 106-7)

At the murder trial of Walker, Norm Sanders, shipmate of Tom Wolfe, was called as a witness on behalf of Walker. During final argument prosecutor Enoki reviewed a portion of Sander's trial testimony:

"Dr. Sanders testified he thought things were so bad he wanted to convince the Grahams to leave. There was a discussion about — Dr. Sander's testimony about how there was — almost a war in terms of a war, one part of the island was someone's territory and the other part of the island someone else's territory, and the bathtub was neutral territory." (Volume 11, page 57, transcript from Walker murder trial.)

Not only did Marilyn Pollock urge the Grahams to leave, but Sanders, a casual acquaintance, after just a few days on the island, also perceived the same tensions and made an effort to persuade the Grahams to leave. The observations of Wolfe and Sanders, were noted while visiting the island August 13th through the 17th — less than two weeks before the murder of the Grahams.

Bill Larson and Don Stevens, sailing aboard the Shearwater, stopped by Palmyra for nine days on return to Hawaii. (p. 332)

Desiring to present the relationship between the Grahams and defendants in an amiable light, Weinglass asked Larson:

"Based on your observations of Jennifer with the Grahams, how would you describe their relationship?"

Larson replied: *"It was friendly."*

"Did you detect any animosity or hostility?"

"No, I didn't." Stated Larson.

Weinglass continues:

"Now, did you see or hear any comments or behavior by Muff Graham, in Jennifer's presence, that would lead you to believe that Muff and Jennifer were unfriendly or hostile to each other?"

Larson responds: *"No. I did not."*

"Did you see any or hear and behavior or comment of Muff Graham, in Jennifer's presence, that would lead you to believe that Muff and Jennifer were unfriendly or hostile to each other?" (p. 376)

Muff's background would not permit an outward show of anger in a normal social setting regardless of her dislike and fear of the defendants. Later when Larson was aboard the Sea Wind he suggested the defendants be invited to share an ice cold drink. Muff's response to his suggestion startled Larson:

"She said that she didn't want the other two to actually be on her boat." (p. 376)

Bugliosi, treating the fictitious diary/log of Stearns as if it were truth from on high, requests she read portions of the diary dealing with her supposed relationship with the Grahams to the jury during the trial.

"July 9th: On our way to bathe took some coconut butter to Mac and Muff. Never got to bathe but had a very enjoyable evening

with them, drinking wine....got pretty drunk...."   (Vol. 11,   pp. 1616-7)

The above supposed event never occurred. Only under the most unusual circumstances would Muff ever allow Walker on board her boat.   The only exception to Muff's hard and fast rule was the bon voyage dinner of the 28th. This deviation was permitted because both Grahams believed the Iola was departing the morning of the 29th and the defendants would never be seen again.

One fact is certain — Muff would not tolerate the defendants aboard the Sea Wind on a casual social basis.   Stearns' diary is replete with notations alleging she visited the Sea Wind. With the exception of the 28th bon voyage dinner, which is not noted in the log, neither Stearns nor Walker ever set foot on the Sea Wind while the Grahams were alive — any suggestion by Stearns to the contrary is a lie advanced to obscure her role in the murder of the Grahams.

Rosencrans and Guildenstern

There are two characters in this murder drama flitting about more real in their absence than in person: Richard ("Dickie") and Carlos Musick. Assistants to the murderous defendants they play a small but significant role in aiding and abetting defendants in the murder of the Grahams, and theft of the Sea Wind. (Bugliosi chose to assign different names to the MUSICKS.   RICHARD ('DICKIE") TAYLOR was in fact RICHARD MUSICK   and CARLOS TAYLOR is his brother CHARLES MUSICK.)

Prior to departure from Hawaii defendants anticipated problems explaining their impoverished presence at Palmyra aboard a derelict sailboat with no money and little food. To this end they created a cover story to disguise their purpose of piracy. To this end they enlisted   their friends Richard and Carlos Musick.   Before leaving for Palmyra defendants informed the Musicks they intended an act of murder and mayhem and their intent   to disguise their purpose by pretending to be engaged in a marijuana growing business with them.   Seeing no harm, Richard "Dickie" Musick agreed to play a supporting role and went along with the scheme.

Bugliosi outlines their purported role:

"Buck and Jennifer were planning to rendezvous on Palmyra with their friend Richard Musick and his brother, Carlos at the end of August. They'd all become acquainted at Maalaea Bay when Dickie was outfitting his thirty-two foot sailboat beside the dry-docked Iola." (p. 50)

Stearns, confides:

"Before leaving for Palmyra, Walker   had worked out a business deal with the Musick brothers they hoped would make them all rich. From seeds they would take with them, Buck and Jennifer would grow a large crop of marijuana on Palmyra......Dickie and Carlos were to handle the distribution end of the business, smuggling the dope into Hawaii and selling it for big profits. As part of the deal, they would bring supplies with them to Palmyra in late August." (p. 50)

On arrival at Palmyra Stearns informed all who would listen the primary purpose for their presence was to grow marijuana in sufficient quantities return to Hawaii and make their fortune selling the proceeds of their labor.

While hawking the supposed marijuana operation, shortly after arrival, Stearns also began spreading the rumor they might go to Fanning Island to purchase supplies if the Musicks did not show up on a resupply mission as scheduled. This misinformation was spread by defendants knowing all along the Musicks had no intention of sailing two thousand miles to Palmyra and back to deliver groceries.

Richard   Musick was the owner of a *"small fixed base operation which dealt with aircraft charter, maintenance, and flights"* . (Vol. 5, p. 2, Walker murder trial transcript.) He claimed only a passing friendship with defendants who he met on Maui while they were repairing the Iola. He assisted them with sailing advice and adjusted the compass of the Iola. He also gave them advice on navigation claiming he thought defendants were planning a trip to the South Seas with a possible visit to the Marquesas Islands. (Vol. 5, p. 3, Walker murder trial transcript.)

Testifying at the murder trial of Walker, Musick mentioned nothing about engaging in a marijuana growing operation with defendants. Instead he testified defendants planned a trip to the South Seas suggesting they were going to the Line Islands, then beating eastward hundreds of miles to the Marquesas, eventually heading west downwind to Samoa hundreds of miles away. (Vol. 5, p. 8, Walker murder trial transcript.)

(The suggested path of travel makes little sense, in that the Marquesas are hundreds of miles south and east of Palmyra. Samoa is located hundreds of mile west of the Marquesas. It would have been impossible for the Iola to beat into prevailing winds and travel eastward against prevailing currents for nearly a thousand miles to the Marquesas. Had Musick the sailing experience he claims, he would have advised against such a proposed voyage particularly given the woefully inadequate Iola and the total ignorance of Stearns and Walker regarding sailing.)

Prosecutor Schroeder examining Richard Musick at the murder trial of Walker:

"Did Buck ever mention whether he was planning on taking the Iola anywhere?"

"Yes. They were planning a trip down to the South Seas, through the Line Islands perhaps the Marquesas to Samoa." (Vol. 5, pp. 7-8, Walker murder trial transcript.)

After the Iola departed Hawaii for Palmyra aside from the radio contact with Stearns via Wheeler, Musick also was in contact with defendants in July when Wheeler arrived in Honolulu and mailed Stearns' letter to them.

Richard Musick testified:

"I received a letter that had been mailed in Honolulu. I believe I was in Lahaina at the time I received it. It had been brought to the Hawaiian Islands by another boat that had been on the island of Palmyra."

"Do you recall the name of the individual who brought it to Hawaii?"

"I believe it was Mr. Wheeler."

Jack Wheeler, before departing Palmyra in early July, contacted the Musicks on Stearns' behalf via his radio. During the direct examination of Wheeler at the murder trial of Stearns, mentioned making a radio call for Stearns to someone in Honolulu. He could not remember the name of the party he contacted, but *"It was in regard to another boat coming down with food."* (pp. 100, 315)

The letter requested underwater epoxy, flour, and sugar. In the letter Musick was further instructed to contact Curt Shoemaker to relay messages to defendants. Schroeder inquires of Musick:

"In this letter, did they request you to bring anything?"

Musick: *"Yes, sir. They requested me to bring down some...a product called sea-going epoxy."*

109

"What is the purpose of sea-going epoxy?"

"It is a two-part epoxy which you can mix together to patch fiberglass if you are under water." (Vol. 5, p. 9, Walker murder trial transcript.)

(This same letter gave Musick the name, address and phone number of Curtis Shoemaker.)

Prosecutor Schroeder continues:

"Did you in fact, attempt to respond to them through this person?"

Musick stated, he *"wrote a letter"* to defendants informing them he and his brother, *"would bring down whatever they needed"*. (Vol. 5, p. 10, Walker murder trial transcript.)

Schroeder asks Musick about the nature of the relationship:

"Mr. Musick, how many times would you estimate altogether you met with Mr. — well, you didn't know his last name at the time. How many times did you meet with Buck and Stephanie?"

"Maybe five times, maybe six."

"How well did you know them?"

"Not very well. I mean you meet people, you live next door to somebody for ten days or so, and you see them on the street a couple of times."

"Could you describe your relationship with them?"

"They were just some other people interested in sailing...cruising."

"Would you say you had not reached a level of relationship that you would refer to as being friends with them? Would that be a correct statement?"

Partington, defense attorney for Walker, objects as leading. King sustains the objection and Schroeder rephrases the question:

"What term would you use to describe your relationship with them?"

"New acquaintances. We were friendly with most people."

Musick testified he planned to go to Palmyra sometime around Thanksgiving, but did not make the voyage, claiming he lost his storm jib during a severe storm. (Vol. 5, pp. 10-13, transcript, Walker murder trial.)

Schroeder asks if he ever heard from defendants again; Musick testified he heard from them again in October of 1974 by mail. (The letter was mailed from Honolulu.) He also had further conversations with Walker on October 27, 1974 after defendants had murdered the Grahams and returned to Hawaii. Defendants now back in Hawaii had the Graham's boat and wanted to know about documentation. Musick claimed he thought Walker was talking about the old Iola and advised:

"That it would take three or four months to do so, and he should probably get a ....customs broker to do it for him."

Musick: *I went into a fairly detailed explanation of the requirements of documenting a boat such as tracing the ownership of it."*

Schroeder: *"Then what did he say?"*

"Well, I also went on to explain that the alternative method would be to register the boat with the state." (Vol. 5, p. 15, transcript, Walker murder trial.)

Musick explained the problems of changing boat registration including the necessity of a Bill of Sale from the prior owner. He gave defendants detailed information on how they could register the stolen Sea Wind with the state and avoid interference by the U.S. Coast Guard. He advised defendants about the timing of the Harbor Patrol and their frequency of making the rounds. Walker was nervous about being demanded papers by the Harbor Patrol, and Musick assured him that they were not in the habit of doing this. (Vol. 5, p 18, Walker murder trial.)

Although Richard Musick was called by the prosecution in the murder trial of Walker he was an adverse witness. At every opportunity he attempted to assist the defense while claiming to be merely casual friends with defendants. Eager to be of assistance he trips himself up. One such example is found as he explains why defendants wanted sea-going epoxy. Rather than admit there were underwater cracks in the Iola which rendered the vessel a derelict, he states:

"They wanted the epoxy so the worms would not get to the wood and destroy the wood....this is normal."

The problem with this comment is that, assuming the hull of the Iola was properly glassed over, it is not possible for worms to penetrate the fiberglass covering. (The fact that worms do not penetrate fiberglass is one of the chief reason boats made of fiberglass are so popular today.) This is a well known fact and Richard Musick was undoubtably aware of it.

Musick, purportedly agreed to ferry down the requested supplies, assisted by his brother, (Vol. 5, p. 10, Walker murder trial transcript.) yet, he claimed not to know defendants last names and alleged to have only met them five or six times. (Vol. 5, p. 11, Walker murder trial transcript.) Musick stated he intended sailing to Palmyra in late November around the time of

Thanksgiving.   (This would be an ill-advised time in that coincides with the commencement of typhoon season in the Southern Pacific Ocean.) (p. 120)

Questions arise from the above narrative: Musick asserts he was going to embark on a two thousand mile voyage to deliver groceries to people he had only known casually.   Why bother?   Why go to all the expense and trouble of buying food and supplies for defendants, endangering his life and that of his brother, for people who he had met five or six times?   He testified he did not know them "very well." (Vol. 5, pp. 11-12, Walker murder trial transcript.)   Musick testified his trip was because he *"lost"* his storm jib *"overboard"* on a trip to Lahaina to see some friends. (Vol. 5, p. 13)

On cross-examination by defense attorney Findlay during the murder trial of Walker,   Richard Musick admitted going to Palmyra Island on two occasions mentioning the year 1977.   He testified he stayed for three or four weeks.   He does not speak of the supposed second visit nor does counsel inquire about it. (Vol. 5, p. 25, Walker murder trial transcript.)

Given the testimony of Uberlaker, suggesting there was a later burning of the aluminum container holding Muff's remains one might expect the prosecution to examine Musick about this issue.   Was he the person that dug up Muff's remains and attempted to burn them on Walker's instructions? Why did he go to the island twice? Who went with him? When was the second visit made?   What was its purpose? Did he contact Walker at the time he was in prison, and etc.   However none of these issues were raised.

Weighing in on behalf of the defendants, Musick issues a series of patently false   remarks pertaining to the safety of a small boat compared to that of a larger boat, when queried by defense attorney.

Findlay examines:

"....a small boat, that in and of itself   makes it less seaworthy or less safe, compared with the big vessel?"

Musick responds:

"Yes sir, the reverse is true. The smaller boats are quite safer." (sic)

Findlay: *"Would you explain why that is true?"*

"The larger boat has a bigger mast to handle, requires a larger crew, a larger sail area, which in high seas and larger winds is more difficult to take care of. A smaller boat has only to worry about taking one sea at a time, while a large ship is subject to multiple stresses on the hull.   In fact, storms that would sink ships, large ships, oftentimes a smaller boat up to about 40, 45 feet will ride it out quite well." (Vol. 5, p. 34, Walker murder trial transcript.)

Obviously where there are two equally equipped sailboats each with competent crew, a larger boat will respond to high wind and seas better than a small boat.   In fact a larger vessel may well outrun a storm while a smaller slower boat will be unable to do so. Applying Musick's partisan logic the safest boat in high wind and seas would be a twelve foot row boat.

Crossed Wires

The proposed Musick visit raises many questions. Shoemaker did not know the Musicks nor did he have their address. When the murder scheme was first formulated defendants had no idea the Musicks would be able to communicate with them once they departed for Palmyra. Defendants anticipated one way communication in the form of a letter from Stearns sent via sailors returning to Hawaii. Defendants reasoned that merely discussing with other sailors a resupply mission by the Musicks would suffice to mask their purpose of murder and theft. Sending Richard Musick letters in addition to radio contact via Mac and Shoemaker lent credibility to her ruse.

After agreeing to play along with defendant's piracy scheme the Musick did not expect to hear anything more about the supposed business deal to sell dope or the fate of the unfortunate victims selected as defendant's target. Nor did he intend to have any direct involvement assisting defendants in their venture. It was by chance Mac possessed a long range ham radio permitting Stearns to receive communications from Richard Musick via Shoemaker in Hawaii. It was this chance occurrence that drew the Richard Musick deeper into Stearns' murderous web of lies.

(One wonders why Stearns did not request Mac contact Richard Musick directly via radio much in the same manner Wheeler had done? Obviously she had Richard's radio information since she had previously contacted him via Wheeler's radio when he was on the island early in the summer.)

Stearns claimed to have written a letter to Richard Musick for Mac to forward to Shoemaker via radio the evening of August 21st. She alleges giving it to Muff that same day. (Vol. 11, p. 1623) However, it is unlikely this letter existed. If Stearns supposed note of the 21st to Richard Musick truly existed and Stearns gave it to Muff on the 21st why did Mac not relay the information contained within the letter during his conversation with Shoemaker the same evening of the 21st? Had the letter existed, presumably Stearns would have informed the Musicks of her intent to sail to Fanning for resupply thus saving the Musicks the expense, time-wasting and life endangering two thousand mile ocean voyage during typhoon season only to arrive at Palmyra to discover defendants had departed for Fanning island and were no longer there.

The ham radio transmissions and letters between Stearns and the Musicks played a major role in the deception of the Grahams. Stearns' fabricated messages delivered via Mac, Wheeler, and other sailors, were concocted to convince the Grahams, and others present on the island, that defendants truly intended to depart for Fanning Island. One can observe her ploy in action in Shoemaker's carefully hand-written memorandum wherein he outlines Richard Musick's communication to him of August 21, 1974. (p. 120)

"We have been delayed by unforeseen circumstances, but hope to see you in October. We've enjoyed your letters very much. Of interest is the fact that bird eggs are considered superior eating to chicken eggs in many European countries. Hopefully, we will bring everything you need. We promise to

116

bring a turkey for Thanksgiving dinner. See you. Richard Taylor." (p. 120)

During the murder trial of Stearns, on direct examination of Shoemaker, one finds a different version of the above letter. Shoemaker is asked by prosecutor to read the letter written by Richard Musick to defendants of the 21st. (The underlined portions were deleted by Bugliosi from his book version of the letter.)

"Dear Mr. Shoemaker, would you please relay this message to my friend Roy Allen the next time you are in radio contact with Mac Graham. Thank you for your assistance."

Message: We have been delayed by unforeseen circumstances, but hope to see you in October. We've enjoyed your letters very much. Of interest is the fact that the sea gull eggs are considered superior eating to the chicken eggs in many European countries, not only in nutrition but in taste as well. Hopefully, we will bring everything necessary to repair your engine and so forth. Patty promises to bring a turkey for Thanksgiving dinner. See you there. Richard." (Vol. 5, p. 757-8))

Musick claimed not to know Walker's last name, yet he addresses the letter to his *"friend, Roy Allen"*.

There is nothing mentioned about repairing the engine in the book version. (p. 120) Presumably, this references the twenty horse outboard motor, which had been examined by Mac and was beyond repair.

Bugliosi deleted the portion of Richard Musick's letter to Stearns, of August 21, 1974 mentioning a person by the name of

"Patty". There is no follow up or testimony relating to a person with this name during the trial. Not a single question to identify this person, and what role, if any, she played in the charade and subterfuge. Why include her as part of the delivery team as if she were on friendly terms with Stearns? Who is she and what relationship did she have with the defendants? How well did "Patty" know Stearns and Walker?

On the 22nd of August 1974, advised by Mac the Musicks would not be down until October or November Stearns set her plot in action by informing the Grahams they were departing for Fanning Island on Thursday, August 29th. The following day, August 23rd, Stearns sold her generator to Mac for a paltry $50.00, borrowing it back ostensibly for the purpose of recharging the battery of the Iola. (p. 120)

It was on this date, August 23, 1974 the Grahams, convinced defendants were departing for Fanning Island on Thursday, August 29th, invited them to the Sea Wind for a bon voyage dinner the evening of Wednesday, August 28, 1974.

Had the marijuana business enterprise truly existed the Musicks, not knowing defendants were departing for Fanning Island, would have continued preparing for their resupply mission to Palmyra purchasing much needed supplies such as cooking oil, flour, sugar, and beans and after purchase, departing for Palmyra as soon as possible. After a perilous voyage, arriving at Palmyra, the Musicks would discover defendants were no longer there. They then faced a difficult thousand mile beat back to Hawaii during typhoon season — all their effort and expenditures would have been for nought.

Of course this scenario never occurred, defendants and the Musicks knew the purported marijuana business enterprise was a sham. It was never the intent of either party to proceed with the business as outlined by Stearns. Richard Musick having aided and abetted defendants in their murderous scheme by sending the untruthful message of August 21st remained in Hawaii awaiting the triumphal return of defendants in their newly stolen sailboat.

Moreover *at* no time during trial of Walker or Stearns did any attorney inquire about the alleged "business" deal. Not a single question. (Had Musick been questioned he may have refused to answer on the grounds of self-incrimination and demanded an attorney.) After Musick sent the message to defendants on the 21st of August there was no effort to follow up by either party until they met at the Ala Wei Harbor on the island of Oahu, October 27, 1974.

An example of Richard Musick's open partisanship, is found in his testimony:

"A wooden-hull boat generally leaks quite a lot. In your....That's why people put automatic bilge pumps in them." (Vol. 5, p. 39)

(A well maintained wooden hull scarcely leaks significantly more than a fiberglass hull. All small sailing vessels intent on a blue water voyage should have both an automatic 12 volt bilge pump and a manual pump.)

Another spurious example of Richard's supposed advice is advanced by Stearns as she explains a method of combatting sea sickness that runs contrary to all known remedies. On direct

119

examination Stearns testified she was upset with Walker's eating too much. Shortly thereafter he became seasick:

Bugliosi: *"So you were somewhat upset over his eating so much?"*

Stearns: *"Yes."*

"If Buck was seasick, how was he able to eat so much?" Asks Bugliosi.

"He was told — Mr. Musick told him that eating would help his nausea."

Bugliosi: *"But it just intensified if or —"*

"No, it helped. It did help." Interrupts, Stearns.

Even a landlubber like Bugliosi, is doubtful about Stearns' response:

"It actually helped?" He asks in astonishment.

"Yes." Responds Stearns — presumably with a straight face.

Again the jury is treated to Stearns' nonsense. When one is seasick, for most, the affliction is severe, the state of discomfort extreme. The ingesting of a large quantity of food by a sea-sick person will guarantee one result — an exceedingly quick trip to the rail as the food ingested comes back up in a great rush to exit the stomach. One cannot hold down a sip of water once the malady has set in. Sometimes saltine crackers in moderation can be retained. No one reasonably experienced in matters of sailing as Musick claimed to be would recommend eating a large amount of food to correct sea-sickness.

There are numerous remedies available to lessen the effect — pills, patches, and wrist-bands. For most within a few days the inner-ear adjusts to the gyrations of the vessel and all is back to normal.

Musick went to great lengths to advise defendants how they could escape notice of law enforcement and still obtain title to the Sea Wind. He pointed out the difficulties of registration with the Coast Guard and the several months it would take to obtain title. Also the possibility of an investigation into the background of the previous owners. If Walker applied for a change in ownership with the Coast Guard there was a possibility they would discover the prior owner was Mac Graham.

Musick advised Walker the absence of a Bill of Sale could present major problems for him in his quest for title if he attempted to renew title through the Coast Guard. The Coast Guard documentation number which is usually carved into a timber on the hull of the vessel is a permanently assigned number. As long as the boat is documented with the Coast Guard it retains the same number. The name of the owner may change, the name of the vessel or hailing port may change, but for the life of the vessel, the documentation number does not change.)

After pointing out all the problems the defendants might have attempting to continue the title with the Coast Guard, Musick suggested there would be far less likelihood of discovery of their crime if they registered the Sea Wind with the Department of Motor Vehicles in the State of Hawaii. The process would be speedy, and there would be far less chance of the authorities discovering the Lokahi was the Sea Wind and that her prior owner was Mac Graham.

One wonders why the constant allusion to Richard Musick's brother Carlos by Stearns as a person involved in the drug operation when there is only fleeting reference to him in the testimony of Richard during the trial? (Vol. 5, p. 10)

After years in Hawaii, owning a small company, why did Richard Musick pull up stakes and move to the east coast? Was it purely a personal decision or did things get too hot for him in Hawaii?

Richard Musick is a shadowy, ill defined villain in ATSWT, yet his obituary after dying from cancer makes him out to be a candidate for sainthood. How does that come about? Getting his hands sullied in the murder of the Grahams and drug trafficking in Hawaii did he repent his sinful ways and seek to atone? No one knows. Was he the saintly person suggested by his obituary? If so why his association with the likes of Stearns and Walker? Why his dogged defense of Stearns in his trial testimony? With his passing these questions and dozens more will never be answered.

BEATING WINDWARD

Wheeler Opines

In need of masking her true purpose of piracy Stearns spoke to Wheeler within a few days of her arrival on Palmyra about a possible voyage to Fanning Island, approximately 175 nautical miles to the southeast of Palmyra. Wheeler was of the opinion the Iola was not in condition to sail to Fanning. Not only was the proposed voyage against the prevailing southeast trade winds, but there is an opposing two knot current the entire distance.   Wheeler suggested Stearns   would be better off sailing over a thousand miles south and west to Samoa to replenish their supplies rather than a difficult beat into south east trades fighting the current all the way. (p. 100)

"Before Jack Wheeler left the island, she asked him if food was available at the nearest island shown on the chart......Wheeler said...The
nearest island that could be reached where food could be purchased was Fanning Island, 175 miles to the southeast." (p. 100)

"Wheeler warned her Fanning Island would be too difficult a voyage for a sailboat without a motor because they would be going against the wind."   He suggested American Samoa *"because of favorable winds and currents the whole way."* (p. 100)

Gentlemen Never Sail to Windward

There is an old adage that "gentlemen never sail to the windward".   That is to say if a skipper has regard for his passengers he avoids sailing windward whenever possible.   A pleasant off wind sail can become a wet, tossed about experience, merely by changing course and heading into a strong wind.

123

"Beating windward" is an apt term for the experience because everyone and everything on board gets beaten up. Following seas which help push the boat forward while sailing downwind become an adversary pounding the hull incessantly. The hull flexes and works shaking off endless assaults one wave after another. Fastenings securing wooden planks to the frames strain to hold the hull together as it flexes with each passing wave. The vessel heels at a precarious angle as the center of effort battles with the center of lateral resistance.

Excessive weight aloft in a heavy mast adds to the stress. Standing rigging goes taut, oncoming waves sweep the deck and "green water" submerges the bow. The bow drives through each wave lifting skyward as the crest of the wave passes under only to plunge into the oncoming trough. The smallest crack admits enormous amounts of water below soaking bedding and occupants as the vessel drives forward with the ever present threat of being thrown on her beam ends by a breaking wave and driven under. Doubts arise as the mariner looks up at the rigging and questions shortcuts that in fair weather seemed permissible, but with the vessel under stress raise grave concerns.

When beating windward modest winds can actually enhance the speed as the apparent wind over the deck increases due to the forward motion of the boat. However oncoming seas never enhance vessel speed and can be a major factor in reducing forward momentum. If severe they can impede forward progress to the point where the vessel is forced backward if attacked at the same time by adverse currents.

All You Have to Do is Tack

Defendant naively states to sail into the wind, *"all you have to do is tack"*. She is correct in that assertion but glosses over the problems inherent in sailing to windward. Supposing a vessel is sailing windward on a starboard tack (wind coming over the starboard rail) and the skipper decides to change course. He orders, "ready about". The crew acknowledges the order, and when prepared responds, "ready". The helmsman announces, "helms-a-lee," and turns the helm hard over. Meanwhile the crew is busy controlling the movement of the boom as it swings across the deck, at the same time slacking the sheet controlling the headsail and winching in the sheet on the opposite side of the vessel making the sail taut. Once on a new tack the skipper will make small adjustments to obtain the maximum drive from the sails.

In any appreciable wind as the boat comes about the sails loudly protest as the boom sweeps across the deck. (Uncontrolled movement of the boom during this maneuver is dangerous and could snap the mast or injure crew.) Tacking in darkness adds an additional element of confusion and danger. Tacking windward without benefit of winches to control the sheets , as was the instance with the Iola, is a perilous exercise and even more so at night. It is no wonder the defendants inexperienced in sailing feared sailing at night, claiming they did not do so because the were "leisure" sailors.

A sailboat cannot sail directly into the eye of the wind which is why it must tack. Sailors speak of "apparent wind".....

the actual flow of the air over the sails — the wind as it appears to the sailor from a moving vessel. Most well designed sailboats can sail at an angle of approximately 45 degrees into the eye of "apparent" wind. This means when tacking is necessary, the voyage becomes considerably longer than a direct line between the point of departure and point arrival.

Much attention is given by sailboat designers to design a boat that will sail at a close angle to the wind. In racing most skippers will sail their vessels "close-hauled" if it permits advantage. However if they point too high into the eye of the wind, (a maneuver known as "pinching") the vessel will lose speed. Higher still and forward motion will come to a halt and the sails will flail about emitting thunderous protest; a condition known as being "in irons" will result and all forward progress will halt. Most racing skippers will sail on a tack that will deliver maximum speed and pinch only if it is for a short time, and gives them a tactical racing advantage.

Tacking, depending on the conditions, can add considerable mileage to the voyage perhaps as much as doubling the distance depending on many variables. For the Iola, a voyage of 175 nautical miles to Fanning Island, against a two knot current and adverse trade winds could easily become 400 miles or more So much for a "simple" tack while sailing to windward as mandated on a voyage to Fanning from Palmyra.

Leeway

Leeway is another factor extending the distance and time of a windward sailing voyage.   As a sailboat beats forward through the water it drifts sideways away from the wind, because of the pressure of the wind on hull and sails.   As a windward boat is tacking towards its destination it is constantly being driven off course and away from its goal by the very wind that propels it forward. One cannot be certain exactly how many miles leeway drift would add to the proposed voyage to Fanning Island.   With the decrepit Iola it could be considerable depending on the wind direction, wind speed, steering error, condition of the bottom of the vessel re marine growth, design of the boat, the number of times the vessel must tack to achieve its destination, seamanship of the skipper, and etc.

Steering Error

Steering error can prolong a voyage, particularly where all steering must be performed by an inexperienced hand. It is difficult even for an experienced helmsman to keep his vessel moving precisely on the right course.   Under normal sea conditions an auto pilot tied into the helm with an electronic compass will navigate far more accurately than a human. This is especially true at night where the helmsman must rely on is his dimly lit compass.   (It is unlikely the Iola possessed a binnacle light.)   Without a binnacle light defendants could not read the compass card while sailing during the hours of darkness.

The romance of the sea is always in the forefront of sea stories —   truth is long stints at the wheel are boring and fatiguing. How is the watch split? Two hours on and two hours off with a crew of two would not work out. When would anyone get sleep? Four hours on, four off may be a bit better. Six on and six off would provide for proper rest, but to sit or stand behind a wheel for long periods of time causes fatigue, tedium and inattention. Fatigue and inattention encourage steering error and lengthens the voyage.

Jib Sail Alone

While it is possible to sail down wind under jib alone any effort to beat to windward with only a jib would fail. With nothing to balance the headsail, hit with fifteen or twenty knot trade winds, the Iola would spin about, comply with the demand of the wind, and commence sailing downwind away from the destination ignoring the rudder and helmsperson.

It is generally accepted in design of a sailboat that the center of effort in the sail must be forward of the center of lateral resistance located in the keel. This enables the vessel to move forward as the wind pressure builds. If the center of effort is aft of the center of lateral resistance the vessel will not move forward. However, if the center of effort greatly exceeds the center of lateral resistance the vessel will be out of balance and will have difficulty in moving forward.

Sailing downwind to Palmyra under jib alone presented no problems for defendants. Sailing windward to Fanning Island would not be possible without use of the mainsail. Handling the sails would present great challenges for an inexperienced crew given the fact that the Iola had no winches for the halyards, main or jib sheets.

128

Beating windward to Fanning aboard the Iola would require a small jib depending on wind conditions. Best, perhaps a storm jib coupled with a double or triple reefed main. Once the proper balance was achieved modest forward progress may have been made. Then again, perhaps the sea and wind conditions were so severe that while there may be an appearance of forward progress, the vessel is actually losing ground.

This all supposes sailing skills on the part of the crew and a sound vessel. Obviously the Iola and crew were severely lacking in both departments. With on coming waves and a rotten hull breaking up with each hammer-like blow, in all probability she would not have survived twenty-four hours of pounding. This fact was made clear to both defendants as they bailed for their lives, knee-deep in water, on the easy voyage down to Palmyra.

Two Knot Current

All of the above factors add to difficulty of sailing to windward. However these obstacles pale in comparison to the problems presented by the two knot current Wheeler and others warned defendant the Iola would face. The record clearly shows the Iola under the most favorable conditions scarcely exceeded two knots per hour on the voyage to Palmyra. (That speed would be reduced further, if the true passage to Palmyra was 26 days, and not the twenty, as alleged by Stearns.)

When all the above considerations are factored in there is no possible way Iola could ever succeed in arriving at Fanning

129

Island. Faced with above adverse conditions and circumstances with an inexperienced crew the Iola would lose ground with every passing hour. It would have been a voyage to nowhere. Tacking windward in the dark without winches would be pure hell. Food supplies and water would quickly run out, seams would open even further, and the Iola buried by on coming seas would be driven to the bottom.

LOG OF THE IOLA

Daylight Saving Time

Stearns stated she "usually" made her log/diary entries during daylight hours of the day in question. This practice assured an accurate account because the events were "fresh" in her mind.

Bugliosi inquires of Stearns:

"And would you make daily entries in this diary; is that correct?"

"Yes." Replied, Stearns.

"When would you usually make your entries? What time of day?"

"Well, I would usually make them in the late afternoon, before dark, and after some things had already transpired during the day."

"It would always be during daylight hours, however?"

"During the daylight hours," responds Stearns, in agreement with Bugliosi's leading question.

"Was there a reason for that?"

"Well, it was very difficult to write, with the lighting that I had on the Iola, after dark. So it was much easier to make those entries during the daylight hours."

"You made your entries at a time when those incidents to which referred in your diary were still relatively fresh in your mind?" Leads, Bugliosi.

"Yes." Responds Stearns. (Vol. 10, pp. 1587-8)

(The above testimony regarding the preparation of her log/diary was repeated by Stearns several times during her trial.)

July 1974

" July 16. .....Talked awhile, then Mac and Muff bid goodnite. (sic) After which R and I smoked some hash and had an exquisite fuck — all and all, a fine birthday." (p. 94)

The street language is not surprising in that Bugliosi noted as late as 1982 Stearns had a "latrine mouth". (p. 334) Dannell Peterson concurred. (pp. 298-99) There is more to this entry than the above, but it is the above excerpt that is relevant. Stearns had a birthday party allegedly attended by the Grahams.

The purpose of this entry is to impress upon the authorities the supposed private and personal quality of the log. After all who in manufacturing a fake log would use vulgar language or admit to a minor crime? Stearns has a subtle mind — knowing it is this kind of entry that argues in favor of

131

authenticity and will assist in misleading authorities or a future jury.

This part of the salacious note was not read to the jury. A reference to the log entry of July 16, 1974 is found in Volume 11, page 1620, of the court reporter's transcript from the murder trial of Stearns. Bugliosi quizzes Stearns on direct examination:

"Okay. You may continue reading your diary entries of your association with the Grahams."

"On July 16th — that was my birthday — it says: 'Mac and Muff delivered my second present. They had retrieved our anchor. Invited them to partake of cake and coffee at 6:00 which they accepted. Mac and Muff wrapped some roasted soy nuts and sachet as a present — all sang Happy Birthday and I blew out one of our large votive candles atop the cake after making a wish. Talked awhile, then bid each other goodnite." (sic)

There is another more subtle message found within this log note in reference to the part that was not read to the jury. Sociopathic criminals often believe they are inherently superior to others. They enjoy flaunting criminal activities before their pursuers. Stearns places the note in the log all the while thumbing her nose at the authorities.

In the log entry for July 16, 1974, Stearns makes five different references to Walker. However, she does not refer to him using his moniker, "Buck" but only as "R", abbreviating his Palmyra name Roy. Why resort to this subterfuge in a supposed log if it is for her eyes only? She has no need to mislead herself. The use of "R" indicates she expects others to read her log/diary at some time in the future. (pp. 94-5)

132

What is Stearns' purpose in abbreviating the word marijuana using the letter "m" in her log note of the 16th? On the 16th she admitted to smoking hash with Walker, so what is the big deal about marijuana? Who does she expect to find reading her so-called log? Why the misdirection if not to confuse future authorities? (p. 101)

Her judgment regarding the role of her diary/log was correct. During her murder trial Bugliosi had her read every entry in the log referencing her relationship with the Grahams lending authenticity and an air of truth to the entries even though many were false, particularly those that characterize defendant's relationship with the Grahams and Stearns' alleged activities near the time of the murders.

"July 22. Carried loads of dirt in the A.M.— after five trips I was ready to pass out. Another boat came in, the Shearwater from Portland, Oregon. Two guys — Don Stevens and Bill Larson — on board. Have toured the South Pacific, heading back to Hawaii. R rowed out and helped moor them where Journeyer (Tempest) had been. More fish for dinner." (p. 101)

Log entries for July 22 and 23, describe what purports to be a typical Palmyra day for Stearns; carrying dirt, planting marijuana seeds, making sourdough starter, reading, and meeting Stevens and Larson of the Shearwater, which had just arrived. *(p. 101)d'être*

It is interesting to observe Stearns is still planting marijuana seeds, having been on the island for nearly a month.

133

(If growing marijuana was the "raison d'être" for the trip to Palmyra why did she delay planting for nearly a month?)

The following two paragraphs, from the log of the Iola for July 23rd, are found on page 101. The first entry is found in ATSWT and the second, which varies considerably, is found in the official murder trial transcript of Stearns.

"July 23. (Book Version) *Rainy day. Put up batch of sourdough starter. Also planted some m seeds. R came over and both of us stayed on the boat and read. Mac brought over a good group of books--1984, a Harold Robbins, some Zane Grey, and another Agatha Christie. We gave them some books we'd already read."*

"Another favorite for dinner — papio and coconut cake, some baked in shell, some fried. In the evening, the two guys on Shearwater invited us to their boat. We were treated to rum and Cokes and cocktail peanuts. Made a deal to trade magazines and books the next day. They gave R two packs of South Sea Cigarettes. Don showed me his ship's log, full of pictures of Tonga, Fiji, and etc. A very enjoyable evening."
(p. 101)

However, the following underlined dialogue, unlike the above, is a direct quote of the original court reporter's transcript from the murder trial of Stearns for date of July 23rd, read to jury by Stearns during her murder trial.

"July 23rd. <u>'Mac and Muff came by. He gashed his leg with a machete. Tried to sew himself up, but ended up just pushing the skin together and bandaging it that way. They gave us the address of someone on the big island who the boys can</u>

contact to say when they'll be down and by ham radio when Mac talks to him will relay the message on."

(The underlined portion is *not* included in the book version of the log note for July 23rd. Also, in the trial transcript Stearns alleges *both* Mac and Muff coming by the Iola to visit her whereas the book version only references Mac coming by.)

Bugliosi: *"Before you go on...to whom are you referring when you say 'who the boys can contact?'"*

"Richard Musick and his brother Carlos were planning — those were the people that were going to come down after three months —",
replied Stearns. (Vol. 11, p. 1620.)

"Okay." Encourages, Bugliosi.

Stearns: *"and join us."*

Bugliosi: *"Is there any other reference in the July 23rd entry to Mac and Muff, and you and Buck?"*

Stearns: *"Yes, it says: 'Earlier Mac brought us over a good group of books; Justine — 1984 — a Harold Robbins — some Zane Grey and another Agatha Christie."*   *(Vol. 11,   p. 1620)*

Clearly, there is a substantial difference between the alleged log note set forth on page 101 of the book ATSWT and that found in the official court reporter's transcript from the murder trial of Stearns.

Why present a false transcript to the reader of ATSWT? Was the purported log note found in the book altered because few, if any, would believe Muff accompanied Mac to the Iola

135

given her fear dislike and distrust of both defendants? Was the alteration an accident...poor editing or was it an attempt to obscure the fact that on July 23rd, 1974, Mac gave defendants the address of Curtis Shoemaker allowing the Musicks to contact him by mail to update Stearns?

Why would Stearns need the mail address of Shoemaker sent to the Musicks? Why involve Shoemaker when she had already contacted the Richard Musick by radio when Wheeler was present on Palmyra. (Vol. 2, p. 219) If she wanted to talk to Musick why not have Mac directly contact him directly via radio as Wheeler had done? Curtis Shoemaker's radio reputation was well known throughout Hawaii and the South Pacific. The Musicks, running a small flight operation, must have heard of him and could contact him at any time through ham or single-side band radio had they chosen to do so.

There is another factor indicating Stearns is lying about this supposed log entry. Stearns had previously mailed to Richard Musick, Shoemaker's address in her letter to him posted by Wheeler when he arrived in Hawaii in mid July. This point is made by prosecutor Schroeder during the murder trial of Walker as he examines Richard Musick:

"Do you recall when you next heard from them?"

Musick: *"I received a letter that had been mailed in Honolulu, I believe I was in Lahaina at the time I received it. It had been brought to the Hawaiian Islands by another boat that had been on the island of Palmyra."*

"Do you recall the name of the individual that brought it to Hawaii?"

136

"I believe it was a Mr. Wheeler."

"Was this letter, in fact delivered to you?"

"I picked it up at the post office."   (Meaning defendants already had the address of the Musicks.)

"Who was the letter from, if you recall?"

"I don't recall actually who wrote the letter, although I believe that there was — I believe both of them wrote the letter. I don't know who did the majority of the writing."

"That is Buck and Stephanie?"

"Yes."

"In this letter did they request you do anything?"

"Yes, sir.   They requested me to bring down some, a product called sea-going epoxy."

"What was the purpose of sea-going epoxy?"

"It is a two part epoxy which you can mix together to patch fiberglass if you are underwater."

"Did they ask you to bring anything else?"

"They asked for some specific food supplies, mostly, I believe it was sugar and flour."

"How were you to respond to this request?"

"They said, in the letter, that there was a ham radio operator in Honolulu who was in contact with some people on another boat on Palmyra and that I could write to him or contact him and have him radio down a message."

"Did you, in fact, attempt to respond to them through this person?"

"Yes. I wrote a letter to him and told him to relay down that we would bring down whatever they needed, whatever was in the letter." *(Vol. 5, pp. 9-10, transcript, Walker murder trial.)*

The Wheelers were on Palmyra from June 19 through July 6th. (Vol. 2, p. 200) Defendants arrived at Palmyra on the 27th of June. (p.71) While on Palmyra, Jack Wheeler contacted the Musicks directly over his radio at the request and direction of Stearns. Weinglass makes this point in the course of his cross examination of Wheeler during the trial of Stearns for the murder of Muff Graham:

"Mr. Wheeler, yesterday do you recall just at the end of your testimony being asked the question: did the defendant — page 144, line 3 — Did the defendant, Stephanie Stearns, ever come aboard your boat and use your two way radio?"

Wheeler: *"At one time."*

Weinglass continues:

"Did he ask you if Stephanie Stearns ever used the radio on your boat?"

"That's why I say...I think I did the talking for her. I'm not sure. But I believe I did the talking. She just told me what to say, I believe." Responded Wheeler. (Vol. 2, p. 219)

There is no need for the Musicks to contact Shoemaker by mail. Richard Musick owned a small inter-island flying service and was familiar with radio contact of one type and another. So why involve Shoemaker? Why the charade of August 21st where Shoemaker relays Musick's letter to Mac when he could have contacted Mac directly by radio just as Wheeler had dome on behalf of Stearns earlier in the summer?

The logical inference one might draw from Stearns unnecessarily involving Shoemaker in the communication link between defendants and the Musicks was to advance her misinformation campaign about the need to sail to Fanning Island. The letter from Richard Musick to Stearns sent via Shoemaker and forwarded by radio to Mac Graham did much to convince the Grahams that the purported voyage to Fanning Island by defendants was for real.

Palmyra Dreaming (and Drooling)

The log of the Iola was partially true, but where it mattered most, completely false. Written as Enoki correctly asserted, after the fact, to confuse pursuers and hide the murder of the Grahams. From time to time within the log there were comments relating to island life…something that would give an aura of authenticity. Most strange is the entry dated August 5, 1974.

"Enoki reminded the jurors of Jennifer's "curious diary entry" of August 5, 1974, just weeks before the Grahams' disappearance, that she and Mr. Walker spent the night 'drooling and dreaming' about their next boat." (p. 470)

The entry obviously references the anticipated death of the Grahams, theft of the Sea Wind, and access to the food supplies on board. A tantalizing admission of guilt, Stearns, thumbing her nose at the court and jury as if to say: Yeah we did

139

it...so what are you going to do about it? You are all too dumb to understand my role in the murder of the Grahams.

We are not treated to the entire entry only a portion thereof. The entry is significant not only because of Stearns' *"drooling and dreaming"* comment, but because she places herself in the murder plot. The night of August 5th, just a few weeks before the murder of the Grahams, not only is Walker dreaming and drooling over the prospect of the murder of the Grahams, the theft of their yacht, and access to the Graham's bountiful stores, but Stearns, herself, is *"dreaming and drooling"* in anticipation of the death of the Grahams.   The log entry is tantamount to an admission of guilt by Stearns in the murder of the Grahams.

Settling on the Grahams as their target, the only remaining question was when and how to take their lives? Obviously there could be no witnesses. The executions of the Grahams could only take place when all other sailors had departed.   It was just a question of time before Stearns formulated her murder plot and the window of opportunity arose.

"August 20. Transferred dirt to roof. Gave R a haircut. Soybeans for dinner. And a beautiful sunset." (p. 120)

Apparently her supplies have dwindled to virtually nothing — she had only soybeans for dinner. Why note soybeans for dinner? Perhaps to remind her off the paucity of her diet and status of supplies. Nearly two months after their arrival Stearns is still in the process of putting her garden together.

140

The above entry finds Stearns, once again, not using Walker's name or his alias but referencing him as R. Why the subterfuge? Who does she expect to find reading her notes? If reading her log was restricted to herself and Walker as she claimed why obscure his identity? The logical conclusion is that she is writing her log for those in a position of authority to read. The use of "R" allows her to raise the inference that she was protecting Walker and in so doing is excused for lying — a ploy Bugliosi employs to the fullest in his defense of Stearns at trial.

Strangely, Stearns testified she made her log/diary notes during the daylight hours. One wonders how it was that she entered a "daylight" notation about a *"beautiful sunset,"* on August 20th when the sun had not set?

Shoemaker's Message

Stearns' log of August 21, 1974:

"Very calm day — no wind. Dug 5 loads of dirt. Wrote another note to Dickie. Will have Mac relay via ham radio to Curt Shoemaker if we don't hear something soon...." (p. 120)

The evening of August 21st, a Wednesday, Mac received a message from Shoemaker regarding the supposed resupply trip by the Musicks. Mac carefully wrote down the message from Shoemaker. On the 22nd he delivered his hand written memorandum to Stearns.

Bugliosi observes:

" Mac had written down Curt Shoemaker's message in full."

"We have been delayed by unforeseen circumstances, but hope to see you in October. We've enjoyed your letters very much. Of interest is the fact that bird eggs are considered superior eating to chicken eggs in many European countries. Hopefully, we will bring everything you need. We promise to bring a turkey for Thanksgiving dinner. See you. Richard Taylor." (p. 120)

The above message from Richard "Dickie" Musick to Stearns played a major role in removing all doubt from the minds of the Grahams that defendants were leaving Fanning Island. The Musicks were responding to a letter from Stearns, mailed in Honolulu by Wheeler on his return to Hawaii in mid July. The note informed Stearns that Musick was unable to deliver her requested supplies until late November. Musick excuses his delay blaming it on "unforeseen circumstances". Later Musick claimed he lost his storm jib overboard while sailing. It was this alleged loss that supposedly delayed his departure. The court reporter transcript shows that Shoemaker had carefully written down Musick's message to Mac on August 21, 1974, in his personal radio log book. It was mailed to him by Richard Musick with a request he read it over the radio to Mac allowing him to forward it Stearns. (Vol. 5, page 757)

Stearns' murder trial transcript of the letter addressed to Shoemaker differs considerably from the the ATSWT version:

"Dear Mr. Shoemaker,

Would you please relay this message to my friend Roy Allen the next time you are in radio contact with Mac Graham. Thank you for your assistance.

142

Message: *We have been delayed by unforeseen circumstances, but hope to see you in October. We've enjoyed your letters very much. Of interest is the fact that the sea gull eggs are considered superior eating to the chicken eggs in many European countries, not only in nutrition but in taste as well.*

    Hopefully <u>*we will bring everything necessary to repair your engine and so forth.*</u>   <u>*Patty*</u> *promises to bring a turkey for Thanksgiving dinner.*

    See you <u>there.</u> Richard   (Vol. 5, p. 757)

Once again Bugliosi tampers with the official transcript. in that he deletes the introductory paragraph, the reference to "Patty" and the comments pertaining to the repair of the outboard motor of the Iola.   (The deleted material is set forth above, underlined.)

In the trial transcript version of the letter Musick states he hopes to see defendants in October, yet testified during the trial of Walker, he intended to come down near Thanksgiving. There is a vague reference to repair of the 20 horse power outboard engine of the Iola and mention of a traveling companion named Patty.   The letter is unrealistic and superficial. How does one repair a 20 horse-power engine that is seized because of repeated exposure to salt-water as waves washed over the transom of the Iola during the voyage to Palmyra?   Aluminum exposed to salt water corrodes quickly. In all probability the internal workings of the engine are completely useless making any repair useless.

It would have been far more effective for Musick to bring down a used nine horse outboard which would have been sufficient to propel the Iola. It also would have been far more convenient to move it about on the vessel — it would be half the weight of the twenty horse-power engine…something Walker could easily lift over the stern.

Musick's letter was used by Stearns to reinforce in the mind of the Grahams the notion defendants intended to sail to Fanning Island on the 29th. Mac's receipt of the note from Musick on the 21st greatly assisted Stearns in that she could argue the resupply time by the Musicks was too remote, necessitating an immediate voyage to Fanning Island.

The communications between Richard Musick and defendants had only one purpose and that was to provide cover for defendant's murderous scheme. At the time the Iola sailed from Hawaii, Richard Musick was in on the plan of defendants to murder some unknown sailing couple and steal their boat. He knowingly agreed to further that purpose by providing a cover story. "Dickie" Musick was a conspirator to murder in aiding and abetting the defendants. He was an "accessory after the fact" and should have been charged as such. It was Musick's communication with Stearns on the 21st that convinced the Grahams defendants were in earnest about voyaging to Fanning Island. It was this letter that caused the Grahams to lower their guard and invite defendants aboard the Sea Wind for the bon voyage dinner the evening of the 28th.

Into the Vortex

"August 22.   Today was a day of good news and bad news. The good news is that Dickie and Carlos finally sent word via Mac that they'd be down. The bad news is that they would not be able to make it until the end of October."   (p. 120)

The above log note of August 22, 1974, from the official transcript, varies substantially from the alleged entry Bugliosi claims   Stearns read to the jury during her murder trial testimony.   In the trial transcript we find Stearns reading the above portion of the note, but there is more as she lays it on thick for the jury:

"Mac didn't seem overjoyed at buying our generator. But said he would let us have fifty dollars for it." (Vol. 11, p. 1623)

Contrary to Stearns' trial testimony that Mac was indifferent about the opportunity to purchase Stearn's portable gas powered generator for a trifling fifty dollars, one can be certain he was over-joyed. Stearns' generator was the exact same model he considered purchasing before he left Hawaii. (p. 119) The generator was essential to Mac as it served to charge the batteries of the Sea Wind and run the 120 volt power tools in his shop.   Without it his shop work would come to a halt.   With limited ability to charge his ship's batteries   via the ship's alternator before his supply of diesel fuel ran out, possession of a functional gas powered generator was critical.   Without a functioning generator his frozen food would spoil and his comfortable life in the blistering equatorial heat would come to a screeching halt.   Because of prior activities on the island, there were barrels of gasoline available for use — unlike the limited diesel fuel for the engine of the Sea Wind, it was not a fuel source he would exhaust. His generator was on it's last legs, returning a thousand miles to Hawaii to purchase another during the height of the typhoon was out of the question.

August 23rd

On the 23rd of August 1974, Stearns put her plan to murder the Grahams and steal the Sea Wind into action.

Bugliosi writes:

"The first thing Jennifer did was to remind Mac of his offer to buy their portable generator." (p. 120)

"August 23. Mac gave us $50.00 for the generator. I started cleaning up and hauling things not needed to shore. R took motor off compost shredder and converted it to a bilge pump, in case manual pump breaks down." (p. 120)

The generator was sold to Mac for an absurdly low price of $50.00. The transaction is all the more suspect in that defendants were poverty stricken and greatly in need on many food items. (A more reasonable price would have been $600.00 and even at that price it would have been cheap.) But it gets more bizarre. Bugliosi writes that Stearns considered giving Mac the generator outright as a gift. Defendants were in dire straits, the notion of giving away the portable generator under the circumstances, borders on madness.

Stearns states: *"We were just going to give him the generator before we left."* (p. 410)

The portable generator was central to her plan to execute Mac. The "borrowing back" of the generator which was aboard

146

the Iola on the day of Mac's execution, was essential to achieve success in her plot to kill the Grahams. The gambit of "selling" the generator to Mac and then borrowing it back insured he would keep his appointment with death. Had they given the generator to Mac there is no way they would have known the Mac would show up on the appointed day to meet his death. By selling the generator to Mac there was a much greater likelihood Mac would show up to collect the generator since he had paid $50.00 for it.

The log entry of the 23rd is troubling for another reason. Stearns asserts Walker, the lazy all-time mechanical klutz had constructed a *"mechanical compost shredder"* the motor of which he purportedly adapted to run off 120 volt alternating current supplied by the portable gas generator. After use as a compost shredder he allegedly converts the device into a bilge pump. (The reader is not informed whether the supposed converted bilge pump is manual or electric.)

Throughout ATSWT one is led to believe Walker is not competent when it comes to machinery (or little else for that matter). Reading the log entry for the 23rd of August the jury is asked to accept the proposition Walker constructed a mechanical shredder running off 120 volt alternating current supplied by his generator, After constructing this device he supposedly dismantles it, removes the motor from the shredder and constructs a back-up bilge pump. (One wonders how the alleged motor of the compost shredder was obtained or where it came from? In all probability this device did not exist.)

Stearns' note is ambiguous, she writes:

147

"R took motor off compost shredder and converted it to bilge pump,...."

Did she mean to inform the reader that Walker converted the motor of the shredder to a bilge pump or that the supposed shredding device itself, was converted to a bilge pump? Presumably, what she meant to say was the shredding device was converted to a manual bilge pump, without the electric motor. The motor was 120 volt and could not function without the portable generator which she had sold to Mac.

It is a confused line Stearns and Bugliosi draw in defining Walker; clumsy, ignorant, strong, possibly deranged, comes through in a pinch, a bully, ignorant of machinery, yet mechanically adept, clever enough to fashion a shredding device driven by a 120 volt generator and when necessary, magically convert the machine to a manual bilge pump.

Aside from the above discussed issues, further questions arise when reviewing Stearns' testimony from her official murder trial transcript — it reads differently. On page 1623, Volume 11, Stearns' murder trial transcript, her purported log states:

"On August 23rd: '*Took outboard motor'* — '*Took outboard* — *sorry* — *over to Mac's. He gave us fifty dollars for the generator."*

The actual trial transcript above does not vaguely resemble the entry set forth in ATSWT. Why the considerable disparity between the actual trial transcript and that proffered by Bugliosi in his book? Time and again, we find Bugliosi intentionally misleading his readers. Stearns court transcript references the Iola's outboard motor. This notation is followed by a comment that Mac gave Stearns fifty dollars for her generator.   There is *nothing* in the trial transcript about Stearns cleaning up the boat, hauling things to shore or Walker taking the motor off the compost shredder and converting (presumably) the motor to a bilge pump.

The disparity continues in the August 24th log note testimony of Stearns found on the same page.

The testimony, given under oath by Stearns is as follows:

"On August 24th: Mac passed final death sentence on our poor old outboard." (Vol. 11, p. 1623.)   Nothing more. Compare Stearns actual trial testimony as revealed by the official court reporter's transcript to that of her alleged testimony set forth below, taken from "And The Sea Will Tell":

"August 24.   Made further strides in getting boat seaworthy, tho hardly looks it at a cursory glance.   R started in on front hatch — he's going to fiberglass it watertight.   Mac passed final death sentence of our poor old outboard.   It's too far gone to be fixed.   So ends our day — no dinner other than coconut milk shake." (pp. 120-1)

The reader of ATSWT is supposedly being told the truth about the testimony given by Stearns and others during her murder trial, yet it is often patently false. This fabricated testimony must have originated from him because it certainly is not found in the Official Court Reporter's transcript. Why is Bugliosi permitted to present false testimony in his book?

"Further strides in getting the boat seaworthy". (Apparently the Iola is not seaworthy at this time in the opinion

149

of Stearns.) One wonders how it is Walker can repair the front hatch of the Iola when the Musicks have not brought down the necessary epoxy, resin and fiberglass materials? When prosecutor Eggers went to Palmyra shortly after the murders in November 1974, he found the forward hatch of the Iola on the beach. (p. 140) Also, in the photo of the Iola, as she is scuttled by defendants, the forward hatch is missing. (pp. 120-21)

"August 25. Not what I consider a high energy day—but then we have not been eating high energy food lately. Collected 19 sprouted coconuts and R husked some for the trip. I resumed trying to get the boat stowed and orderly but another day is needed to finish the job. For the first time in 3 days, we'll have something other than coconut for dinner — beans. Maybe we'll generate more energy tomorrow." (p. 121)

Nothing much of note deserving comment. Apparently because of a restrictive diet both defendants are suffering from a low energy level.   It is hard to understand the several days it is taking Stearns to get things stowed on the Iola. The Iola was a small boat and neither had many possessions.

Another fact that strongly argues the log entries are, for the most part, fiction: When prosecutor Eggers arrived on Palmyra Island, shortly after the arrest of Stearns, he discovered the camp of Walker completely in tact.   Walker's books were present. The tent which he had been using was still up and had not been disturbed. With only a few days before the supposed departure of the Iola for Fanning Island one would expect his belongings to be stowed aboard ship. One would expect Walker to take his place aboard the Iola prior to the day of departure.

150

How is it that after allegedly receiving an invitation to attend a bon voyage dinner aboard the Sea Wind on the 30th of August, with an intended departure the following day, Walker's few camp shows no indication of his preparation for departure? (p. 415)

" *August 26.   Got a few things accomplished today. Between R and me, we must have gathered 20 plus sprouted coconuts. Started charging the batteries.   Mac brought by Fanning chart, which I copied. R put fiberglass over bow hatch due to leakage.*" (p. 121)

How is it that without materials Walker can effect repairs to the forward hatch ? Stearns notation of August 26 is another admission the forward hatch is leaking and needs repair. The log does not specifically state Walker repaired the hatch, she merely notes that he *"put fiberglass over the bow hatch due to leakage."*

The log claims that Stearns started charging the batteries on this date. If there were batteries present on the Iola why did Stearns wait until the 26th to start charging them?   The generator was a device she had in her possession during the summer and could have employed it to charge the batteries at any time convenient to her schedule. Had the Iola possessed a 12 volt automatic bilge pump that was functional it would have been essential to keep the battery charged in order for the pump to operate while at anchor.

Another significant entry in the August 26th log note:

"Mac brought by Fanning chart which I copied."

Mac, persuaded defendants are sailing to Fanning Island, eagerly brought the Fanning Island chart to the Iola so Stearns could copy it. This was a clever ploy by Stearns which did much to support her pretension that she intended to   sail for Fanning Island.

By bringing the chart of Fanning Island to the Iola Mac confirmed Stearns suspicions he had been duped.   On the 26th Stearns was certain the Grahams had bought into her murderous scheme.

Oddly enough, Stearns log entry of the 26th contradicts her comments re the hatch repair by Walker entered on the 28th. (Vol. 10, pp. 1455-7)

"August 27. A rainy, day. Gathered another 16 coconuts. Charged batteries for another several hours. At this rate we'll be here another week." (p. 121)

The log notation alleging charging of the batteries is suspect. Bugliosi comments that during the voyage to Palmyra from Hawaii the generator ran "daily" to recharge the batteries. (p. 52)   Both battery references employ the plural form, indicating more than one battery aboard the Iola. While it would be unwise to set sail with only one marine, deep cycle battery, we know defendants budget was lacking and they had a history of making unwise decisions in selecting gear for the Iola. Had they more than one battery there would have been no need to run the generator every day to keep them charged. Two batteries in good condition would have more than enough reserve capacity to service a small 12 volt bilge pump. If it was necessary for defendants to run the generator everyday to recharge two batteries, it would indicate that an extraordinary demand was placed on the bilge pump during the voyage south from Hawaii.

Implied from the log entry on the 27th is that Stearns could ascertain the charge status of the batteries; *"at this rate we will be here another week"*.   There is no showing she had this capability.   It appears her charging efforts were not successful. If the rate of charging did not improve Stearns thought they may be forced to delay the voyage for another week.

Looming over the entire battery issue is the question of whether or not the Iola possessed any batteries whatsoever. Without a VHF radio,   12 volt automatic bilge pump, binnacle light — (Why have a binnacle light when Stearns, as a "leisure sailor" does not sail during the hours of darkness?) The only use for a 12 volt battery would be to furnish power for running lights,   hardly something one would worry about in the vast reaches of the Southern Pacific Ocean.   If a ship came near at night one could shine a flashlight, (if they had one) onto the sail.

August 28. I husked coconuts. <u>R fixed bow hatch and did some worked on bilge pump.</u>   All the while the hum of the generator attests to the charging of the batteries — from morning till night. Today's Wednesday, winds willing, we shall be ready Saturday.

According to the above log entry, the bow hatch is now fully repaired. Walker's testimony during his theft trial in December 1975,   contradicts Stearns log entry of the 28th.   At his theft trial he testified he repaired the forward hatch on the 30th   of August, and not the 28th.   Stearns recounting her supposed activities on the 30th of August makes no reference to Walker working aboard the Iola on that day. She was probably unaware of Walker's theft trial testimony until her trial for the

153

murder of the Grahams, by then it was too late to make alterations to her log which was in evidence. (Vol. 10, pp. 1455-7)

Not only does Walker dispute the supposed date of the hatch repair, but Stearns herself claims in her log entry of the 26th that the alleged date was the 26th. (p. 121)

Walker's testimony from his 1975 theft trial regarding his activities on the 30th of August became a contested issue during Stearns' murder trial when Bugliosi demanded a right to introduce it hoping to point out to the jury that Walker was a liar. Bugliosi argued at length with the court and Enoki in an effort to introduce prior testimony of Walker about his activities on the 30th of August 1974.   Why Enoki opposed the introduction of Walker's theft trial testimony is difficult to understand in that it impeached Stearns account of the hatch repair that never occurred!

Bugliosi, referencing Walker's 1975 theft trial transcript, argues:

"On page 612 he (Walker) said that on the date, August 30th, he was on the Iola, among other things, patching fiberglass in the hatch cover."   (Vol. 10, pp. 1455-7)

After a half dozen pages of argument King puts its off his ruling on the motion to a time later in the trial.   Several days later, King addresses the issues Bugliosi raised, but does so in a cryptic manner; he only permits certain numbered pages to be read to the jury.   Without a copy of the original theft trial transcript of Walker one cannot know with certainty if Bugliosi prevailed.   In all probability King, in his desire to protect

Stearns' interests, prohibited Bugliosi from referring to Walker's testimony, fearing most jurors would conclude it proved Stearns as well as Walker was lying about the activities of the 30th. (Vol. 12, pp. 1921-23)

Battery Charging

One must exercise caution when charging boat batteries, not only because batteries give off explosive hydrogen gas as they charge, but over charging a battery can destroy it. Severe over charging can cause a battery to overheat and explode. When charging a battery a skipper must constantly monitor the rate of charge and when the battery has reached the proper charge, cease charging.

In a lead/acid battery the most accurate method of monitoring the charge level is by use of an inexpensive hydrometer. One should not commence charging a lead-acid battery in a boat without a monitoring device showing the level of charge. There are more sophisticated methods employing electronic monitors, but it is highly unlikely the Iola would have such a system on board. Usually these systems are integrated with the engine alternator which the Iola did not possess. It is unlikely Stearns was educated in the use of a hydrometer or proper battery charging techniques.

One would expect the Iola's 120 volt generator to charge at a maximum rate of approximately 15 amps per hour. As the battery regains its charge, the charging amperage tapers off. Two days of charging may be required for two 12 volt, one hundred ampere hour, deep cycle marine batteries hooked up in parallel.   Stearns assertion she was charging the batteries four days *morning to night* is not credible.   Running the generator *"dawn to dusk"* four days would over charge two batteries and destroy them. (p. 121)

There is another annoyance with her entry of the 28th.

Stearns writes,   *"All the while the hum of the generator attests to the charging of the batteries--from morning to night".* The notation, while poetic does not ring true.   A 1973-4 Sears generator capable of generating 1200 watts of alternating current was an expensive, noisy machine. It did not hum, but made a hell of a racket.   To listen to it all day would be a difficult proposition. It would have to be placed in the cockpit or better on deck   to avoid the loud noise caused by the motor, which only a deaf person would describe as a "hum".   It also gives off carbon monoxide fumes which can kill in very short order. Carbon monoxide fumes are odorless, and heavier than air making the interior of a sailboat a place of potential danger. Running a gas powered generator in the interior of a boat, even for a short time, without proper ventilation, would invite death by carbon-monoxide poisoning to anyone below.

Stearns Misspeaks

Stearns tripped herself up during her first interview with FBI Special Agent, Calvin Shishido, October 29, 1974, as she delineates her purported activities while on Palmyra Island. During her initial interview, Stearns told Shishido   she and

Walker were invited over to the Sea Wind on August 28th by the Grahams for a bon voyage dinner.

The fact that a bon voyage dinner took place aboard the Sea Wind on August 28th, does not sit well with Enoki or Bugliosi. Bugliosi believed it was in his client's best interest to deny the invitation ever existed although overwhelming evidence indicates defendants attended a dinner aboard the Sea Wind on Wednesday, the 28th of August 1974.

Enoki was completely befuddled about the issue. He denies its existence throughout the trial. At the last minute, during final argument, he implies defendants attended the dinner on the 28th.

Stearns defense stands or falls on the proposition that the invitation was for the 30th of August. Enoki, in a muddle about the facts of the case, bent on convincing the jury the relationship between the Grahams and defendants would prohibit an invitation, erroneously supports Stearns' testimony that the invitation was for the 30th. Bugliosi's game plan pretends the invitation was an invention of Walker, and was never extended to Stearns by the Grahams.

Quoting from Stearns murder trial transcript we find the following colloquy between Enoki and Stearns as he exams her about the bon voyage dinner.

Enoki: *"Now that's the day that you were invited over to the Sea Wind and boarded the Sea Wind, that was the last Friday in August according to you, correct?"*

The question clearly directs Stearns to focus on the last Friday in August and *not* the 28th which was a Wednesday.

157

Following Enoki's lead Stearns answers:

"Yes", replies Stearns as she follows Enoki's direction.

Enoki undermines his prosecution against Stearns by directing focus away from the date of August 28th as the date of the cake/truce incident:

"You recall that agent Shishido said that you gave him the date of August 28 when you — when you talked to him as an estimation?"

"Yes". Replies, Stearns.

Surprisingly, Stearns admits she told Shishido during her initial interview of October 29, 1974, just a few weeks after killing the Grahams, she was invited to the Sea Wind for a bon voyage dinner on the 28th. Twelve years later she finds this admission a hindrance to her defense and recants explaining:

"I misspoke myself."

(The volume and page number from which the above dialogue is taken is somewhat blurred....it appears to be Volume 12, page 1825 from Stearns' murder trial transcript.)

Down the Hatch

In an effort to obscure the patent absurdities of her hatch repair story, we find the following exchange with Enoki cross-examining Stearns:

"Now, you were going to make the trip to Fanning without a hatch cover; is that right?"

Stearns: *"The hatch cover leaked. So Buck fiberglassed over the entire hatch."*

(Apparently, meaning that Walker completely fiberglassed over the entire hatch opening.)

"And that fiberglassing was completed prior to August 30th; is that right?" Continues, Enoki.

"Yes". Stearns, replies.

Enoki, timidly inquires: *"The hatch...that's the forward hatch is that correct?"*

Stearns: *"Yes".*

Enoki: *" And did that hatch provide ventilation for the cabin when it was open?"*

Stearns: *"Yes".*

Enoki: *"and he had fiberglassed it for the trip to Fanning, correct?"*

"He had fiberglassed it because on the way down it leaked." States Stearns.

Disbelieving, Enoki asks: *"So in order to go to Fanning he — instead of using that hatch cover he fiberglassed it?"*

(The idea of completely fiberglassing over the entire hatch opening is too much even for our gullible prosecutor to accept.)

"Yes, in order to sail any place without the boat leaking into that forward area where we used to store everything." Responds, Stearns.

Puzzled, Enoki continues: *"Would it cause considerable damage to the hatch to take the fiberglass out of the hatch cover or hatch area, I guess?"*

(Enoki demands to know if, at some time in the future, if defendants wished to bring back ventilation to the forward hatch, cutting out the fiberglass covering the hatch opening might cause damage to the boat.)

The court flummoxed because Stearns is not making sense interrupts Enoki:

"You mean...after he..."

Enoki responds: *After he fiberglassed it, to remove the fiberglass?"*

Stearns: *"I don't know for sure. I would think that if he fiberglassed it over and decided he then preferred having a hatch, that he could figure out how to do that."*

The court totally confused and wishing to protect throws a life-ring to Stearns instructing:

"You don't fiberglass over a hole...I guess you put something there."

Enoki inquires: *"Do you know how he did it?"*

She answers: *"No I don't."*

"You remember seeing it afterward?" suggests Enoki.

Stearns seeing where her idiocy is leading, picking up on the hints from Judge King, backs away from her stupidities:

"Well, yeah, you know, I can look back and assume that he put a piece of plywood on top of the opening and then

160

fiberglassed over it, but I didn't help him do it and I didn't watch him do it."

(Inundated with the strong odor of fresh set resin, purportedly working along side Walker on a small boat in the tropical heat — and Stearns claims did not notice what he was doing.)

Puzzled, Enoki plods onward assisting Stearns in her absurd lies:

"Would it be fair to say, whatever it was that he fiberglassed over, that it was a — as it was put there would be permanent;   it wasn't something you could open and close and so forth?"

Stearns, caught in her imbecilic lies doubles down: *"That's correct."*   (Vol. 12, pp. 1826-7)

If one were so foolish as to believe Stearns,   after Walker's supposedly repaired the Iola there was no longer a forward hatch opening. This leaves the Iola in the tropical heat, humidity and animal stench with only the companionway for ventilation.

New Math

The dire food situation of defendants is noticeable in Stearns' comments about preparing for the voyage to Fanning by collecting coconuts as defendants primary food source. She had little idea of what lay ahead, nor could she know if food will be available when, and if, they were to reach Fanning Island.

Impoverished defendants had no choice but to gather what they could for food. It strikes a discordant note to observe sailors about to engage in a difficult voyage of unknown duration relying almost exclusively on coconuts as a food source.   (Nothing is said about the collection and storage of drinking water for defendants and their dogs.)

One wonders, why this alleged math student is unable to add simple figures?   According to her log on August 25th, she collected 19 coconuts.   The following day, August 26th, she collected 20 plus coconuts.   August 27th, she allegedly gathered another 16 coconuts.   Fifty- five in all, yet in her August 29th log posting she observes she has *"30 to take with us"*.   (Is the jury to suppose defendants consumed twenty-five coconuts in a day or two, or was Stearns careless in producing her fraudulent log, or is she incapable of performing simple addition?)   (pp. 120-1)

Aside from her math fumblings regarding coconut gathering of August 25th through 27th, there are the coconuts she allegedly gathered on the 21st. She writes in her log:

"Loaded up on some sprouted coconuts."

Not only does she claim to have the coconuts collected of the 25th through 27th , but must have some left over from her efforts on the 21st when   she claims to have "loaded up" whatever that means.

Log notes such as these cause one to doubt Stearns ever studied math and cast doubt on her educations claims in general. (p.120-1) It is difficult to believe any sensible jury could ever buy the coconut stores routine.   It is laughable to think defendants were going to commit themselves to a dangerous and difficult voyage against prevailing trade winds and an opposing two knot current, on a derelict vessel, unable able to sail at night, with no more than coconuts for sustenance.

Unforced Errors

Another glaring example exposing the so called log as a fraud is showcased in Stearns notation about the arrival of the Sea Wind at Palmyra Island.   In Stearns' murder trial transcript we find the following testimony as Bugliosi examines Stearns:

"Would you please read for the jury and Judge King the entries you made in your diary dealing with your relationship with Mac and Muff. You said you've underlined those in red."

Stearns: *"On July 6th it says; Mac and Muff of ship — and I didn't put the ship's name in because I couldn't remember it then.   They had just come in — out of San Diego came by. Mac had an outboard motor on his dinghy so helped R swing boat around — Mac's a smoker so R would love to get tight with him."* (Vol. 11, p. 1616)   This log/diary entry is directly contradicted by several entries in ATSWT wherein Bugliosi asserts the Grahams *entered* the Palmyra lagoon on July 2, 1974 — the same day the Pollocks arrived.

Bugliosi writes: *".....two boats glided into the lagoon the following day, July 2. First in was the double-masted boat she'd seen, its name was Sea Wind, now legible on the stern."* (p. 82)

How is it that Stearns can be so careless in the preparation of her log note of July 6th? It was well established that the Sea Wind entered Palmyra lagoon on the 2nd. Why should her log state the date was the 6th? The logical inference from this patent contradiction is that the log was not prepared on a daily basis, but in one effort, thus causing making the likelihood of obvious errors more probable. Regarding the inherent contradictions one can only conclude the document is a fraud conceived to assist Stearns in avoiding punishment for her part in the murder and torture of the Grahams.

Swabbies All

"August 29. Husked rest of the coconuts — we have 30 to take with us. Still charging batteries. Have decks cleared and ready for swabbing —swabbed cockpit."

It is significant Stearns is allegedly still charging her non-existent, and/or useless batteries, presumably morning to night. (The jury is never informed exactly when, or if, the batteries were ever fully charged.)

One of Stearns' goofy assertions, attempting to sound like a sailor, is found in her reference to "swabbing" the deck. To *"swab"* means to clean with a swab like device. In the case of a sailor presumably a mop. There was a time in sailing history when sailors may have cleaned decks with a mop. The term "swabby" was at one time used in reference to a sailor although it has been out of favor for many years. In any event someone should have informed Stearns the term is seldom used among the sailing community these days. (Cleaning the deck with a scrub brush, usually attached to a broom handle, is described as cleaning the deck or scrubbing down the deck.)

No doubt she employed this term in an effort to appear knowledgeable as a sailor, much as she describes how careful she was to use a limited amount of fresh drinking water to wash and rinse her dishes while on the voyage down to Palmyra (It is the practice of experienced blue water sailors to use salt water to wash and rinse dishes if there is a remote possibility they may run short of drinking water.)

Sleep Over on the 29th

Stearns makes another grievous error as she recounts her activities of the 29th of August, 1974, and inadvertently she tells the truth and in so doing implicates herself in the murder of the Grahams.

Enkoi cross-examines:

"Now on the morning of August 30th, when you woke up in the morning, where had you slept that night — the night of August 29th and 30th?"

Stearns replies:

"Well, I hadn't slept very much the night of August 29th."

Enoki responding in wonderment:

"What had you been doing? Working or what?"

Stearns clarifies:

"The night of August 29th?"

Enoki:

"Yes."

Stearns confesses:

"I was on board the Sea Wind."

As indeed she was. The morning of the 29th both Mac and Muff were executed. On this same day the Iola with Mac's body was scuttled in the waters off Palmyra, soon thereafter Muff was tortured, murdered and buried on Strawn Island in a shallow grave by defendants. The evening of the August 29, 1974, a Thursday, defendants slept aboard their prize.

Enoki, at his Hamilton Burger best, having caught Stearns telling the truth apparently feels sorry for her, realizing she has made a catastrophically damaging admission, tries to help her out:

"Was that the 29th or the 30th?" Suggests Enoki.

Stearns, not realizing the horrendous injury she has just done to her defense about the supposed happenings of the 30th, ignores Enoki's warning and repeats her testimony:

"I believe that was the night of the 29th."

Enoki dismayed she did not pick up on his warning continues to assist:

The night before...," he cues.

Stearns, after a second warning from Enoki, realizing that she has just destroyed her defense finally picks up his suggestion:

"Oh. no. I'm sorry. That was the night of the 30th."

Enoki, pleased to see Stearns is now aware of the danger inherent in her admission that on the 29th of August she slept aboard the Sea Wind, (meaning her log note of the 30th and all her testimony about what supposedly happened on that day was fabricated) courteously gives her a way out of her self-imposed trap, prompts:

"I'm talking about the night before the 30th. Where had you slept?"

Finally comprehending her error, Stearns regains consciousness, taking the hint from her protective prosecutor, and corrects her statement.

"On board the Iola." (Vol. 8, pp. 1306-7)

Thereafter they engage in a pas-de-deux about the alleged events of the 30th.

(The above is an example of the worst cross-examination I have ever encountered in my years as a trial lawyer. If one did not know better, he would suspect Enoki intentionally scuttled his own prosecution. Most reasonably competent trial attorneys would let Stearns' admission stand, say nothing further about it until final argument and then hammer the defense with her admissions when it was too late to offer more fabricated testimony.)

LOG — AUGUST 30, 1974

Although the evidence proves beyond a reasonable doubt the Grahams were murdered by Stearns and Walker on the Thursday morning of August 29, 1974, for purposes of argument, let us address the log note of August 30, 1974 and demonstrate within the limited confines of Stearns false testimony and the conflicting false testimony of her co-defendant, there is more than sufficient evidence proving her log notes are fallacious and her defense fraudulent.

Stearns read her log notes of August 30th to the jury during her murder trial at the request of Bugliosi:

"Would you please read to the jury that part of your August 30th entry, that part which you wrote on August 30th?"

Stearns begins reading:

"All-out effort day. R was up bright and early, scavenging butts at Mac's workshop. R wrangled a couple of games of chess, a stash of coffee and tobacco to go, plus an invitation to dinner. Not bad for before 9:00 a.m. Next was coffee. Cleaning, swabbing, stowing — removed canopy, baking bread, all around cleanup effort both on boat and ashore. Was going to bake bread in outdoor oven to conserve fuel, but time and energy would not allow it. Undoubtably, upon return. I'll have no alternative — only hope the fuel lasts till then." (p. 413)

The murder trial transcript concurs with the above, but continues:

"South winds have been blowing pretty steady for over a week. Most south wind we've had — and I'm not sure we can get out of the channel with it. Mac said if the winds are not too strong he could probably push us out with the 9.5 horsepower outboard. Here's hoping." (Vol. 11, pp. 1637-8)

As usual there are several supposed facts that do not ring true. How would Stearns know that Walker got up bright and early? Certainly this does not sound like the Walker we know. Why would Walker want to scavenge cigarette butts in Mac's work area if Mac had just given him a stash of tobacco? Even if Walker had scavenged cigarette butts in Mac's work shop why would he bother to tell Stearns about this insignificant, and somewhat embarrassing fact?

Consider:

("Youhoo, Stephanie! I had a great morning. I was over at Mac's work area scrounging for cigarette butts off the ground....aren't I the successful, clever fellow?")

Why would Stearns enter such a demeaning and insignificant event in her so called log? Why would Walker want to bring this embarrassing act to the attention of Stearns? It does not add up.

Stearns alleges in her log note of the 30th that Mac and Walker played a couple of games of chess on board the Sea Wind before 9:00 a.m. This assertion is a lie. Unless an alleged chess game is corroborated by an unbiased observer, (there is one such instance in ATSWT) there is no reason to believe Mac engaged either defendant in a game of chess as alleged. Muff did not like either defendant, Muff would not approve of Mac playing chess with either Stearns or Walker; doing so aboard her home, the Sea Wind, would be out of the question. It was an activity which would encourage familiarity followed by begging for food. Admittedly, chess playing gives the patina of a normal social atmosphere, but it is doubtful few of Stearns alleged games of chess ever took place. Moreover, it is highly unlikely that Stearns is the accomplished chess player she claims to be. A detailed cross-examination of her supposed chess skills would prove interesting.

She portrays herself as a "tournament" level chess player. It would have been a simple matter to demonstrate her prowess, or lack thereof, by posing a few tournament level chess hypotheticals for her to solve while on the stand. (p. 155)

Likewise, without seeing Stearns Junior College transcript there is no reason to believe she completed a two year course of

169

study which included mathematics. (p. 56) Admittedly, making this claim helps sell   the jury on the idea she could teach herself navigation while on the way to Palmyra,   yet when one observes her confusion upon arrival at Palmyra and her inability to ascertain the location of the Iola, or plot a Line of Position, it is obvious she cannot navigate by sextant.   The extraordinary length of time required for the return voyage of the Sea Wind to Hawaii also casts doubt on her claim to be a competent navigator.

Her alleged math skills appear to be woefully lacking in the simple task of adding the number of coconuts she claims to have accumulated, in preparation for the purported voyage to Fanning Island. Her addition is clearly incorrect. If she cannot add coconuts, why should the juror believe she completed a course in Junior College math, wherein one would expect trigonometry and calculus to be included? (p. 56)

Her claim to have attended UC Santa Barbara falls under the same cloud of suspicion.   Without seeing a transcript there is no reason to accept her claims of attendance. With just a few deft words she creates an appearance of a semi-educated person when, nothing could be further from the truth.

Close By

A troubling aspect of Stearns testimony concerning the supposed activities of the 30th is her comment Walker's tent was *"close to the Iola"*. (p. 415)   When reviewing the chart on page 531 of ATSWT using the   scale provided on the chart, measuring a straight-line distance between the Iola and the X marking Walker's tent, one measures approximately three to four hundred yards.

There would be several means of traversing this distance. If Stearns intended to walk over to Walker's tent, she could row ashore, secure the dinghy, walk fifty yards through the jungle to the airstrip, walk approximately three to four hundred yards in an easterly direction down the strip, then cut back into the jungle where she would walk another fifty yards to Walker's tent. Including the jungle and the airstrip, one would reasonably estimate a distance of four to five hundred yards total. Most would not describe this distance as *close by*, particularly given the fact that it must be covered in the equatorial heat and humidity.

Probably the easiest method for Stearns to visit Walker during the daytime would be to get into her dinghy, row easterly along the shore until she reached the approximate location of Walker's tent, secure the dinghy and walk fifty yards through the jungle to the camp area.

Neither attorney attempted to correct Stearns characterizing Walker's tent as *"close by"*, nor did they clarify her comments about the number of trips she allegedly made that morning, in the hour or hour and a half she had available. (p. 415)

Up In Smoke

Before moving on there is an aspect of the events of the 30th that is not mentioned by Stearns...something is missing. In her diary of the 29th she notes the supposed batteries were still in need of *"charging"*. (p. 121)

Why was there no reference to battery charging on the 30th? Since the portable generator belonged to Mac, if the batteries were fully charged, why would he not come by and collect it?

The complex scenario of events created by Stearns requires the absence of the noise-making generator on the 30th.   If Stearns was still engaged in charging the batteries on the 30th (as her alleged log note of August 29th suggests),   she would be unable to hear anything aside from the loud, unpleasant racket made by the generator. With the generator running, she would be unable to hear Walker if he came and attempted to get her attention from shore, nor could she hear the alleged sound of the motor from Mac's dinghy moving away from the Iola in late afternoon.

Stearns bemoans the lack of progress in the charging of the batteries in her alleged log note of the 27th:

"Charged batteries for another several hours.   At this rate we'll be here another week."   (p. 121)   This entry presupposes Stearns has the ability to comprehend the state of charge of the batteries.   How would she know the state of the charge?

The log note for the 29th observes: *"Still charging batteries."* (p. 121)   The alleged battery charging episode, which gave an air of authenticity to the purported log, disappears into thin air.   The process, supposedly commenced on the 26th, in full swing on the 29th and then, is heard no more.

The sudden absence of reference to the battery charging process in full swing on the 29th suggests, like most of the entires in the log of the Iola, the battery charging references were a fiction. All the fol-de-rol about the endless charging process in the log, and then suddenly, without explanation — silence.   The battery charging ruse having served its purpose now is banished from the script and our ever alert jury takes no notice of this fact.

The fate of the generator was the same as that of Mac. The interior of the Iola was a bloody, god-awful mess. Walker did not have the stomach to retrieve the generator and clean it up. Useful though it was, along with Mac's body, it was consigned to the deep on the 29th of August 1974.

Oops!

Stearns was assisted in thwarting justice through the ignorance of the prosecutorial team and lack of attention by the jury. An example of this inattention involves the alleged activities of the defendants on the 30th of August.

The Sea Wind was anchored in the lagoon near Cooper Island. The distance of the anchorage by sea from the Iola was approximately a quarter of a mile. (Vol. 8, p. 1309) Stearns claimed, while on her way to bathe the evening of August 30th, she met Walker coming back from bathing around 6:00 p.m., They purportedly agreed to meet at the lanai near Mac's anchorage around 6:15 p.m. to await the return of the Grahams. (Vol. 8, pp. 1309-10)

The distances depicted in the chart on pages 72-3 cause one to question her testimony. After passing Walker she must go to the bathing area, take a bath, dry off, get dressed, walk back approximately a third of a mile to the Iola, get in her dinghy, row a short distance to the Iola, clamber aboard, deposit her toiletries and towel, get back in the dinghy, row ashore, secure the dinghy, walk a quarter mile through the jungle and meet Walker at 6:15 p.m. at the lanai — all in fifteen minutes.

There is another more serious problem with this scenario. When Stearns arrived at the lanai she claimed the Zodiac was not present at the Sea Wind. She alleges talking with Walker for fifteen or twenty minutes at the lanai. After that, around 6:40 p.m., they *"went on board"* the Sea Wind. (Vol. 8, pp. 1310-11)

173

Any alert juror would want to know, how this was accomplished? How did the defendants get *"on board"* the Sea Wind? There is no mention Stearns rowed over in her dinghy to the lanai after finishing her bath — that would take considerable time. The Sea Wind was surrounded by water as she sat at anchor and the lagoon supposedly teeming with aggressive black tipped sharks. The only way defendants could safely access the Sea Wind was by getting into a dinghy and row over to her. However, there was no dinghy present which would enable them to do this. Admittedly, the Sea Wind also had a hard fiberglass dinghy as well as the Zodiac, but this was kept secured to the Sea Wind when not in use.

Stearns fictional account of going aboard the Sea Wind August 30th has a gaping hole — there was no safe method by which Stearns and Walker could get to the Sea Wind unless by dinghy.

Walker's supposed setting up the table aboard the Sea Wind presents the same problem. On the 30th Stearns supposedly possessed the dinghy. At no time does she allege she turned use of the dinghy over to Walker. How could Walker board the Sea Wind to kill the Grahams without a dinghy?

Stearns could offer one supposition or another, but *the lack of a dinghy to access the Sea Wind at times appropriate on the evening* of the 30th is a major stumbling block for the defense. Fortunately for Stearns, Enoki and the jury completely missed the issue.

Selective Hearing

A key aspect of Stearns' defense was to blame Walker for the murder of the Grahams. To succeed, Bugliosi had to convince the jury Stearns had nothing to do with the murders and no knowledge of them. Bugliosi argued that Walker killed the Grahams sometime on the 30th and disposed of their bodies in the lagoon while Stearns was busy readying the Iola for the voyage to Fanning Island.

Around 4:30 p.m. the afternoon of the 30th, while allegedly working below in the cabin of the Iola, Stearns testified she heard the outboard motor of Mac's Zodiac going away from the Sea Wind, heading in a westerly direction.   She claims to have heard Mac's outboard motor at a distance of over two hundred and fifty yards. She alleges she was able to distinguish the sound of the outboard motor from the noise made by the incessant screeching of the thousands of birds nesting on the island; the sound muted by the dense foliage; a jut of land; and the sound of the wind and waves. Unbelievably, she not only heard the outboard motor, but could ascertain its direction of movement. (pp. 416-17)

Compare the above assertions when hearing above the din of the island works to her favor, versus a situation where acute hearing undermines her position.

Bugliosi examines:

"Did you hear any screaming or gun shots ?"

"No, I didn't."

"Or any other sound that aroused your attention."

"No."

"During the period of time when you were on Palmyra, other than when Buck fired at a fish in the lagoon, were you aware of any guns being fired on the island?"

"Well, once — I don't remember if it was someone from the Shearwater or the Toloa--they told me they were with Mac and Muff when they had been target practicing."

"Did you hear any gun shots at that time?"

"No, I didn't."

"Was it difficult to hear things on the island?"

"It was difficult."

Bugliosi: *"Would you relate for the jury the various sounds that inhibited one's ability to hear things on the island?"*

Stearns; *"The birds made a terrific racket with their squawking. And there were the sounds of the ocean breaking on the outside shore, and the water in the lagoon lapping against the boat. There were also winds, and the winds rustling through the trees would make quite a bit of noise. The dense foliage muted sounds, too."* (p. 419)

The contention Stearns could hear the Zodiac the afternoon of the 30th, and was able to tell the direction of movement, is patently false and unbelievable. Her above testimony, unequivocally, establishes this fact.

Time Out of Joint

Bugliosi has the unenviable task of convincing the jury Walker was the killer of both the Grahams without assistance by Stearns. While there is not a shred of truth in Stearns assertions as to the events of August 30th, nonetheless, for purposes of argument, let us address some of the issues.

August 30, 1974. Stearns' log reveals:

" All-out effort today. R was up bright and early, scavenging butts at Mac's workshop. R wrangled a couple of games of chess, a stash of coffee and tobacco to go, plus an invitation to dinner. Not bad for before 9:00 A.M. Next was coffee. Cleaning, swabbing. stowing--removed canopy, baking bread, all around cleanup effort both on boat and ashore. Was going to bake bread in outdoor oven

to conserve fuel, but time and energy would not allow it. Undoubtably, upon return, I'll have no alternative--only hope the fuel lasts till then.'" (p. 413)

Stearns continues to read her log entry for August 30th, 1974 to the jury:

"And then tragedy.   And overnight a whole new set of alternatives beset us." (p. 425)

One notices the log entry for the 30th is devoid of any reference to the disappearance of the Grahams.   Stearns explains, she thought she had written the so-called log note the afternoon of the 30th, while she was baking bread on board the Iola. (p. 413)

She commences her concocted log asserting that Walker was up "bright and early" although she would have no way of knowing this supposed fact since his camp is located in the middle of the jungle approximately 300 to 400 yards distant from the Iola.   (pp. 72-3)

Since Stearns wrote the log entries during the day in question, how is it that she would know on the afternoon of the 30th,   the Grahams would be missing that night?   Obviously, she could not have known the Grahams would be missing *in advance of their disappearance.*

It is only many years later, as she prepares for her murder trial, that Bugliosi quizzed Stearns about this obvious faux pas. Stearns looking in her bag of tricks finds a solution, claiming an exception to her rule, alleging she wrote the last line of her August 30th entry, on the 4th of September. (Vol. 12, p. 1849)

If this were true, one wonders why she did not write an entry that supposedly was observed on the 31st, on the 31st.   Why include an event that was observed on the 31st in the log entry for the 30th?   Why not include the log note as an entry for the 31st ?

Of course the reason for this error was that the log is a fiction and the events therein, are for the most part, lies. At the time she wrote her counterfeit log she did not notice the inherent contradictions.

Bugliosi, fearful the jury might look with disbelief on the accuracy of her memory recounting a nondescript day that occurred nearly twelve years ago quizzed Stearns during her trial preparation. She responded, claiming she recalled the events of the 30th because she was supposedly preparing for the Fanning trip the next day. This answer satisfied Bugliosi. However, a less biased observer might want to know why, prior to the disappearance of the Grahams, was the 30th any different than any other day commencing on the 23rd when she began preparing for the voyage? (p. 414)

During trial Stearns testified she didn't remember everything:

"But it is more clear in my mind, I guess, than a number of other days because we were getting ready to go to Fanning the next day. That was the reason for all the activity, all the things to get ready to go." (p. 414)

Not satisfied Bugliosi comes to the rescue once again with a leading question — as usual there is no objection from Enoki:

"However, because it was almost twelve years ago, your memory is not perfectly clear. Is that correct?" (p. 414)

Stearns, following his lead, dutifully agrees:

"That's correct."

It is incumbent upon the reader (and juror) to understand that any desperate accused will fabricate whatever defense his or her mind can conjure (unfortunately all too often with the assistance of a defense attorney) to secure a not guilty verdict.

Bugliosi asks Stearns to *expand* on what Walker told her when he came to the Iola the morning of the 30th for the first time.

Stearns, replies:

178

"Well, he said Mac had said that he and Muff were going fishing, and they'd catch all the fish they could. Anything we didn't eat that night for dinner he wanted us to take on our trip."

This is the point where Stearns was supposed to talk about the bon voyage dinner invitation but did not. Observing her failure to mention the bon voyage dinner invitation Bugliosi again takes matters into his own hands and with a leading question introduces the "bon voyage dinner".

"Was this going to be somewhat of a bon voyage dinner for you and Buck?"

Stearns, reminded of her forgotten story line picks up on the cue and obediently responds:

"Yes." (p. 415)

The above testimony is confused, and if carefully examined, borders on weirdness. Bugliosi asks Stearns to expand on the information Walker purportedly gave her around 9:00 a.m., the morning of the 30th. As usual she gets her lies confused inadvertently including in the alleged 9:00 a.m. conversation matters she says were imparted to her during Walker's 4:00 p.m., conversation

After the above conversation Stearns claims she got into her dinghy, rowed ashore and went to Walker's camp for a cup of coffee. Stearns alleges she and Walker made several trips removing items and bringing them to the Iola. Stearns does not mention what items were removed from Walker's tent and brought to the Iola. Neither of them had much to begin with. Walker had furniture he found in the ruins but it remained in his tent. Other than a few clothing items what else would he have? Walker had a few books but we know they were not moved aboard the Iola because

179

prosecutor Eggers, when he arrived on Palmyra in search of the Grahams in November of 1974, found Walker's camp untouched with furniture and books in place. Stearns alleges after a few trips she stayed on the Iola and stored whatever was brought over from the camp. (p. 415)

She exaggerates the proximity of the Iola from shore. The authors inform the Iola was 15 yards from shore when tied to the dolphins. (p. 71) Stearns challenges this in her testimony claiming the Iola was on 10 to 15 feet from shore. (Vol. 11, p. 1646) (This is a lie as it would be virtually impossible with the Iola drawing close to five feet....she would be aground or lying on her side in the sand at low tide.)

Stearns alleges Walker appeared at the Iola between one and two in the afternoon and said something she did not remember. Stearns claimed Walker again appeared at the Iola around 4:00 p.m. and told her he was off to bathe and the Grahams had not yet gone fishing, that they still intended to go fishing and if they were not back by 6:30 p.m. defendants were to go aboard the Sea Wind and *"make themselves at home."* (It was supposedly during this 4:00 p.m. conversation with Walker that Stearns was informed of the invitation to go aboard the Sea Wind if the Grahams were not back from fishing.) (p. 415)

Continuing the direct examination of Stearns, not satisfied with Stearns' response, Bugliosi prompts Stearns with another leading question, per their script:

"Would there be anything set out for you?"

Remembering her lines, Stearns channeling her Little Miss Puffer alter ego stated:

"They said they would leave out some nibbles or something."

(Who, but a sweet little girl, would employ the child-like word, nibbles?) (p. 415)

The above testimony places Stearns directly speaking with one or both of the Grahams. She does not say, "Buck said, we were invited by the Grahams, to make ourselves at home and they would leave something out to eat." Nor would Mac employ the cutesy-pie noun "nibbles". (Neither would Walker for that matter.)

Stearns unequivocally states:

"They said they would leave out some "nibbles..."

Unaware she has undone her position regarding the purported events of the 30th, Stearns stumbles on   claiming around 4:30 p.m. she heard the sound of the the Zodiac near the anchorage of the Sea Wind, moving in a westerly direction. (Bugliosi speculates the sound of the Zodiac was Walker on his way across the lagoon to dispose of both the bodies of the Grahams.)(p. 503)

If one were to accept Stearn's narrative of the events of the 30th, between 4:00 p.m. and 4:30 p.m. Walker had time to capture both Mac and Muff Graham, time to rape and torture Muff Graham, beat her to a pulp, bust her bones, burn her with an acetylene torch, execute them, chop up their bodies, stuff both of them into two small aluminum containers, load the containers into the Zodiac, and dump their bodies in the lagoon.

After dumping their bodies, he then had to take the Zodiac ashore, wash the blood and gore off the dinghy, overturn it on the beach, go back to the Sea Wind, clean up the site of slaughter, discard his bloody clothes in the burn pit, set fire to the clothes, go over to the bathhouse, clean up, wash the blood off himself, put on a change of clothes, go over to the Sea Wind, go aboard and set the table with "nibbles". After doing all this he finds time to run back to the Iola

181

around 5:30 p.m. and inform Stearns he is, once again, on his way to bathe.   Purportedly, around 6:00 p.m., he has bathed and is on his way back to his camp, when he runs into Stearns, who is on her way to the bathhouse.   (p. 416)

After all this supposed activity, Walker reports to Stearns around 5:30 p.m. to see if she wants to go bathe with him. (p. 417) How is it that Stearns would not notice he is covered with bloody gore from the dismemberment of the two bodies when he asks her to join him?

No matter what time of day Walker supposedly accomplished these foul deeds, the narrative has problems.   How is it that Walker can race around, murder and butcher the Grahams, viciously assault Muff, cover himself with blood and gore, and whenever meeting with Stearns, appear composed and carefree?

Of course this is all pretend, none of the above ever occurred. The Grahams were brutally murdered by both defendants on the morning of August 29th as previously described.   On the 30th of August Mac's body lay at rest in several thousand feet of water and Muff's remains lay buried in a shallow grave on Strawn Island where they were found by Sharon Jordan several years later.

Stearns Disagrees (With Herself)

Anytime Stearns testifies to supposed factual events the juror is inundated with different versions depending on her immediate needs. When first detained for questioning by Shishido, Stearns told him about the purported events of the 30th of August. Shishido took detailed notes of the conversation and the following day prepared a summary of his interview in what is referred to as a 302 report.   At the time of her initial interview with Shishido, October 29, 1974,

Stearns stated Walker came by the Iola around 9:00 a.m. the morning of August 30, 1974 with an outline of his activities of the morning, including information the Grahams had invited them for "bon voyage dinner" aboard the Sea Wind that evening. (Vol. 11, pp. 1637-40)

Shishido's 302 report agrees, alleging that Walker returned to the Iola a *"short time"* after 9:00 a.m. and told Stearns about the dinner invitation, informing her that the Grahams were going fishing and would be late returning that evening.

Enoki inquires of Stearns:

"Do you recall agent Shishido testifying that you told him that after Mr. Walker told you about this invitation, he came back to the Iola shortly thereafter, and then told you about the....Grahams being delayed, and they were going fishing and they would be late?"

(The record is blurred, but it appears the page reference is Volume 12, page 1881 of the court reporter's transcript from Stearns' murder trial.)

Obviously, Stearns statement to Shishido that Walker returned "shortly" after 9:00 a.m., informing her the Grahams would be delayed for the dinner and *"would be late"* makes no sense whatsoever. (How is it Mac would know, "shortly" after nine in the morning, he would be delayed and would be late for a dinner scheduled in the early evening?)

To correct this glaring defect, in preparation for her murder trial, Stearns came up with an improved version that contradicted her 1974 statement to Shishido. Her 1986 version has Walker coming by the Iola around 4:00 p.m. informing her that Mac might be late in getting back to the Sea Wind in time for dinner.   Supposedly it was at this time that Walker informed Stearns they could make

183

themselves at home aboard the Sea Wind if the Grahams were not back at 6:30 p.m.

Bugliosi, quizzing Stearns:

"When was the next time that day that you recall seeing Buck?"

Stearns: *"I guess it was several hours later. Sometime — maybe around 4:00."*

Bugliosi: *"And what happened at that time?"*

Stearns: *"He came by, and he said that he'd been on his way to bathe and he had run into Mac, or, Mac called him over, something like that. And that Mac had said that he and Muff were still working — they were doing all kinds of things around the camp — and they hadn't gotten a chance to go fishing yet.*

But he said they were still going to do that. And so we should still come over at the same time. And that if they weren't back by 6:30 we should just go on board and make ourselves at home, and they would be along presently." (Vol. 11, pp. 1646-7)

Bugliosi Battens Down The Hatch
(Supposed Hatch Repair)

There were four trials involving Stearns and Walker as defendants. Stearns theft trial was held in June of 1975, with Walker's following in December 1975. In both instances the juries refused to accept defendants lies, both were convicted on all counts. (Walker's theft conviction was generously overturned by the Court of Appeal.)

Walker's trial for theft was the only trial in which he testified. Run of the mill theft charges although concerning a well publicized case did not demand the careful preparation the defense of a first degree murder charge.   At the time of the theft trials defendant's goals were to beat theft and transportation of stolen property charges not the far more serious charge of murder which was to follow eleven years later.   In 1975 there was little need for Walker to worry about co-ordinating his testimony with that of Stearns. Her trial preceded his. She had already been convicted of various felony charges and was off to the slammer by the time he went to trial. At the time of defendants theft trials both thought they had evaded murder charges. Thus, one might expect both Walker and Stearns to venture "off script" on numerous occasions.   (Enoki, for reasons unknown, failed to employ these early theft transcripts as impeaching documents during the murder trial of Stearns).

An example of Bugliosi's confused trial strategy can be found when he insisted on introducing into evidence a portion of Walkers 1975 theft trial testimony with the intent of showing that Walker was a liar because it contradicted Stearns log notes of August 30th.

Predictably, in a knee-jerk reaction, Enoki opposes the introduction of Walker's testimony and attempts to prohibit his testimony from being introduced to the jury even though it makes shambles of Stearns account of the supposed events of August 30th.

Several pages of the Stearns' murder trial transcript are devoted to the argument between counsel. (Vol.10, 1455 et al.)   At issue was the testimony of Walker, found on page 612 from his 1975 theft trial transcript, wherein Walker states on August 30, 1974, he was aboard the Iola working on the forward hatch, repairing and fiberglassing it and was not busying himself darting to and fro through the jungle as Stearns' log and testimony suggests. (This is the same hatch Wheeler observed sitting on shore when the FBI search party arrived at Palmyra Island looking for the evidence

185

of foul play.) Not only does his theft trial testimony impeach Stearns testimony pertaining to the 30th of August, but it directly contradicts her log relating to his alleged activities of the 26th and 28th. (p. 121)

Incomprehensibly Bugliosi argues to Judge King:

"On page 612 he (Walker) *said that on the date, August 30th, he was on the Iola, among other things, patching fiberglass in the hatch cover." (Vol. 10, p. 1455)*

Bugliosi, in a confused haze, is persuaded this tidbit of testimony is important because it demonstrates that Walker is a liar and that Stearns is telling the truth:

"Ms. Stearns will testify that he was not on the Iola on August 30th, and the diary of hers, August 26th, says that Buck fiberglassed the Iola on that day." (Vol. 10, p. 1455)

The debate rages on for several pages with Bugliosi pushing his point with Judge King:

"I think the jury — since Walker is one of the co-defendants in the indictment, and since the purpose of a trial, at least allegedly, is the ascertainment of the truth, the jury should know what this fellow, Buck Walker, said about the — the key date in question." (Vol. 10, p. 1457)

Bugliosi, misses the larger point — Walker's testimony contradicts and impeaches Stearns alleged log activities of the 26th, 28th and 30th of August. (p. 121) Moreover, his testimony was given during his theft trial of 1975 at a time when events were fresh in his mind. If anything, the testimony of Walker at his theft trial relating to his supposed activities on the 30th emphasizes the fact that both defendants are liars out to save themselves and their testimony is not to be trusted under any circumstances — each contradicts the other concerning their alleged activities on the crucial date of August 30, 1974:

One would think Enoki rather than opposing the admission of the theft trial testimony of Walker would welcome Walker's testimony that on August 30,1974, he spent the day fiberglassing the forward hatch of the Iola. His theft trial testimony makes shambles of Stearns murder trial testimony and log notes regarding their purported activities of August 26th, 28th and 30th.

The court does not immediately rule on the admissibility of Walker's theft trial testimony. In the end, goaded by Bugliosi, King permits the introduction of Walker's 1975 theft trial testimony. Again, Enoki misses a golden opportunity to capitalize on Bugliosi's strategy miasma when he fails to point out in his summation that Walker's 1975 theft trial testimony directly contradicts Stearns version of the alleged events August 30,1975.

DEATH OF THE GRAHAMS

Murder of Mac Graham

The Thursday morning of August 29, 1974, shortly before 8:00 a.m. Stearns rowed over to the Sea Wind and knocked on the hull to announce her arrival. She informed the Grahams that her (non-existent) batteries were fully charged and Mac could retrieve his generator. Receiving the news Mac stepped into his Zodiac and motored off to claim his prize. Arriving at the Iola he climbed aboard and entered the cabin below to pick up his generator. Walker was seemingly engaged in cleaning the galley.

As Mac bent down to retrieve his generator he employed both hands to lift the heavy machine. This action exposed the back of his head. At this moment Walker, grasping a nearby hammer, struck Mac a death dealing blow to he back of his head. Falling unconscious to the cabin sole, Walker beat Mac's head to a pulp. With the execution of Mac complete, Walker vaulted into Mac's Zodiac and raced back to the Sea Wind to assist Stearns in subduing Muff.

For the plot to succeed it was necessary for Stearns to gain entry to the cockpit of the Sea Wind.   She had to be in a position to stop Muff from fleeing down the companionway and obtaining her derringer when Walker rounded the point in Mac's Zodiac. Stearns presence in the cockpit alongside Muff would put her in a position to prevent this from happening. Anticipating   a life-death struggle in the cockpit Stearns knew every second counted once Muff saw Walker in Mac's Zodiac.   In what must have been a subdued, but extremely tense tete-a-tete, ever so innocently, Stearns asked Muff's permission to come aboard while they waited for Mac to return. Muff, believing defendants were departing for Fanning Island in an hour or two, granted permission to come aboard.

Predator and prey sat in the cockpit of the Sea Wind the morning of August 29, 1974. Stearns on edge, adrenalin pumping, expecting to see Walker come around the point in Mac's Zodiac at any moment and in so doing set off a savage battle for survival. Muff, uncomfortable in the presence of Stearns, felt her anxiety rise as she heard the far off sound of Mac's outboard motor. View of the approaching dinghy was obscured by the point… but something was not right. The sound of the motor had a high-pitched whine as if the throttle was full out. Muff knew this was not the manner in which Mac would drive the Zodiac with his precious generator aboard.

Stearns casually, but intensely, observing Muff saw a shadow of doubt cross her brow — something was setting her off.   Stearns, tense, giddy with excitement and anger, prepared for a fight, yet tried not to show it.   Suddenly the Zodiac rounded the point and Muff's long and tortured nightmare began. She saw Walker, a hound from the rictus of hell, charging at her with the outboard motor at full throttle. Stunned, her leadened feet were unable to respond, as precious seconds passed. Suddenly, she sprang into action lunging down the companionway seeking her derringer.   Stearns, leaping after her in an effort to block her way, was carried down the companionway along with Muff, who despite Stearns efforts, obtained her derringer and attempted to bring it to bear on her tormentor. Stearns fighting for her life was in a rage cursing and screaming for Walker's help as she struggled for possession of the weapon. Surprised by the strength of Muff, Stearns was barely able to force the pistol away as both rounds harmlessly discharged into the side of the hull just below the water line.

Walker cut the motor as the Zodiac slammed into the hull of the Sea Wind. Not stopping to secure the dinghy he vaulted over the life-lines.   Dashing below he disabled Muff with a vicious blow to the head, sending her writhing in pain to the floor.

Stearns' plan had succeeded; Mac was dead and they had secured the object of their desire, the Sea Wind.   Muff was trussed up and left on the cabin floor.   Walker found a tapered wooden plug and jammed it into the bullet holes to stanch the influx of water. He then went topside and clambered aboard Mac's hard dinghy to pursue the Zodiac which had drifted out into the lagoon. Securing the Zodiac, he took the hard dinghy in tow and motored back to the Sea Wind.   After securing the hard dinghy he proceeded to the Iola aboard the Zodiac.

Stepping aboard he placed a few personal items in the Zodiac and   picked up the netting attached to the stanchions which had been

189

employed to prevent the dogs from falling over board. As he climbed the companionway which was covered with Mac's blood and brains his foot slipped causing him to fall backward. Cursing, he landed atop Mac's lifeless body. Regaining his composure he headed back to the Sea Wind. On return to the Sea Wind he started the diesel engine and showed Stearns how to use the controls. He then sped back to the Iola to prepare her for tow.

Walker cut the lines securing Iola to the dolphins. The Iola free, he stepped forward on the bow, and threw a line to Stearns who was idling nearby on the Sea Wind. Stearns slowly eased the Sea Wind out into the lagoon with Iola in tow.

A funeral procession fit for a Viking, Mac's body aboard the Iola, laying atop the bloodied generator which was rested on the cabin floor. His head disfigured beyond recognition, blood and brains everywhere. Behind the Iola dragged the Zodiac which would carry Walker back to the Sea Wind once the Iola's sails were set and sea cocks opened (although hardly necessary given the amount of water that would naturally enter her hull through the cracks in the hull).

The final act of Mac's death was to take a victory photo of the Iola as she sank to her watery grave. (Defendants could show it about and fear nothing all the while relishing the secret knowledge of her cargo.)

On Thursday, August 29, 1974 around 10:00 a.m., a mile or two south-southwest of Palmyra Island, the Iola with Mac's body aboard, was committed to the deep. Defendants in the cockpit of the Sea Wind toasted as they watched the Iola sink beneath the waves. They mocked Muff as she lay trussed up, giving her a blow by blow account as the Iola disappeared. Their first objective of the day was

190

achieved — Mac was dead and all evidence of his murder lay several thousand feet under water.

Murder and Torture of Muff Graham

Defendants had planned a far different exit for Muff.   For Muff they had created, well in advance, a special scenario — a violent and cruel end to her life.   (So fixated was Stearns on the murder and torture of Muff that she was willing to take a chance on being caught at a later date. It would have been easy after executing Mac to place her aboard the ill-fated Iola and dispose of her at the same time.)

Why the difference in treatment if all they had in mind was stealing the Sea Wind? Why not insure success by executing Muff and dumping her body in thousands of feet of water along with Mac? There can be only one response to these questions and that is the phantasy both defendants had planned and savored for many weeks. A helpless victim and all the time in the world to wreak upon her every assault and torture their demented minds could conjure.

This was their childhood phantasies come to life. Muff's execution would wash away all the the years of hatred and insult, both real and imagined, heaped upon them by life.   A safe and simple execution would not do. Weeks before the appointed day they discussed and debated the scenario and   selected the aluminum container that was to be her coffin.   They located the tidal sands where her body would be dismembered and hacked to pieces and examined her place of burial nearby.   They gave thought to what they would wear for the celebratory occasion and the drugs they would take to stimulate this macabre act.

191

Having taken their "trophy" photos of the scuttled Iola, they returned to the lagoon to play out the final demonic chapter in their Palmyra adventure. Before returning to the lagoon Walker made a final sweep of the horizon with Mac's binoculars, to be certain there were no approaching vessels. Observing none, they entered the lagoon and secured the Sea Wind.

Before commencing defendants consumed a potpourri of pharmacy drugs and alcohol. With the Sea Wind secure Walker dropped Muff into the Zodiac and with Stearns headed off to his camp. On arrival he picked up his helpless victim, threw her over his shoulder and marched off to a location near his tent with Stearns leading the way.

They decided on Walker's camp as the place for Muff's macabre execution because it was convenient and, in the unlikely event another vessel entered the lagoon during their "entertainment", they could dispatch Muff immediately, hide her body in the tent, and dispose of her remains at sea when the coast was clear.

Dropping Muff to the ground Walker went back to the Zodiac retrieving Mac's propane torch. Both retired to Walker's tent to dress for the show. He donned a pirate mask adorned with long black fiberglass like hair and tied on a make-shift sash. Stearns put on a pair of sun glasses, wrapped a scarf around her head in pirate style — they were ready. Walker carried with him his .22 caliber pistol and Mac's large machete.

With hands and feet bound Muff could offer no resistance. When necessary to achieve their purpose her legs were untied and held by Stearns while Walker had his way only to be tied when he reached completion. Stearns jumped into the act and forced herself upon Muff. All the while Muff's screams rang throughout the island. She violently resisted suffering powerful blows to her head and body

192

in an effort to render her more compliant and break her will. However, this they could not do. Muff was far stronger than either imagined. Trussed and tortured, bloodied and screaming, she would not give in, and fought her tormentors until her last dying breath.

When tiring of this sport, defendants commenced on her person with foreign objects, delighting in Muff's agony. Finally, when both were satiated, Walker brought forth the tool of hell itself, the propane torch. He fired it up and approached as Muff screamed and struggled in fear and agony. Walker handed the torch to Stearns, who applied it to Muff's left eye then ran it over her blood soaked scalp. Walker no longer able to endure Muff's death agonies drew his pistol, placed it against her skull and with one shot mercifully ended her life. It was an unimaginable prelude to Muff's death. One so seeped in pain and horror it reached out over time and space. It was the end Muff had foreseen in her nightmares before leaving San Diego. (pp. 30, 43-5)

Walker threw Muff's corpse over his shoulder and walked to the Zodiac tossing it, like a rag doll, into the dinghy. Stearns secured the aluminum coffin placing it in as well. They motored to the pre-selected location on the tidal sands of Strawn Island, to dismember her body.

There they both set to work in their shop of horrors on the tidal sands; hacking and chopping, all the while marveling at the difficulty involved in the dismemberment of a human body. Now and then cutting off a piece of flesh, and with gleeful remarks, throwing it to the sharks circling at the water's edge.

Finally the deed was done but there was a problem. The dismembered body parts would not fit into the aluminum container— it was too small. They could not close the lid. Walker obtained a strand of wire which he wrapped around the container to keep the lid closed. Transporting the container to the place of burial Walker hastily dug a shallow grave and placed the coffin in it. The coffin was buried in the sand among the shrubbery on Strawn Island precisely where Sharon Jordan was to discover it seven years later.

As they motored back to camp the on-coming tide was already at work cleansing the sands. Arriving at the Sea Wind they stripped off their blood soaked clothing and placed it in a burn pit near the Sea Wind along with fantasy paraphernalia and empty prescription drug vials from the Sea Wind pharmacy. Once assembled, Walker poured gas on the pile and set it alight. They then retired to the shower and cleansed Muff's blood from their bodies. Returning to the Zodiac, they rinsed it several times with sea water to wash away evidence of their crime.

So violent and vicious was the attack and so great the pain and suffering of their victim, neither Stearns or Walker desired to revisit the scene of the crime. Buck's camp had become cursed and haunted. An hour before, Muffs unheeded screams of pain and terror rang out across the lagoon, blood and gore on the tidal sands....now, only the cry of birds, sparkling crystal waters, and palms waving in the breeze. A tropical paradise. Gone was the Iola, gone was Mac and Muff — defendant's ghoulish fantasy complete.

RETURN TO HAWAII

Detention and Arrest of Stearns

Almost immediately after the murders defendants commenced a thorough examination of the contents of the Sea Wind. Amazed at the amount of food Muff had so carefully purchased and stored away. Along with the food was a plentiful supply of wine and alcohol.   Eventually they discovered Mac's "cruising kitty" of nearly five thousand dollars in small bills. They were elated—they had hit the jackpot.

With the discovery of Mac's cruising cash reserves of nearly five thousand dollars, and possession of the Sea Wind with all her stores and equipment defendants were eager to leave Palmyra, get back to Hawaii, obtain new papers for the Sea Wind and sail off into the blood-drenched sunset.   They had achieved their purpose — enacted two bloody murders, and had stolen a fine sailing vessel.

Walker removed the figurehead the following day; it was a unique   signature clue to the identity of the Sea Wind. He painted over the ship's name and crudely painted in "Iola". For almost two weeks, undisturbed by others, they lolled about the island. During the days before returning to Hawaii to obtain cruising papers they were careful not to revisit   the area where they had tortured and murdered Muff.   Both sociopaths, typically devoid of guilt, but *not* fear of retribution.   It slowly dawned on them that they had committed a horrendous crime — fear of apprehension, possibly the death penalty, begin to invade their thoughts. Weighing anchor they departed Palmyra for Hawaii the morning of September 11, 1974. (p. 432)

The return trip to Hawaii afforded plenty of time to co-ordinate defendant's stories coming up with a scenario that would cast them in an innocent light. They finally settled on the one Stearns presented at her theft trial.   Stearns on the Iola, Walker on shore meeting up with Mac, the dinner invitation, the Grahams going fishing for supper in the late afternoon, finding the table set, searching for the Grahams, remaining on board the boat overnight, discovery of the Zodiac floating in the lagoon with no sign of the bodies, and etc.   The same scenario   Stearns, babbling away, presented to Shishido on her arrest for the theft of the Sea Wind October 29, 1974. The same song and dance that bound Bugliosi to the nonsensical defense narrative presented by Stearns during her trial for murder.

Stearns highly touted navigational skills mysteriously disappeared on the return to Hawaii. Sailing to Hawaii from Palmyra in the month of September, on a proper yacht, such as to Sea Wind, one would expect a passage of 7 to 10 days. However, defendants did not make landfall until October 12, 1974, an extraordinarily lengthy passage of 31 days. Sailing the Sea Wind, a boat vastly superior to the Iola, it took Walker and Stearns *more than a month to return to Hawaii* — so much for the supposed navigational skills of Stearns.

Allegedly, their first port of call on return, October 12, 1974, was Nawiliwili Harbor on Kauai. The following evening, October 13, they visited an adjacent sailboat at anchor owned by the Mehaffys. It was during this visit Stearns told the MeHaffys there was a hole in the Sea Wind near the waterline caused by a swordfish. The Mehaffys were skeptical and demanded to see the remains of the swordfish bill, supposedly still lodged in the hull. But defendants refused to permit them to come aboard citing the need to get to a yard and repair the damage. (p. 354)

The next day, defendants proceeded to Pokai Bay, Oahu where the stayed for a week. Departing they arrived at the Keehi lagoon on Oahu, October 21, 1974. The following day they hauled out the Sea Wind at Tuna Packers' boatyard to replace the plank penetrated by the .38 caliber bullets from Muff's the derringer. A week later, the Sea Wind went back in the water. Defendants sailed to Ala Wai harbor arriving on the 28th of October. While at Tuna Packers, the Sea Wind's name and home port had been painted over, also the trim had been repainted lavender. Foolishly defendants failed to paint the new name or hailing port of the boat on the stern.

Shortly after arrival at Ala Wai harbor on the 28th of October 1974, Edwin Pollock, friend of the Grahams and member of the Ala Wai Yacht Club, spotted Walker rowing away from the Sea Wind. He contacted the Coast Guard and advised them it was the missing vessel and that the Grahams were not aboard. The Coast Guard contacted the FBI

When first notified, FBI Special Agent Shishido thought it was not an FBI matter and properly belonged to the Coast Guard as a crime on high seas. Despite some reservation an "office special" for the following day was decal
red and all available agents were alerted to be present. The Coast Guard informed Shishido they planned to board the Sea Wind and invited him to come along. Edwin Pollock agreed to accompany them since he could identify Walker and Stearns. (pp. 128-9)

The next morning October 29, 1974, the Coast Guard informed FBI Special Agent Shishido a man and woman were getting ready to leave the vessel and that they intended to pursue. Shishido hurried over to the Coast Guard cutter and they got under way. (p. 129)

Stearns had taken Walker to the dock and was returning to the Sea Wind to put their barking dogs below. Observing the Coast Guard cutter approaching at high speed, she reversed her direction and headed back to land, rowing as fast as she could. On the dock Walker pursued by the Coast Guard dived into the water to escape. With the Coast Guard cutter bearing down on her Stearns redoubled her effort reaching shore before apprehension. Scrambling over the rocks, with the Coast Guard in hot pursuit, she ducked into a hotel

197

lobby where she was apprehended attempting to hide behind a potted plant. (pp. 128-31)

The Coast Guard placed Stearns in a dinghy, supervised by Edwin Pollock, and towed them back to the cutter. While being towed back to the cutter, Stearns told Pollock, she *"had found the Zodiac capsized on the beach at Paradise Island "*. (p. 322, footnote)

Aboard the cutter, a few minutes later, when questioned by FBI Special Agent Shishido, Stearns changed her story telling him they found the Zodiac belonging to Mac *overturned in the lagoon at Cooper islet.* The outboard motor was also overturned and they *"found the gas tank floating nearby."* On discovery, they *"turned the dinghy upright, reattached the gas tank, and continued searching in the Zodiac."* (p. 133)

At the time of her initial conversation with Shishido, Stearns did not realize an outboard motor exposed to sea water for twelve hours would not run without a through cleaning. Approaching trial for the theft of the Sea Wind the summer of 1975, she realized her error and changed her testimony for a
third time, claiming they found the Zodiac, overturned on the beach on *Cooper Island,* with motor attached and the gas tank lying on the sand nearby. (pp. 132-3)

After giving Shishido a statement she was escorted off the Coast Guard cutter and taken to the Ala Wai Yacht Club. Arriving at the Yacht Club Stearns made a request to use the bathroom. Edwin Pollock, a club member, had a key. Along with several FBI officers they walked Stearns over to the rest room and waited outside. Stearns took her purse with her. While in the bathroom those present heard her repeatedly flush the toilet which was equipped with a valve type flush device allowing for rapid repeated flushing. A few

198

minutes later Pollock's wife Marilyn appeared and went into the restroom; finding Stearns, they exited together. (p. 319)

Shortly thereafter Stearns was taken down to the FBI headquarters and further questioned. After questioning she was arrested for theft of the Sea Wind and taken to jail. The charges included transporting stolen property over state lines, theft of the Sea Wind, and stealing four hundred dollars from Mac's cruising funds.

Botched C.S.I.

The arrest of Stearns and Walker caused great consternation among the public and sailing community in Hawaii. On arrest, an investigative party was immediately dispatched to Palmyra.

Since Palmyra came under the jurisdiction of the federal government the FBI and US Attorney's office became involved. Forty hours after the arrest of Stearns at Ala Wai Harbor on November 1, 1974, two months after the murder of the Grahams, an ocean-going tug from Fanning Island captained by Martin Vitousek, the University of Hawaii's Man For All Seasons, pulled into Palmyra lagoon carrying a ten man search team including Jack Wheeler, FBI agents Calvin Shishido and Tom Bridges as well as U.S. Attorney, Bill Eggers. As the search party entered the lagoon they observed the Iola was not on the coral reef where Stearns stated it had run aground. Nor was there any indication of another boat visiting Palmyra between the death of the Grahams on the 29th of August and the visit of the investigation team on November 1, 1974. (pp. 137-8)

Wheeler spotted the forward hatch of the Iola on the beach near the dolphins to which the Iola had been tied. As they walked around the west lagoon shoreline in the area of the Sea Wind's former anchorage they came across a burn pit. In the residue were unmarked prescription bottles, a small piece of fabric that had survived the fire, one non-prescription dark lens from a pair of sunglasses, and another clear prescription lens. Also found in the burn pit was a pair of earrings. On later examination the prosecution was unable to associate the lens of the glasses with the decedents or defendants. For reasons unknown, the earrings probably made by Mac for his wife, were not recovered. (pp. 138-40, 166)

Wheeler, on direct-examination by Schroeder during murder trial of Stearns testified:

"Okay, it was women's clothing, and specifically, there was a pair of earrings and eyeglasses on the pile."

"And these items had been burned?"

"Scorched."

"Now you mentioned items of clothing. Do you recall how many items of clothing you saw?"

"We don't know, because we didn't...we didn't dig in."

The court in disbelief, intercedes: *Well, you didn't?*

"Nobody did."

Schroeder: *"Now you mention that these were women's clothing. Were they all women's clothing, or could you tell?"*

"From what I saw I would say they were all women's."

"Could you tell about how many items of clothing were there?"

"It looked like the contents of a drawer, perhaps." (Vol. 1, p. 128)

"Now, how far was the Graham's boat? How far had it been from this fire site that you found?"

"30 to 40 feet."

On cross-examination Weinglass, dumbfounded, inquires:

200

"Is it your testimony that three or four law enforcement officials down there looking for Muff Graham — that earrings were pointed out to them and they just left them there?"

"They left the clothing....they didn't take it?" Repeats Weinglass.

"Didn't take it because, like you just pointed out, we couldn't tell who it belonged to." Agrees, Wheeler.

Weinglass, still disbelieving: *"And they didn't take it back?"*

"They didn't take it."

"Okay. Was a picture taken of it?"

"I'm not sure?"

"Have you ever seen a picture showing earrings?"

"No.   The rubble was still there in '77 when I went down again, but by that time, of course, it was shot."

"The earrings were gone?"

"Well, there were no earrings there. In fact, even the clothing — you could still see where it was."

"The fireplace was?"

"Right."

"But in '77, there were no earrings there?"

"Nothing there then." (Vol. 2, p. 202.)

Continuing on cross examination by Weinglass, Wheeler a veteran of the South Pacific, opines the trip from Hawaii for defendants was cold and wet.

Weinglass inquires:

"And did she tell you that was her experience in fact coming down?"

"That's the way I got acquainted with their heavy weather gear, because they had it up to dry when — when they came in."

"I see. Okay. Now again, with respect to the heavy weather gear, to your knowledge that was never picked up and brought back by the FBI or anyone else?"

"We just went through the brick — the cement building where they had it hanging. And I don't think anything was brought back."

"No. And, no pictures were taken either."

"Right."

"You've never seen photographs of it."

" I don't believe I have." Responded, Wheeler. (Vol. 2, p. 206)

Unlike their TV counterparts, the FBI during their search of Palmyra for evidence relating to the disappearance of the Grahams, were grossly negligent in collecting evidence that may have related to the murder of the Grahams. The burned clothing probably was that of Muff discarded by Stearns. If so, relatives of the Grahams might have identified the items. The earrings may have been worn by Muff during her murder and were discarded when Stearns thought they might be recognized by someone or were bad karma. Of note is the fact that Mac made jewelry for Muff.

Another item described by Bugliosi as a *"fright wig"*, such as one might expect to be attached to a Halloween pirate mask, was also found in the ashes. (With this brief note, there is no further reference to the "fright wig" in ATSWT.) We do not know if the wig was recovered or if Enoki attempted to tie the wig to the murder of the Grahams. (pp.137-9)

The search party found Walker's camp virtually undisturbed, his tent still standing. Inside the tent was a cot, a work project left

202

untouched, and a bookshelf with books and magazines. It was as if after the murders, defendants moved aboard the Sea Wind and never went back; purposely avoiding the scene of the torture and murder of Muff Graham. (Even for someone as depraved and sociopathic as defendants it must have been unnerving to be in such close proximity to the gruesome scene of Muff's final hours.) (pp. 137-9)

ERRANT SWORDFISH — Differing Accounts

Version One (Book)

There were many contradictions that made sorting out fact from fiction in Bugliosi's account of his defense of Stearns difficult to comprehend; the confusion brought on by the changing of names of various principle witnesses without informing the reader;   the compulsive lying of Stearns; Bugliosi's reporting of trial testimony that was misleading, and patently false; the failure of the authors to clearly define the facts — often offering two different version of the same scenario, and, of course the constant lying by Stearns.

The following is a prime example:

Defendants returning to Hawaii from Palmyra Island aboard the Sea Wind dropped anchor in Nawiliwili Harbor, Kauai October 12, 1974.   The following evening, just after supper, they went over to a nearby sailboat skippered by Frank Mehaffy and introduced themselves. They stayed for several hours conversing with Mehaffy and his wife.   Bugliosi alleges that during the meeting Roy Allen (Walker) brought up the subject of a *mysterious hole in the hull of the Sea Wind just below the waterline.   Roy Allen explained that a swordfish had speared his boat just below the water line on the trip from Palmyra."* (p. 235) Later, on pages 354-5, the reader is treated to a different version of the same facts.

On page 235 defendants on the Sea Wind pulled *"up to a pier"*. On page 354 they *"anchor"* next to the Mehaffys. Page 235 has Walker informing the Mehaffys of the swordfish attack; on page 354 it is Stearns who brings up the attack and elaborates. On page 354 Bugliosi alleges Mehaffy stated he and his wife were at anchor in Nawiliwili Harbor on the evening of October 12, 1974 when the Sea Wind appeared with defendants aboard *"setting anchor next to his boat"*. (Not tied up to a pier as in the p. 235 account.) The following day *"just after dinner"*, defendants *"knocked on the hull"* and were invited aboard where *"they stayed about three hours."* (p. 354)

"Stearns did most of the talking."

In this version it was Stearns who told the Mehaffys the story of the hole in the hull of the Sea Wind, *"just below the waterline"*. She attributed the hole to a swordfish attacking the boat on the return to Hawaii. According to Stearns, they heard a *"thump"* but did not think much of it, until *"later"* when *"they went below and found the boat taking on water."* Stearns claimed after they noticed the water in the boat, they pumped it out; alleging *"they found the bill of the swordfish sticking through the hull into the bilge area"*. Stearns stated Walker put an *"outside patch"* on the hole. (pp. 354-5)

Mehaffy doubted the account of the swordfish and said he would like to see the hole. Defendants demurred, stating they had to find a place to haul the boat out and make repairs. (pp. 354-5)

(Differing accounts of the same event confuse the reader. It must have been Stearns who brought up the swordfish subject not Walker. It is the kind of nonsensical tale she makes up without

204

thinking, at the drop of a hat. The conflicting stories on pages 235 and 354 are probably the result of the input of two different writers and sloppy editing. What ever the cause, it is a recurring problem and adds another layer of confusion in the quest to ascertain the truth of the matter in the death of the Grahams.)

Version Two, (Stearns' Murder Trial Transcript)

In the course of Stearns' murder trial on direct-examination, Bugliosi inquires:

"Going back to your trip from Palmyra to Hawaii, did anything unusual happen to your boat en route?"

Stearns: *"Yes. We were becalmed one day, and the dog started barking, and they were all over on the one side of the boat barking, looking down into the ocean. And, I went over there and looked, and there was this huge fish, possibly 14 feet long, with a — it was a swordfish and it had a bill on it that extended out. It was a huge fish, the biggest fish I had ever seen. And we were becalmed, and the boat was rocking back and forth and the fish was just swimming around us, under the boat and around the boat.*

And after a while, I went below and started making dinner. And I was below and I heard this sound, kind of sounded like a "kheeeh," and it sounded like something fell off the mast and hit the deck.

I went topside and looked around. Buck was up there. He had heard it too, and he was looking around. And I looked over the side and I saw this fish, just the tail end of the fish diving down. I just didn't think any more of it, and I went back down and finished making dinner.

Buck and I had eaten, and after we were through with dinner, I leaned down and I was petting Puffer and her whole backside was wet. So I felt the rug where she was laying and the rug was all wet. And Buck picked up the floorboards of the bilge and the bilge was full to overflowing. It was filled with water.

(Stearns claims the bilge of the Sea Wind was completely full of water and overflowing on to the floorboards.)

So Buck got the pump started, and we started searching, and we had our heads down on the side of the boat and we could kind of hear a trickling sound of water running. So Buck pulled up the floor boards of the interior where we heard the noise, and we found this bill of the swordfish had penetrated the hull and water was gushing in all around it.

(In this version of the supposed swordfish attack, Stearns locates the alleged point of intrusion by the swordfish *below* the floorboards, *not* above them.)

"Buck tried to jiggle the bill like he wanted to pull it in or push it out, and the water gushed in, and so I said, 'don't. That's the only thing between us and the ocean. I went and got some cotton. I had read about this in a book. We started stuffing cotton all around where the bill was, and when the cotton gets wet it swells. And it slowed down the flow of the water, and gradually, as we stuffed, almost stopped."

"And Buck spent the evening getting a board together where —He had a wooden board that he cut out in a square size and put calking on it and <u>*screws*</u> *on it, and next morning, he hung from his feet over the side of the boat and attached the board to where the swordfish — and it had broken off flush with the deck....so he attached the board over that."* (Vol. 11, pp. 1695-7)

(Presumably, Stearns meant to say the bill of the swordfish broke off "flush with the hull" — not deck. Her misuse of words is common when she is lying.)

Bugliosi, leads: *"This swordfish incident occurred where on the high seas?"*

Stearns: *"I don't remember, maybe halfway. Maybe three quarters of the way to Hawaii. I'm not sure."*

Bugliosi inquires: *"You heard Mr. Mehaffy testify that you told him the swordfish attack was inter-island in Hawaii?"*

(Mehaffy's memory of the swordfish encounter told by Stearns is that it occurred *after* defendants returned to Hawaii as they were sailing between the islands comprising the state of Hawaii.)

"Yeah, I don't know why he said that."

"It did not happen inter-island?"

"No."   (Vol. 11, p.1697)

Version Three (Inter-Island Encounter)

In recalling Mehaffy's account of defendant's swordfish story Bugliosi leaves out a portion of her testimony which exposes the story for what it was — a bold-faced lie. The version Bugliosi mentions in ATSWT says nothing about Stearns first returning to the big island of Hawaii directly from Palmyra, nor of a subsequent five day passage to Nawiliwili, Kauai.

In the murder trial transcript, contrary to the version of the sword fish attack found in ATSWT, Stearns testified she told Mehaffy they sailed from the island of Hawaii, near Hanamalo Point, to Nawiliwili harbor located on the island of Kauai.

Schroeder, questioning Mehaffy on direct examination:

207

" And did she tell you how long it had taken them to sail from Hanamalo?"* (Located on the island of Hawaii.)

" Yes. It took five days to sail from Hanamalo. "

"During the conversation did Stephanie say anything about any incident that might have happened on the way from Hanamalo to Nawiliwili?"

"Well, only one that stuck in our minds. And that was the....occurrence of a large sailfish or swordfish. They were kind of becalmed out quite a way up — quite a ways west of Honolulu. (The island of Kauai is west of Oahu where Honolulu is located.) *And this fish kept circling the boat. And so at that point they watched if for a while. And then they heard a thump, and didn't think anything about it...until later. "*

" And later why the dog came up to Stephanie, and the small dog was wet. And then ...later on, Roy (Walker) went down to find out why there was water. And they pumped out the boat, and found the bill of a swordfish sticking through the hull into the bilge area."

"Did you ever in any way ask Stephanie or Roy to show you evidence of this swordfish attack?"

"Well they were talking about it, I just simply said: I would like to see that — a hole a fish could put through the boat."

"But I didn't ask specifically to go aboard and look at the hole."

"Did Stephanie or Roy every offer to show you this swordfish hole?"

"No. They mentioned that they had to leave the next day because the boat was still taking on water, and they wanted to get

back to...Maalaea to haul it out, to effect repairs, more permanent repairs." (Vol. 5, pp. 857-8)

(Mehaffey's version differs substantially from Stearns account of the incident. The purported attack, according the Mehaffys, occurred *after* defendants have reached Hawaii and were sailing from the island of Hawaii to Kauai.)

Unbelievably Stearns claimed, after piercing the hull of the Sea Wind and leaving a portion of his bill in the boat, the fish was able to swim away. She also told Mehaffy it took five days to sail from Hanamalo Point, Hawaii to Nawiliwili, Kauai.

Version Four — Suicidal Marlin

Stearns had not thought out the details of her lie concerning the alleged swordfish attack when she first spoke to FBI agent Shishido on the 29th of October 1974. A forth version of the supposed attack is recorded by FBI agent Shishido as he questions Stearns on the 29th of October, 1974. It is in this version that he incorporates into his 302 report. (Bugliosi fails to include it in that portion of Shishido's report which he furnishes to the reader in his book ATSWT.)

On direct-examination we find Enoki inquiring of Shishido:

"Did she indicate what they did to the boat when they dry docked it?"

Agent Shishido replies:

"She said that they patched up a hole that was caused by a 'marlin spearing' the boat while they were in route to Honolulu. And they had repainted the boat. And they had also scraped off the name Sea Wind and had repainted over that."

209

In this version Stearns changes the species of fish from that of a swordfish to a marlin. (A marlin has a long, sharp, pointed bill, as opposed to the long, wide, flat, toothed bill of a swordfish.) (Vol. 6, p. 958)

Version Five — Walker Pipes Up

Defendants got maximum mileage out of the attacking swordfish routine. Walker as usual got a bit carried way and added a different spin asserting that a swordfish attack was responsible for loss of the Iola according to a report by the Associated Press in a release dated June 1, 1985.   Reporter, Jack Schreibman, notes; *"Walker had told others his boat was lost after it was holed by a swordfish."*

The Tuscaloosa News, June 2, 1985 picked up the same AP story, repeating the statement by Walker, that *"the reason he lost the Iola was because of a swordfish attack."*

In the same news release the Associate Press quoted Marilyn Pollock, wife of Edwin Pollock. She stated the reason they left Palmyra early was because *"she was frightened by Walker."*   The release also notes: *Marilyn Pollock choked back tears, as she stated Mrs. Graham told her she "knew she would never leave the island alive."*

Thus we have at least four differing accounts of the supposed swordfish attack on the Sea Wind, and one version of the attack by Walker wherein the swordfish supposedly sunk the Iola.   So there you have it; not merely two different versions of an alleged event that never occurred, but five.   Take your pick — which, in the vernacular of Stearns, is *"more close to the truth"*?

Stearns Tutors Enoki

There was considerable confusion identifying the location of the supposed intrusion of the swordfish bill into the hull of the Sea Wind. Enoki cross-examining Stearns:

"Okay. and then — I think you described it. You discovered the bilge was full of water."

"Yes."

"And eventually — and after you got to the bottom of the water you saw the swordfish bill sticking out."

Stearns corrects Enoki: *"No, not to the bottom of the water. The swordfish had penetrated the hull...on the port side of the boat."*

Enoki: *"Okay. The port is left; correct?"*

"It was under the kitchen table where we actually found it. And the kitchen table in a boat kind of butts up against..." (Volume 11, page 1751, is missing.) Resuming on page 1752, Enoki responds to Stearns assertion:

"Okay. Now the swordfish struck the boat at some area below that floor?"

Stearns corrects Enoki, informing him the purported intrusion occurred above the floorboards:

" No. No. The swordfish struck the boat — I don't believe it was below the floor. It was in between the floorboard, and just above to some degree. I'm almost positive."

"Buck had to pull it off — there was some type of covering to the wood, like...wall covering; but I think it was...rug I'm not exactly — I don't exactly remember what was covering it."

"But he had to pull out those planks, and some kind of insulate, to get to the swordfish bill."

"We had heard water running, and he started...pulling pieces of wood out and looking for it. And it was under table there. Not below what you would consider the floor. (The hole was allegedly under the table, but not below the floorboards. If so, this would mean the bill of the swordfish was intruding into the galley area above the floorboards.)

"More on the side of the boat, under the waterline."

"Okay. And just so I get it straight."

"Obviously the bill was not sticking right into the room where you guys — where you people were."

Stearns, picking up on Enoki's ignorance and confusion, just after informing him the supposed swordfish bill was in the same cabin (room), below the water line, but *above* the floorboards, meaning it would be visible, gives up and following his lead, contradicts herself:

"No."

Enoki finishing: *"—eating or whatever?"*

(After testifying the swordfish bill was allegedly visible above the floorboards in the galley area she describes Walker's actions as he plugged the bullet hole caused by Muff's derringer.)

"No. Buck had to pull off whatever this decorative paneling was so that you didn't actually see the ribs of the boat, and the studs, or whatever they call that."

"And when he pulled that part away, then we saw the swordfish bill penetrating the hull, and the water gushing in around it." (Vol. 11, pp. 1750-3)

(The above testimony by Stearns probably describes Walker's actions as he stanched the leak in the hull of the Sea Wind caused by the discharge of Muff's derringer. To plug the leak in the galley Walker had to tear away a piece of thin veneer panelling, or a rug, to access the bullet holes allowing him to insert the wooden plug.)

Enoki continues:

"Okay. And — but you still didn't know at that point what had happened; correct?"

"That's correct."

"You didn't know until later when you discovered your dog was wet, and so forth."

" Yes."

"Now — but it was right after dinner. I patted her, and her backside was all wet."

"Okay. And then — I think you described it."

"You discovered the bilge was full of water?"

" Yes." (Vol. 11, p. 1750)

There are two ways by which Puffer's fur could have been exposed to water had the alleged event actually occurred. Puffer could have encountered the leak under the galley table; or catastrophically, the boat was endanger of sinking because water had filled the entire bilge and was coming up over the floor boards.

If the floor boards were underwater, this fact would signify the automatic 12 volt bilge pump was over-whelmed by the influx of water, or worse, non-functional. All this gets silly when one considers the transmission, diesel motor, many electrical connections and devices, to say nothing of the food stored in the bilge, would all have been inundated by destructive salt water.

213

The entire proposition is preposterous particularly in light of the fact that the Sea Wind unlike the Iola, had at least one and perhaps two automatic 12 volt bilge pumps that would cycle on immediately after sensing of water in the bilge. The water would be expelled without a need for Walker to "turn on" the bilge pump. The water level sensing switch automatically detects the presence of sea water and activates the bilge pump.

Apple Bobbing Time

More hilarity ensues as the jury attempts to follow Stearns account of patching the hole left by the alleged penetration of the swordfish bill.

Enoki cross-examining Stearns:

"All right. And it was your testimony that — that <u>the next day</u> Mr. Walker repaired the hole from the outside?"

Stearns: *" He put a patch on it, with caulking, to try and cut down on whatever waters might seep in through it."*

"And, in order to do this, Mr Walker hung by his feet over the railing of the Sea Wind?", queries a skeptical Enoki.

Stearns, committed to a ridiculous lie about Walker hanging over the side of the Sea Wind upside down, feet somehow "clamped" to the rail, continues:

"Right. He kind of took the netting that was there to protect the dogs from falling overboard, and he clipped his feet over the top, and I held his feet. And he went headfirst down. And from that position he screwed the...patch onto the hull."

"Okay. And — and how long would you say this took?"

(Pause.) *"I — will guess and say maybe he it took — twenty minutes, or something like that."*

"Okay.   And were you holding him the whole — holding his feet the whole time?" Enoki asks, in disbelief:

"His feet were clamped on to and over the gunnel, and I was holding him so he wouldn't fall overboard."

This explanation is too much for our gullible prosecutor:

"Okay.   Was — was his — well, I — and at this time the boat is also pitching in the water, is it not?"

"Yes."

Enoki, incredulous: *"Was his head underwater?"*

"It was about three or four inches under the waterline."

(Enoki should have left the jury with the absurd spectacle of Walker bobbing up and down for twenty minutes.   Bewildered, he gives away his advantage.)

"His head was?"

Stearns picks up on the absurdity of her testimony and backs away suddenly changing in direction:

"No, the hole."

Enoki: "Oh, I see."

Stearns, attempts clarification:

" So — he didn't have — I mean, he would have to go under to see where to put the screwdriver into the screw holes. But then he would come up, and he would just (indicating) turn the screwdriver with his head above the water. So it was kind of dunking down and coming up."

(Stearns depicts Walker hanging over the side of the Sea Wind, feet somehow clamped to the gunnel, head bobbing under water with each roll of the boat, alleging he had to go under water to

215

locate the screw holes that he had set in the patch. Once the target hole was located, with his head above the water, he would turn the screwdriver, all while he was upside down.)

Enoki, with his quarry on the ropes, immediately gives up his small victory and lets Stearns off the hook by correcting her fallacious testimony:

"So the swordfish had penetrated in an area where he could reach with his hands, but his head was still above the water. Would that be a fair way of saying it?" (Hamilton Burger of Perry Mason fame strikes again.)

Relieved, off the hook, Stearns agrees: *"Yes."*

(No, Elliott, it is not a "fair way of saying it". Stearns just told you that Walker was hanging over the side of the boat upside down, his feet somehow clamped over the rail, his head under the water, bobbing up and down as the waves passed under the hull. It is virtually impossible! How does one *"clamp"* his feet over the gunnel? I suppose it might be possible to hook your toes over the rail, but how long could that go on? Since Walker is six feet tall, his head would be immersed between two and three feet over the side of the Sea Wind given her three and a half foot freeboard observed in the photo on page 92 of ATSWT.)

How could Walker, upside down, take a dunking for twenty minutes, without water entering the nose? It would be nearly impossible to expel the water because of the position. When Enoki responds in disbelief Stearns, sees the error of her testimony and attempts correction; stating it was the hole that was three of four inches under water and not Walker's head.

Her response still does not solve the problem of Walker hanging over the side with his six foot frame dangling from the gunnel, totally immersing his head, and portion of his upper body, with Stearns hanging onto him for dear life. How is it that Stearns would have the strength to hold Walker, weighing nearly two hundred pounds, by the feet, upside down for twenty minutes? There is another unmentioned problem: Walker is completing this task without benefit of a mask or goggles. Salt water severely stings the eyes and blurs the vision making any underwater repair extremely difficult without eye protection. (Vol. 11, 1753-4)

Lying Larry Begs to Differ

The testimony of Larry Seibert concerning the alleged swordfish attack varies substantially from the version Stearns presented to the jury. Seibert had known defendants for over a year. Shortly before hauling out the Sea Wind for repairs relating to the gun-shot damage to the hull defendants invited Seibert aboard the Sea Wind. During this visit Seibert testified he saw the remains of the bill of the swordfish sticking through the hull.

On direct-examination by Weinglass, Seibert wanders off script in a big way as he explains what defendants told him about the swordfish attack and in so doing contradicts Stearns:

"And did they relate anything to what happened on the return trip from Palmyra to Hawaii?"

"Yes, they did."

"And what did they tell you?"

"They told me that the boat was rammed by a large fish that they seen swim away after ramming the boat. And initially, they didn't think anything about it, but later, somehow or another they heard a trickling noise or something. Anyway, they investigated later and found there to be a leak where the bill of the fish stuck in the side of the boat. And Buck said he jumped over the side with the hammer

217

and nails and a piece of plywood and put a temporary patch on the outside of the boat."

Stearns testified that Walker fixed the hole by hanging upside down with his head under water and *fastened the patch by means of screws.* Seibert has Walker jumping over the side, no mention how he hung onto the side of the hull, while he swung a hammer in the water fastening the patch with nails. There is further departure from the script: Seibert has Walker repairing the hole the *same day* the intrusion purportedly occurred.

Seibert continues to deviate from the script, describing the intrusion of the swordfish bill in the hull of the boat.

Schroeder on cross-examination:

"Can you recall exactly where this swordfish bill was protruding from the floorboard?"

Seibert claimed he saw the swordfish bill protruding *under* the floorboards and *not* above as Stearns lectured Enoki.

"It wasn't protruding from the floorboard. It was protruding through the hull underneath the floorboard, from between the water — the ocean, and the inside of the boat, through the hull, not the floorboard." (Vol. 8, p. 1368)

Seibert's testimony contradicts that of Stearns, and in so doing, exposes the swordfish routine for exactly what it was; an untruth to distract the jury and investigators from the fact that the hole was the result of the untimely discharge of Muff's derringer as she struggle for her life against Stearns and Walker.

What does one glean from the two completely different versions of the location of the supposed swordfish hole and the efforts of Walker to make repairs? They are completely at odds with one another for the obvious reason the entire swordfish episode is a collage of lies prepared by Stearns to explain away the bullet hole left in the hull of the Sea Wind as Muff fought for her life the morning of August 29, 1974.

The One That Got Away

Bugliosi states he contemplated hiring an expert re the swordfish. Had he enlisted the services of an expert on the behavior of swordfish, in the end, the expert would have to admit that he never personally examined a wooden hull that had been penetrated by a swordfish let alone have personal knowledge of the incident. Having never observed the hole, nor seen a photo of it, he could not vouch that it was caused by a swordfish and not by a doubled barrelled .38 caliber derringer that Muff Graham fired in the struggle for her life against Stearns and Walker — Weinglass was right, had the expert been called, his testimony would have weakened defendant's position. (pp. 395, 396)

If defendants had been telling the truth about the swordfish intrusion the best proof of the event would have been to preserve the broken bill of the fish and the portion of the plank that it supposedly impaled. The least they could have done was take a few photos of the Sea Wind once she was hauled out showing the bill as it protruded through the hull. (This was not done for the obvious reason that the attack never occurred.)

Like so many of the lies Stearns spews across the pages of ATSWT, her comments to the Mehaffys raise more questions than they answer. Why bring up the hole in the hull at all? Until Stearns mentioned the hole and the alleged swordfish attack to the MeHaffys no one would have known about the bullet holes in the hull or of Muff's courageous struggle with Stearns and Walker in effort to save herself. Once Stearns told the MeHaffys about the hole and the swordfish, the cat was out of the bag. There could be no going back. Stearns then had to defend another one of her brainless lies with more dumb lies.

It is curious how in the world of lying one lie begets another and another. A single gossamer strand becomes a convoluted mess in a short time. It starts when Stearns blurts out to the MeHaffys there is a hole in hull of the Sea Wind just below the waterline caused by a swordfish. Having called attention to the hole in the hull of the Sea Wind, she is obligated to explain how it got there. Rather than saying something with a degree of credibility, such as alleging it was caused by impact with a reef as they were leaving Palmyra, or inadvertent contact with a navigational buoy, she comes up with cockamamy nonsense about a swordfish attack.

The subsequent lies that follow include more lies about the fish circling the boat after shadowing them for a period of time. She follows this with another whopper: When the swordfish allegedly attacked the boat *"they heard a thump, but did not think anything about it until later."* The jury is to believe a fourteen foot swordfish rams the hull of the Sea Wind near the waterline with such force it shattered a plank of the hull and the defendants did not notice it? (p. 364)

Bugliosi goes on and on with this absurd proposition. He cites as proof positive the occurrence truly happened because we have the testimony of his lying client who has her freedom to gain if she can convince the jury the hole was caused by a swordfish. (p. 488)

In addition to the word of Stearns he gives us another proven, unreliable source, Larry Siebert, (*a witness that should have been charged in the underlying murder case as an accessory after the fact*). This is the same witness of sterling character who committed felony-perjury lying about Walker's identity to the passport authorities, allowing Walker to obtain a false passport, and title papers to the Sea Wind under the alias of Roy Allen.

How Enoki missed this issue is difficult to understand since Seibert assisted Walker in 1973-74 in obtaining a false passport and Walker was tried and convicted of perjury in obtaining a false passport under the name of Roy Allen in December 1975 at his theft trial.

Where is Bugliosi's statistical analysis in the instance of the swordfish attack? Given the millions of boats on the ocean on any given day and the rarity of a swordfish attack, what are the odds of an unprovoked swordfish attacking a boat by ramming it for no apparent reason? Probably about the same as stepping out of your house on a sunny day and being struck by a bolt of lightening — or winning the lottery.

Stearns' treatment of Mehaffy's request to examine the alleged hole is suspect; when he asked to see the hole and protruding bill of the swordfish they refused the request. (p. 354) Had they shown Mehaffy the hole allegedly made by the swordfish with the bill protruding it would have ended all arguments. It would have been in the best interest of defendants to preserve the plank with the hole and the supposed portion of the swordfish bill to prove the veracity of their contentions. (The obvious reason they did not do this is because the plank would show the hole was caused by bullets from Muff's derringer, and the broken bill of the swordfish did not exist.)

Bugliosi plays on the naïveté of the jury when he suggests forensics could have analyzed the hole and found evidence of the passage of a bullet through the hull. Of course forensics could have easily determined whether or not a bullet made the hole in the hull.

In presenting his argument Bugliosi ignores the fact that the defendants destroyed the plank in the boat yard shortly upon return to Hawaii.

It was defendant's first order of business upon their return to Hawaii to change the color of the trim, the name, and replace a portion of the plank that had been pierced by the bullets. If Bugliosi had rudimentary knowledge of wooden boat repair, he would have known, rather than put a plug in the plank that had been pierced by the bullets, the shipwright would have cut out a section of the plank and replaced the damaged section of the plank leaving nothing for forensics to examine. Under cover of the "swordfish attack" the critical section of plank was thrown away and disposed of by the boatyard. It was only years later, after the discovery of the remains of Muff, an inquiry into the Graham's disappearance rose to the level of a murder investigation — by then it was too late to find the plank. (p. 488)

The great benefit passed on to the juror and reader by Stearns' swordfish story, is that it reveals the confrontation Muff had with Stearns in the cabin of the Sea Wind as she bravely fought for her life. Without Stearns blather about hole in the hull of the Sea Wind we would not have a clear picture of Muff's final moments and her death struggle with Stearns and Walker aboard the Sea Wind.

TRIAL OF STEPHANIE K. STEARNS FOR THEFT OF SEA WIND

Stephanie K. Stearns was indicted on three counts for her part in the theft of the Sea Wind; Count I, a felony, charged her with theft of the Sea Wind; Count II, a misdemeanor, petty theft of $400.00

belonging to the Grahams; and Count III, a felony, interstate transportation of stolen property of a value in excess of $5,000.00.

Stearns' trial was held in June of 1975. After listening to her absurd series of lies about the final days of the Grahams and the Sea Wind the jury rejected her obviously fabricated testimony, convicting her on two counts of theft of personal property within the special maritime and territorial jurisdiction of the United States, violations of 18 USC 661, and on one count of transporting stolen property in interstate commerce, a violation of 18 USC 2314. She appealed her conviction on all counts. Her appeal was denied by the US Court of Appeal, Ninth Circuit, March 2, 1977. United States of America v. Stephanie K. Stearns. (550 F.2d, 1167)

After serving just seven months in prison she was conditionally released.

TRIAL OF WESLEY DUANE WALKER FOR THEFT OF SEA WIND

Buck Duane Walker was tried by jury in December 1975 on a three count indictment; Count I, charged Walker with theft within the special maritime and territorial jurisdiction of the United States, a violation of 18 USC 661; Count II, charged Walker with transporting stolen property in interstate commerce, a violation of 18 USC 2314; and Count III, charged him with making a false statement in an application for a passport, a violation of 18 USC 1542. Walker was convicted on all three counts. He appealed his conviction on the first two counts, contending that photographic evidence used against him was discovered by an illegal search, and further that the trial court erred in some of it's jury instructions, and in denying a defense motion to consolidate the two counts.

223

The court sided with Walker as to Count I and reversed his conviction for theft of the Sea Wind based upon a flawed jury instruction. (United States of America v. Buck Duane Walker, 575 F 2d 209.)

SHARON JORDAN DISCOVERS THE REMAINS OF MUFF GRAHAM

South African, Sharon Jordan (Jordan) and her husband Robert were sailing around the world on Moya, a boat they had built. They became familiar with the death of the Grahams when they stopped by Palmyra Island and happened across an old newspaper which reported the murders. Quite happy with the discovery of the island paradise, they stayed for several months.

On January 25, 1981, while beach-combing on Strawn Island, Jordan was attracted by something gleaming in the sand. Approaching, she discovered numerous bones of Muff, her skull and an aluminum container partially buried in the sand. In the container were several bones and Muff's wrist watch. (p. 162-4)

The Jordans retrieved the remains of Muff and the aluminum container and advised the authorities. The Coast Guard relayed the news to the FBI. On the 4th of February 1981, a team of investigators including FBI Special Agent Calvin Shishido was dispatched to Palmyra to pick up Muff's remains and search for evidence. (p. 166)

Returning to Hawaii six days later, the remains of Muff were examined. On February 17, 1981, the FBI verified they were those of Muff Graham. Three days later, February 20, 1981, a federal grand jury indicted Walker and Stearns for first degree murder in the death of Muff Graham.

TRIAL OF WESLEY DUANE WALKER FOR THE MURDER OF MUFF GRAHAM

With Judge Samuel King presiding, numerous pretrial motions were filed by lawyers for the defense. Motions for a Separate Trial as well as Change of Venue were granted. After years of preparation and delay on May 28, 1985, the trial of Wesley "Buck" Walker began in San Francisco. Walker chose not to testify on his own behalf. Closing argument was presented on June 11, 1985. After a mere hour and a half of deliberation the jury returned a verdict of guilty. Walker was sentenced to life in prison; sentence to run consecutively to the prior sentences he had previously received for past crimes. (pp. 258-9)

Vincent Bugliosi attended the murder trial of Walker to observe the court in action. He carefully noted prosecutor Eliott Enoki's presentation expecting much of the same for his client Stearns. There was an obvious advantage to see a preview of coming attractions; Stearns' defense team benefitted immensely from Bugliosi's observing the presentation of the prosecution case and Enoki's interaction with the court.

TRIAL OF STEPHANIE K. STEARNS FOR TORTURE/ MURDER OF MUFF GRAHAM

Vincent Bugliosi

Vincent Bugliosi had an illustrious career as a prosecuting attorney for the District Attorney's office of the County of Los Angeles. He was respected as an effective, aggressive prosecutor and

225

made his reputation in the prosecution of Charles Manson and his gang. Resigning from office after the successful prosecution of Manson, he turned to defense work and found time to write several books.

In April of 1982 Bugliosi agreed to take on the defense of Stephanie Stearns, assisted by Leonard Weinglass of "Chicago Seven" fame. He immediately settled on the strategy of defending Stearns by shifting blame to Walker as the sole killer and began to construct a tenuous   defense defined and limited by Stearns statements to FBI Special Agent Calvin Shishido. (p.187)

Bugliosi informs he first made acquaintance with Stearns in Los Angeles, on March 8, 1982.   She appeared at her first interview along with her small dog Puffer, the same pet that had voyaged with her to Palmyra.   Bugliosi noted she had a *"little girl quality about her"*. (p. 177)

Bugliosi made an issue as to whether or not Stearns was involved in the murders claiming in good conscience he could not represent anyone he suspected had committed murder. He requested she take a polygraph exam which she marginally passed. (p. 177)

Pretrial Considerations

There was considerable delay in the trial of the defendants; Evidence gathered, witnesses interviewed, and numerous pre-trial motions considered by the court.

Weinglass filed a motion asserting double jeopardy based on Stearn's theft trial conviction. On September 7, 1982, Judge Burns denied his motion; Weinglass appealed to the Ninth Circuit Court of Appeal. On the 31st of May, 1983, the Court of Appeal denied the motion. Six months later, the Supreme Court of the United States refused to hear the appeal which put the issue to rest.

So obvious was the guilt of Stearns almost everyone in Hawaii held the opinion both she and Walker were guilty of murder. Fearing Stearns would not get a fair trial her defense attorneys prior to Bugliosi's involvement, filed a Motion for a Change of Venue, which allowed for trial in a location far removed from Hawaii. The motion was presented on two different occasions before two separate judges, Heen and Burns. Both refused to grant the motion. (p. 194)

Later, Judge King was assigned to hear both the trials of Walker and Stearns. Weinglass and Bugliosi renewed the Motion for Change of Venue, this time the motion was granted by King. The trials were scheduled to be heard in San Francisco. In accord with the traditions of the federal court, King was assigned to follow the case, commenting he'd *"like to be in San Francisco for the opera season."* (pp. 200-1)

On motion by Bugliosi, Judge King made two orders that turned the trial upside down. Incomprehensibly he prohibited the prosecution, or any witness, from informing the jury Stearns was tried and convicted for theft of the Sea Wind in a trial by jury in 1975. Witnesses were instructed to refer generically to Stearns' theft trial as an *"earlier proceeding"*.   To make matters worse, on numerous occasions during trial, King allowed Stearns to testify that at no time did she ever intend to steal the Sea Wind. (This ruling introduced massive confusion into the trial and was a factor in the jury's not guilty verdict.) (p. 221)

As outrageous as the above ruling was, King in an even more egregious ruling, denied the prosecution the right to proceed against Stearns on the basis of the felony/murder rule. (p. 373)

The felony/murder rule holds that:

"Any death which occurs during the commission, or attempt to commit certain felonies, which include arson, rape, robbery.....is first degree murder and all participants in the felony can be held equally culpable, including those who did no harm, had no weapon, and did not intend to hurt anyone. Intent does not have to be proven for anything but the underlying felony."

If ever there was an instance where the rule applied it was in the facts of the case against Stearns. Along with transportation of stolen property across interstate lines, Stearns and Walker were convicted of theft of the Sea Wind. The charges should have included robbery, (the taking of property by force or fear) but, defendants had successfully hidden the murder of the Grahams. (Walker was convicted of murder for his role in the death of Muff Graham before commencement of the trial of Stearns for murder.)

Jury knowledge of Walker's conviction for the murder of Muff Graham and Stearns previous conviction for the theft of the Sea Wind and transportation on of stolen property would have insured an easy verdict of guilty against Stearns for the murder of Muff Graham. Under the Felony/Murder rule even if Stearns was *not* involved in the death plot nor engaged in any overt actions to assist Walker in killing the Grahams, she could have been found guilty based on her participation in the theft/robbery.

Calculated Risk

Criminal defense attorneys spend endless hours haggling and arguing with District Attorneys and City Prosecutors concerning the proper charge that should be levied against a defendant. The usual procedure for a prosecuting attorney is to "over-charge" the defendant; a misdemeanant who jay-walks is charged with

228

disturbing the peace, resisting arrest, and anything else a creative prosecutor can come up with. (Probably ninety-eight percent off all cases against criminal defendants are "plea-bargained" away during, or after arraignment, but before trial.)

Endless arguments go on between the defense attorney and the prosecutor aimed at *reducing the charges*...separating the wheat from the chaff. During these negotiations the defense attorney often suggests an additional charge be lodged as a substitute to those facing the defendant. Almost invariably the suggested charge is accompanied by lesser punishment and is amenable to the defendant.

In what has to be the greatest single stratagem of the contest, Bugliosi in a daring move during pretrial proceedings, suggested to Judge King in addition to the existing charge against Stearns under the felony/murder rule she should be charged with Murder in the First Degree. A charge that could substantially increase punishment should Stearns be found guilty. (pp. 216 — 20) Admittedly, it would have been be a far easier task for Enoki to convince a jury Stearns was guilty of murder under the felony/murder rule, however, there was a probability her punishment would not be nearly so severe as Walker would be perceived as the "heavy" in the killing.

To suggest the prosecution supplement the indictment against Stearns with a charge of First Degree Murder was an extraordinary gamble, upping the ante considerably. Bugliosi's reputation was on the line. Should he fail in his efforts to obtain a verdict of not guilty, his reputation would be substantially diminished.

Then too, there is another consideration. Just as Sherlock Holmes had his Moriarty, Bugliosi had his nemesis — a villain of the first rank he put in prison for life — Charlie Manson. Manson lurks in the background of Bugliosi's subconscious like a bad dream that does not go away. Always on the alert to observe a misstep or an error..... anything that could be a reason to gloat. Most certainly a failure to successfully defend Stearns would have been such an occasion, especially since Bugliosi requested the additional charge of First Degree Murder be lodged against Stearns.

On February 3, 1986, nine months after the trial of Walker, the murder trial of Stearns began. (p. 301) Scarcely more than a week into trial Bugliosi played his trump card by way of a Motion to Dismiss the charge against Stearns under the Felony/Murder Rule. As Bugliosi correctly anticipated, Judge King dismissed the felony/murder count against Stearns leaving only a charge of murder in the first degree. Bugliosi's high stakes gamble proved correct, and payed big dividends later. (pp. 373-4)

Bugliosi rightly observed had Judge King not allowed amending the complaint against Stearns alleging First Degree Murder there was no possibility he would have dismissed the felony/murder charge against Stearns. With the felony/murder charge out of the way the burden on the prosecution was considerably enhanced.

EXPERT WITNESSES

Douglas Uberlaker

Douglas Uberlaker, forensic anthropologist at the Smithsonian Institute, on studying the skeletal remains of Muff during the Walker trial concluded the bones came from one person *"a Caucasian woman approximately five feet four inches tall."* There was a stipulation by both sides the remains were those of Eleanor Graham. (p. 243)

Uberlaker, during trial, held up Muff's skull and studied it; in response to a question from Enoki about a whitish area on the top part of the skull, he described the area as "calcination". The whitish area was found on the *"upper left part of the skull that extends more or less, from the eye area over the left top of the skull, and then back down to about the center (of the rear) of the skull."* (p. 243)

In all probability, Stearns' torture of Muff with a torch started by burning out her left eye, then proceeding over her scalp to the back of her head.

(For purposes of continuity I refer to the torch used in the torture of Muff as an "acetylene" torch, however it is unlikely this a correct assessment. An acetylene torch requires two separate tanks of gas; one of pure oxygen, and the other acetylene. The two gases mixed together, in the presence of a source if ignition, can be explosive if not properly handled. Because of the danger inherent in v pure oxygen and acetylene and the fact that the use would require two separate tanks, it is more likely the torch involved was propane of the variety used in sweating copper pipes together. Such a torch is capable of generating intense heat and requires only one small tank. Moreover they are relatively safe and easy to ignite.)

Enoki presses onward asking about the cause the calcination, Uberlaker opines;

"Given the extreme whiteness of the area, the best causal factor I would attach to that is extreme heat applied to that very localized area over a period of time."

Later, in reference to questioning from Enoki, he stated it would be *"some sort of heat source that could generate extreme temperatures."*

When Enoki asked if an acetylene torch could supply such heat, Uberlaker answered in the affirmative.

Enoki continues:

"Were you able to determine when this heat was applied to the skull in relation to death or decomposition?"

Uberlaker in response states;

"The borders of the calcination area suggest that something had to have been present to protect the non-affected bone from also getting that extreme heat. In other cases I have seen like this , that has always been flesh."

Uberlaker goes on to note portions of the skull show *"coffin wear."* (p. 244)

As Uberlaker's testimony was drawing to a close in the murder trial of Walker, under cross examination by one of Walker's defense attorneys, he testified he found: *"several blackish deposits on the top of the skull which appeared to be remnants of burn material."*

He was of the opinion the burning which caused the "blackish deposits" unlike the burning that caused the "calcination" had "taken place years after death." (p. 245)

This observation and conclusion causes Bugliosi to speculate: *"Was it possible that someone had set fire to Muff's remains years after she was murdered? If so, who? And why?"* (p. 245)

Uberlaker's response to this causal question raises some very interesting questions. The "blackish deposits" were a result of burning that *occurred years after* her death. If true, it means someone returned to the grave site, dug up Muff's remains and set fire to them.

Importantly, Uberlaker's expert opinion scotches Bugliosi's claim that Muff's remains were dumped in the waters of the lagoon. It was only after her remains were buried that someone returned to the grave site, dug them up, and attempted to burn them beyond recognition. Obviously, if Muff's remains had been jettisoned into the lagoon as suggested by Bugliosi this would have not been possible.

Dr. Boyd Stephens

Stephens was Chief Medical Examiner and Coroner for the city and county of San Francisco. Examining the skeletal remains of Muff, he opined:

"The radius and ulna-the forearm bones-on the left forearm have transverse fractures, meaning they are broken across. Both the right and left tibia-the lower leg bones-have a twisting fracture."

In response to a question from Enoki regarding the amount of force necessary to cause such fractures he opines:

" A considerable amount of force in a living individual. It's usually a rotational force, frequently seen in skiing accidents. It usually implies that some part of the extremity is fixed while the body is rotated around it, or the body is fixed while the extremity is rotated." (p. 245)

Stephens agreed with Uberlaker in regard to extreme heat being applied to the skull, noting:

"This is not the type of heat we see from sun exposure. We are talking about an accelerant or a gas that is burning. To burn something like that, you would need about eleven hundred degrees Fahrenheit or higher. "This burning, I believe took place while there was tissue on the skull. The tissue and moisture protection are the explanation for the irregular margins. The burning happened at or near the time of death." (p. 246)

233

Stephens supports the findings of Uberlaker regarding the calcination found on the skull of Muff. He explains that the *"irregular margins"* of the calcination indicate at the time of the burning of the skull of Muff there was tissue and moisture protecting that area of the scalp where the intense heat was not directly applied. He is of the opinion the application of this kind of damage to the bone would require *"intense heat"* above *"eleven hundred degrees Fahrenheit."* He also believes the burning occurred *"at or near the time of death."*

One pictures Muff bound, but not gagged, suffering the torture visited upon her person by defendants. (Why bother with a gag at this point, there is no one to hear her screams of terror and agony, but those involved in the torture themselves.) Her screams were no doubt music to the drugged ears of her assailants. She thought she was better … she did not approve of their behavior … she looked upon them with scorn and now the bill was due. Muff would pay not only with her life, but with an agonizing exit from this world. The only reasonable conclusion one can draw when studying the evidence of the acetylene burning of her skull and scalp is that she was alive at the time of the application of the torch — there would be little point in applying an extremely hot torch to her eye and scalp if defendants could not enjoy the agonies of her death.

William Tobin, Metallurgist

During the trial of Walker for the murder of Muff, an issue was raised by the defense, arguing Muff's body was not in the aluminum coffin. Tobin was one of several expert witnesses who were called by the prosecution to demonstrate Muff's remains were placed in the coffin shortly after she was butchered. (pp. 247-8)

After a series of examinations Tobin made various findings concerning the aluminum "coffin" containing Muff's remains. He concluded *"there had been intense heat inside, evidently produced with the aid of a hydrocarbon accelerant — something like gasoline, kerosene or fuel oils."*

After cutting open a section of the aluminum coffin, he examined it with a powerful microscope and discovered there was a " *very abnormal variation in grain size"* of the metal between the inside and outside of the container. *"The larger grains on the inside showed that the surface was subjected to elevated temperatures while the outside was not."*

While Bugliosi does not state the final conclusion of Tobin in his book, it is obvious that Tobin concurred with Uberlaker — someone had set fire to the aluminum coffin containing Muff's remains, well after her death. Bugliosi speculates about this possibility and asks, *"If so, who? And when?"* (It is an intriguing question with no definite answer, however, Bugliosi informs, Richard Musick voyaged to Palmyra Island in 1977.) (pp. 245, 247-8)

Dr. Oliver Harris

Harris, a forensic odontologist, called as an expert witness in the Walker trial, examined the skull and lower, detached jaw bone, of Muff Graham. After study, he concluded the jaw bone was *"fractured out by blunt trauma"* and detached from the skull. He found other evidence of blunt trauma :

"Fractures to an upper left molar of Muff's skull and a lower right molar in the jawbone, as well as to the crown of tooth number

235

13 at the gum line and the apices (tips) of the roots of tooth number 30."

There were *"fracture lines"* in the lower jaw. He opined, *"These fractures most probably occurred either pari-mortem (at or near the time of death) or post-mortem."*

" Harris also stated that the injuries to the teeth would cause 'intolerable' pain and that the fracture of the jawbone would cause death if left untreated." (p. 242)

In response to a question from Enoki about the degree of force necessary to cause these fractures he was of the opinion that to split the jawbone from the skull and fracture the roots of Muff's teeth which are *"deeply embedded in bone, would require extreme force.....more characteristic of a sledgehammer, a ball peen hammer or some other heavy round object. Multiple blows were involved"* (In other words, defendants beat her face in with a hammer or a heavy bronze winch handle.)

The question for the jury to consider is: who was delivering these death dealing blows? Was it Stearns or Walker? We will never know for sure, but either, or both, could be involved in this sadistic act. Probably delivered in the final stages of her life as she lay helpless on the ground. Defendants were infuriated because Muff, to the very end, bravely resisted their efforts. She proved to be much stronger than either imagined and refused to comply with their demands and, in so doing, paid a terrible price.

After this horrible assault, Muff, screaming in extreme pain, blood flowing profusely from her mouth, with her jaw hanging askew, no longer fixed to her skull, continued to resist. Bound hand and foot, knowing death was near, still conscious, Muff courageously resisted to the very end, which came when Walker placed his pistol to her head and fired .

Ken White

Ken White, an expert on outboard motors, was assigned the task of taking the outboard motor of the Zodiac apart to ascertain if there was evidence of saltwater exposure to the inner workings of the engine, as one would expect if the Zodiac had capsized and the engine submersed in salt water. On careful examination he found *"It was a very clean engine."* Examining the cowling of the motor, he found no evidence of abrasion on the cowling indicating it had been dragged over coral. (p. 358)

Thus, White's expert opinion directly refuted Stearns lies about the Zodiac being overturned in the water or dragged by force of wind or tide across the sand.

EDWIN AND MARILYN POLLOCK

There was considerable overlap of witnesses in both trials. Expert testimony was necessary to assist the prosecution in setting forth the cause and details of death of Muff Graham. The experts called on behalf of the prosecution in the murder case against Walker were the same as those called in the trial of Stearns.

While their testimony was important in the prosecution of both Walker and Stearns, no one could sort out the time-line of the events leading up to the murders and theft of the Sea Wind, nor expose with certainty, the compulsive lying of Stearns. To complicate the issue of culpability, neither the prosecutor, nor the defense team, had a clue about the death plot, who formulated it or how it was carried out.

The prosecutorial burden fell most heavily upon the shoulders of five witnesses; Edwin Pollock and his wife Marilyn, Curtis Shoemaker, FBI Special Agent Calvin Shishido, and to some extent, FBI Special Agent Hilton Lui. The Pollocks were present on Palmyra Island for a short period of time during the summer of 1974. They planned to spend the summer on Palmyra, however after a few weeks, feeling uneasy about Walker and Stearns, they wisely chose to return to Hawaii rather than risk becoming their victims.

Curt Shoemaker, a friend of the Grahams living in Hawaii, spoke with Mac on Palmyra Island via ham radio twice weekly, including Wednesday evening between the hours of seven and eight p.m. (The final conversation Curtis Shoemaker had with Mac the evening of Wednesday, August 28, 1974 plays a pivotal role in resolving the mystery of their murders.) (pp. 352-4)

FBI special agent Calvin Shishido was the first law enforcement officer in contact with Stearns on the day of her detention and arrest. His careful interview notes reflecting Stearns comments to him, shortly after her detention on October 29th 1974, were hotly contested during trial.

For Bugliosi to prevail it was necessary to undermine the credibility of the Pollocks, Shoemaker, Shishido and FBI Special Agent, Lui. Should he fail to do so the jury would see Stearns as a compulsive, sociopathic liar, disbelieve her obviously contrived story, and convict her of planning and assisting Walker in the torture, murder and butchery of Muff Graham.

To achieve this goal, with his reputation on the line, Bugliosi in his methodical and detailed manner, commenced preparing for Stearns' trial several years in advance. He obtained a transcripts of

Stearns' and Walker's 1975 theft trials and sat as an observer in the murder trial of Walker which preceded the murder trial of Stearns.

(Bugliosi and Henderson, authors of "And the Sea Will Tell" (ATSWT) chose not to use the true names of EDWIN and MARILYN POLLOCK in their book. In place thereof the Pollocks were assigned the names BERNARD and EVELYN LEONARD. I prefer to use their true names. Along with CURTIS SHOEMAKER they are the true heroes of this saga. The Pollocks sailed aboard their boat, TEMPEST, a Calkins 50, which was labeled JOURNEYER, in Bugliosi's book.)

The Pollocks were experienced, "blue water" sailors, cruising thousands miles in the Southern Pacific Ocean. Both school teachers, they received threats of death and expulsion from work for their involvement and testimony in the trials of Walker and Stearns. Like Curtis Shoemaker and his family, they paid a heavy price standing up for truth and justice as they testified on behalf of their brutally murdered friends.

The Pollocks observed at first-hand the events that transpired on Palmyra the summer of 1974. Exposed to the sociopathy of Stearns and Walker, fearing for their lives, they abandoned their plans for a pleasant summer on Palmyra Island and returned to Hawaii. Before departure they had several emotionally packed conversations with the Grahams advising them to leave Palmyra.

Edwin and Marilyn Pollock sailed to Palmyra Island the summer of 1974 aboard their boat, arriving on the same day as the Grahams, July 2, 1974. They tied up to dolphins next to the Iola. In a short time they became good friends with the Grahams and were frequently entertained aboard the Sea Wind.

On occasion Walker would row his dinghy near their boat, acting in an intimidating manner towards Mrs. Pollock. After a

239

couple of weeks of this treatment the Pollocks thought it wise to return to Hawaii. Before departing they warned the Grahams about the behavior of the defendants and advised
them to leave as well. Muff, in tears wanted to go, but Mac refused to heed her entreaties foolishly thinking he was well armed and could handle any situation that might arise. (pp. 326-7)

(One speculates about the motives of Walker as he engaged in the above activity intimidating Marilyn Pollock. He could have been observing the Pollocks thinking they might be a possible target, however I suspect he had another motive. Defendants could not make a move on the Grahams so long as there were other sailors about in the lagoon. The Pollocks presence interfered with defendants plan to murder the Grahams and steal the Sea Wind. As far as the defendants were concerned, the sooner the Pollocks left the better.)

The Bug Melts Down

During Stearns murder trial we find an unusual exchange between Judge King, Bugliosi and Edwin Pollock, occurring when prosecutor Schroeder asks a question of Pollock the answer to which might incorporate hearsay evidence.

Prosecutor Schroeder:

"After you sailed away from Palmyra, did you learn from your wife why Mrs. Graham had been crying?"

Bugliosi objects:

"Your honor, it obviously calls for hearsay."

Pollock, ignoring Bugliosi's objection, answers:

"Yes."

Bugliosi continues:

"There is no problem, but there should be an offer of proof."

Judge King counseling Bugliosi as if he is new to the art of cross-examination:

"Just make your objection."

Bugliosi responds:

"I am a little upset, too."

The court, holding Bugliosi's hand, again instructs:

"Just make your objection."

Whereupon Bugliosi states:

"I object."

Attempting to assist and support an obviously distressed Bugliosi, King commiserates:

"You are much too competent a lawyer to get upset."

Obediently, Bugliosi agrees:

"Yes, your honor."

King reiterates:

"Just object."

Bugliosi, not fully recovered, comments:

"That's part of being a trial lawyer."

In the meantime Pollock, undeterred, continues his answer:

"All those yes's don't tell the story."

Judge King admonishes Pollock:

"You are not on trial for anything."

Pollock, no shrinking violet, responds:

"But I like the story."

Getting things back on track the court instructs Pollock:

"Just answer the questions that are asked."

The curious thing about the above exchange is the contrast found in the above colloquy and how Bugliosi presented an inflated image of himself as a powerhouse lawyer in ATSWT.   Edwin Pollock, confident in the truth of his own testimony, pays no heed to Bugliosi's presence or objection. Pollock's testimony and demeanor overwhelm Bugliosi.   In the above exchange, rather than the combative persona suggested when he supposedly rebukes Judge King by implying he is a "pompous ass" at the commencement of trial. (p. 296) We find Bugliosi acting in a confused and submissive manner, seemingly lost in the trial process and overwhelmed by Schroeder and Pollock.   Needless to say for obvious reasons this contretemps was not mentioned in ATSWT and is found only in the official court reporter's transcript. (Vol. 2, p 280)

Knee Deep in Water

Stearns,   in discussing the voyage to Palmyra Island from Hawaii, informed Edwin Pollock they were   *"knee deep"* in water aboard the Iola, while making the passage.

Prosecutor Schroeder, on direct-examination,   inquires of Pollock:

"Did she say anything else about their trip, do you know?"

"She said that at times during the trip, she was knee-deep in water down below."   (Vol. 2, p. 256)

Schroeder:

"Did you ever have occasion to talk to Stephanie Allen (Stearns) about how they would manage to leave the island?"

Pollock replies: *"There was just the one statement —"*.

Protective of Stearns, the court jumps in:

"First of all, did she mention anything like?"

In response to this vague demand by Judge King, Pollock replies:

"At one time, she said that she wasn't going to leave the island on that boat."

Schroeder: *"Was she specific as to what boat she was talking about?"*

"Iola." Stated Pollock.

Schroeder: *"Did she add anything when she said that? Was there any additional part to that conversation?"*

Pollock: *"Well, I think it was in reference to the outboard motor and whether it could be repaired. And along that line, she said she wasn't going to leave. The outboard wasn't of importance."*

"And that she wouldn't leave on the Iola ?" Finishes Schroeder.

Pollock agrees: *"Um-hum. (Vol. 2, p. 256)*

On further direct examination prosecutor Schroeder elicited the following testimony from Edwin Pollock, who disparaged the Iola, stating she was in

"Very poor shape and very unseaworthy. It was a carvel-planked boat ....As the boat gets old and tired, the planks start to wobble and warp, letting water in......So this boat had all those problems, and was also fiberglassed. When you fiberglass a carvel-planked boat it's a last ditch effort." (p. 317)

While on Palmyra, Stearns told Pollock *"that she wasn't going to leave the island on that boat."* (p. 317)

Pollock testified he had *"personally visited the Sea Wind close to twenty times* and *had never once seen the Grahams associating with the defendants."* He stated the reason they left Palmyra early was because they had an *"uncomfortable feeling"* about the defendants. (p. 318)

243

Pollock testified as he and Stearns were towed back to the Coast Guard cutter on the day of her arrest she told him *"they found the Zodiac capsized 'over at' Paradise Island"* and that she and Buck *"attempted to sail away from Palmyra Island on the Iola but got stuck on a reef in the channel."* (p. 319)

Ten Dollars To Her Name

Shortly after the Pollocks secured their boat to the dolphins next to the Iola, Stearns came a begging. She was in need of flour, cooking oil and sugar. She had various items removed from the Iola for "barter". In addition to her last $10.00 in cash, she offered to trade her am/fm radio and the ship's compass. Marilyn Pollock refused to barter with Stearns, but did give her a small amount of flour and supplies before returning to Hawaii.

Schroeder continues his direct of Edwin Pollock:

"Did you ever have an occasion to talk to Stephanie about the state of their food provisions?"

"Yes."

"What did she say in that regard?"

"One of the first times, she said they were low on food. They would like to barter. They had a compass and a radio and a few other boat pieces they would like to barter for some food. They also had $10,00."

"So she offered to barter some equipment; is that it?"

"True."

"And $10.00 in cash?"

"Right."

244

"Now did either you or your wife ever give Stephanie and Roy (Walker) any food?"

" My wife was in charge of the stores. So she had to check that out, and she gave Stephanie a few things as we left — not very much." (Vol. 2, p. 257)

Desperate for food and a change of diet, Stearns was willing to part with her last $10.00 and cannibalize essential equipment from the Iola. She offers her small, no doubt cheap and useless, am/fm radio for barter. Ominously, she offers the ship's compass in exchange for flour, sugar and oil, demonstrating her need for food, hinting of terrible deeds to come.

What could be more of a tip-off than for Stearns to offer up the ship's compass? What value would there be to a boat without a compass? What does it mean in terms of future sailing prospects? Admittedly, there are more effective ways of ascertaining the zenith of the sun's transit at noon than the use of a cheap, and for the most part, worthless radio, but it is extremely difficult to navigate without a compass. The Iola, without winches to control the main or jib sheets, was in a perilously poor condition to put to sea, the loss of the ship's compass would be the final blow to the Iola and the myth of seaworthiness.

Don't Mess With Popeye

There are numerous inconsistencies between what Bugliosi represents as the testimony during the trial of Stearns and the Court Reporter's Transcript of Stearns' murder trial, but none more glaring than his editing the trial testimony of Edwin Pollock and Curtis Shoemaker. Unwilling to be cowered by the judicial process, weary

245

of the innumerable times they were called to testify, in four separate jury trials, the countless times they were interviewed by the FBI on a case that dragged out over eleven years, the Pollocks and Shoemaker stood up for what was right and in the process paid a heavy price for their principles.

Those inexperienced in trial work might imagine direct and cross-examination to run smoothly like a Hollywood script. However, as can be observed from the following pages set forth, *verbatim,* from the Court Reporter's Transcripts, one can see that things do not always go smoothly even for a supposed master of the courtroom. There is always a certain tension between the judge who, when fair, acts as an unbiased referee and the contesting attorneys. On another level, caught up in all this, are the confused witnesses adding to the cacophony.

The court reporter's transcript is an important record of the proceedings. It is often produced under pressure with the court reporter working late into the night to complete the transcript for the following day. Often the grammar is poor, spelling not always correct, and occasionally words are left out. When a judge misbehaves and says things that are improper, these matters are frequently edited out by the reporter who sits at "the pleasure of the judge."

What follows are excerpts from the court reporter's transcript from Stearns' murder trial. The excerpts are a revealing and contentious contretemps between the defense attorney, Vincent Bugliosi, the prosecuting attorneys, and the witness; Edwin Pollock trying to tell his story to the jury with Judge King, not always impartial, acting as referee.

Bulgiosi had prepared what he expected to be a withering cross-examination of the Edwin Pollock. His set piece revolves around Stearns visit to the Ala Wai Marina bathroom the day of her arrest, October 29, 1974. Just as the "cake-truce incident" was promulgated to confuse and entrap Shoemaker, the "toilet flushing incident" was designed to confuse and undermine the testimony of Pollock. However, Pollock, a math teacher and experienced seaman was not easily intimidated, (nor was Shoemaker for that matter).

Pollock, under going cross-examination by Bugliosi:

"During the interview — about a half an hour into the interview — you said Stephanie requested to go to the bathroom; Is that correct?"

"That's correct."

"And she was permitted to do so?"

"Yes."

"I believe you told me personally before you — during one of the recesses that everyone ....the FBI agents, everyone who was on the Coast Guard cutter involved in the interrogation of Ms. Stearns went with you to the restroom; is that correct?"

"I believe that's true. Yes."

"And Stephanie entered the rest room by herself?"

"That's correct."

"Was anyone else in the restroom as far as you know?"

"As far as I know, no. But there's some question."

"You say there's some question. You've heard that other people were in the rest room?" (Vol. 2, p. 315)

"That's true."

"Can we assume, Mr. Pollock, that you felt — again, going to state of mind — that maybe Stephanie was flushing something down the toilet she should not have been flushing? Did that enter your mind?

"That entered my mind."

"So you were very suspicious; is that correct?"

"I'm not sure whether it was me or the Coast Guard."

"But I'm asking you now, Mr. Pollock."

"I don't remember what my feelings were at the time."

"Did the thought cross your mind at all that what she was flushing down the toilet may have had some connection with what happened on Palmyra? Did that thought cross your mind, Mr. Pollock?"

"I...suppose it would naturally follow. I don't remember exactly."

"Well, looking back now, do you believe that that thought crossed your mind?"

"The only thing I remember was that the FBI said; 'Well, what's going on in there?' Or, somebody said; 'What's going on in there?' And my wife appeared about that time, and they said; why don't you go in and see what's happening?"

"Well — ." (Vol. 2, p. 318)

"So I don't know whether I had any thought process of that, or whether I was reflecting on something else. I can't — I can't put that together."

"So you're testifying then that as far as you know, your state of mind back then may have been — it was totally innocent what she was doing; is that correct?"

"I don't remember that part of a reflection ten years ago."

"Haven't you testified that you thought that what she was doing was very unusual? Didn't you just say that about half a minute ago?"

248

"They were in there for an unusual length of time, and...it was in — it was of concern what she was doing. Yes."

"All right. And it could have been something that she should not have been doing: isn't that true?"

"I suppose it would follow."

"Okay.   As a reasonable man, you could draw that inference..... and you are a reasonable man; Is that correct?"

" I hope so."

"All right.   It's conceivable she could have been flushing down evidence; isn't that true, sir."

"I suppose you could say that."

"Well, these other members of law enforcement they were right outside the door there, right?"

"That's correct."   (Vol. 2, p. 319)

After attempting to lay the groundwork,   Bugliosi asks Pollock a question that is objectionable for many different reasons:

"You were a little suspicious what Stephanie Stearns was doing inside that restroom, can you tell this jury why you never sought fit to tell the FBI agents about the toilet flushing incident?"

One would expect an objection from prosecutor Schroeder: *"Objection your honor, the question is vague, ambiguous, and assumes a fact not in evidence".*   (He may have told one or more agents about the incident and his comments were not reported in the particular 302 report. There may have been several 302 reports on the subject, and etc.   Moreover, Bugliosi, himself,   previously furnished the answer to the question when he stated there were *"other members of law enforcement were right outside the door"....* why would it be necessary for Pollock to inform the FBI of Stearns' actions inside the bathroom when they could all observe it for themselves?) (Vol. 2, p. 319.)

Pollock agrees: *"I think it was in our testimony the other time."* (Referencing one of three prior trials.)

"Well — I think it's been in every one of the trials." Comments, Pollock.

Bugliosi's grand strategy is slipping away.   He loses all semblance of self control and out of the blue personally and unprofessionally attacks Pollock with an argumentative insult:

"Well, we already know whose side you're on.   Okay?   We know that."

Startled, King not waiting for an objection from the prosecution, chides:

"Mr. Bugliosi —."

Pollock, not intimidated, is unperturbed by Bugliosi's insults:

"But the answer to your question —."

The court jumps back in: *"Just a minute. Both of you."*

Schroeder decides to join in the melee: *"Your Honor, Mr. Bugliosi   —."*

Judge King, struggling to maintain order, reins everybody in:

"Just a minute. Mr. Bugliosi if you have a question, go ahead and ask it."

Bugliosi: *"Okay. I'm not talking about your testimony in — on any other occasion; we'll get into that, by the way.* (Another threat.)   *I'm asking you why, the very day that this toilet flushing incident happened, you're interviewed by the FBI, and you don't tell them about it. Why?"*

Pollock responds with the obvious: *"They were there."*

In effect he is telling Bugliosi there is no need to tell the FBI agents because they could see and hear the same thing he did. (Vol. 2, p. 322)

Pollock continues: *"I — we answered the questions that they asked us. And....they experienced that.....(followed by a jab at Bugliosi).... That wasn't novel, was it?"*

Bugliosi: *"Do you remember—"*

The court admonishes Pollock: *"Don't ask any questions....just answer."*

Bugliosi: *"Do you remember talking to me as the jury was walking into the courtroom about ten minutes ago, and I asked you if the agents who interviewed you on October the 29th were present outside — outside the rest room, and you said 'no'. Do you remember telling me that?"*

Pollock: *"I don't remember which agents questioned me. But the FBI certainly knew about the flushing incident. Whether — which agents interviewed me, and which agents were there, I have no recollection."*

"Bugliosi, threatens: So it's your testimony...I want to remind you of something, Mr. Pollock. It's ....that you are—since other people are involved here — in other words, it's not just your word against someone else; there are third, fourth, and fifth and sixth parties, by your own testimony, that you are testifying under penalty of perjury."

Again. Bugliosi attempts to intimidate Pollock. His comments should have drawn a firestorm of objections. One would expect...*"Objection, vague and ambiguous; counsel is attempting to intimidate, badger and bully the witness!"*

251

Not waiting to hear from Schroeder, Judge King again weighs in and up-braids Bugliosi in front of the jury:

"Mr. Bugliosi, I will do the warnings of the witness if that is necessary."

Reprimanded once again in front of the jury, Bugliosi backs down: *"All right."*

The Court: *"— Thank you very much."*

Chastened, Bugliosi, wanting to get in the last word, replies: *"Thank you, your honor."* (Vol. 2, p. 323.)

Bugliosi continues to attempt to set Pollock up much in the same way he attempted to set up Shoemaker:

"So, in other words, your state of mind was that when you were interviewed by the FBI, if they didn't ask you something you weren't about to tell them; is that right?"

Pollock: *"We told them quite a few things. but, we didn't tell them — we told them mainly things that the asked for."*

Bugliosi: *"And if they — ."*

Pollock interrupts: *They knew most of the story by the time....I don't remember that specific interview, because it was one of many and I didn't know any of those officers before. I have gotten to know some of them since.*

"So it's your testimony then that they may have known what happen and, therefore, you didn't have to tell them; is that correct? Is that correct?"

Pollock responds: *"I suppose."*

"Okay." Bugliosi agrees.

"They communicate." Stated, Pollock.

Doggedly, sticking to his game plan, Bugliosi plows ahead:

"Would you have had to tell these agents then that Stephanie Stearns was seen rowing in a dinghy in the harbor, and was subsequently caught by the Coast Guard?

"Would you have to tell the FBI that information?"

(One would expect an objection as the supposed question is unintelligible, vague and ambiguous and not relevant.)

"I don't remember that I told them that information. They were there. It was probably part of the report, but did I say it?" — Pollock, incredulously asks.

Bugliosi, out of control, once again attempts to intimidate:

"Mr. Pollock, again, the judge has reminded you — or...by talking to me, you've picked up the drift that this is under very serious circumstances here."

(Again, an objectionable and amateurish effort to intimidate Pollock...but no objection is forthcoming. Not only is it a blatant effort to intimidate the witness, but Bugliosi mis-states the comment of Judge King, also, the question is unintelligible.)

Bugliosi continues:

"On June 15th, 1975, you were interviewed by a William Eggers, an assistant US Attorney, occupying essentially the same type of position that Mr.Schroeder and Mr. Enoki occupy. And he talked to you about this case in Honolulu: is that correct?"

Not permitting Pollock to answer, Bugliosi piles on, asking another question:

"Do you know Mr. Eggers?"

Pollock: *"I talked to Mr. Eggers many times."* (William Eggers was the prosecutor in Stearns theft trial in 1975.)

"Okay."

"I don't know (about) that date." States, Pollock.

253

Bugliosi now moves in for the kill with what he presumes is a block-buster question:

"Okay. Are you prepared to testify now under oath...that you told Mr. Eggers about this toilet flushing incident? Are you prepared to testify under oath on that point?"

Disappointingly, Pollock does not bite, and worse, lectures Bugliosi:

"I don't remember having told anybody about it.   But it is something the FBI knew, and...I don't — I don't remember....It's an insignificant item as far as I'm concerned."

(In other words all the nonsense about toilet flushing is inconsequential....just another defense lawyer's trick — something to distract the jury from the real issues in the death of the Grahams.)

Bugliosi ignores being called out, and continues:

"In fact, the first time that you've told anyone about this toilet flushing incident is today in court, almost twelve years after it happened; isn't that true, Mr. Pollock?"

Pollock: *"It's the first time I've mentioned it.   I think it's been mentioned in the other trials."*

Bugliosi takes offense at Pollock's answer and tells him not to volunteer information — after just chiding him for not giving more information:

"You don't have to volunteer all this stuff."

Thinking it over, Bugliosi's curiosity is aroused:

"You mentioned other trials?"

Schroeder starts to object: *"Mr. Bugliosi —."*

Pollock responds: *"It was mentioned."*

Schroeder: *"— continues to cut off the witness."*

The court, confused, interrupts: *"Just a minute. Just a minute."*

Pollock not the least bit intimidated by Bugliosi reminds him:

"I believe it's part of my wife's testimony, which it should be. In other trials, I think you'll find it in the testimony."

Bugliosi: *"But as far as —."*

Pollock chides:

"That's an insignificant thing in my mind." (In other words, the toilet flushing incident has little relevance to the murder of the Grahams and is a mere distraction.)

Bugliosi, not comprehending Pollock's point, responds with his intimidating best:

"Okay. Are you willing to tell this jury then that the toilet flushing incident is an insignificant thing?"

"The significant thing is what happened." Scolds, Pollock.

Schroeder rightly objects to Bugliosi's question: *"Your honor, it's argumentative."*

At this point, undeterred by Bugliosi's bullying, Pollock continues:

" — to the Grahams." (i.e. The murder of the Grahams.)

The Court, belatedly: *"He may answer."*

Bugliosi, — incensed: *"Are you willing to tell this jury that the toilet flushing incident, in your mind, is an insignificant thing?"*

Pollock responds: *"Sure, I think it's — it's not the main thing at all. It's just one little item."*

Observing his carefully planned trap falling apart in front of the jury, a stunned Bugliosi repeats the question for a third time in shock and total disbelief:

"Is it insignificant?"

Bugliosi hoped to set Pollock up for a fall, using the multiple toilet flushing by Stearns, while Stearns was in the restroom flushing the Grahams cruising money down the drain, but the gambit fails miserably, flabbergasted he repeats himself.

    With Bugliosi on the ropes   at this point an aggressive prosecutor would have stated: *"Objection your honor, asked and answered"*.   But Pollock, intent on educating Bugliosi about the relevant facts of the case, needs no help — he rebukes:

    "It's insignificant in relationship to (the loss of) *Mac's life and Muff's life."*

    Bugliosi: *"But as far as you know, the first time you — forget the other people — the first time you have ever told anyone about this toilet flushing incident is today in court, over eleven years after it happened; is that correct?"*

    "Right. I was asked —."

    Bugliosi attempts to cut off Pollock's answer:

"You answered the question."

Pollock ignores Bugliosi admonition, and continues driving his own steam-roller:

    " — for those specific events —"

Schroeder dives back in supporting Pollock: *"Objection your honor. Let him answer the question."*

    The court intercedes: *"He may explain his answer."*

Pollock testifies:

    "I say I was asked today for those specific events. If I wasn't asked, I have a hard time getting out anything of the story. So if I wasn't asked before, then ..... I'm sure that I was closed up and not permitted to answer."

Bugliosi continues to argue with Pollock:

"So you — what? You were closed up and not permitted to talk to the FBI?"

"If you read —". Pollock gets no further:

"No. No." Interrupts the court.

Schroeder offering to help: *I think the witness is —."*

The Court: *"Just a minute, Mr. Pollock."*

Bugliosi: *"Okay."*

Schroeder: *"I think the witness is confused as to court appearances."* (Vol. 2, p. 327.)

The Court issues a clarifying comment directed to both lawyers, supporting Pollock and chastising Bugliosi:

"He's not confused. The lawyers may be but he is not. He doesn't answer anything unless he's asked in court under oath. And you may inquire whether he told anybody else."

Bugliosi, recovering:

"Have you ever been called to court in any proceeding in this case where...the lawyer who talked to you while you were on the witness stand did not interview you before he called you on the witness stand? Has that ever happened?"

Pollock responds: *"Yes."*

"When?"

"Neither of the cases, did I talk to the defense lawyer before the —"

Bugliosi interrupts and refines his question:

"I'm not talking about the defense lawyer, though. I'm talking about the prosecutor. He would be the one calling you to the stand."

257

(Of course, a defense lawyer can call Pollock to the stand as well.)

Bugliosi continues:

"Are you saying that....the lawyers that have called you to the stand on the part of the prosecution have never interviewed you before they called you to the stand?"

"No, I was interviewed by the prosecution." Corrects, Pollock.

Bugliosi: *"Okay."*

Pollock, attempting to clarify: *"It's the first time I've been asked to be interviewed by the defense, however."*

Bugliosi: *"Okay. Now, granted when you're on the witness stand, (Vol. 2, p. 328.) normally, you can only answer questions. I say 'normally.' You get the drift of what I'm saying; right? Okay?* (At this point Bugliosi's question is unintelligible and an objection should be lodged.)

"But when you're out of court, people talk to other people; and if they think they have valuable information, they volunteer it, don't they, Mr. Pollock?"

Another poorly framed, unintelligible and argumentative question, nonetheless, Pollock agrees:

"That's true, too."

"Now are you prepared to testify under oath that you never — that you did volunteer the information out of court to previous prosecutors and to the FBI agents?"

(Another vague, ambiguous, compound and unintelligible question.) Pollock responds:

"I don't remember."

The Court confused, intervenes: *"About the...?"*

Bugliosi re-focuses his inquiry harking back to the flushing incident clarifies:

"About this toilet flushing incident?"

"I don't remember.   It was — everybody knew about it." States Pollock.

Not happy with Pollock's response,   Bugliosi objects and moves to strike:

"I move to strike that—".

Pollock attempts to finish his answer: *"All the FBI knew. That was an important —".*

Bugliosi continues his effort to shut Pollock down: *"I move to strike that your honor."*

The court concurs:

"Yes. Don't add anything more than you have to, Mr. Pollock. And the — everything after, 'I don't remember' is stricken, and the jury is instructed to disregard it."

With the above brouhaha resolving nothing, Bugliosi goes off on another tack:

"This statement about Stephanie allegedly telling you she would never leave —"

Pollock interrupts and corrects Bugliosi:

"Told my wife."

"Oh, she told your wife, but you were there, right?"

"I was there."

"Okay. All right. So this statement that Stephanie allegedly made to your wife in your presence that she would never leave Palmyra on the Iola, surely you thought that was relevant to what may have happened to the Grahams, and to Stephanie and Buck Walker being — being on the Sea Wind; isn't that true?"

Pollock agrees: *"That's true."*

"Again, Mr. Pollock, can you tell the judge, and this jury, why, when you were interviewed on October the 29th, you never told them about this statement that she made to you?" Asks Bugliosi.

Schroeder objects: *"Objection, your honor, that's an improper foundation."*

(The question is also improper because it misconstrues the evidence, assumes a fact not in evidence and has been asked and answered — Stearns did not make the statement to Pollock...she made it too his wife, Bugliosi is confused on this point.)

The court asks Schroeder: *"Why?"*

"Well, he's trying to impeach him with someone else's statement is what it amounts to."

"Well...you have a chance to redirect." Responds the court.

"All I can say is we answered the questions that were asked. And, if they asked us about those things — we testified in each of the other trials about that" responds Pollock.

Bugliosi does not like the answer and exclaims: *"Wait. Wait."* Pollock: *"So —."*

The Court: *"Well...."* (Vol. 2, p. 330)

"It isn't something that's new evidence; there was no new trial." Reproaches, Pollock.

Sensing another blow up, the court intervenes: *"Hold it. Just answer it,"* the court orders, although there is *no* question pending.

Bugliosi jumps back into the confusion with an argumentative, incomprehensible question:

"There were no new trials on October the 29th?"

Not allowing Pollock to answer, he follows this comment with a question:

260

"I want to know why you didn't tell the FBI agents about this statement that Stephanie Stearns allegedly made? Why didn't you tell them?"

Pollock: *"They probably didn't ask that particular...."*

Bugliosi, not allowing Pollock to answer, again interrupts:

"Well, Mr. Pollock, how could they have asked you that question? How would they know if you didn't tell them"

Pollock responds: *"We told the story. And...so...what they asked were particulars that they wanted to know; we repeated them back. And, if we left that detail out...then I don't know. I don't remember — that's — I don't remember those parts."*

Bugliosi follows with an objectionable, sarcastic comment to Pollock:

"So I guess your state of mind then was...even though in your state — your frame of mind, the toilet flushing incident was suspicious, and Stephanie Stearns saying she's never going to leave Palmyra on the Iola — even though you believed that — by golly, if they didn't ask you the magic question, you weren't about to tell them; isn't that correct, sir?"

Pollock is faced with an unintelligible, compound, sarcastic and ambiguous question: It had been asked and answered, was argumentative and assumed a fact not in evidence.

Pollock clearly stated he felt it was not necessary to inform the FBI agents Stearns was flushing the toilet numerous times because they were standing right next to him and could hear it as well as he. Furthermore, he thought the toilet flushing incident was "insignificant" in the grand scheme of things. Flushing drugs (or in this case the money stolen from the Grahams) was not important compared to the murder of the Grahams.

261

In responding to a poorly framed, and improper question from Bugliosi, Pollock lays out the basis for his belief Bugliosi's question violates the Rules of Evidence, by "assuming a fact not in evidence".

"We told them many things. I don't know whether that happened to be one of them or not or whether the transcribed it or whether we told them, and they didn't transcribe it." (Vol. 2, p. 331)

Pollock does not remember informing the FBI about the comment Stearns made to his wife. He may have mentioned it and they did not write it down. The FBI may have written it down in a report, and the attorney does not have the report. He doesn't remember.

Bugliosi responds: *"Okay."*

Pollock states: *"I don't know."*

The Court clarifies: *"You don't remember?"*

Pollock: *"I don't remember."*

With a lull in the battle, Bugliosi, frustrated and unable to contain himself, once again, out of the blue, takes a cheap shot, personally attacking Pollock accusing him of being a liar

"You've come up with a lot of these things just — just out of whole cloth, haven't you —."

If an experienced trial lawyer was opposing Bugliosi, this comment would amount to a declaration of war. Bugliosi, without cause, is calling Pollock a liar.

The court, recognizing the gravity of the error, not waiting for an objection from Schroeder again reprimands Bugliosi:

"Mr. Bugliosi, please. Questions. You'll get a chance to argue the case."

"Okay." Bugliosi, promises to be good. (Vol. 2, p. 332.)

A few minutes later, Bugliosi questions Pollock's attitude toward Walker. Pollock responds:

"I had no fear of Buck Walker. I had no feelings on the basis of — my wife generated the — the feelings on the basis of —."

"Okay. You know, as I say, Mr. Pollock —" Bugliosi begins another question, but is cut off by Judge King.

"Just ...you had no feelings," instructs, King to Pollock.

Bugliosi, off on another track, unable to contain himself, ignoring Judge King's admonition, steps out of line again with another personal attack:

"You're very experienced as a witness; Right?

Pollock is taken aback:

"Pardon?"

Bugliosi, out of control and on a rampage continues: *"You're a very experienced witness. You know you're only supposed to answer questions —"*

Pollock responds: *"I try to get at the truth."*

Unrestrained, Bugliosi continues with his attack, which has nothing to do with the issues:

"Bugliosi: *Mr. Pollock —."*

Judge King, hearing no objection from the prosecution, steps in again, fearing things will quickly spin out of control:

"Let's have no exchange between the parties. Thank you very much."

Bugliosi: *"Mr. Pollock — "*

Judge King admonishes Bugliosi; *"Just ask him a question, and we'll..."* (Vol. 2, p. 340)

Bugliosi, ignoring the order of the court, goes back to his personal vendetta with Pollock:

"I want to ask you something — you said that you could only answer questions in court; correct?"

This is not what Pollock stated. No objection is made, Pollock proceeds to answer a question that has no foundation, is vague, ambiguous, argumentative and misstates testimony.

Pollock: "Well, I try, you see."

"But haven't you volunteered a lot of information for this jury today, Mr. Pollock, in court, without being asked?" Argues, Bugliosi.

"I tried." Pollock, replies gamely.

"But out of court, where you can volunteer, you have to be asked that magic question; Is that correct?"

Again Pollock is faced with an argumentative, sarcastic and non-relevant question. With no objection from the prosecution, the Court again, reins in Bugliosi:

"Well, that's pretty argumentative, Mr. Bugliosi."

Bugliosi: "I'll withdraw the question. I'll withdraw the question."

After the above imbroglio, Bugliosi changes the subject and starts quizzing Pollock about dinghies, first prefacing his questions by admitting total ignorance of sea-faring ways:

"Incidentally, I know nothing about the sea, or boats, or anything like that." (Vol. 2, p. 341)

A few minutes later we find Bugliosi inquiring about Pollock's discovery of Stearns hiding place on the day of her apprehension. Uncharacteristically apologizing:

"Okay. On October 29th — Oh, I'm skipping around. I apologize for that."

(Bugliosi, attempting to promote the jury's notion of the closeness that existed between Stearns and her small dog Puffer,

264

embarks on a rambling cross-examination about what Pollock observed on the day Stearns was taken into custody.)

When you and Mr. Wallish pursued Stephanie, you found her sitting on the ground holding on to her little dog, Puffer, is that correct?"

"No." Responds, Pollock.

"Where was Puffer? Had he taken off?"

Pollock reprimands Bugliosi:

"You're not listening to the testimony."

Picking up the gauntlet, Bugliosi comments: *"Well, I — You don't have to get sarcastic with me."*

Judge King again chastises Bugliosi: *"Well, yes. But neither of you need get sarcastic with either one. Now he didn't say that on direct examination."*

Bugliosi admits he is wrong: — *"I know. I'm asking."*

Getting impatient, King abruptly interrupts Bugliosi: *"I know that. So he said, no. So next question."*

"Where was Puffer?" Demands Bugliosi.

Pollock: *"Puffer followed her, and Puffer led her — led us to her. She ran from the dinghy, and threw her dog to the side, and ran for cover, and... Puffer followed.* (Vol. 2, p. 344.) *When we got to the Ilikai Marina, we didn't know which way to turn. And then Puffer came along. And we just followed Puffer to where Stephanie was."*

"You didn't see Puffer when Stephanie got off the boat there...doing whatever..."

"We were following Stephanie. Puffer was no concern."

"So you didn't see Puffer go to the bathroom, as soon as they landed. You didn't see Stephanie stop for that?"

"Stephanie did not stop." Replies Pollock.

"Okay. So...there is no question in your mind that Puffer was not with Stephanie at the time that you and Mr. Wallish approached her? There's no question in your mind about it?"

Pollock corrects Bugliosi: *"Puffer was with Stephanie at the time that we found Stephanie. Puffer led us to Stephanie. We might not have found Stephanie—"*

"Okay.'

"Without Puffer."

Having lost ground, Bugliosi shifts his attention to Pollock and Stearns, while they were towed back to the Coast Guard cutter, on the day of her apprehension.

"When you spoke to her as you rowed her out to the Coast Guard Cutter, you obviously were not taking any notes. You — You were the one who was rowing the boat; is that correct?"

"Only for a few feet."

"Well, who rowed it thereafter?"

"After that it was towed by the Coast Guard." (Vol. 2, p. 345.)

"You testified earlier that she told you that they — they had found the Zodiac dinghy capsized at Paradise Island. Specifically, she told you that they had found the dinghy on the ….. or is it your testimony they found the dinghy on the beach at Paradise Island? Is that correct?"

"Capsized on the beach." Reiterates, Pollock.

"Okay. She used the word "beach" to you."

"I believe that was true."

"Okay. Could she have told you , Mr. Pollock, inasmuch as you did not take notes — and this happened....almost eleven — or

over eleven years ago — could she have told you that they thought the dinghy had capsized near Paradise Island? Is that a possibility?"

Pollock, refusing to follow his lead, replies: *"She told me where she found it; not where she thought it had capsized. She said she found it capsized on the beach at Paradise Island."*

"So she didn't use words like; we thought the dinghy had been capsized near Paradise Island?"

"I don't remember that." States Pollock.

"Are you positive about this?" (Vol. 2, p. 346)

"I — I'm...sure, positive."

"There's no way you can be confused about this eleven years later; is that correct?"

Pollock: "I've testified to that — ."

"Well —."

Pollock: *" — several times. I think that...I said it that way the first time. And I'm sure that that's the way it is."* (Vol. 2, p. 347)

With the loss of more ground, Bugliosi moves on to other lose ends.

On close of cross-examination prosecutor Schroeder on re-direct, brings out some interesting points about the adversities of the Pollocks suffered during the years, dealing with the murder of their friends:

Mr. Pollock, on the day that Stephanie was apprehended, on October 29th, (1974) the day you rowed her out to the Coast Guard vessel, would it be safe to say that things were pretty hectic around the Ala Wai that day?

"That's true," responds Pollock.

"A lot of people were running around, and the FBI agents, and Coast Guard, and such —."

"That's true."

(Shishido previously testified the 29th was labeled an "Office Special" day where all available FBI agents are required to be present and participate in the apprehension of defendants.)

"— scurrying around.,... now...on that day — at some point did the FBI come to see you?"

"I don't remember that. But I had — you know, I was with them all day; I was up all night with them. I was trying to get lessons out to my classes; the Board of Education was giving me a bad time. It was hectic.....it was a hectic time." (Vol. 2, p. 350.)

"And...so I don't — I know that we had an interview. We had several interviews. But — at least one on the boat, several at school. I don't remember the specific one. That must have been in the evening if it happened."

"So there were a lot of things going on that day at Ala Wai, and there were a lot of things going on in your life; is that correct?" Quizzes, Schroeder.

"I had — I had boats and people in front of me, threatening me. Thought it was a drug bust. Thought I was responsible for a drug bust. and....threatening my life. The FBI put a guard on me. There were all sorts of things taking place."

"And you testified that you were with the Coast Guard or the FBI intermittently most of the day?"

"That's true."

Schroeder: *"In addition to try to....trying to teach classes at the school that you taught at?"*

"I didn't teach that day. But...I put my lessons on the board early in the morning, and I called for substitute. At that time we had no personal leave. I had to either say I was sick or be there. (Vol. 2,

p. 351) *So I told them I couldn't be there. And I almost got fired for it."*

"At some — sometime that day...you spoke with FBI agents;"

"Well we went through that." : the court admonishes Bugliosi.

Pollock agrees: *"Several times."*

Schroeder: *"Over the span of...what has it been now, eleven years, twelve years, I presume that there have been times when you have been questioned by FBI agents?"*

"Many times." (Vol. 2, p. 352)

With that, the questioning of Edwin Pollock winds down.

"And The Sea Will Tell" presents a very different version of the encounter between Edwin Pollock and Bugliosi.   In ATSWT Pollock is portrayed as a witness that is humbled by Bugliosi's supposed peerless cross examination. (pps. 317-24) The murder trial transcript reveals that Bugliosi was lying about his supposed expert examination and that it was Bugliosi that was "schooled" by Pollock. Much of Bugliosi's presentation of   Pollocks supposed cross-examination set forth in the above listed pages of "And The Sea Will Tell" was a lie to cover his lack of cross-examination skills. (pps. 317-24)

Testimony of Marilyn Pollock

(Bugliosi's version of the following cross examination is found on pages 325-330 ATSWT)

Marilyn Pollock, wife of Edwin Pollock, also a school teacher, essentially testified to the same events and conversations her husband addressed previously. Bugliosi was prepared to attack her credibility using the same techniques he employed against her husband. He was fearful her emotional testimony could sway the jury if he was not successful in destroying her credibility.

So great was this fear, he filed an unusual motion attempting to prohibit the jury from hearing her testimony, describing it as "inflammatory". The court denied the motion and permitted her to testify. (p. 325) Later, while on record, but out of the presence of the jury, the following discussion occurred between the court and counsel which exposes the extraordinary defense bias of Judge King:

Judge King advises Bugliosi: *"In fact, if you really want to scare her (Marilyn Pollock) you can tell her that if she opens her mouth once too often, we'll, one, have a new trial; or, two….we'll have to throw the whole thing out. That might help."*

Enoki counters: *"I — I feel compelled to say that by our not objecting at this point — we are not agreeing that she is a biased witness by our lack of objection."*

Schroeder concurs: *"Not at all."*

Enoki finishing his comment: *"— to Mr. Bugliosi's comment of bias."*

Judge King wishing to assist Bugliosi further advises: *"Well, I'm talking from my own remembrance of her having testified three time before. And she was emotionally involved as long as she was on the stand, which is something you've got to look out for, too, when you cross-examine her.*

Bugliosi: *"Yes." "Okay."*

(The trial of Stearns for the murder of Muff Graham, was Marilyn Pollock's fourth time she was called to give testimony concerning her observations and conversations about the events that occurred on Palmyra Island the summer of 1974. During her prior testimony Judge King remembers she showed great distress as she

270

recounted   the events occurring on Palmyra Island the summer of 1974.)

Judge King advises Bugliosi not to allow his anger to get the best of him:

"You know. I — have a hard enough time keeping you from showing emotion, without trying to do it to every female witness who gets on the stand.",   (i.e., the court has a difficult time keeping Bugliosi's anger in check when he cross-examines female witnesses.)

When Marilyn Pollock finally does take the stand,   Bugliosi noticed her demeanor was very different than it had been at the trial for Walker.   She spoke with a flat intonation, as if she had taken a tranquilizer.   Co-counsel Leonard Weinglass notices the flat affect as well, gloating to Bugliosi:

"her husband's undoubted report to her of what he had been put through on cross-examination had probably had an effect."   (p. 326)

The Pollock's boat was tied to dolphins a mere fifty feet away from the Iola.   When asked if she had been aboard the Iola, Marilyn Pollock's response was *"never."* She testified Stearns told her she would never leave Palmyra Island on the Iola; also that Walker was a frightening figure who made her feel uncomfortable with his stares. (pp. 326-7)

(Although Walker and Stearns had their sights set on the Sea Wind, any vessel in reasonable condition and well equipped, given the right circumstances could have become the target.   Edwin and Marilyn Pollock could have been murdered and tortured rather than the Grahams.   It was this un-named fear that drove them away from a pleasant summer vacation in what most would consider a tropical paradise.)

Under questioning by Schroeder, Marilyn Pollock informed the jury they had intended to stay for the summer, but because she felt threatened and uncomfortable she asked her husband to leave after only two weeks.   She knew Muff was also anxious, upset and wanted to leave, but Mac was not interested in leaving. At the time of this discussion Muff was in tears.

"She was afraid for her life — she knew she would never leave the island alive." (pp. 326-7)

Further evidence the testimony of Marilyn Pollock was not of recent manufacture can be found in her handling of a letter Stearns gave the Pollocks to mail upon return to Hawaii. Instead of mailing the letter to Stearns' mother, Marilyn Pollock set it aside in a drawer on the boat, eventually turning it over to the authorities after the theft of the Sea Wind had occurred. Her retention of the letter in 1974 supports her testimony re the nature of her relationship with the defendants at the time of her presence on the island. (pp. 327-28)

Prosecutor Schroeder questions Marilyn Pollock, recounting her last conversations with Muff Graham:

"Did you talk with Mrs. Graham at that time, during this last meeting?"

"Yes, I did."

"And was Edwin talking to Mr. Graham during that...last meeting?"

"Yes."

"Do you recall what you said to Muff and how she responded?"

"I.... I was quite...This is so hard".

"We were — I was fairly anxious about the situation. And I knew Muff was very anxious—."

272

The Court: *"What did you say to her?"*

"I....I told — I asked her if she couldn't try to leave — try to persuade Mac to leave Palmyra."

Schroeder: *"And did you — what did you say to her in that regard?"* *"Did you tell her she should leave?"*

"Yes. I said this is not a safe place to be. It would be — it would be wise if they would leave."

"And do you recall how she responded when you told her this?"

"She — was crying. And she realized —"

King, supporting Bugliosi, admonishes Marilyn Pollock: *"Just no matter — what did she say?"*

"She — she would have liked to have left, she said. But Mac was not interested in leaving."

"And did she say anything else?"

"She — she was afraid for her life. Yes. She said she knew she would not leave the island alive."

"Now was this the first occasion at which Mrs. Graham had become upset?"

"No, it was not the first occasion."

"Had you ever seen her upset on other occasions."

"Yes. Yes, several times."

"About the same subject?"

"Yes."

"Now, after you spoke with Mrs. Graham, and she said these things to you, did you thereafter leave the island?"

"Yes. We left that day."

"The same day?"

273

"Yes."

"And when was the last time you saw the Grahams?"

"That was the last day we saw the Grahams." (Vol. 3, pp. 380-1)

At a point during cross-examination Bugliosi discusses the letter Stearns had given Marilyn Pollock to mail upon her return to Hawaii. Rather than mail the letter she kept it and later gave it to the FBI:

"There are some things I did, I will never know why I did them. I kept the letter. I put it in a drawer in my lower part of the boat; it was — I ended up — when this all came about, I gave it to the FBI."

Bugliosi, losing his temper, for no apparent reason yells at the witness:

"Okay. Do you have the letter? Well, cough it up!"

There was no objection made to Bugliosi's demand that Marilyn "cough up" the letter; however, King, shocked by Bugliosi's rude and improper demand, admonishes, sua sponte: *"Well, just — Mr. Bugliosi —*

Bugliosi, realizing he was out-of-bounds, distances himself from his improper outburst and attempts to backtrack:

"That's just a joke. I'm sorry."

King, still unhappy with Bugliosi's outburst, reprimands: *We'll get to it when we get to it."* (Vol. 3, p. 394)

Bugliosi examines Marilyn Pollock about why she did not allow Stearns aboard her boat:

Marilyn Pollock patiently explains:

" I did not let her aboard, because I was uncomfortable about letting her on board the boat."

274

"How did you communicate to her that you did not want her aboard?"

"She asked to come aboard: I refused."

"Did you say: No, you cannot come aboard?"

"I said: No." (Vol. 3, p. 398)

An example of the "different lifestyle" of defendants can be observed during the testimony of Larson, shipmate of Stevens as he described the Iola:

"Just that there was no head on board. They were using the back of the boat for the head." (Vol. 8, p. 1340)

(Larson testified that defendants were urinating and defecating off the stern because there was no head on the Iola. *Walker* was scruffy, no front teeth, had prison tattoos, and possessed few social skills......not exactly an ideal couple one would casually invite into one's home.)

Bugliosi moves on to Marilyn Pollock's testimony regarding Stearns' statement she would never leave Palmyra aboard the Iola. He starts out with a preamble:

"I have a series of questions to ask you, Mrs. Pollock; and I would ask you in advance to just try answering the question without volunteering anything. I'm sure you and your husband have discussed — "

Bugliosi commences with an argumentative statement, the court, rebukes:

"Now, Mr. Bugliosi..."

"Pardon." Replies Bugliosi.

"Just ask the question."

Bugliosi agrees: *"Okay,"*

"About this conversation that you say you had with Stephanie wherein she said she would never leave Palmyra on the Iola — "

Confused, the court chides: *"No, not Stephanie....Muff."*

Bugliosi responds: *"Stephanie."*

In error, the court corrects: *"Stephanie. Oh, yes."*

"Yes." Echoes, Bugliosi.

The court: *"Okay. Excuse me."*

Bugliosi, hoping to misdirect the jury, prefaces his remarks with an objectionable comment in an effort to prejudice the jury in his favor:

"I have a few questions in this area, and if I sound a little harsh, Mrs. Pollock, please know that I feel nothing but tremendous sorrow for what happened."

Once again King, growing impatient with Bugliosi's excesses, not waiting for an objection, corrects him: *"Mr. Bugliosi, Please."*

"All right." Concedes, Bugliosi.

King, chastising: *"You're a professional lawyer—."*

Bugliosi agrees: *"Yes, sir."*

King, reprimands: *"— and you don't feel anything, except to ask the question. Thank you. Go ahead."* (Vol. 3, p. 399)

(In other words stop trying to con the jury.)

Bugliosi ignoring the admonition of the court, commences to lecture Marilyn Pollock and the jury, on the law — a job normally reserved for the judge at the close of trial.

"You realize, Mrs. Pollock, that although Buck Walker and Stephanie Stearns were together on Palmyra, he and she are two separated and distinct people in the eyes of the law? You realize that, do you — do you not?"

276

(The question is not relevant, vague, ambiguous, completely improper, but no objection is forth coming from Enoki.)

He then returns to cross-examination inquiring about a letter he had sent to her husband with the intent of intimidating Pollock; subject that had come up during cross-examination of Edwin Pollock.

"Okay. Before I go any further, did you read this letter that I wrote to your husband?"

The court, flabbergasted: *"You wrote to her husband?"*

"Yes."

"Did you read a letter that I wrote to your husband in 1984?"

"I read it, but I wasn't — I — I really didn't pay attention to it, but I read it. He showed it to me, okay. I read it."

Still exasperated with her husband's testimony, Bugliosi continues:

"Okay. He testified yesterday about (how) I tried to create the impression of being a high-powered lawyer. Isn't it true that...since he brought up the issue of 'high-powered" that the only thing I said in that letter —"

Finally, the opposition wakes up and objects this vague and non-relevant question:

"Objection your honor. Mr. Bugliosi is trying to testify."

"I'll sustain the objection." States the court.

With that Bugliosi, gets back to relevant issues at hand:

"When Stephanie...told you, or allegedly told you, that she would never leave Palmyra on the Iola —"

"Uh-huh."

"— did you take this, at the moment she told you this, to be an idle loose statement by Stephanie; or did you feel this was

277

potentially threatening and foreboding to the owners of the other boats on the island?"

"I felt she meant what she said."

"Okay. Did you think it was potentially threatening to the other people on the island?"

"Well, it threatened me."

"Okay."

"I—"

"So..."

"It — it was a threatening remark. I discussed it with Mac and Muff."

"Okay."

"It was unusual."

Okay. So at the very moment she said it, it sounded a little foreboding to you, frightening; and you felt a potential danger to the other people on the island?

"I felt threatened myself."

"Okay. And you've testified that you felt very close to the Grahams"

"That's true."

"— they became good friends or yours." (Vol. 3, p. 401)

Several pages of transcript later we find Bugliosi, demanding to know why, if she thought Stearns' statement was threatening, did she not tell the FBI, or others such as prosecutor Eggers, about the statement. Her response was that if they did not ask her about any given situation she did not volunteer the information assuming the officials had a reason for asking the questions they did and knew what they were doing.

Unfortunately the Pollocks were as much in the dark about what had transpired on Palmyra during the summer of '74. Bugliosi pretends to be perplexed about the Pollocks not volunteering information that may have helped in fixing blame. On the other hand, whenever they attempt to enlarge on an answer in response to his questioning, he immediately cuts them off.

As if the authorities could not ask a question until the witness first volunteered the answer. Only then could they inquire about the incident. All an FBI agent had to do was ask if Stearns made any threatening statements to her. Did she say or do anything that caused Marilyn Pollock to fear for your own safety? Did she fear for her safety? Why did she fear for her safety, and etc. There is no "magic" involved. Just a few simple questions. Why did the Pollocks cut their vacation short and return to Hawaii in only two weeks after planning to stay on Palmyra for the summer?

The authorities, themselves, backed into this case. On the initial investigation they left large amounts of evidence untouched. They did very little to engage in proper crime-scene investigation. Why did they not immediately upon the detention of Stearns, go to Tuna Packers and talk to the yard people that repaired the Sea Wind? It may be that the plank which was penetrated by the bullets from Muff's pistol was still in the yard sitting in a pile of trash. Certainly the shipwright that repaired the hull could be questioned about his work and observations.....had there been the bill of a swordfish penetrating the hull, he would have had to remove it. A copy of the yard bill would demonstrate what work defendants had done on the Sea Wind.

Bugliosi demanded to know why Mrs. Pollock did not tell prosecutor Eggers about the threatening behavior of Stearns and Walker. Without the complete FBI file we cannot be sure of what she did, or did not divulge.   Perhaps it is all there, but like so much of the evidence it was   over looked by the prosecution and advantageously ignored by Bugliosi.

Bugliosi's character assassination   of the Pollocks and Shoemaker is found throughout ATSWT. One cannot blame a trial attorney who, during trial, assaults an opposing witness with every weapon in his arsenal....it's just all part of the game.

However, our thin skinned defense lawyer, aka "the Bug" continues his vendetta in his book for no reason other than to vent his spleen on three innocent witnesses who refused to knuckle-under to his harassment during trial. In so doing exposes himself as a near incompetent trial lawyer who lost his focus during cross-examination of three crucial witnesses and gratuitously introduced damning evidence against his client.

Accusations of Bias

Bugliosi ends his comments re the cross-examination of Pollock arguing he had a twelve year campaign to see Stearns was tried and convicted for the murder of the Grahams. To some extent this is probably true.   Being true, is not the same as to imply the Pollocks were willing to perjure themselves. Several times, during cross-examination Pollock could have cast aspersions on Stearns, but did not do so. When asked by Enoki on direct-examination why they left the island early, he stated:

"There was an uncomfortable feeling. The Iola people were not the usual type of people that we were used to meeting on cruises."

There was nothing "wrong" in him expanding on his answer. Moreover, it was truthful and did not substantially damage Stearns. He could have said much worse about Stearns and did not.

If Pollock harbored animosities against Stearns why did he courteously allow her to use of the club house restroom when she came off the Coast Guard cutter?   He went so far as to escort her, opening it with his key. Later, he informed the jury he and his wife had many *"friendly conversations"* with Stearns, and his wife *"discussed recipes"* with Stearns.   The day the Pollocks departed Palmyra, they took a picture of Stearns with her dog Puffer, admitting they were not on unfriendly terms with her. This is not the testimony or actions of a person with an agenda to frame an innocent defendant. (Vol. 3, p. 322.)

During his FBI interview, Pollock could have made many negative comments about the relationship between the defendants and the Grahams,   but he merely stated   the relationship was: *"friendly.....however, not extremely friendly because of their different life-styles."*

Pollock admits, under questioning by Bugliosi,   he would have told the FBI something like the above statement.

Bugliosi follows it up: *"And that is your present testimony?"*

To which Pollock responds: *"That's my feeling."*

When asked if that was still his opinion as he sat there on the stand, he stated it was.   He concurred with Bugliosi — the Grahams gave fish to defendants and   there was plenty to eat on the island. (p. 323)

The above questioning presented Pollock with an opportunity to trash defendants and cast them in a negative light, he chose not to do so.   He did believe Stearns had participated in the planning, torture and murder of his friends, but there is no showing he fabricated evidence against them.   He merely testified as to what he heard and observed while he was on Palmyra, and what he observed when defendants returned to Hawaii on the Sea Wind. (p. 323)

Bugliosi peevishly notes Pollock expanded his answer to Schroeder when quizzed about the length of time Stearns spent in the restroom. He stated, *"It seemed like a long time. Longer than was necessary."* The *"longer than necessary"* comment draws Bugliosi's ire although most attorneys would think it within the ambit of a proper response to the question. (p. 319)

Bugliosi's approach to discrediting Pollock presumes he had a grasp of the prosecution's case. A completely absurd notion: Stearns had carefully obscured the facts of the murders and her role in them. Neither attorney, nor any of the witnesses on either side, including the FBI, or other authorities had a clue about what had really happened.

Without a clear understanding of the facts surrounding the murders any effort to apply pressure on the scales of justice would come to nought. How could anyone unschooled in law and not cognizant of crucial facts possibly know what testimony would help and what would be harmful?

A more aggressive witness with a vendetta to convict Stearns could have "explained" his answer, but Pollock did not, and merely nodded in modest agreement, *"That's correct."*

CURTIS SHOEMAKER

Curtis Shoemaker (Shoemaker) was a telephone engineer and experienced south seas, blue water sailor, as well as a ham radio enthusiast. He built his own 57 foot sailboat. Like the Pollocks and Martin Vitousek of the University of Hawaii was held in high esteem by the sailing community. He was the last person from the outside world to hear the voice of Mac Graham before he was murdered. His testimony established beyond a reasonable doubt the date the

Grahams were murdered was Thursday, August 29, 1974, and not Friday, August 30, 1974, as Stearns alleged in her so-called log of the Iola and in her perjurious testimony during trial.

The Grahams met Shoemaker during his stop over in Hawaii before setting off for Palmyra. They became good friends. Shoemaker suggested they keep in contact via short-wave radio as long as Mac was at Palmyra.

Contrary to the information supplied to the reader in ATSWT, which implies that Shoemaker and Mac spoke *once* a week on Wednesday evenings between 7:00 and 8:00 p.m., the two friends agreed to talk via radio, *twice weekly*. Eventually, they settled into Monday and Wednesday evenings, between 7:00 p.m. and 8:00 p.m. to exchange information. (p. 65, Vol. 5, p. 770)

(Bugliosi's recounting of Shoemaker's cross-examination is found in ATSWT on pages 350-4. Like Edwin Pollock's cross-examination it is, for the most part, a collection of lies designed to make Bugliosi appear to be competent when he clearly was not. Bugliosi's ATSWT account of his cross-examination skills are at odds with the official record. Wisely, he makes no mention of the muddled mess he created at the close of Shoemaker's examination.)

Shoemaker Informed Edwin Pollock About His Final Conversation With Mac Graham on October 30, 1974.

Reading ATSWT one has the impression Shoemaker knew the Pollocks and were friends. While their relationship was friendly, living on different islands, they did not know each other well. Although the Pollocks and Shoemaker were interviewed numerous times by various FBI agents and members of various prosecutorial teams, neither knew much about the testimony of the other. On one

283

notable exception Shoemaker met with Edwin Pollock and discussed various aspects of the case. Other than this one meeting there is no indication of any further exchange of information between them.

From various newspaper clippings given to him by Enoki shortly before trial Bugliosi happened across a front-page article in the Honolulu Star Advertiser of October 30, 1974, written by reporter BRUCE BENSON. (Benson)   In the article *"Benson wrote about Curt Shoemaker's last radio contact with the Grahams and extensively quoted Edwin Pollock."*   Bugliosi underlined the following paragraph in red:

"Pollock said Shoemaker was told during the last radio transmission from the Grahams that they had invited Allen (Walker) and Jenkins (Stearns) to dinner, presumably as a going-away party, since the man and woman were to depart from Palmyra aboard the Iola the next day."   (p. 397)

Benson's interview of Edwin Pollock discussing Shoemaker's last conversation with Mac established that Mac had invited defendants for dinner on the 28th of August and thought defendants were departing for Fanning Island the next day, Thursday, August 29, 1974. Significantly, the discussion between Shoemaker and Pollock occurred less than two months after the death of the Grahams; long before lawyers interceded attempting to spin the facts, and years before anyone knew with certainty the Grahams had been murdered.

Benson's interview of Pollock is important for two reasons; it refutes Bugliosi's argument made during the murder trial of Stearns, that Pollock's testimony was of recent manufacture; and that Mac thought the defendants were departing for Fanning Island the "next day" August 29, 1974, and not the 30th of August as Stearns testified.

Shoemaker's Testimony at the Murder Trial of Buck Walker
(June 1985)

During the murder trial of Buck Walker in June of 1985, on direct examination, Shoemaker was questioned by prosecutor Schroeder:

"Do you recall if the subject of your last conversation with Mac Graham on August 28th ever turned to something that was taking place?"

"Well, toward the end of the contact, I could hear a voice in the distance. Then Mac said, 'Wait a minute. Something is going on.' So he went up topside and he came back and said, 'There is a dinghy coming over to the boat.' And his comment was, 'I guess they've made a truce,' or something like that. Then he told me to hang on while he went topside again."

"Did he return to the radio?"

"Yes, he did," Shoemaker said. *"He came back in ten or fifteen-seconds and said something about they're bringing a cake over. And he said, 'I better find out what's happening.' Mac signed off at that point."*

"Did you hear anything in the background while Mac was telling you about these events?"

"Yes. I heard woman's voice, and there was laughter, and I believe Muff was talking too. It sounded like two female's (sic) voices." (p. 233)

Shoemaker's Testimony At Stearns Murder Trial.
(February 1986)

Prosecutor Schroeder examining Shoemaker on direct-examination during the trial of Stearns for the murder of Muff Graham:

"Now, as you maintained regular radio contact with Mr. and Mrs. Graham, did you ever relay any third party messages to or from Palmyra?"

"Yes, I did. Several messages."

"And what form did these communications take?"

"I received letter from relatives and friends of people who were on the island at the time. And, I would read them over the air for Mac."

"Do you recall any letters to the people on the Iola from a man by the name of Richard Musick?"

"Yes, I do."

"And how did that communication get to you from Mr. Musick?"

"It was mailed to my address at home."

"And did you in fact relay it to the people on board the Iola?"

"No. I relayed it to Mac."   (Vol. 5, pp. 755-6)

Shortly thereafter Schroeder addresses the crucial aspects of Shoemaker's testimony:

"Mr. Shoemaker, do you specifically recall your last contact with the Grahams?"

"Yes."

"And on what date did that last contact occur?"

"That was....(witness reviewing his log)...August 28th."

"Does your log specifically reflect August 28th?"

286

"Yes, it does."

"And did you enter the information about that contact in your log book immediately after it occurred?"

"Yes."

"Does the log reflect the time of day the contact began?"

"Yes."

"What time did it begin?"

"Ten minutes after seven."

"What general subject did you discuss during the conversation on the 28th?"

"Well, the first part of the conversation was like the previous ones with activities he had been involved in during the day and...like before."

This is followed by a brief discussion about the clarity of the radio contact and then Schroeder returns to the subject:

"Now, during this conversation did the subject ever turn to something that seemed to be then taking place?"

Shoemaker responds:

"Well, towards the end of the conversation he...he said: there's something going on up topside, or above."

"And I could hear voices....someone talking. It sounded like women." (Shoemaker could hear the voices of Stearns and Muff in the background.)

"All right, to the best of your recollection, what did Mac Graham say at that point?"

"Well, he — he said: I guess they've formed a truce. I'm going to go up and see what's going on."

"So he went up topside, and then he came back down again. And he said: 'They're (meaning Walker and Stearns) *bringing the cake over. So I don't know what is going on.*

I'll — I'll have to look into it.'   And that he would meet me on the next contact.   You know the next scheduled contact."

"So I said: *Okay.   And that was it."*

"Now he specifically said the word 'they' as in they are bringing a cake over?"

"He said they".

"Did you understand the term 'they' to indicate the people on board the Iola?"

"I would...yeah.   That would have to be, because they were the only people —."

Judge King,   protecting Stearns, intercedes instructing Shoemaker to narrowly answer the question and not attempt to explain his answer, admonishes: "Well, that — just — Yes?"

Shoemaker: "Yes."

Schroeder: "And what do you base that on?"

Shoemaker: "You mean base the what on?"

"All right.   Your understanding that 'they' referred to the people on board ?"

Schroeder: "What do you base that on?"

"Well, they were the only other two living inhabitants on the island."

"Now after he said 'I'd better find out what's happening,' did the two of you schedule any further contacts?"

"Yes we did.   That was the last thing we decided."

"Now the voices that you heard in the background...did any of those — or was any of those voices a feminine voice, a woman's voice?"

"Yes."

"And how could you tell that....well, strike that."

Could you tell whether or not the voice belonged to Muff Graham?"

"Well, there was apparently laughter and conversation between the women in the distance. It was...background noise."

"Now, at any time during this conversation did Mac say anything about inviting them over for dinner?"

"I don't remember that. No."

The above quoted testimony is found in the original court reporter's transcript of Stearns' murder trial. (Vol. 5, p. 755-761)

Bugliosi Blunders On

Bugliosi, seeking a method to attack and discredit Shoemaker, studied his testimony given during the 1985 murder trial of Buck Walker. He noticed Shoemaker testified that Mac told him Stearns and Walker approached the Sea Wind in their dinghy the evening of August 28th with a cake she had baked. Mac hearing laughter between the Stearns and Muff casually remarked a truce had been declared (between Muff and defendants) and went topside, terminating his conversation with Shoemaker.

He noticed in Shoemaker's testimony at the murder trial of Walker as set forth above, there was no reference to Stearns bringing a *"cake"* to the Sea Wind the evening of August 28, 1974. Also absent was Mac's comment that a *"truce"* had been declared.

289

Reading FBI agent Hilton Lui's 302 summary of October 30, 1974, pertaining to his interview of Shoemaker, Bugliosi also noticed there was no mention of a *"cake"* in Lui's 302 summary.

Armed with this information, Bugliosi using the same tactic he unsuccessfully employed in his impeachment efforts of Edwin and Marilyn Pollock, formulated a plan to diminish the impact of Shoemaker's testimony.

Bugliosi writes:

"I headed toward the podium to commence my cross-examination of Shoemaker. After explaining to him that for convenience's sake I intended to refer collectively to his testimony about the cake and truce as the cake-truce incident." (p. 351)

Bugliosi commencing his cross examination of Shoemaker:

"Good morning Mr. Shoemaker."

"Mr. Shoemaker, for purposes of convenience these events you've testified took place at the end of your last conversation with Mr. Graham; that is, someone coming over to the Sea Wind, the cake, the statement about....Mac telling you something about a truce, his going up topside to see what was happening, his returning to the radio, and your hearing voices in the background. I'm going to refer to all of these things in my questioning, collectively, as the cake/truce incidents." (p. 351)

"I take it you have no problem by my referring to it as such; is that correct?"

(At this juncture Enoki should have objected on the basis that the question is based upon a multitude of facts would cause confusion and the question was vague, ambiguous, unintelligible and compound.)

"No," he agrees.

Bugliosi: *"This last contact with Mr. Graham on the evening of August the 28th, 1974, you say commenced at 7:10 p.m. is that correct?"*

"Yes."

"And you signed off at 7:50 p.m. is that correct?"

"Yes."

"So this cake/truce incident would have taken place right near the...very end of your radio contact; is that correct?"

"That's right." Replies Shoemaker. (Vol. 5, p. 767)

"So this would have been somewhere around — referring to the cake/truce incident — somewhere — around eleven or twelve minutes before 8:00 p.m. on the evening of August 28th, 1974; is that correct?"

Shoemaker corrects Bugliosi:

"Maybe fifteen minutes before."

He then questions Shoemaker about a conversation they had in the course of Walker's murder trial a few months before:

"Okay. Mr. Shoemaker, you recall speaking to me personally before this trial here, do you not?"

"Uh-hum."

"And this was the first time I ever spoke to you here in San Francisco at Mr. Walker's trial....in a little room across from the courtroom, about five months ago?"

"Yes"

"Do you recall telling me that during this last conversation that you had with Mr. Graham he told you that the couple on the Iola were about — about to leave the island?"

"Do you remember telling me that?"

291

(Referencing a private conversation he had with Shoemaker, Bugliosi recalls Shoemaker telling him Mac thought defendants were "about" to leave Palmyra for Fanning Island, but Shoemaker does not remember the conversation.)

"No, I don't." Shoemaker responds.

Bugliosi attempting to refresh Shoemaker's recollection continues:

"Okay. You don't remember using words to the effect that....they were about to leave, and you assumed that that meant they were going to leave the very next day?"

(Shoemaker still does not remember the conversation with Bugliosi in the little room. However, the reader can glean from Bugliosi's comments that during the conversation in question Shoemaker informed Bugliosi, Mac had told him defendants were leaving Palmyra Island the next day, Thursday, August 29, 1974.)

"No." replies Shoemaker.

Finally, it dawns on Bugliosi (as so often happened during the trial) that he is building a case against Stearns...with this realization he moves off in another direction:

"Okay. Apart from this....apart from this cake/truce incident, about which you've testified, was the rest of our conversation with Mr. Graham on the evening of August the 28th basically about typical things? Just routine conversation, as it were?" (Vol. 5 , p. 768)

"Prior to that, yes."

"Nothing stands out in your mind certainly?"

"No."

"Okay, so the cake/truce incident is what you remember most about this conversation you had with Mr. Graham on the evening of August the 28th, 1974."

"Yes."

"It sticks out in your mind above anything else; is that correct?"

"Yes."

"Is it the type of thing — I'm referring to the cake/truce incident — that if you live to be a hundred years old — and I hope you do, sir — if you live to be a hundred years old, and someone asks you to relate what was said, and what took place during this very last contact that you ever had with Mr. Graham, it would be the very first thing that entered your mind, something you would never forget; is that correct?"

In the ATSWT Bugliosi continues with the observation:

"Shoemaker emphatically agreed it was something he'd never forget."

The court reporter's transcript demonstrates the above characterization is false, revealing merely a one word response from Shoemaker to the above question :

"Yes."

Bugliosi then drops this line of inquiry and changes direction examining Shoemaker about FBI Special Agent Hilton Lui's report. (Vol. 5, p.769)

"Mr. Shoemaker, about two months after your last contact with Mr. Graham, specifically on October the 30th, 1974, do you remember being interviewed by a Special Agent for the FBI by the name of Hilton Lui at the Hawaii County police station in Hilo, Hawaii? Do you remember that?"

"Yes, I do."

"And the express purpose of this interview was …(blurred) ….what you knew about the Grahams, and their disappearance, is that correct?"

"Yes."

"And you certainly wanted to be helpful to Mr. Lui, the Special

Agent, and tell him whatever you knew that you felt was relevant; is that correct?"

"Yes."

"In fact, Mr. Graham — you considered him to be a friend of yours; is that correct?"

"Yes."

And you told Mr. Lui — this is a report that I have here of your interview with Mr. Lui — you told Mr. Lui about your twice weekly radio contacts with Mac Graham, did you not?

"Yes." (Vol. 5, p. 770)

"And you told the FBI agent — I'm holding in my hand a report of your interview with Mr. Lui — about your radio contacts with the Grahams, did you not?" (p. 351)

"And you told him your last contact with Mac Graham was on August the 28th, 1974, did you not?"

"Yes."

"You also told Mr. Lui what Mr. Graham told you about his and his wife's daily activities on Palmyra?"

"Yes."

"And what Mac Graham told you about the other people on Palmyra, and the activities of these other people?"

"Yes."

294

"The Court: *"Did you say yes or no?"*

The witness, *"Yes."*

Bugliosi continues:

"All in all did you talk to Special Agent Lui about this case, and the disappearance of Mac and Muff Graham for about three hours? It was a very long conversation?"

"With Lui?" Asks Shoemaker.

"Yes, the Special Agent from the FBI."

"It wasn't three hours. It was probably more like forty-five minutes." (Shoemaker corrects Bugliosi's exaggeration of the time taken for the interview.) (Vol. 8, p. 1292)

"Mr. Shoemaker, is there any reason why during this entire interview with Mr. Lui you failed to mention the cake/truce incident that you have testified to here today. Any reason at all, sir?"

(At this juncture the prosecution failed to object to Bugliosi's question in that it "assumed a fact not in evidence". Simply because cake and truce were not mentioned in Lui's report does not mean that Shoemaker did not tell him about the incident. Agent Lui may have excluded the information because it did not seem relevant to a theft investigation.)

Shoemaker, a cautious witness, unfamiliar with the courtroom, disagrees with Bugliosi's assumed facts.

"No. If I did fail to.... I don't remember. I'm sure I did, though."

The court intercedes: *"You're sure you did what?"*

"Mentioned the last contact. The radio contact and the termination of the contact." (Vol. 5, p. 772.)

"Okay. You're testifying under oath that you are positive you told Mr. Lui about this cake/truce incident."

"You're positive about this?"

Shoemaker, abandoned by Enoki, fights back:

"Well, I'm not positive; but I'm — I feel that I did at that time. Because I was relating everything I knew to him."

"Certainly you would want to tell him about that, because that's the thing that sticks out in your mind above everything else; isn't that right?"

"Well, yes, yes."

"Mr. Shoemaker, on June the 25th, 1975, you testified at a court proceeding in Honolulu. The clerk will hand you a photostatic copy...of your testimony at that court proceeding." (Vol. 5, p. 772)

Bugliosi returns to his "bully-boy" tactics...

"Before you testified at that court proceeding you took an oath to tell the truth —."

Suspecting the prosecution will fail to object Judge King intervenes on behalf of Shoemaker admonishing Bugliosi to refrain from his bully-boy tactics:

"I wish you wouldn't go into that. That —" (Vol. 5, p. 772.)

Brought up short, Bugliosi acquiesces:

"Okay."

"At that proceeding on June 20th, 1975, which would be less than one year after the alleged cake/truce incident, to these questions, Mr. Shoemaker, did you give the following answers?"

Reading the direct examination of Shoemaker by prosecutor Eggers from Stearns' theft trial transcript of 1975, Bugliosi continues:

"Question: Well, did you continue to have regular contacts throughout the month of July?"

"Answer: Oh, yes, right through July."

296

"Question: And did you have continuous contacts throughout the month of August?"

"Answer: Well, August there was — up until August and then I think it was the 27th or so was the last contact I believe I had with him."

Bugliosi interrupts his reading of the transcript....

"Before — before we go any further, you...misspoke when you said the 27th; you meant the 28th. Is that correct?"

Shoemaker responds: *"Yes. At that time I don't believe I had a copy of the log."*

Bugliosi: *"Yes. All right."* and goes back to reading a portion of the 1975 theft trial transcript of Stearns into the record.

"Answer: —up until August and then I think it was the 27th or so was the last contact I believe I had with him."

"Question: And what was the nature of that contact?"

(Bill Eggers, the prosecuting attorney in the theft trial of Stearns, quizzing Shoemaker asks the above non-specific general question. Compare the trial transcript above to the following "book" version below.)

Question: What was the nature of that <u>last radio</u> contact <u>with Mac Graham on August 28th.</u> (The underlined words are *not found* in the original transcript and were gratuitously added by Bugliosi to bolster his position.) (p. 353)

"Answer: Like all the other contacts. He related his experiences on the island. What he was doing, what he found, and talked about everything from rain to birds, sharks in the lagoon, and everything. How to fish, and what fish were poisonous. I was trying to help him out as much as I could." (Vol. 5, p. 774.)

" that there were other boats on the island, and I was relaying messages from some of these other boats to their parents, and I was acting, in other words, third party traffic."

"Question: Were you able to establish the — through speaking with Mr. Graham, were you able to establish who the other people were on the island?"

"Answer: No. Just an identity of people. He didn't say too much about them. There was a, there were some young people going to Samoa, is one, but he didn't mention any names. There was a young fellow and a girl there. In one case there was some.....There were some young people going to Samoa, is one, but he didn't mention any names."

"Question: Did he speak to you about a couple with dogs on the island?"

"Answer: Yes, yes."

"Question: What was the nature of that — this is on the last conversation with now. What was the nature of that communication with you?"

"Answer: Well, he said spoken about this prior to it. (sic) I think one of the dogs had almost attacked his wife, and he did mention that the dog had previously bitten some other people on the island, so...."

"Question: Did he make any other statements to you with respect to that couple with the dogs?" (Vol. 5, p. 775.)

"Answer: Well there seemed to be a problem. It was a boat that had gone down there that was — according to him, he said it was unseaworthy and leaking badly, and the people on the boat were having a hard time, apparently, running out of food and these were *the ones with the dogs. There were several dogs, but I think there was only one that was causing trouble."*

(Skipping a few lines.)

"Question: That was approximately on the 27th of August?" (Vol. 5, p.776.)

"Answer: This was on the 27th, was my last time that I heard from them."

"Question: Did you have another contact with him after that?"

"Answer: No. That was the — that's the last time I heard from him was he said that the other boat, as he referred to, was leaving the next day."

Shoemaker confuses the dates, mistakenly calling the 28th of August the 27th. However the significant point made by Shoemaker during his testimony given at the Stearns theft trial in June of 1975 was that Mac thought the Iola was *"leaving the next day."* Mac had the impression defendants were departing for Fanning Island on Thursday, August 29th, and not Saturday, August 31st as Stearns suggested during her murder trial.

Bugliosi continues reading from the 1975 theft trial transcript of Stearns.

"Question: What did you do next after that point in time? After the last conversation that you said you had no other contact with him, did you do anything with respect to attempting to contact him?" (Vol. 5, p. 776.)

"Answer: Well, this was, I believe, a Wednesday night, so the next scheduled contact would have been the following Monday, and he didn't — there was no, you know, communication from him."

Finished reading from the 1975 theft trial transcript of Stearns, Bugliosi inquires:

"Did I read the questions and answers correctly, sir?"

"It sounds — yes." Answers, Shoemaker.

Having laid a somewhat confused groundwork Bugliosi continues his cross-examination hoping to ensnare Shoemaker:

"Okay. Mr, Shoemaker, I've counted seven, seven references in the transcript I've just read to the fact that this was the last contact you ever had with Mac Graham. So there was no confusion as to which conversation this was?"

"You've testified earlier how this cake/truce incident stood out in your mind above everything else; something you would never forget as long as you live."

With the above lead-up, Bugliosi springs the following question:

"Can you tell this jury and Judge King....why, when you were specifically asked to relate what was said, and what was done, what took place during this very last contact that you ever had with Mac Graham, that you never felt the cake and truce incident was memorable enough or important enough to mention? Can you tell the jury and judge why?" (Vol. 5, p. 777)

(There is a problem with this question: it completely mischaracterizes the question put to Shoemaker by prosecutor Eggers. Shoemaker was asked a *general question* by Eggers, not a *specific*. Moreover, Bugliosi's question is vague, ambiguous, assumes a fact not in evidence and is argumentative.)

Bugliosi is seemingly irate because Shoemaker did not mention the word "cake" or "truce" in recounting the last 5 minutes of his final conversation with Mac during his testimony at Stearns' theft trial in 1975.   However Shoemaker did inform Eggers that Mac believed the Iola was leaking badly and was not seaworthy;   that the defendants were in dire need of food and; and most importantly, Mac thought defendants were sailing to Fanning Island the next day, Thursday, August 29, 1974.   These facts are the   heart of the prosecution case and are far more important and probative than a tangential reference to a "truce" or presence of a "cake" Stearns was bringing to the Sea Wind.

Shoemaker, puzzled by Bugliosi's   question, attempts to clarify:

"To mention to who?" He asks.

Bugliosi in his usual "short fuse" mode starting to lose his cool angrily replies:

"To the lawyer who asked you to relate what took place during that conversation."

Shoemaker, still confused wanting to know what lawyer Bugliosi is talking about, again demands:

"What lawyer?" (Vol. 5, p. 777)

Bugliosi, impatiently:

"The person that was asking you the questions, sir, that I just read to you.   Someone was asking you questions, and you were answering them."

Shoemaker: "Well, I was only answering the questions that were asked of me —."

"And you were"— Bugliosi interrupts.

Shoemaker cuts him off continues:

"—- as I was told.   So if the question wasn't asked, I wouldn't....I wouldn't have added this information."

"So, in other words, you would only discuss this cake/truce incident if the lawyer asked you to tell the jury about the cake/truce incident; is that correct?"

"Well, he didn't know there was such an incident. So he couldn't ask me about it." Responds Shoemaker.

"Well, why didn't you tell him sir?" Demands an irritated Bugliosi.

Shoemaker explains: *"Because I was instructed to either answer yes or no.....at the beginning of the trial. Be brief, and answer either yes or no truthfully. So —"*

Bugliosi, interrupting Shoemaker follows with a series of poorly worded, vague and rambling questions:

"Before you took the witness stand this lawyer who asked you these questions — this was not the first time you ever saw him. In other words, he wasn't a stranger to you?"

Shoemaker: *"Not quite, no."*

Bugliosi follows up with another unintelligible question:

"In other words, you didn't look at him like you're looking at me now, and saying, I wonder who that guy is, I've never seen him before. You had talked to him, is that correct?

"That's correct." Answers Shoemaker.

"He had interviewed you; is that correct?" Inquires Bugliosi.

"Briefly."

"Why didn't you tell him during that interview about this cake/truce incident?"

"There was many things that I told him. But at the time....he didn't — we didn't lead up to that particular point. It was a very

brief discussion, as I recall. And...the case....was a different nature, to begin with, at that time." (Vol. 5, p. 779)

(Shoemaker is referring to the fact that it was a theft case and not a murder trial.)

Getting nowhere with his grand strategy Bugliosi moves off in another direction:

"Mr. Shoemaker, you know this fellow Buck Walker, of course? You testified at his trial."

Shoemaker questions: *"Buck Walker?"*

"Yes. You testified at his murder trial last June, here in San Francisco, did you not?"

"Yes." States Shoemaker.

"And that was the first time you have testified to this cake-truce incident; is that correct?"

"I don't know. I — I can't be sure of that. I may have testified or mentioned that in the previous trial. I have no......recollection of it."

Bugliosi, not understanding Shoemaker's testimony, incredulously asks;

"Buck Walker's trial?"

"Yes." Replied, Shoemaker.

Bugliosi: *"— That would have been in June of '75. That's eleven years, eleven years, after this last contact; is that correct?"*

(Now, it is Bugliosi who is confused — Walker's murder trial was in June of 1985, not June of 1975 when Stearns was tried for theft of the Sea Wind.)

Shoemaker picks up on Bugliosi's confusion and attempts to clarify:

"Buck Walker's trial — which one are you referring to?"

303

Bugliosi does not acknowledge Shoemaker's cue, nor does he recognize his own confusion and impatiently scolds Shoemaker:

"June of 1975, you came to this courtroom —"

Observing no engagement on the part of the Enoki to clear up Bugliosi's misunderstanding, sensing impending chaos, King rebukes Bugliosi:

"No, No, that's not it. You're talking about —"

Bugliosi realizing his confusion apologizes: *"I'm sorry."*

The court, impatiently: *" Last year. Last year."*

Bugliosi chastened, apologizes again: *"I'm sorry....in June of 1985"*.

"The court concurs: *That would be better."*

"Yes." Bugliosi agrees.

"In June of 1985 you testified at Buck Walker's trial here in San Francisco."

"That's right". States, Shoemaker .

With the above apology to the court his supposed brilliant cross-examination in a state of confusion, an embarrassed Bugliosi bows out.

"Okay. No further questions, your honor." (Vol. 5, pp. 772-80)

What might have been an effective cross-examination (as Bugliosi falsely alleges in ATSWT) ends in a pointless tangle. By cherry picking the questions and answers and misrepresenting Shoemaker's demeanor and the trial transcript, Bugliosi in ATSWT presents the above testimony in a different light, causing it to appear effective, when in fact it all fizzles out leaving a confused and chastened Bugliosi limping off stage. (ATSWT pp. 351-354)

And worse, by introducing Shoemaker's testimony given at Stearns June 1975 theft trial, he undermines Stearns murder trial defense in that Shoemaker recalls the Grahams were under the impression that defendants were sailing for Fanning Island the next day, Thursday, August 29, 1975, not Saturday, August 30, 1975. Significantly, Shoemaker gave this testimony at Stearns' theft trial less than a year after the murder of the Grahams, and eleven years before Stearns trial for the murder of Muff Graham.

FBI Special Agent Hilton Lui Affirms Shoemaker Testimony

On direct-examination by prosecutor Schroeder during the murder trial of Stearns in 1986, FBI Special Agent, Hilton Lui, testified Shoemaker told him about the cake incident during an interview on October 30, 1974. (pp. 370-1)

Schroeder examines:

"Agent Lui, did Mr. Shoemaker tell you about his last radio contact with the Grahams?"

"Yes."

"Did he tell you about the incident with the cake coming from the other boat?"

"Yes. He mentioned to me that the people from the other boat, who I was led to believe were the Allens, (Stearns and Walker) *were either there,* (aboard the Sea Wind) *or they were to be with them at a later time."*

"And what did he say that they had with them, or were bringing with them?"

"A cake....."

"Now, did you include that cake incident in your 302 report?"

"No. No I did not."

"The agent explained that he didn't imagine, at the time, that the cake had anything to do with the disappearance of the Grahams."

"Was the case classified as a homicide investigation at that time?"

"No, it was not. It was classified as a crime on the high seas."

Bugliosi, cross-examining:

"Mr. Lui...when is the very first time anyone ever asked you if you recalled Mr. Shoemaker telling you about the cake?"

"A couple of days ago."

"No one, prior to a couple of days ago, asked you if you recalled Mr. Shoemaker telling you about the cake?"

"That's correct."

"Your interview with Mr. Shoemaker took place on October 30, 1974. This is mid-February, 1986, Almost twelve years later. Right?"

"Yes."

"And you've investigated hundreds of cases since then, have you not"

"Yes."

"At the time Mr. Shoemaker supposedly told you about this cake incident, in your mind, this was just two people bringing a cake to two other people. Right?"

"Yes."

"It was totally insignificant to you at the time you heard it. Is that correct?"

"The obvious question: How can you possibly remember, twelve years later, something which, at the time you heard it, you admit was totally insignificant?"

(Bugliosi has a habit of jumping to another question without permitting the witness time to answer the first.)

Lui replies:

" I recall that particular instance of a cake, simply because.....that it was quite difficult for someone to bake a cake on a boat."

"You mean you haven't heard before people making cakes on boats?"

"I have never had someone serve me a cake on a boat." (pp. 370-1)

Although there is no complete description of the cooking device defendants used on board the Iola, it was likely a small one burner gimbaled device powered by a one quart propane canister popular among campers.

Stearns testified to the contrary; that the Iola possessed a *butane stove* and oven. (Vol. 11, p. 1643) However, this assertion is probably untrue. A butane stove with oven (if one were available) would cost in the neighborhood of $750.00 in 1973, perhaps more. Defendants were so impoverished they could not afford to purchase a used toilet for the head, nor did they have money to purchase used winches to control their main and jib sheets or assist in raising the sails.

Bugliosi scoffs at Lui's testimony that he could remember Shoemaker's comment about the Stearns' cake because he had never been served cake on a boat. Bugliosi, with no boating experience or understanding of the sea believes Stearns' testimony that there was a household oven aboard the primitive Iola. He was unaware Stearns, in all probability, did her baking aboard the Iola using an alcohol or kerosene burner, cooking the cake in a pot on a stove top. To bake a cake on a cooktop burner or oven in tropical heat would create an intolerable furnace like condition in the small cabin of the Iola particularly since, according to Stearns, the forward hatch was entirely sealed off preventing proper ventilation. (More than likely Stearns baked her bon voyage cake in the outdoor oven ashore which she mentioned previously.)

Associated Press Sides With Shoemaker
(August 28, 1981)

After the murder of the Grahams nearly seven years passed before the remains of Muff were discovered on Strawn Islet. Once discovered, the press again became active in reporting news concerning the disappearance of the Grahams.

Lindy Washburn, a reporter investigating the incident interviewed Shoemaker on or about August 18, 1981, and quoted Shoemaker in the Associated Press release of that day. (See Google, Free Lance Star, Fredericksburg, Virginia, August 28, 1981)

"I remember Mac saying, I guess they're going to declare a truce. They're bringing over a cake tonight. That's the last I ever heard from him, Shoemaker said."

In above press release we have Shoemaker, not prompted by a lawyer, speaking with Associated Press reporter Lindy Washburn about his last conversation with Mac of the 28th of August 1974. In this interview Shoemaker mentioned both Stearns' cake and Mac's comment concerning the truce between Muff and defendants.

There is another highly probative comment found in the above Associated Press release. Washburn interviewing Stearns on this same date writes in the same article:

"The next day according to Miss Stearns, the Grahams overturned dinghy was found in the lagoon."

This statement by Stearns directly contradicts her murder trial testimony of February 1986. In the above statement made to reporter Washburn, Stearns uncontrolled by an attorney, reverts to her initial story that she told Shishido when first detained — *defendants discovered the Zodiac overturned in the lagoon and not on the beach.*

(The above excerpts were carried by numerous other papers throughout the United States that use the Associated Press news releases.)

FBI SPECIAL AGENT CALVIN SHISHIDO

FBI Special Agent Calvin Shishido (Shishido) plays an important role in resolving the murder of the Grahams because his notes and testimony expose Stearns for the liar she is. He was witness to her contrived story, carefully recording her comments about how the Grahams disappeared, the "make yourself at home" routine, and her concocted story about the over turned dinghy in the lagoon near Cooper Island.

To evaluate the testimony of Shishido it is necessary to step back and look at the players. On one side we have highly motivated, intelligent, sociopathic criminal, compulsive liar, convicted thief, admitted perjurer, and murderess, fighting for her freedom. Her defense is orchestrated by a determined, well known trial lawyer, Vincent Bugliosi who is not above suborning perjury or cutting

309

corners to win an acquittal for his obviously guilty client.   The prosecution is led by Elliott Enoki, a pleasant,   well mannered, poorly prepared, federal prosecutor who has difficulty going "for the jugular".

Shishido's 302 Report

Shishido detained Stearns in Honolulu for questioning when she and Walker appeared in Ala Wai harbor aboard the Sea Wind, October 29, 1974. Stearns had rehearsed her spiel in the event of her arrest for many days during the return voyage of the Sea Wind to Hawaii; on questioning at the time of her apprehension she spewed a torrent of lies.   So careful and concise was FBI Special Agent Shishido's summary it merits inclusion.   (Only a limited portion of Shishido's report was made available in ATSWT.)   What was made available follows:

"Jennifer Jenkins (Stearns) furnished the following information: On the last Friday in August 1974, she and Roy Allen were making preparations to leave Palmyra the next day. She was on the boat Iola while ALLEN was on shore. He returned shortly after and told her they were invited to dinner at the GRAHAM'S boat the Sea Wind. Allen left the Iola and stated he was going to take a bath and went ashore.   He returned shortly after and told her that the GRAHAMS told him they were going fishing for the evening dinner and would be a little late but to make themselves at home.   The dinner invitation was for 6:30 P.M. that evening.   At about 6:30 P.M., she and ALLEN went aboard the Sea Wind to await the Grahams' return. The Grahams did not return that evening, and she and ALLEN spent the night aboard the Sea Wind.

The next morning she and ALLEN conducted a search of the area and located a dinghy overturned in the lagoon at Cooper islet, part of Palmyra Island. The dinghy was the Zodiac dinghy which was used by the Grahams the day before when they went fishing. The outboard motor on the dinghy was also overturned, and they found the gas tank floating in the lagoon nearby. They turned the dinghy upright, reattached the gas tank, and continued further searching in the Zodiac. They continued the search for the GRAHAMS until September 11, 1974, and finally decided the GRAHAMS were gone. Since they did not know how to operate a radio, they were unable to call for assistance or to report the incident.

They rationalized the GRAHAMS last statement to them to make themselves at home to mean the GRAHAMS would like for her and ROY ALLEN to keep the boat if anything happened to them. They therefore tied a 50-foot tow rope to the Iola and attempted to tow it back to Honolulu with the Sea Wind. She was on the Iola steering and ROY ALLEN was on the Sea Wind. On September 11, the Iola ran into a reef while being towed out of Palmyra and when last seen was still stuck on the reef.

They arrived at Nawiliwili, Kauai, on the Sea Wind October 12, 1974. They stayed at Nawiliwili overnight and sailed to Pokai Bay, Oahu, arriving October 15, 1974. They stayed at Pokai Bay about one week, left and arrived at Keehi Lagoon on October 21, 1974. The next day, they docked at Kewalo Basin and dry docked the Sea Wind at the Tuna Packers. There she and ALLEN repainted the boat another color. The boat was in dry dock for a week, and on October 28, it went back into the water, and they went to the Ala Wai Yacht Harbor, arriving there in the late afternoon.

She and ALLEN found $400 in currency on the Sea Wind, consisting of $20 bills — $300.00 in a book, and $100.00 in

311

MALCOLM GRAHAM'S wallet located under the floor board of the Sea Wind.

She stated the Sea Wind did not belong to them but they loved it as much as the GRAHAMS and thought the Grahams would like for them to have it. She also stated they did not report the incident at Palmyra to proper authorities upon arrival in Hawaii because they knew the boat would be taken from them." (p. 133)

Stearns rehashed her story over and over while sailing back from Palmyra, but had not worked out the fine details when first arrested. Thus, she told Edwin Pollock one story about the alleged discovery of the Zodiac and a few moments later told FBI agent Shishido another. Her fabrications were not fool proof, but sufficient to put off prosecution for murder so long as she stuck to her story line and the remains of Muff were not discovered.

No Golf Today

In the afternoon on his day off Special Agent Shishido received a phone call pertaining to a sailboat reported missing for over a month. He felt it was a crime on high seas and was a Coast Guard matter not an FBI responsibility. However, he did respond to a request to come to Ala Wai Harbor and assist the Coast Guard. He met with Coast Guard Lieutenant Bruce Wallish and Edwin Pollock who related his experiences at Palmyra Island with the defendants and the Grahams. Pollock informed agent Shishido he had just seen a person he knew as Roy Allen leave the Sea Wind and row away. (pp. 126-7)

Unconvinced a federal crime had been committed Shishido agreed to take a closer look at the vessel and climbed into a skiff along with Pollock and Wallish. Approaching the Sea Wind they observed she had been repainted, the figurehead was missing and netting Pollock had seen aboard the Iola was draped about the stanchions. Returning to the yacht club the Coast Guard agreed to post a watch and report to Shishido if they saw anyone boarding the Sea Wind.

On reflection, the circumstances were sufficient to convince Shishido something big was going down and an "Office Special" was declared requiring all available FBI officers to assist. (Vol. 8, p. 1351) The next morning October 29, 1974, Shishido received a call that a man and woman were about to leave the Sea Wind and was requested to come down to the harbor. By the time he arrived Stearns had dropped the Walker off on the dock and was returning to the Sea Wind. A Coast Guard team pursued the Walker who dived into the water and escaped by hiding under the docks.

The Coast Guard cutter pursued Stearns who was frantically rowing to shore. Reaching the breakwater she abandoned her dinghy and raced off into a hotel where she was subsequently apprehended by Officer Wallish and Pollock while hiding in the lobby behind a potted plant. Wallish requested she come back to the cutter for questioning and placed her in a dinghy accompanied by Pollock. (p. 131)

During the trip back to the cutter, Stearns gave Pollock a general outline of her story:

"You'll never believe what happened. They invited us over for dinner. They were going fishing and they knew they were going to be late. They told us to make ourselves at home. They never showed up. The next morning, we went looking for them and found the Zodiac capsized. We searched for days and didn't find any sign of them. We left a few days later on the Iola, but she got hung up on the reef, and

313

when we couldn't get her off, we went back and got the Sea Wind." (p. 131)

Aboard the Coast Guard cutter FBI Special Agent Shishido questioning Stearns taking notes of her comments.

"The next morning she and Allen conducted a search of the area and located a dinghy overturned in the lagoon at Cooper Islet, part of Palmyra Island. The dinghy was the Zodiac dinghy that was used by the Grahams the day before when they went fishing. The outboard motor on the dinghy was overturned, and they found the gas tank floating in the lagoon nearby. They turned the dinghy upright, reattached the gas tank, and continued searching in the Zodiac." (p. 133)

Some of the supposed facts found in the above paragraph were lies created by Stearns to mislead the authorities. Not only were they lies, but they were inherently unbelievable — she purportedly, finds the dinghy with motor attached *"overturned in the lagoon at Cooper islet"* with the *"gas tank floating nearby"* and shortly thereafter turns the dinghy upright, reattaches the gas tank, starts up the outboard motor, and goes off in search of the Grahams.

It was only later as she was approaching trial for theft of the Sea Wind in June 1975 that Stearns learned an outboard motor would not start if it had been immersed in salt water for twelve hours unless it had a through cleaning. Armed with this information Stearns changed her story. In her third version of the facts she alleges the overturned dinghy was discovered the morning of August 31st overturned on the beach on Cooper Islet. (p. 155)

Lagoon Blues

314

On October 29, 1974, Shishido had only a passing interest in the observations of Pollock and the theft of the Sea Wind. (p. 126) He was indifferent to the sea and sailing and possessed a limited knowledge of the South Pacific.

Years later during Stearns' murder trial Bugliosi focuses on Shishido's 302 report which memorialized his interview with Stearns. It is almost verbatim the same song and dance Stearns testified to in the murder trial.

Herein we find the fictitious dates and time lines of August 30 and 31; the purported events that supposedly occurred during those days; Stearn's lies about losing the Iola on the reef as it was being towed back to Hawaii by the Sea Wind; finding the dinghy the next day over turned in the lagoon; and etc. (p. 133)

Nothing speaks more eloquently of the accuracy of agent Shishido's trial testimony as his 302 report. It was written shortly after Stearns' capture on October 29, 1974, at a period in time when no one understood what had transpired on Palmyra. A careful reading of excerpts of Shishido's 302 report reveal the outline of Stearns' trial posture, except for a few lines in the second paragraph, where she talks about the Iola running aground in the channel.

Shishido writes in his 302 report:

"The next morning she and Allen conducted a search of the area and located a dinghy overturned in the lagoon at Cooper Islet, part of Palmyra Island. The dinghy was the Zodiac dinghy which was used by the Grahams the day before when they went fishing. The outboard motor on the dinghy was also overturned, and they found the gas tank floating in the lagoon nearby. They turned the dinghy upright, reattached the gas tank, and continued further searching in the Zodiac...." (p. 133)

It is the above paragraph that causes Bugliosi to become exercised. Except for these few lines, every matter discussed in the report is part and parcel of Stearns' defense. A few lines are disavowed by Bugliosi because Stearns was caught in bold faced lies such as her comments that the Iola ran aground on the reef as she was being towed out of the lagoon.

The biggest problem for Bugliosi is Stearns' assertion she discovered the dinghy *overturned in the lagoon at Cooper Islet.* This information could only come from one source and that is Stearns. How can one know this for a fact? Shishido at the time of the interview with Stearns was not familiar with the Palmyra atoll. He did not know Palmyra Island was composed of at least sixteen different islets. At the time he took the report in October 1974 he had no knowledge that one of the islets within the atoll was known as Cooper Islet; Palmyra could have been a reef island possessing no lagoon. If Stearns had not told him this information how is it that Shishido would have knowledge that Palmyra had an islet known as Cooper and that it was part of the Palmyra lagoon?

Bugliosi could argue it was Pollock who got together with Shishido to concoct a lie about Stearns to entrap her by telling Shishido about Cooper Island. The problem with this argument (aside from the absurd notion that an FBI Special Agent would collude with a witness to falsely change testimony) is that Pollock was told by Stearns the Zodiac was found over turned on the beach at *Paradise Island* and not *Cooper Island.* If there was collusion between Pollock and Shishido, the FBI report would have read Paradise Island and not Cooper Island. (p. 322…footnote) Moreover how would even the most clever Special Agent know what might be probative when there are no murder charges pending and Muff's body had not been discovered? After all, this was nothing

316

more than an instance of theft and illegal transportation of stolen property.

Stearns told Shishido they found the *dinghy overturned in the lagoon at Cooper Islet.* Twelve years later during her murder trial Stearns does not challenge this statement head on but attempts to place a different spin on it.

Bugliosi inquiring of Stearns:

" Jennifer did you tell the FBI agent Calvin Shishido that you found the dinghy in the lagoon?"

Stearns: *"I don't remember what I said to Mr. Shishido, but I found the dinghy on the beach. If I said in the lagoon, it could have been to differentiate between finding the dinghy on the beach in the lagoon as opposed to on the beach on the ocean side."* (p. 423)

Suddenly she is at a loss for words and does not know the meaning of the word lagoon. The wording of Shishido's report is clear and concise; Stearns told Shishido they did a search and, *"located a dinghy overturned in the lagoon over at Cooper Islet."* (p. 423) Nothing could be more clear. Her explanation was an effort to confuse the jury and undermine Shishido's report. Finding the dinghy overturned on the beach with motor attached was fundamental to her defense although she did not understand this point when she spoke to Shishido the day of her arrest.

Stearns the Spinmeister

Bugliosi, on direct examination, inquires of Stearns:

"Mr. Pollock testified that while you and he were going back to the Coast Guard cutter you told him you had found the Graham's dinghy on the beach on Paradise Island. Did you tell him that?"

317

"No. He misunderstood if he thought I said I found the dinghy on Paradise Island. That was just where I thought it had flipped over, by Paradise Island." (p. 437)

This is another example of Stearns' lies that make little sense. If one takes her testimony at face value she tells Pollock while being towed in the dinghy back to the Coast Guard cutter she thought the Zodiac had flipped over by Paradise Island. Why didn't she tell him she found the Zodiac overturned on Cooper Island? A few minutes later while speaking with Shishido aboard the Coast Guard cutter she realizes her error and changes the supposed place of discovery of the Zodiac to Cooper Island.

After dancing around the statement that she found the dinghy *overturned in the lagoon* she later modifies it during cross-examination by Enoki:

"You remember Agent Shishido testifying that you told him that you found the Zodiac overturned in the lagoon and the gas tank was floating nearby."

"Yes."

"And you deny telling him this?"

" I told him that I thought the dinghy had overturned in the lagoon, and that both the gas tank and dinghy had floated ashore." (p. 455)

In this revision of her testimony Stearns admits telling Shishido she thought the dinghy *had overturned in the lagoon* as Shishido's report specifically states, but with a twist, adds she also told him she thought both the gas tank and dinghy had *"floated ashore"*. This is a further revision of her lie

about the alleged discovery of Mac's dinghy the morning after the supposed disappearance of the Grahams.

Bugliosi employs another gambit attempting to prop up Stearns flagging testimony by introducing consistent testimony. (The Rules of Evidence mandate consistent testimony can only be introduced if it was made before the statement at issue was made.) Ignoring the Rules of Evidence Bugliosi introduces a consistent statement made by Stearns about the location of the discovery of the Zodiac made after Stearns comments to Shishido and Pollock on October 29, 1974.

Knowing his question contravenes the Rules of Evidence, Bugliosi proceeds anticipating Enoki will not object:

"At your theft trial, did you testify that you found the Zodiac dinghy overturned on the beach about a half a mile or so to the west of the Sea Wind?"

Stearns responds: *"Yes."* (p. 462)

While the above statement is consistent with her murder trial testimony it is improper in that it is proffered *"after"* she made her initial statement to Shishido and was "lawyered up" preparing for her theft trial. It was also proffered after Stearns discovered that an outboard engine exposed to salt water would not start without a careful cleaning.

There is another issue to consider; we know that Shishido was a conscientious note taker because everything in his report with the exception of the comments about the location of the Zodiac and gas tank were part of Stearns defense during trial.

To accept Bugliosi's point we must imagine Shishido during his interview of Stearns in October of 1974 intentionally changed the comments of Stearns. When she purportedly says the Zodiac was found on the beach, he must intentionally change her commentary and write down it was found in the lagoon. Why would an FBI agent falsely report an alleged fact about something that at the time seemed

319

inconsequential? At the time of the interview he knew nothing about the case. He was hearing about Palmyra Island for the first time. He did not know what was probative of what. If he changed her comments how would he know he was helping or hindering the prosecution of the case? What would be his motivation? And besides, this was all over a seemingly small potatoes case of boat theft. There is no way in October of 1974 Shishido could have known twelve years later he would find himself in San Francisco as a witness in a murder trial and that his notes and recollection of his interview with Stearns would be at issue.

At the close of Shishido's cross-examination Bugliosi critiques his own performance noting:

"During Shishido's testimony on the witness stand, the defense had clocked some serious mileage." (p. 368)

Admittedly this may be what Bugliosi believed, but a more dispassionate observer might arrive at a different conclusion. There was nothing in his cross-examination that was particularly devastating. There are few that would accept Stearns new version of the alleged facts as *"more close to the truth"* than her prior statement carefully noted by Shishido in his 302 summary of October 29, 1974. There are many reasons why the defense prevailed over the prosecution in this contest, but the cross-examination of FBI agent Shishido by Bugliosi was not one of them.

Shishido Stands His Ground

FBI Special Agent Shishido testified during direct examination by Enoki:

"...she said they found the Zodiac dinghy with the outboard motor over-turned in the water the following morning. The gas tank was detached and floating nearby......"

"Do you specifically remember her mentioning that the Zodiac was found overturned in the water?"

"Yes." responded Shishido. (p. 359)

Bugliosi reviews his cross-examination of Shishido;

"First, I elicited that although Shishido testified on direct examination that Jennifer told him the Zodiac was found three quarters of a mile west of the Sea Wind, his report did not reflect this allegation."

Next Bugliosi brings out a minor inconsistency in that Shishido had testified at a hearing on November 8, 1974, Stearns had told him the dinghy was only a *"half-mile"* away.

Bugliosi obtained a copy a transcript of a judicial hearing of November 8, 1974 in which Shishido testified regarding the statements Stearns made to him the day of her arrest. (The reader is not informed of the nature of this hearing which occurred just a few days after Stearns arrest. Probably a Preliminary Hearing to enable the court to determine if there was sufficient evidence against Stearns to hold her to answer on a felony charge.) (p. 364)

Using this 1974 transcript Bugliosi questions Shishido about his testimony:

"She told me they searched the next morning for the Grahams. During the search they found the Zodiac dinghy that was used by the Grahams the night before. The dinghy was overturned. It had an outboard motor that was also overturned. They also found a gas tank that belonged to the dinghy floating nearby in the lagoon."

Bugliosi having laid the groundwork, challenges Shishido:

321

"*Mr. Shishido, when you say 'they found the dinghy overturned' and then say they found the gas tank 'floating nearby in the lagoon,' doesn't it sound from the context as if you recalled her telling you they found the dinghy on shore, and the gas can floating in the water nearby?*"

Shishido, undaunted, gives as good as he gets:

"*No, sir, it does not. When you are on the stand testifying, you just go into the general details oftentimes. And I may have done that in this instance. But at the time of investigation, my recollection is that she said the dinghy was found overturned in the lagoon. But if the motor had overturned in the lagoon, how could they have turned it upright, attached a gas can, started the motor, and continued the search? Because the motor, I doubt, would have run.*"

Losing ground Bugliosi shifts his attention to the memory of Shishido and suggests he does not have the best recollection of the events that had occurred over ten years ago. To his credit, Shishido admits that he does not have *perfect recollection*. (In this instance his written report was prepared *one day after* the interview with Stearns on October 29, 1974 at a time when his memory was fresh and long before any accusations of murder.) (pp. 363, 365)

Where the Zodiac Was Found

Pollock testified as he and Stearns were being towed out to the awaiting Coast Guard cutter on the October 29, 1974, the day of her arrest, "*she told him that she and Buck had found the Zodiac capsized, on the beach, over at Paradise Island*". (p. 322, footnote.) A few minutes later aboard the Coast Guard cutter to Pollock's astonishment   Stearns   told to Shishido   the Zodiac was found *"overturned in the lagoon at Cooper Islet."* (p. 133)

Once she is "lawyered up" at her theft trial in 1975 these versions of the discovery of the Zodiac morph into finding the Zodiac over turned on the beach on Cooper Island in a westerly direction a half mile from where the Sea Wind is anchored.

It is difficult to know exactly when this metamorphosis occurred, but by the time she took the stand during her theft trial in 1975 the transformation was complete.   (This third revision of the supposed discovery of the Zodiac surfaces in defendants letter to Kit Graham in March of 1975.)   (p. 154-6)

If the jury decided   Pollock and Shishido were telling the truth about Stearns alleged discovery of the Zodiac overturned in the lagoon with the gas can floating nearby her defense would crumble. Realizing the potential for great harm to her defense, Bugliosi attempts to patch things up during his direct examination of Stearns:

"Jennifer did you tell the FBI agent Calvin Shishido that you found the dinghy on the beach?" (p. 423)

It is here Stearns attempts to weasel out of her original statement to Shishido about finding the Zodiac *"overturned in the lagoon at Cooper Islet"* with *" the gas tank floating in the lagoon nearby."* (p. 133)

Squirming to avoid a direct confrontation with Shishido, Stearns hedges her position employing one of her favorite routines by claiming she did not remember what she told Shishido, followed by a modifying comment. Attempting to dodge the issue she says if she used the word *lagoon* she really meant *"on the beach in the lagoon"* . (p. 133)

"I don't remember exactly what I told Mr. Shishido, but I found the dinghy on the beach. If I said in the lagoon, it could have been to differentiate between finding the dinghy on the beach in the lagoon, as opposed to on the beach on the ocean side." (p. 423)

Bugliosi, continues;

"Did you tell the Agent Shishido that you saw the gas tank of the dinghy floating in the lagoon near the dinghy?

"No, he got that wrong. I told him that I thought the gas tank had floated to shore."

Bugliosi, again leading:

"After you found the gas tank, did Buck reattach it to the dinghy?"

The above question makes little sense. It may be possible to "attach" a gas tank to a dinghy but there is no reason to do so. An external gas tank in an inflatable dinghy normally sits on the floor. An external dinghy gas tank is usually attached to an outboard motor by means of rubber tubing which allows the transfer of fuel to the motor as needed. The proper wording should have been reattach it to the *outboard motor".*

Stearns nonetheless answers the question rather than correct Bugliosi.

"Yes."

(If one were to take Stearns statement at face value we have the fuel tank attached to the dinghy and not the motor.)

"What happened next?"

Stearns responds by stating: *"Buck tried starting up the Zodiac dinghy..."*

"Buck tried starting up the Zodiac dinghy, and he pulled the cord a bunch of times, and the motor finally started. And we took the

wooden dinghy back to the Sea Wind and started searching for Mac and Muff in the Zodiac." (p. 423)

Again more goofiness — one cannot *"start up"* the Zodiac dinghy. One can *"start up"* an outboard motor attached to a dinghy. What one presumes Stearns meant was:

"Buck tried starting up the outboard motor, he pulled the cord a bunch of times, and the motor finally started."

The above exchange between Stearns and attorneys for both sides clearly demonstrate the limited understanding both Enoki and Bugliosi possessed concerning sailing matters. Bugliosi erroneously frames the question to Stearns who, following his lead, agrees although it does not make sense. She adds further confusion by alleging Walker "started up the dinghy", when what she meant was started up the motor.   Small points that out of ignorance add to the confusion, but go unchallenged by Enoki.

Bugliosi attacks both Shishido and Pollock with gusto realizing the danger his defense of Stearns could be in if the jury were to believe Pollock and Shishido accurately reported what Stearns had told them on October 29, 1974.

In an aside to the reader Bugliosi observes:

"Concerning Shishido's extremely critical testimony that Jennifer told him she and Buck found the dinghy overturned in the waters of the lagoon, I said, 'The decided weight of the evidence shows that Cal Shishido is wrong about what he says Jennifer told him." (p. 513)

For all Bugliosi's blather and fault finding about the accuracy of Shishido's FBI report, if one takes the time to carefully read Shishido's report presented on page 133 of ATSWT, it reflects precisely, the defense Stearns prepared.   The only particular that changed is the Zodiac was no longer found in the water, but discovered overturned on the beach on Cooper Islet.

The reason for this deviation is obvious; between October 29, 1974 when she told Pollock and Shishido of her discovery of the dinghy and the time she went to trial for theft in 1975 someone informed her that it would not be possible to start the outboard motor if it had been in the water for several hours. Advised of this fact she changed her testimony to fit the circumstances.

One might argue that Shishido got together with Pollock who gave him the name of Cooper Island, but we know this did not happen because Stearns told Pollock she first saw the overturned Zodiac on the beach at *Paradise Island*. If Pollock had collaborated with Shishido the report would have read Paradise Island.

The mention of Cooper Islet, the existence of which Shishido could not possibly have known about at the time of the interview, proves Shishido's report contained the exact words of Stearns as she wove her complex skein of lies about the events of Palmyra. The same reasoning applies to Stearns' comment about the gas tank floating nearby. How would Shishido know, years later the exact location where Stearns first found the gas tank would be an issue in trial.

If all the king's horses and all the king's men could not comprehend this case, (including the attorneys for both sides) how is it Shishido would have the foresight to place the gas tank in the water as opposed to being on the beach? How is it Shishido would know twelve years in advance of trial the alleged location of the discovery of the Zodiac on the morning of August 31, 1974 would be an issue? He could not possibly have known this at the time he wrote the report. At the time he believed he was dealing with a minor boat theft case that was a concern for the Coast Guard and not the FBI. He may have had suspected defendants murdered the Grahams, but could not have anticipated 12 years after his initial interview with Stearns, facts he had faithfully recorded would be at issue in the murder trial of Stearns.

BRUCE BENSON — THE MAN WHO WASN'T THERE

Jail House Rock

Enoki entertained calling BRUCE BENSON, (Benson) reporter for the Honolulu Star Advertiser, as a witness to testify concerning a jail-house interview he had with Stearns while she was awaiting arraignment on the charge of grand theft for stealing the Sea Wind. Benson's article appeared on the front page to the Honolulu Star Advertiser published October 31, 1974, two days after Stearns' arrest. (p. 396)

Three weeks before the Stearns' murder trial Enoki sent Bugliosi several news clippings. One of these was a copy of Benson's October 31, 1974, Honolulu Star Advertiser interview of Stearns. Reading the article, Bugliosi characterized Stearns' comments as *"explosive", "outrageous",* and *"damaging".* (p. 396)

Stearns made the following statements to Benson:

"Mac's last words to us were, 'Make yourselves at home until we get back. I'm sure he didn't expect to go out and die. But that's what we did: We made the boat our home."

Bugliosi stated Stearns gave Benson the following explanation for not reporting the disappearance of the Grahams to the authorities when she and Buck reached Hawaii.

"They would have confiscated it — they would have taken the boat. We didn't have anything to prove that it was ours. He didn't really give us the boat. He just said make yourselves at home. I realize that's a rationalization on my part, to keep something that I love." (pp. 396-7)

The interview reported Stearn's lie about the Iola *"running aground on the reef"* and concluded with what Bugliosi labeled a "disturbingly flip quote", *"The Sea Wind wanted to go around the world again, and I wanted to go with it."* (p. 397)

Bugliosi writes: *"Characteristically, Jennifer had never mentioned anything to me about this article, but she did confirm, when I asked, that Benson had quoted her accurately."* (pp. 396-398)

Until discovery of the interview shortly before trial, Bugliosi was unaware of its existence and was justifiably upset about Stearns not informing him of it. He fulminates:

"Jennifer, how in the living hell could you tell this guy Benson something so outrageous as the Sea Wind wanted to go around the world again, and you wanted to go with it? I bellowed.....thanks Jen. We really need crazy things like this in our case. I retorted." (p. 397)

Bugliosi was caught off guard by Benson's interview of Stearns, however for the most part, the information contained therein was rather harmless. He was prepared to concede there had been no "dinner invitation" contrary to Stearns' expected testimony and he intended to explain away her lie about the Iola running aground on the reef.

Lost in Transmission

328

Continuing to review old news clippings furnished by Enoki, Bugliosi happened across *another* interview by Benson printed a day earlier in the same newspaper.   The article focused on Benson's interview of Edwin Pollock concerning a conversation Pollock had with Curt Shoemaker about his final conversation with Mac Graham on the 28th of August 1974.

Bugliosi underlined one paragraph of Benson's article in red:

"Pollock said Shoemaker was told during the last radio transmission from the Grahams that they had invited Allen and Jenkins to dinner, presumably as a going away party, since the man and woman were to depart from Palmyra aboard the Iola the next day." (p. 397)

Bugliosi, agitated, observes:

"Most assuredly, this was wrong, and something had been lost or garbled in transmission between Shoemaker, Pollock and Benson. I didn't believe for a moment that there had been such an invitation, (even if there had, this in no way would have militated against Buck still having murdered the Grahams), but I knew that Enoki, at all costs, would try to prevent the jury from hearing that there may have been, for it directly contradicted his position that no invitation ever existed." (pp. 397-98)

In his comment regarding the paragraph underlined in red, one finds Bugliosi focusing on the issue of whether or not the invitation to the dinner had been made, ignoring the most important implication of the interview — Mac thought the defendants were departing for Fanning Island the day after the bon voyage dinner — *"since the man and woman were to depart from Palmyra aboard the Iola the next day."*

Mac's statement defendants were departing for Fanning the day following the bon voyage dinner when coupled with Shoemaker's testimony regarding his final communication with Mac on the 28th of August establishes the supposed departure date of the defendants for Fanning Island as Thursday, August 29th.   Thus implicating not only Walker in the murders of the Grahams, but Stearns as well.

In October 1974 when Shoemaker informed Pollock of Mac's last words he had no idea twelve years later Stearns would argue the Grahams disappeared on the 30th and not the 29th.   Shoemaker's final conversation with Mac did not become a focal point until the murder trials of Walker and Stearns.   Even then no one quite understood the implications of the last words of Mac Graham — including the attorneys themselves.

There is another reason the conversation between Pollock and Shoemaker, reported by Benson on October 30, 1974,   is notable: Bugliosi planned to attack the anticipated testimony of Shoemaker and Pollock by suggesting it was something they made up *shortly before* the trial of Walker in June of 1985. The fact that Shoemaker told Pollock about the conversation he had with Mac just two months after Mac's death and nearly twelve years before the murder trial of Stearns, would weigh heavily against the success of such a stratagem. (p. 397)

It is clarifying to re-examine the testimony Shoemaker gave at the murder trial of Stearns in February 1986.

Prosecutor, Walter Schroeder, questioning Curtis Shoemaker:

"Mr. Shoemaker, do you specifically recall your last contact with the Grahams?"

"Yes."

"And on what date did that last contact occur?"

"That was....(witness reviewing his log)...August 28th."

"Does your log specifically reflect August 28th?"

"Yes, it does."

"And did you enter the information about that contact in your log book immediately after it occurred?"

"Yes."

"Does the log reflect the time of day the contact began?"

"Yes."

"What time did it begin?"

"Ten minutes after seven."

"What general subject did you discuss during the conversation on the 28th?"

"Well, the first part of the conversation was like the previous ones with activities he had been involved in during the day and...like before."

(This is followed by a brief discussion about the clarity of the radio contact and then returns to the subject.)

"Now, during this conversation did the subject ever turn to something that seemed to be then taking place?" Inquires, Schroeder.

Shoemaker responds:

"Well, towards the end of the conversation he...he said: there's something going on up topside, or above.   And I could hear voices....someone talking. It sounded like women."

"All right, to the best of your recollection, what did Mac Graham say at that point?"

"Well, he — he said: I guess they've formed a truce. I'm going to go up and see what's going on."

"So he went up topside, and then he came back down again. And he said: 'They're bringing the cake over. So I don't know what is going on. I'll — I'll have to look into it.' And that he would meet me on the next contact. You know the next scheduled contact."

"So I said: Okay. And that was it."

"Now he specifically said the word 'they' as in they are bringing a cake over?"

"He said they."

"Did you understand the term "they" to indicate the people on board the Iola?"

"I would...yeah. That would have to be, because they were the only people —."

Judge King intercedes, instructing Shoemaker to answer the question narrowly, admonishes:

"Well, that — just — Yes?"   (An example of what the witnesses have complained about during their many appearances in court; when Shoemaker attempts to fully answer the question put to him by Schroeder he is cut off by the court.)

The witness: *"Yes."*

Schroeder:

"And what do you base that on?"

Shoemaker: *"You mean base the what on?"*

"All right. Your understanding that 'they' referred to the people on board. What do you base that on?"

"Well, they were the only other two living inhabitants on the island."

"Now after he said 'I'd better find out what's happening,' did the two of you schedule any further contacts?"

332

"Yes we did.   That was the last thing we decided."

"Now the voices that you heard in the background...did any of those — or was any of those voices a feminine voice, a woman's voice?"

"Yes."

"And how could you tell that....well, strike that."

"Could you tell whether or not the voice belonged to Muff Graham?"

"Well, there was apparently laughter and conversation between the women in the distance. It was...background noise."

"Now, at any time during this conversation did Mac say anything about inviting them over for dinner?"

"I don't remember that. No." (Vol. 5, p. 755-761)

At the time Stearns created her log following the murder of the Grahams she had no knowledge her arrival at the Sea Wind with Walker the evening of August 28, 1974,   interrupted Mac's conversation with Shoemaker.   Nor at the time of the creation of the log did Stearns know   Mac announced her arrival to Shoemaker cutting short his conversation to accommodate the defendants and assist Muff.   Stearns did not know that on the other end of the radio Curtis Shoemaker heard her voice and laughter as she and Walker approached the Sea Wind.   (No doubt to her great surprise all this was discovered by Stearns as she sat in court at the time of her theft trial, when Shoemaker took the stand and testified about his last contact with Mac on the 28th of August 1974.)

Under the Bamboozle Bush

Erroneously believing it was in the best interest of the prosecution to take the position there was no bon voyage dinner invitation extended to defendants by the Grahams, Enoki entered into a disastrous stipulation with Bugliosi. Enoki's confused purpose in entering into the Benson Stipulation was to prevent the jury from hearing Stearns' allegations that the Grahams had invited defendants to a bon voyage dinner aboard the Sea Wind. (pp. 398, 513-14)

Enoki, not understanding the thrust of his prosecution, approached the trial of Stearns from the viewpoint there was complete distrust and animosity between the Grahams and the defendants at all times despite considerable evidence to the contrary. The idea the Grahams might extend an invitation to the defendants to come aboard the Sea Wind for a bon voyage dinner prior to departure for Fanning Island did not fit in with his prosecution plan. At no time did he comprehend the Grahams had been taken in by the voyage to Fanning Island ruse advanced by Stearns. Nor for that matter did Enoki understand that the voyage to Fanning Island was a ruse whose purpose was to encourage the Graham's to drop their guard allowing for their execution.

The Benson Stipulation served an important function for Bugliosi in that it eliminated the need for Enoki to call Benson as a witness. (Bugliosi feared in so doing Enoki might inadvertently stumble upon the highly damaging Benson interview of Edwin Pollock of October 30, 1974, which established August 29, 1974, as the alleged date for the departure of the Iola to Fanning Island.)

Bruce Benson, a reporter for the Honolulu Star Advertiser, played an important "off-stage" role in that he interviewed Stearns within a few days of her arrest in 1974, reporting his conversation with her in the October 31, 1974, issue of the Honolulu Star Advertiser. (pp. 396-8)

334

More importantly, the day before, on October 30th 1974, Benson reported an interview he had with Edwin Pollock, wherein Pollock revealed a conversation he had with Curt Shoemaker, pertaining to Shoemaker's last contact with Mac Graham on August 28, 1974. It was this final conversation with Mac Graham that became the focal point of an intense battle between prosecution and defense during trial. (pp. 396-8)

Bugliosi formulated the Benson stipulation with the purpose of undermining the testimony of the Pollocks, Shishido and Shoemaker. Moreover, the stipulation supported Stearns' false narrative of the events as they supposedly unfolded the last week of August 1974.

By dangling the carrot of omitting the allegation defendants had received a bon voyage dinner invitation Bugliosi induced Enoki to agree to stipulated facts pertaining to a fictional conversation between Benson and Stearns that never occurred. The fictitious facts of the Benson stipulation greatly favored the defense of Stearns. (p. 398)

Contemplating his ploy concerning the non-existent Benson's jailhouse interview of Stearns, a gleeful Bugliosi chortles:

"I knew that Enoki, at all costs, would try to prevent the jury from hearing that there may have been, (a bon voyage party invitation) for it directly contradicted his position that no invitation ever existed."

"He would have to shoot down this article while defending the accuracy of the same author's jailhouse interview. I was soon on the phone negotiating long distance with my courtroom opponent. We ended up agreeing that neither of us would call Benson and worked out a stipulation." (pp. 397-98)

335

The Benson Stipulation

(In law a stipulation is a contractual agreement between contesting parties as to issues or facts. It often has the effect of shortening litigation. It is binding on the parties to the stipulation; even the court is not permitted to make findings to the contrary. When made as to questions of fact, a stipulation is conclusive.)

Enoki and Bugliosi stipulated to the following, for the most part non-existent facts, regarding Benson's jail house interview of Stearns October 31, 1974.

"It is stipulated that if Bruce Benson, a former reporter with the Honolulu Star Advertiser, were called as a witness, he would testify as follows;"

"That he interviewed Jennifer (Stearns) on October 31, 1974, and among other things, Ms. Jenkins told him that the day after the Grahams did not return to their boat, the Sea Wind, she and Roy Allen found the Graham's dinghy about a half-mile down the beach in a westerly direction from where the Sea Wind was anchored, and that it was overturned as if it had flipped over."

"Also, that since the wind was from the southeast, she and Roy Allen figured the dinghy flipped over around Paradise Island."

" Furthermore, as she and Allen were taking their boat and the Sea Wind out of the channel on Palmyra, their boat got hung up on the reef and they unloaded things from their boat onto the Sea Wind." (p. 398)

The stipulation to facts of a conversation that never occurred greatly favored Stearns defense. With the exception of the lie about the Iola running aground on the reef, the alleged facts of the stipulation were an integral part of Bugliosi's defense of Stearns.

With the above-noted exception *none of these statements were made by Stearns to Benson during her jailhouse interview.* The Benson Stipulation encompassed the lies that hid and obscured the truth about the murders of the Grahams the defense had been hawking from the start.

Bugliosi celebrates:

"I not only kept out the damaging and outrageous statements Jennifer had made to Benson, but I got into the stipulation the very key fact that she had told Benson she and Buck found the Zodiac on the beach."

"I managed to get in that Jennifer told Benson she and "Roy" had assumed the Zodiac had flipped over near Paradise Island and floated to where they found it on Strawn Island, thereby rebutting Edwin Pollock's testimony on this point." (p. 398)

(In the above paragraph there is a curious aberration in that Bugliosi erroneously references Strawn Island and not Cooper Islet as the location where defendants discovered the Zodiac dinghy belonging to Mac on the morning of the 31st of August. (p. 398) The erroneous reference to Strawn Island rather than Cooper Island appears several times in ATSWT most notably when Weinglass was examining prosecutor Eggers as to his findings.)

The stipulation relieved Bugliosi from having to confront Benson on the stand. Benson was a respected journalist. Bugliosi feared Benson's reportage faithfully reflected the information Pollock had conveyed to him on October 30, 1974 concerning Shoemaker's last conversation with Mac Graham. In tangling with Benson, Bugliosi may have found an articulate and dangerous witness. Moreover, a greater hidden danger lurked in the possibility Enoki might awake from his stupor as he interviewed Benson and

337

discover the true facts surrounding the murder of the Grahams revealed in Benson's October 30, 1974, interview of Pollock.

Bugliosi mulls it over:

" *Enoki had accepted a quid pro quo with me that markedly favored the defense. In exchange for keeping the dinner invitation out (which was of no use to the defense anyway, since I intended to tell the jury I did not believe there had been one), and Stearns would only testify that Buck told her there had been one, and including the story about the Iola's going aground (a lie we already had to explain away anyway, because Stearns had repeated it to Shishido), I not only kept out damaging and outrageous statements Stearns had made to Benson, but I got into the stipulation the very key fact that she had told Benson that she and Buck found the Zodiac on the beach. Also, I managed to get in that Stearns told Benson she and 'Roy" (Walker) had assumed the Zodiac had flipped over near Paradise Island and floated to where they found it on Strawn Island, thereby rebutting Edwin Pollock's testimony on the point.*" *(p. 398)*

The non-lawyer looking at the Benson stipulation must feel bewilderment. How it is that officers of the court can create a non-existent conversation Benson supposedly had with Stearns and turn it into an incontestable series of lies by way of a stipulation greatly favoring the defendant simply because one of the attorneys hasn't a clue about his case and opposing counsel is an aggressive attorney who has little trouble twisting the truth, exploiting his opponents weaknesses and taking shortcuts.

Carefully examining the contents of the stipulation set forth above comparing it with the jailhouse interview of Stearns by Benson reported in the October 31st issue of the Honolulu Advertiser, with the exception of Stearn's nonsense about of Iola going aground, there is not a single common fact. The Benson Stipulation was a fraud

338

perpetrated on the jury by both the prosecution and the defense. Unknown to the jury, and perhaps the judge, the facts signed off on by both attorneys were a total fabrication. (pp. 396-97)

A crucial aspect of the Benson Stipulation from the defense point of view is found in the fact that it was a reflection of a conversation supposedly made at a time many years in advance of Stearns' trial for murder. As such it not only cast doubt on the testimony of the prosecution witnesses, but lends credibility and support to the fabricated testimony of Stearns.

Unmitigated Disaster

The stipulation was an unmitigated disaster for the prosecution. It created the illusion Stearns had told Benson about certain contested matters back in October of 1974, when, in fact, no such discussion ever occurred.

The stipulation was foisted off on the jury by both Enoki and Bugliosi, each with his own motive. Enoki not understanding his case was fearful the cross examination of Benson might reveal to the jury defendants received an invitation from Mac to come aboard the Sea Wind for a bon voyage dinner. (pp. 397-398)

Bugliosi, recognizing Enoki has blinders on, observes:

"I knew that Enoki, at all costs, would try to prevent the jury from hearing that there may have been (a dinner invitation) *for it directly contradicted his position that no invitation ever existed."*

The stipulation undermined the testimony of Pollock, Shishido and Shoemaker on many different levels. It reinforced Stearns' fictitious storyline encouraging the jury to believe just a few months after the murder of the Grahams, before lawyers were involved on her behalf, she divulged the purported information set forth in the stipulation to Benson.

What happens when stipulated facts were never fact to begin with? Judge King's hands were tied. He could not intervene in the stipulation had he been so inclined. One feels sorry for the jury, confused and disoriented it is no wonder they finally gave up and acquitted Stearns.

During summation Bugliosi uses the Benson Stipulation to cast doubt on the testimony of Pollock arguing:

" *It happened with Mr. Pollock, also. Jennifer tells him they found the dinghy on the beach, and she thinks it probably capsized by Paradise Island. I pointed out that this was corroborated by the stipulated testimony of the reporter Bruce Benson. Jennifer told Benson that because of the direction of the wind (from the southeast), she figured that the dinghy had flipped over around Paradise Island. Yet, twelve years later Mr. Pollock's recollection of what Jennifer told him is that they found the dinghy on Paradise Island.*" (p. 514)

He employs it to denigrate the implications of the testimony of Ken White who found the outboard engine salt free:

"But we know that's not so because long before Ken White testified at her theft trial, she told Mr. Pollock and Bruce Benson that the dinghy was found on the beach." (Once again Bugliosi employs the lie of the half truth in partially quoting Pollock with no objection from Enoki.)

As Bugliosi foresaw, the Benson Stipulation was a clever hoax that paid big dividends for Stearns.

CHARACTER EVIDENCE

Getting Away with Murder

The ability of the homicidal sociopath to murder and escape punishment rests in his or her ability to appear non-violent — the ability to deceive. Gary Ridgeway the infamous Green River killer murdered over seventy women, yet was married for many years to a completely unsuspecting wife. As in the case of Stearns he too was fond of animals, detested violence on TV and was repulsed by guns.

Modern psychiatry has not advanced sufficiently to examine the mind of a sociopath who has yet to act on his or her bloody predilections and predict with any degree of accuracy when he or she may act out in a violent manner.   Rather than use terms such as sociopathy or psychopathy, the Diagnostic and Statistical Manual, Fourth Edition, prefers the term "Antisocial Personality Disorder" noting several different symptoms:

"Deception indicated by repeated lying, use of aliases or conning others for personal profit or pleasure; impulsiveness or failure to plan ahead; irritability and aggressiveness, indicated by repeated physical fights and assaults; Reckless disregard for the safety of self or others; Consistent irresponsibility, as indicated by repeated failure to sustain consistent work behavior or honor financial obligations; and, lack of remorse, as indicated by being indifferent to, or rationalizing having hurt, mistreated or stolen from another."

Reviewing the listed traits it can safely be said that Stearns manifests six out the seven traits, the only exception being *"aggressiveness indicated by repeated physical fights and assaults".*

The problem with Bugliosi's thinking re the guilt of Stearns is that he assumes she is a normal person and not a sociopath.   He assumes the actions of the defendants in the killing of the Grahams was done in a normal psychic state and not one enhanced with

341

alcohol and drugs such as hash, MDA and pot.   Since both defendants were drug users it is reasonable   to suspect they kept a supply for themselves and were under the influence of drugs and alcohol during the murder of Muff.   No doubt they found prescription drugs on board the Sea Wind to further distort their disordered personalities.

Normally character evidence during trial is limited to very simple issues such as   reputation in the community for honesty and veracity. A so-called character trait, if there is one, for non-violence is difficult to define. Bugliosi is prohibited from asserting Stearns had a reputation for truth and veracity because she has a flawed record of theft and arrests and would be easy to impeach during cross examination. (p. 34)

No matter the transgression Bugliosi finds one reason after another to excuse her lying and deceptive acts. Assisted by the court Stearns is able to hide much of her past. The jury is completely in the dark about her conviction for theft of the Sea Wind, her petty theft convictions, her arrest for possession and sale of MDA, and her use of an alias. (p. 571)

Bugliosi argues:

"But ladies and gentlemen, when time and time again, as I will shortly point out to you,   a person acts in an innocent way, doesn't it stand to reason that they are innocent?" (p. 520)

Apparently, *in* Bugliosi's world if you are a good enough con and can act innocent, you are innocent. Conversely should one act in a manner others might consider the actions of a guilty person you must be guilty of the crime. Many look and act guilty when they are not. Moreover, it is not uncommon for a person that is innocent to admit to a crime they did not commit.

Bugliosi continues his whitewash of Stearns:

342

"In our case here, although Jennifer did several regrettable things that were induced by the circumstances in which she found herself, on occasion after occasion she acted in a way that only an innocent person would have acted. Guilty people simply don't do that. If they did, they wouldn't be guilty." (p. 520)

Ergo if you act guilty you are guilty, and if you act innocent (in a convincing way) then you must be innocent. Under his system the only issue to be investigated re guilt or innocence is how you acted. Fortunately this is not the basis for law in the United States.

Deborah Noland

Bugliosi began his presentation of character evidence with Debbie Noland, (Noland) a person who lived with defendants in their house in Hawaii between 1973 and 1974. Enoki failed to demand a hearing outside the presence of the jury to limit the testimony of each of the so-called character witnesses. As a result Bugliosi was able to circumvent the Rules of Evidence and parade before the jury various *specific acts* of Stearns in an effort to support his position she was essentially a non-violent person even though specific acts are not usually admissible to prove character.

Bugliosi announces his strategy of cutting corners of the Evidence Code by introducing specific acts of Stearns into evidence even though it is generally not allowed:

"Because of the likelihood of surprise and consumption of time, most courts permit character evidence relating to specific acts only on cross-examination, not direct. However, this was a grey area of the law....and I intended to make an effort to slip in such specific testimony from Noland on my direct." (p. 385)

343

Abiding by Bugliosi's playbook Noland used conclusionary terms such as peaceful, easygoing, loved nature, went to the beach a lot, loved animals, etc. Violating the Rules of Evidence she spoke of Walker's "firecracker personality"; he was "domineering" and he threw stones at Stearns' van when on one occasion he got mad at her. One specific act or irrelevant conclusion after another went unchallenged.

(While demonstrating Walker was not an even tempered individual, throwing stones at Stearns' vehicle is the kind of displaced aggression one might expect from a *subservient* afraid to challenge the authority of the alpha leader Stearns.) Moreover it is not permitted to reference the behavior of Walker to show the so-called character of Stearns. (p. 50)

This line of testimony normally would have been prohibited in advance by an "offer of proof." Each one of these comments gives rise to many questions regarding specifics which is one of the reasons why character testimony should carefully be examined prior to calling the witness. Since Noland opened the door Enoki had the right to walk in, commence cross examination and impeach the witness with examples contrary to her testimony.

It would have been very illuminating to get a blow by blow description of each and every fight and confrontation that occurred between Stearns and Walker during this time. How many times did these fights occur? Who started the fight? What were they fighting over? Did Stearns use foul language during these arguments? What about the tone of her voice and the decibel range and etc?

Noland's comments are completely out of line and not relevant to the issue of Stearns' character for non-violence. Walker's personality traits and actions were not permissible nor relevant. Enoki should have objected and moved to strike, but he did not.

344

Finally Enoki objects on the basis the answer to Bugliosi's question would permit the introduction of specific acts which are generally not prohibited.

Bugliosi was given extremely wide latitude in questioning Noland concerning the character of Stearns by Judge King. Her examples of supposed non-violent behavior on the part of Stearns should have been stricken from the record. The testimony of Noland was improper as Bugliosi concedes — her testimony was *"not generally permissible."* (p. 385)

Finally, Judge King observing lethargy on the part of Enoki as Bugliosi wanders far afield, intervenes with his own objection:

"Are we getting into specific acts now?"...."I thought you weren't supposed to get into that?"

Waking up, Enoki timidly joins in:

"I'm not sure what the answer is going to be, but it could call for a statement about specific acts."

Judge King continues:

"Yes. I thought that what you were getting into was not permissible under the rule."

Bugliosi continues to badger the court:

"I think the bald declaration of the nonviolence certainly is helpful, but what caused the witness to form that opinion I think is important." (p. 386)

True it is important, nonetheless it is not permissible under the law. Bugliosi tries for the third time and is finally foreclosed by the court.

"Mr. Bugliosi, we are going to have a little problem with this. Because you and I both know the rule. It's almost a formula. "

Then King lectures Bugliosi on the proper and accepted method of examination of a character witness:

"Do you know the defendant?" *'Yes."*

"Do you have an opinion?" *'Yes.'*

"What is that opinion?"

Bugliosi's indifference to the rules of evidence are so egregious that King sustains his own objection:

"I'll sustain my own objection." (p. 386)

The witness would be expected to say Stearns has a reputation in the community as a non-violent person. When introducing character evidence the issue is the reputation of the defendant in the community in this instance for non-violence. The mere fact that a person has knowledge of a specific act by the accused for a character trait is not generally admissible to prove character.

It is the reputation of the accused in the community for the trait in question that is the issue.

Prodded by the court Enoki finally objects to Noland's testimony because she may get into specific acts that are prohibited by the Rules of Evidence.

Enoki foolishly ends his examination of Noland with a "soft-ball" question.

"It's your opinion then that in spite of her association with Mr. Walker and knowing the kind of person he was, Jennifer was still capable of being a non-violent person?"

Noland beans him:

"Definitely." (p. 386)

Rick Schulze

Bugliosi called as the next character witness Rick Schulze (Schulze) an attorney who had served briefly as a District Judge in Hawaii.   He met Stearns in 1970 through a mutual friend and claimed to have seen her every week during 1970. He notes Stearns helped around the house in preparation for his marriage.   He describes his relationship with Stearns as *"very close"*. (p. 387)

Even this seemingly innocent description of their relationship goes beyond what is permissible by law. Bugliosi should have asked him if he knew of Stearns' reputation in the community for non-violence. Assuming that his answer would be "yes", the next question should have been,

"And what is that reputation?"

Followed by the expected response: "That she is a non-violent person."   Anything more strays from the path and could open doors that may take hours of cross examination to clear up.

Bugliosi follows by asking Schulze another improper question:

"How would you describe Jennifer to the jury?"

The above questions open the door to just about anything the witness wishes to say about Stearns. Schulze, knowing the question was coming up, exceeds the boundary set by law and unloads with a barrage of improper observations and testimony:

"She is a very giving person. She was always concerned with helping other people. She didn't pay a lot of attention to her own problems. She is a sound and reasonable person." (p. 387)

All the above testimony by Schulze should have been stricken from the record. It is highly improper, moreover it opens the door for the prosecution. Had King been fair in his application of the

Rules of Evidence he would have permitted Enoki to impeach the witness with Stearns conviction for theft of the Sea Wind and all her other crimes. Unfortunately, King did not over-see the trial with a fair hand, Schulze and the defense was given a pass.

If she was such a *"sound and reasonable person"* how is it that she gets involved with very rough types and had been arrested for petty theft twice, grand theft of the Sea Wind and sale of MDA? Why would Schulze describe these actions as those of a *"sound and reasonable person?"* It takes very little imagination to see when once a character witness "opens the door" the chaos that ensues.

No demands for an offer of proof, few objections, fewer restrictions and Bugliosi steam rolls ahead and in so doing succeeds in getting in a touching story (probably fictitious) about how Stearns supposedly cried and slept with her dog when the mean old lawyer Rick Schulze would not let her bring Puffer into his home. Whether true or not the comment was inadmissible.

Enoki and King permit non-relevant observations to be made about nasty Buck Walker with all his guns. At no time did anyone ever quiz Schulze as to the number of guns, the details and circumstances of the viewing, or why it was that Stearns permitted Walker to have a .22 caliber pistol on board the Iola.

Bugliosi, off on a tangent, continues totally unrestrained delving into completely inadmissible testimony:

"I next asked Schulze if he was aware of any of the men in Jennifer's life, and he said he had met two of her boyfriends."

"Did these two men fall into a pattern?"

"Yes they did."

"In what way?"

348

"Contrary to Jennifer's nature, her boyfriends tended to be scruffy, coarse men. Crude-crude men."

Under Bugliosi's unacceptable direct examination Schulze continues to wander speaking about the character of Walker:

"Buck Walker was a burly kind of guy, coarse, crude....He was paranoid...other people were out to get him. He had a fascination with weapons."

Not only did Judge King erroneously rule to keep the conviction of Stearns for the theft of the Sea Wind out the purview of the jury, but typical of his pro-defense bias throughout the trial, he allowed Bugliosi to erroneously interrupt Schroeder's cross examination impeaching the testimony of Schulze.

Schroeder: " Mr. Schulze, I gather you base your opinion as to Jennifer's character for nonviolence on the fact you never witnessed any acts of violence on her part, is that correct?

"In part, that's correct."

"And obviously you never observed Jennifer under circumstances of deprivation or desperation. Would that be correct?"

Bugliosi improperly, objects:

"Your honor.....the question assumes a fact not in evidence. It's an over characterization of the evidence."

King agrees with Bugliosi even though his objection is wide of the mark:

"Yes."

Speaking to Schroeder:

"You used words which really are your conclusion. I'll sustain the objection, and the jury should ignore the question."

King's support of Bugliosi is completely off base. During the trial there was substantial evidence defendants existed in a state of

349

deprivation and desperation. A monotonous diet which for the most part consisted of coconuts and fish. Moreover, defendants were stranded on Palmyra Island in that the Iola could not survive a trip to Fanning Island or return to Hawaii. Defendants existed in an extreme state of poverty dependent for the most part on the largess of other sailors. It is reasonable to assume under these conditions of extreme privation an alleged non-violent person might act in a violent manner. Stearns' conduct in a law abiding society is one thing, her actions when outside the reach of the law, were quite another.

Since Stearns was a drug user and Bugliosi had opened the door Schroeder should have been permitted to ask Schulze about Stearns drug usage. Whether or not he had witnessed Stearns under the influence of marijuana, alcohol, hashish and/or MDA. But Schroeder did not broach the subject probably because he anticipated King would unfairly prohibit such inquiry.

Schroeder exposes Schulze for the partisan he was by first setting up the fact that Schulze thought Walker was violent.

"He talked of violence to the extent that you became weary of it?", asked Schroeder.

"Yes", answers Schulze.

"Jennifer's friends began to shun her--or not to shun her so much as just not wanting to be around her if Buck was with her. And my wife and I—we became that way too a little." (p. 389)

To impeach Schulze, Schroeder offers in evidence a letter Schulze wrote about the character of Walker describing him in the most flattering and non-violent manner. The letter written January 7, 1975 by Schulz was directed to Judge King, who presided over Walker's theft trial on the eve of King's sentencing hearing. (p. 389)

350

Schulze spoke "glowingly" of Walker; *"....saying among other things, that Schulze did not consider him a violent person."* (p. 389)

Schroeder follows up his advantage;

"And just as you once vouched for Buck's character for nonviolence, you are now appearing here today to vouch for Jennifer's character for nonviolence." (Suggesting Schulze's so called character testimony was an untruthful effort to support Stearns defense.)

King, not happy with Schroeder's successful impeachment of Schulze, attempts to discourage Schroeder with mild histrionics and pretends he does not understand why Schroeder would want the letter Schulze had written introduced into evidence.

Schroeder properly responds;

"We want to demonstrate the standards of this witness's ability to assess violence. This letter was a glowing tribute to Mr. Walker, and how Mr. Walker was nonviolent." (p. 390)

King responds:

"I understand that. And that's why I can't understand, for the life of me, why you possibly want it in. And I can't understand, for the life of me, why the defense objects to it. Maybe I am operating in never-never land where rational thought is irrelevant."

To underscore his scorn of Schroeder and the prosecution, the court, in an effort to discourage Schroeder and diminish his stature before the jury, closes his eyes and does the classic nose pinch as if he *"had just seen double"* after making the above remarks — all histrionics meant to demean Schroeder in front of the jury. (p. 390)

Fearing Schroeder was making ground with his impeachment of Schulze, King cuts Schroeder off from any further questioning by commenting in a "testy" manner:

"Haven't we exhausted this subject, Mr. Schroeder, please?" (p. 391)

Bugliosi notes;

"Schroeder instantly realized that he had nothing further."

One of the puzzles in this colloquy is how was it Stearns had a relationship with a former judge? What is the background of the relationship? How did they become acquainted? Why would Schulze trouble himself to appear in court in San Francisco as a character witness for the likes of Stearns? It is expensive to travel and an inconvenience. Moreover one does not think of Stearns traveling in the same circles as Schulz. Where did the money come from to finance Schulze's trial support of Stearns?

Leilah Burns

Bugliosi's so called character witness was Leilah Burns a sailor that lived with her husband aboard a sailboat in Keehi Lagoon on Oahu. Burns, claimed her relationship with Stearns commenced when the Iola sailed into Keehi in early 1974. (p. 392)

The Iola remained for only five days at Keehi and was not until the Sea Wind returned to Hawaii and the subsequent arrest of Stearns that the relationship was renewed. Burns visited Stearns while she was in jail. (p. 392) After her arrest and release on bail Stearns stayed with the Burns' family for eight months probably departing when she was sent off to the federal penitentiary on Terminal Island in Long Beach, CA upon her conviction for theft of the Sea Wind.

There can be little doubt with trial and subsequent sentence to federal prison hanging over her head Stearns was on her best behavior during her stay with Burns. No sooner does Burns take the stand than the defense departs from the Rules of Evidence.

Bugliosi comments:

"Leilah told the court and jury, 'Jennifer is a very gentle, loving, caring, and considerate person. She is not capable of being violent." (p. 392)

This testimony is not permissible under the Rules of Evidence. It could have been eliminated had Enoki insisted on an "Offer of Proof" outside the earshot of the jury wherein the court would admonish the witness (and lawyers) not to transgress the Evidence Code. Inexplicably there were no objections by Enoki.

The defense team continues their assault on the Evidence Code when Weinglass puts an "open ended question" to which Burns responds;

"I got very close to her. I really felt she was a good person."

The answer is not acceptable, Enoki should have moved to "strike" the answer but chooses not to do so. With the door wide open he could have descended on Burns with questions such as:

"Do you think a person that steals is a loving, caring and considerate person?"

"Are you aware that Stephanie, in a trial by jury, was convicted for theft of the Sea Wind, a sailboat belonging to Mac and Muff Graham, and, as a result, served time in a federal prison at terminal island?"

"Are you aware that Stephanie was convicted on two separate occasions of theft of items worth less than five hundred dollars, a crime of moral turpitude?"

"Do you believe that a good person lives with a man convicted of armed robbery, and later, while on parole becomes involved in drug dealing?"

Does a good person use the vulgar and violent language of the street?

"You know her boyfriend, Buck Walker, was convicted of the violent and brutal murder of Eleanor Graham? Does a good person consort with a murderer?"

"The evidence in this trial suggests Mrs. Graham was tortured by acetylene torch before she died. Do you think a good person would live with a convicted murderer with such a reprehensible record and past?"

These types of questions are just a small sample of those Enoki could have asked had he chosen to do so. Admittedly it would have been a colossal waste of court time, but since Weinglass and Bugliosi had opened the door there is no reason why Enoki should not be allowed to walk through it.

Enoki cautiously takes the first step:

"Now, in response to one of Mr. Weinglass' questions, did you describe Jennifer (Stearns) as being a good person?"

"Yes."

Predictably Enoki cautiously approaching the open door finds it slammed in his face by Bugliosi and the court.

Enoki:

"Okay, did you mean to imply by this that she was an honest person also, in your opinion?"

Unable to contain himself, protecting ground gained, Bugliosi interrupts with an objection in violation of King's rule that only the lawyer who calls the witness on direct-examination, can object to a question on cross-examination. (p. 393)

"Objection, ...Beyond the scope of direct examination."

King unfairly and improperly weighs in:

"Mr. Enoki, I'm going to sustain the objection to that. She was called for a limited purpose."

True Burns was called for a limited purpose of testifying to Stearns supposed character trait for nonviolence. However it was Bugliosi who opened the door by permitting Burns to testify Stearns was a "good person". Having done so Enoki should have been able to impeach Stearns with prior acts of theft which would have gone a long way in demonstrating Burns judgment of Stearns' character was seriously flawed. Moreover, the question was not beyond the scope of the direct examination since it was Bugliosi that first broached the subject.

Having been snookered, Enoki properly moves the court to strike from the record the testimony of Burns that Stearns was a "good person".

'Then I would request that her testimony relating to Jennifer Jenkins (Stearns) as being a 'good person' be stricken....because I am not allowed to cross-examine on what that term means to the witness." (p. 393)

Showing extreme bias in favor of the defense the court refuses to do so and unfairly shuts Enoki down by over ruling his objection noting he had already sustained Bugliosi's objection.

King's ruling fails to address the underlying problem that Bugliosi and the court have allowed into evidence improper testimony and having done so now prohibits the prosecution from striking the improper testimony or fairly attacking it. (p. 393)

355

For once Enoki does not give up, and attempts to correct the record with another approach:

"Have you become aware of any information that you know personally, or that you have been told of from other people, that would be inconsistent with Jennifer being a good person?"

Cutting Enoki off, Bugliosi objects:

"It's too broad, your honor. Also, it's beyond the scope of the direct."

King befuddled with the mess in his courtroom which he has permitted and encouraged, intercedes admonishing Enoki:

"She wasn't called to testify that Jennifer was a good person."

Enoki finally getting a little starch in his collar fights back:

"I can't help what she said," ... *"I didn't ask that question, your honor. It came out in her answer to Mr. Weinglass' question."*

King sensing that he is losing control of the situation unloads unfairly on Enoki:

"Let me help you out." He fumes, turning to Burns he asks, *"What do you mean by 'good person'?"*

Burns now totally confused, continues to stray far afield and answers incomprehensibly;

"I love her."

King having created this evidentiary mess looks for a hasty way out:

"You love her? Fine."

Burns with no question pending continues to press her advantage:

"I think she is a good person."

Seeking to end the debacle King asks if there are *"anymore questions"* of Enoki with an edge to his voice indicating there better

356

not be and with that so called character evidence side-show ends. (p. 394)

Once again with the assistance of the court Bugliosi was able to skirt the law by introducing inadmissible evidence. If King was not going to permit Enoki to impeach the witness re the assertion that Stearns was a good person at least these legally impermissible character references should have been struck from the record. Not only was the prosecution unfairly prohibited from striking the improper character evidence from the record, but was denied the right to impeach Stearns for her theft convictions.

Lawrence Seltzer

The final character witness called was Lawrence Seltzer who had known Stearns as a teenager and hired her to work for him after she was released from Terminal Island prison. He stayed within the confines of the Rules of Evidence for the most part but did deviate when he spoke of her work experience. This testimony should have been stricken. Enoki did not object no doubt because he had been chastened by King and did not desire to risk another public flogging by the court.

After stomping all over Enoki and the Evidence Code in summation Bugliosi chides the prosecution for failing to call a single witness to rebut his string of witnesses all friends of Stearns who were called to confirm her alleged character for nonviolence.

Enoki entered into trial not knowing Stearns was going to testify until she took the stand. He had no way of knowing Bugliosi intended to place in evidence Stearns supposed character for nonviolence until she took the stand and testified. By that time it was too late to engage in a lengthly and costly hunt for witnesses Stearns may have met that could counter specific testimony.

Another problem arises with the introduction of character evidence.   Stearns from time to time used aliases, Susan Mallet among others. Without   knowledge of the intention to introduce character evidence in advance of trial it is difficult for the prosecution to counter.   What was the purpose of the alias? Does Stearns manifest a different persona when using this alias? What was Stearns hiding?   Did any of the so-called character witnesses know Stearns when she was using this alias?   Did they know her to use other aliases, and etc?

Examining the logic of character evidence apparently we are all entitled by law to one free pass for murder or violent behavior. It is only after a person has violently assaulted or killed someone and has been successfully prosecuted that they are no longer permitted to play the nonviolent card in trial.

The unfairness of the Evidence Code is obvious in the case at hand: Stearns and Walker were guilty of the crime of robbery — taking the Sea Wind by force or fear. They did not merely steal the Sea Wind from the Grahams   —   they murdered the Grahams to obtain the Sea Wind. This fact was not known at the time of Stearns' theft trial.   In the murder trial of Stearns the prosecutor was prohibited by the court from employing the felony/murder rule or introduce into evidence the facts surrounding the theft of the Sea Wind.   Stearns was involved in not just a robbery but the horrible torture and murder of Muff Graham, a crime from which she was incorrectly absolved.   Judge King improperly tied the hands of the prosecution and assisted Bugliosi in achieving this unjust result. His evidentiary rulings were one of the many ironies of the trial permitting a hate crazed murderess to present herself as non-violent wrongfully accused innocent.

FALSUS IN UNO, FALSUS IN OMNIBUS

(False in one, false in all….two thousand year old Roman Legal Maxim.)

Federal Jury Instruction

If you believe that any witness or party willfully or knowingly testified falsely to any material fact in the case, with the intent to deceive you, you may give such weight to his or her testimony as you may deem it is entitled. You may believe some of it, or you may, in your discretion, disregard all of it. (State v. Samuels, 92 N.J.L. 131, 133, Sup. Ct. 1918; Vol. 3A Wigmore on Evidence (1970) Sec. 1008 et.seq.)

California Jury Instruction

"A witness who is willfully false in one material part of his or her testimony is to be distrusted in others. You may reject the whole testimony of a witness who willfully has testified falsely as to a material point, unless from all the evidence, you believe the probability of truth favors his or her testimony in other particulars." CAL JIC 2.21.2

Hall of Mirrors

Bugliosi argues that Stearns is a peaceable person, yet there are deviant aspects to her personality — she is strongly attracted to men with violent histories. Walker was convicted of the torture/murder of Muff Graham. No sooner does he go off to jail than she gets involved with Joe Buffalo, a man also imprisoned for murder who was mistakenly released. Her relationship with Joe Buffalo only terminated when he was apprehended by authorities and returned to prison. (p. 461) Her pal, Rich Schulze mentions other "rough types" as well.

She excuses her relationship with Joe Buffalo, an escaped con and convicted killer on the run, because he had a rough background and she *"thought she could help him"*. The same rationalization the defense advanced to excuse defendant's relationship with Buck Walker. Bugliosi puzzles over Stearns actions:

"One murderer perhaps an accident, but two and we have a pattern." (p, 461)

Co-counsel Weinglass uncomfortable with Stearns, observes; *"she comes across as 'manipulative and untruthful', and in answering questions she frequently 'shifts her eyes and hesitates, as if she's searching for the right answer.'* He found her mannerisms disturbing".* (p. 92)

Bugliosi mentions the difficulties in preparing her for trial stating he *"had more problems preparing Jennifer for trial than any other witness"* he could remember. She constantly changed her version of the events and these changes *"were endless"*.

Bugliosi ruminates:

"Why was there was always yet another layer of truth to be revealed? Another shadow in this hall of mirrors?" He continues

with his doubts explaining his wife thought Stearns was not trustworthy. (p. 191)

Bugliosi notes Stearns most successful polygraph exam gave her a plus seven out of a possible 30 points. An expert employed by defendant warned:

"Don't get me wrong.....I read the charts as indicating she's innocent. But at plus seven, where the truthfulness factor can go as high as plus thirty, she is only borderline truthful, not dramatically truthful." (p. 212)

Bugliosi excuses Stearns lying while testifying during legal proceedings because it is *"self-defensive in nature"*. In other words he expects guilty defendants to lie under oath during trial in an effort to beat the rap. These lies to his way of thinking are *understandable* as if expected and of no consequence. His only concern about Stearn's defensive lies under oath before a previous jury was that they *"could very possibly destroy her credibility with the jury at her murder trial"*. (p. 190) He is not concerned about the fact that she is lying under oath, only that if her lying is detected it will diminish her credibility.

Reviewing some of the negatives he was facing in the defense of Stearns Bugliosi summarizes:

"There were the preposterous lies she had told to the FBI's Calvin Shishido, the conflicting story she had told to Edwin Pollock, the lies she had told to Lorraine Wollen, and the provable perjury she had committed at her earlier trial in Honolulu." Enoki could not have stated it better. (p. 266)

Obviously her testimony about the alleged occurrences on Palmyra the 30th and 31st of August are complete fabrications as are many of the submissions found in her log/diary. Stearns brain is working 24/7 as she attempts to keep Bugliosi and her defense narrative on track. Her numerous multiple changes wear on Bugliosi. Finally his frustration with Stearns' continuously engineering her defense boils over.

Bugliosi fulminates:

"In the nature of things, there will always be many modifications to my original Q and A, — the changes were endless. Often entire pages of questions became useless because she would add a different twist to an incident we had already covered in detail. Worse, I was constantly having to expand my line of questioning because Jennifer would open up an entirely new area that needed to be explained or covered. The difficulty of preparing her for trial was reflected in my numbering of my pages of questions. It degenerated to the point where it was rare for one consecutively numbered page to follow another. For instance between pages 43 and 44 there soon appeared page 43 (a), 43 (b), 43 (c), and so forth. Then later, for further additions between pages 43 (b) 1, 43 (b) 2, 43 (b) 3...." (p. 191)

Bugliosi with a lucrative book deal and possible TV movie, gambled with Stearns' freedom and encouraged Stearns to reject an offer to plead to the lesser offense of second degree murder with the prospect of an extremely light sentence. Contrary to what Bugliosi alleges, more than likely he was motivated not by a sincere belief in the innocence of Stearns and pursuit of justice, but by the prospect of fame and fortune that would be his should he prevail in the contest.

You Can't Hide Your Lying Eyes

Stearns blamed her lawyers during her theft trial as a source of some of her lies. Bugliosi presents a portion of Enoki's cross-examination of Stearns:

"With respect to Jennifer's testimony on direct that she was cautioned about the inadvisability of changing her story at the theft trial, Enoki asked":

"You're not suggesting that one of your attorneys in that case told you that, are you?"

Stearns: *"I wouldn't say that they told me to lie, but I was advised by one of my attorneys that if I testified inconsistent with statements that I made to the FBI, the trial would probably go poorly against me."* (p. 451)

"Did your attorneys at the theft trial know that the true fact was that the Iola had not run aground and you had not left it there?"

"Yes."

Stearns' propensity to lie was showcased at her theft trial in June of 1975. At issue were the five "trophy" photographs of the Iola a few miles off Palmyra Island the day she was scuttled with Mac's body aboard. There are two boats depicted in the photographs. The Iola is clearly seen under sail with its forward hatch obviously missing. The rigging from the Sea Wind is plainly visible as is a portion of the net defendants draped about the stanchions to keep the dogs from falling overboard.

During her theft trial in 1975 Stearns steadfastly took the position that at no time were the Sea Wind and the Iola sailing together off Palmyra Island. Prosecutor, Bill Eggers showed her the photos and demanded:

363

"Would you explain, please, at what point in time when you and Mr. Walker were on the island of Palmyra were the Sea Wind and the Iola together under full sail out in the ocean?"

Stearns, emphatically replied: *"Never."*

Bugliosi reviewing her theft trial transcript noted she *"stuck mulishly"* to the story she told Shishido about their intent to tow the Iola to Fanning Island and the boat running aground on the reef. (p. 159)

Unlike Stearns' murder trial the jury sitting in judgment of Stearns during the theft prosecution would have none of her patently absurd lies and asinine rationalizations. After a few short hours of deliberation they found her guilty on all three counts. On August 18, 1975, Judge King sentenced her to a mere two years in prison on the theft charges and probation on the other two counts. (pp. 158 - 160)

Stearns "burned" in her theft trial because of *"mulishly lying"* to the jury, was far more cautious when confronted with undeniable truth during her trial for murder. Enoki questioned Stearns about the photos taken of the Iola and Sea Wind under sail off Palmyra:

"That was a lie too? He asked."

"Yes, it was." Answered Stearns as she casually admits to perjury in her former trial.

"Do you recall Edwin Pollock testifying that you also told him that you attempted to sail out of the lagoon on the Iola, and wound up on the reef and that's when you went back to get the Sea Wind?"

"I think I do, yes."

"I gather you deny saying that to Mr. Pollock?" (p. 451)

Stearns refuses to agree with Enoki and makes this peculiar admission:

"No.   With all that was happening that day, I could have easily told Mr. Pollock that story, but then when I was speaking to Mr. Shishido, it got to where I spoke more close to the truth."   (p. 452)

In "Stearns speak", whenever a normal person in the the course of conversation employs the word "yes," Stearns substitutes the word "easily" said, or did, a specified deed. In this instance she admits lying to both Pollock and Shishido when she spoke to them but she was lying less when she spoke to Shishido. In the fractured mind of Stearns there are shades of truth.   Some lies are more truthful than other lies; e.g., one plus one equals ten is more of a lie than one plus one equals five.   One plus one equals five using Stearns' truth scale is less a lie because it is *"more close to the truth"*.

A point scored for the prosecution in that by making this statement, Stearns admits lying to both Pollock and Shishido.   She admits telling Pollock an outright lie and suggests her statement to Shishido was also a lie but one that was a *"more close to the truth."*

Not satisfied, Enoki follows his minor victory with an argumentative question which has no real purpose other than to allow the witness to make another self serving statement which, true to form, she does.

"Isn't it true that the reason your story changed between Pollock and Shishido was because Mr. Pollock told you that you would have never left on the Iola if the Sea Wind was sitting there?"

Coyly, Stearns responds:

"No, it didn't change for that reason." (p. 452)

Unfortunately Enoki does not finish his inquiry into her lying about the scuttling of the Iola. Resuming questioning he goes off in another direction.

365

Sailing in Disguise

Defendants removed the figurehead of the Sea Wind before departure for Hawaii. On arrival at the Tuna Packer's yard the Sea Wind was repainted. Defendants changed the trim color from dark blue to lavender. These changes were meant to disguise the identity of the Sea Wind. Inexplicably they painted over the name Iola and did not paint a new name or hailing port on her stern as mandated by Coast Guard regulations.

Stearns testified she did not think changing the trim color would disguise the Sea Wind. Enoki examines:

"You indicated in your testimony that you were not trying to disguise the Sea Wind by repainting it. Is that right?"

Stearns agrees: *"I did not believe that changing the color of that boat would in any way disguise her."* (p. 443)

"And did you tell Mr. Walker that?"

"I did."

"And what was his response?"

"He just said that he wanted to change the color. He said we were either going to paint her yellow or I could pick a color I like better. Yellow is one of my least favorite color, so I picked lavender." (p. 443)

If Stearns had no interest in the Sea Wind why was her input so important in deciding the color to paint the trim? She was the one who dictated the trim be repainted a "sissy" lavender rather than a "masculine" black, dark blue or dark green. Why was she ordering Walker to repaint the trim if it was not her boat as well? (p. 443) Throughout the trial the question of who played the fiddle and who

366

danced the tune is always at issue.   Repainting the trim is another example where Stearns completely over powers Walker.   Stearns' assertion Walker wanted to paint the trim yellow (another "sissy" color) is also not believable.   (Old salts opine re painting a boat that there are only two colors to paint a boat, white, or black, and only a damn fool would paint his boat black.")

There is another interesting sub-text to the above testimony. If defendants were not concerned about obscuring the identity of the Sea Wind, why were they discussing the question of disguise? Obviously they hoped to conceal the identity of the Sea Wind by destroying the figurehead, changing the color of her accent strip on the hull and painting over her name and home port.

Time and again Enoki allows Stearns to employ weasel words to obscure her answers allowing wiggle room in the event she needs to retract an alleged statement of fact.   Years of lying has taught her to seldom give a straight answer. For the most part her lies and equivocation go unchallenged. The following short colloquy is an example:

"Enoki asked if the gold figurehead of a woman was in place on the bowsprit of the Sea Wind when Jennifer and Buck took possession of the boat at Palmyra."

"Yes, Jennifer said. *'At some point, the figurehead ceased to be on the boat, but....I don't know when it was."* (p. 443)

This is obviously untrue. Stearns was living on the Sea Wind, cutting or knocking the figurehead off the bow of the boat could not go unnoticed. There had to be a discussion about the removal in that it diminished the value of the boat.   Of course she knew of its removal and probably suggested the action.   Moreover there was great danger in removing the figurehead on the prow of the vessel. The prow is exposed to oncoming seas as defendants sailed back to

Hawaii. If Walker had taken a large hammer or crowbar and beaten the figurehead off the prow there would be the possibility of damaged to structural members causing the boat to leak.

One can be certain it was removed while on Palmyra before setting sail to return to Hawaii as removal while under way would have been difficult and extremely hazardous. Waiting until arrival in Hawaii might be unwise in that the activity of removing the figurehead would seem inexplicably strange to most sailors given the traditional design of the Angelman ketch.

The response to Stearns' contention she did not know when the figure head was removed is classic Enoki:

"I gather by your answer you did not remove the figurehead yourself?"

He asks a leading question of Stearns to impeach her testimony and at the same time supplies an answer that exonerates her allowing an easy exit.

Stearns appreciates the assistance and replies, *"Yes."*

(It is true that an attorney on cross-examination may ask a leading question and has a right to do so without objection. Normally this is done for the purpose of impeaching the witness with questions that follow. However, with Enoki, it is rare that impeachment follows.)

Enoki inquires:

"Do you recall whether the name Sea Wind was on the running boards of the vessel when you took possession of it on Palmyra?"

Stearns gives her standby response:

"I don't remember, but it probably was."

Presumably Enoki is asking this question to demonstrate defendants attempted to disguise the identity of the Sea Wind on their return to Hawaii.   From this act one would normally infer a *consciousness of guilt* that they had stolen the boat.

Stearns understands where Enoki is headed and attempts to forestall the inquiry by issuing a vague and incomprehensible answer and then qualifying her answer by speculating ambiguously *"it probably was"*.   By adding the words "it probably was" Stearns has room to later argue the name was on the running boards and she simply had a temporary lapse of memory during testimony.

In response to questioning throughout the trial Stearns responds in the above stated manner.   Curiously, she is never challenged — the prosecution does not ask her to clarify her ambiguous response.

Few jurors would believe Stearns was telling the truth about not knowing the name of the Sea Wind was removed from the running boards. Palmyra is a small island. It was necessary for her to prepare her log in the event of apprehension. She had to be on board during the painting process just as she was there during the removal of the figurehead. Where else would she be....the Iola is at the bottom of the sea and Buck's camp was not disturbed after Muff's torture and murder.

Astonishingly, the Sea Wind had no name or hailing port on her stern when is was launched from the Tuna Packers' yard in October 1974.   Defendants had recently murdered Mac and Muff Graham, stolen their boat, destroyed the figurehead, repainted the trim, and then idiotically, failed to place her name and hailing port on the stern before launching. (Why didn't they simply hang up a sign telling all that passed by they have just stolen the boat?) To top off this masterpiece of stupidity after relaunching the vessel they went to Ala Wai basin and dropped anchor right under the nose of the Coast Guard — idiots in action.   (p. 126)

(All US Coast Guard documented vessels are required to have the name of the vessel and hailing port set forth on the stern. Not only does the Coast Guard mandate a documented vessel have its name and hailing port on the stern, but it further mandates the minimum size of the letters.)

High Seas Joy Ride

Before she gets into the whopper about the swordfish Stearns embellishes her fiction concerning Stearns found an outdated will aboard the Sea Wind while sailing back to Hawaii. It suggested in the event of Mac's death the Sea Wind should be *"returned to the mainland of the United States within the two year period specified in the will".*

Stearns testified about an imaginary conversation she had with Walker:

"He made a promise to me when I showed him Mac's will. Buck promised me that we would get the boat back to the mainland of the United States within the two-year period specified within the will." (p. 443)

During her *theft trial* Stearns alleged it was her desire to return the Sea Wind to the United States after two years of sailing in the South Pacific. How is this goal to be achieved? Is she going to go to the mainland and drop anchor in San Francisco Bay and leave the boat? Is she going to have it hauled out and left ashore? Unfortunately Enoki did not follow up his questioning and expose more of her falsehoods. (p. 445)

Again we see the mark of a practiced liar. Just say something, it does not matter if it is incomplete or meaningless — anything will do; just something that sounds plausible to fill in the

370

gap. It is a technique she has employed time and again to get her out of tight spots. Why does she desire to return the Sea Wind to the mainland? Allegedly because of some vague reference in an outdated will she happened to find aboard the Sea Wind when they were ram-sacking the boat looking for Mac's stash of cruising funds.

Stearns admits lying during her theft trial in telling the jury she was going to go from Ala Wai to the mainland to return the boat to Mac's sister Kit Muncey.   She follows up this admission with another lie:

"Ultimately, I did want to get the boat to Mary Muncey." (p. 445)

The jury is asked to believe after sailing the boat for several years Stearns intended to simply pop on over to the mainland return the boat and escape prosecution.

 What does she mean when she states *"I did want to get the boat back to Mary Muncey."* This lie should have been followed up with many questions: When did she intend to return the boat? To whom would she return the boat? What arrangements did she intend to make when she returned the boat: How did she expect to return stolen property — call up Kit and ask her where she would like the stolen boat dropped off? (p. 445)

Enoki suggests Stearns assertion of returning the boat to Kit was to raise a defense to a theft charge:

"Was this because it would have possibly been a defense to the theft charge that you told that jury that you were returning the boat to Mrs. Muncey?"

Stearns lies:

"No, It was because that's what I knew should be done."

This is followed immediately by two more lies:

371

"And that's what I would have done if it was my choice to make."

The first lie is Stearns' assertion she would have returned the Sea Wind to Kit Muncey when all of her actions including the murder of the Grahams indicated exactly the opposite.

The second lie is the above assertion by Stearns that returning the boat to Kit Muncey was not a matter of her own choosing. She had just as much input into the plan as Walker, if not more. She encouraged the changes made
to the Sea Wind to avoid detection and prosecution for theft and participated in all activities leading up to her prosecution for the crimes that followed. She could have returned the boat but did not because prosecution would have surely followed   as in fact it did. (p. 445)

Enoki continues his weak inquiry with one of his trademark questions where he telegraphs his expected answer to the defendant allowing her to answer in a manner that excuses her false testimony.

"Okay, so you deny that you were setting up the defense of 'return of property' by saying to that jury that you were returning the boat to Mrs. Muncey?"

Following his lead, Stearns repeats her lie:

"I deny that, yes." (p. 445)

Enoki makes a few more weak inquiries and with that his cross-examination finishes for the day.

Weasel Words and Wiggle Room

Once the defendants had murdered the Grahams and taken possession of the Sea Wind they did an intensive investigation of every nook and cranny of the Sea Wind looking for Mac's cruising

372

funds.   During the search Stearns came across the clothes of Muff and commenced using them discarding the rags she had been wearing. Enoki enquires: (p. 444)

"How about Mrs. Graham's clothing?   Did you look through what she had?"

Stearns lies:

"I saw she had clothing there. I didn't go through it, per se."

Time and again we have her familiar lying standard.   She admits she saw Muff's clothes. Then states she did not "go through" them, followed by a qualifier "per se".   Another of the hundreds of explicit and implied lies she told during her short time on the stand. Stearns had access to clothes far
above the quality of anything she could purchase and the jury is to believe she did not carefully examine each and every item?

Enoki: *"Did you wear any of her clothing?"*

"I don't recall wearing any of her clothing. I'm not sure."

One thing Stearns will remember until her dying day is the confrontation she had when Kit Muncey saw the mug shot of Stearns wearing the blouse of Muff Graham.   It shocked Kit to the point where she challenged Stearns who responded that she had purchased the same identical blouse Muff had bought. (p. 444) The *"I'm not sure"* is typical Stearns....always leave the back door open. First she says, *"I don't recall,"*   then she follows it up with, *"I'm not sure".* Plenty of wiggle room if needed.

Enoki follows up:

"Do you recall the outfit in which you were arrested?"

Stearns lies again;

"No".

The clerk hands Enoki two mug shots of Stearns wearing Muff's blouse the day she was arrested and hands them to Stearns.

"Does that refresh your recollection in any way at the time you were arrested?"

"Yes, but, I don't know whether that was ...... Muff's blouse I was wearing. I mean, I've.....I had a blouse just like that too."   (p. 444)

Stearns is lying when she testifies, *"I don't know whether that was....Muff's blouse I was wearing."* Of course she knows the blouse belonged to Muff.

And, lie number two;

"I mean, I've...I had a blouse just like that too."

Enoki could have followed up; Where did she purchase the blouse; What brand name; How much did she pay for it; When did she make the purchase; Did she wear any other clothes belonging to Muff; and etc.

The reader can gain insight into the deranged mind of Stearns, which to a degree explains the horrible butchery of Muff. Muff represented everything Stearns would never be. Because of this Muff paid a heavy price and was selected for a carefully choreographed brutal murder. So great was Stearn's hatred of Muff and all she represented she was willing to gamble her freedom and the freedom of Walker to vent her spleen. Had Muff's body been shipped off with Mac's into the deep that would have been the end to it. There would have been no murder trial and no books would ever have been written. But Stearns had to have her pound of flesh indulging herself and gambled her freedom all the while cleverly setting up Walker to take the fall.

Tangled Webs

("What strange and tangled webs we weave when first we practice to deceive.")

Sir Walter Scott.

Defendants awaiting separate trials for the theft of the Sea Wind, sent an eight page letter to Kit Graham post marked March 11, 1975. Stearns enclosed a short note explaining that Walker had written the letter while they were in dry dock at the Tuna Packer's yard on their return to Hawaii in October of 1974. (p. 155)

The letter was full of lies and bizarre contradictions including the *new third revision* of the alleged discovery of Mac's overturned Zodiac, this time on Cooper Island. Not only was the letter full of lies, but its purpose is incomprehensible. Why was it sent to Kit Graham? What did these two nut-cases expect in return? The letter basically lays out their defense posture for the up coming theft trials. It also showcases a rather strange mentality they both possessed.

An example is found in the letter wherein defendants represent themselves as married.

"My name is Roy Allen and my wife is Jennifer."

Shortly thereafter the letter mentions:

"Last but not least we want to get married."

One wonders what mental process is going on in their heads. They represent themselves as *"married"* and shortly thereafter *suggest they want to get "married"?* A couple of screwballs — one wonders what kind of drug induced the short circuit. (pp. 154-7)

At first glance one speculates they were attempting to curry favor with Kit hoping she will request charges be dropped against

375

them. However this line of thinking is scotched when they mention they want to file *"a salvage claim"* and imply Mac Graham was responsible for their loss of the Iola. They assert the Iola was worth ten thousand dollars. Notably missing— there is no mention of intent to return the Sea Wind. To the contrary the letter informs Kit Graham both Stearns and Walker intend to claim the Sea Wind for themselves. They also tell her they have registered the Sea Wind and changed her name.

"I realize this may be the wrong place to mention this, but we want to file a salvage claim on the Sea Wind.....We love the Sea Wind and we want, eventually, to continue with her in a voyage around the world. Also, I've registered the Sea Wind, renaming her Lokahi, meaning 'of one mind', which we think aptly sums up the spirit of our feelings. We haven't yet notified anyone about the true circumstances. We feel you should be the first to know." (p. 156)

Stearns enclosed a note with the letter lying about Walker writing it while the Sea Wind was in dry dock; lying about the letter being "lost and forgotten in the shuffle"; lying about "October" as the date of preparation; lying about identity of Walker referring to him as Roy Allen; lying about the circumstances surrounding the death of the Grahams; lying about the Iola *"crunching up"* on the reef as they were departing Palmyra; lying about being married to Walker; lying about the wedding; lying about the value of the Iola; lying about an intention to keep Kit Graham fully informed; lying about the amount of money found aboard the Sea Wind, which was closer to $5,000.00 rather than 400.00; and, lying about their intent to return the stolen money. (pp. 154-7)

Stearns rationalized that her lying about the location and time when the letter was written was permissible because the contents of the letter were allegedly true, therefore it is okay to lie about the date the letter was written. (p. 439)

What did defendants hope to gain? Most certainly they knew upon receipt Kit would immediately turn it over to the FBI. Although addressed to Kit it was obviously meant to be read and considered by the authorities.

It probably served other purposes — both theft trials were approaching and it was important for defendants to be on the same page. It was important they repeat the same lies. The eight page letter roughly outlined their defense. It furnished defendants with a script to memorize helping to focus their testimony. The letter outlines Stearns' defense presented in her murder trial and to a great extent repeats the lies she divulged to Shishido when first taken into custody with the exception of changing the location where the Zodiac dinghy was purportedly discovered.

Parts of the letter reflect some of the same issues Stearns faced as she formulated the murder of the Grahams. In writing about the downside of living in a primitive condition on Palmyra there is a passage one can definitely attribute to Stearns as it was an issue which remained high on her list in planning the perfect murder scheme.

"There is the fear of serious injury because the nearest outside help is days away,..." (p. 155)

Stearns contemplated the possibility of injury to herself or Walker. How could defendants kill the Grahams, yet insure no harm would come to themselves? It was this fear that caused Stearns to reject Walker's simple minded ideas such as sneaking up behind Mac and when he was not looking shoot him in the back of the head. It is this concern that caused her to settle on a two phase murder plan wherein Walker kills Mac aboard the Iola as he retrieves his generator, this is then followed by their combined assault against Muff aboard the Sea Wind.

The most important lines in the letter from the standpoint of the prosecution are those referencing the bon voyage dinner that became the focal point of Bugliosi's cross-examination during Stearns' murder trial.

Bugliosi writes:

"Walker mentioned the planned trip to Fanning. He said Mac had invited him and Jennifer for a "bon voyage dinner" the night before the scheduled departure." (p. 155)

This is a letter written on, or about, March 11, 1975 supposedly by Walker and reviewed by Stearns. There is no ambiguity concerning the bon voyage dinner invitation. Defendants specifically state, they were invited to a *"bon voyage dinner"* which was *"the night before the scheduled departure"*. This statement was made by the defendants before either had counsel — no defense attorney to spin the facts. The declaration clearly establishes two facts: Defendants were invited to attend a *"bon voyage dinner"* aboard the Sea Wind celebrating their departure to Fanning Island, and the alleged departure for Fanning Island was scheduled for the *following* day.

(The letter is rich in facts and information that inculpates both Walker and Stearns. Oddly enough, there is little said about it in the trial, as if this source of material was completely ignored by the prosecution.)

Puppet Master

378

Occasionally through inadvertence Stearns gives the jury a glimpse into her thought process. Bugliosi presents just such instance during his direct-examination of Stearns (pp. 437-8)

Attempting to focus the jury in a new direction we find this testimony from Stearns:

"......He asked me why I was on the boat, and why I hadn't turned the boat in. And I couldn't tell him the truth. I couldn't tell him that it was of Buck's fugitive status. So I guess....That was just what popped out of my mouth." (p. 438)

For all her alleged intelligence, Stearns says whatever happens to be convenient at the time. This explains her brief moments of clarity and truth telling to total strangers concerning matters that eventually bear heavily against her such as telling Pollock during the passage from Hawaii to Palmyra she was "knee-deep in water down below"; or on landing at Palmyra "they were nearly out of food" and "were down to their last ten dollars"; .(Vol. 2, p. 257) Comments that just "popped out of" her mouth as she jabbered away without thinking of the future consequences. (p. 317)

The tendency of Stearns to "pop off" without thinking is confirmed a few lines later during direct examination as she attempts to avoid blame for lying to Shishido.

Bugliosi inquires:

"Did you tell Mr. Shishido that you and Buck rationalized Mac's statement — Mac's alleged statement — to Buck to 'make yourselves at home' to mean that the Grahams would have wanted you and Buck to take possession of the boat if anything happened to them? Did you tell Shishido that?"

"I'm sure I said something to that effect."

"Was this a truthful statement on your part?"

379

"No."

"Why did you tell him this?" (After admitting to the above lie she follows it with another lie.)

"Again, he was questioning me as to why we hadn't turned the boat in. And I couldn't tell him the real reason, so....I don't know why I chose those words except that was...as I knew it, the last words that Mac had told to Buck. And they just came out."

Stearns *doesn't know why,* but the words *"just came out"* as if she had no control over what she utters — one moment the truth, the next a lie....it is all beyond her comprehension or control, and perhaps it was. (p. 438)

(The above contretemps is an excellent example of misuse of the "why" question by Enoki. He succeeds in getting Stearns to admit to telling another lie to Shishido. He should have left it at that and later, in final argument, point out to the jury another example of Stearns untruthfulness. Instead he asks "why" which permits her to explain her lying and, in so doing muddy the water and excuse her lie.)

Fearful Stearns might say the wrong thing Bugliosi testified on her behalf as often as he could by use of leading questions. So long as Bugliosi is testifying indirectly by use of leading questions he knows the evidence will stay within the story line and follow the narrative most favorable to his client. (Leading questions are objectionable on direct examination of a witness and most often employed at critical junctures where crucial facts are at issue and the attorney fears the client is likely to get it wrong, or the wishes to emphasize a point the witness has already made. In essence testifying twice to underscore the point.) The following is a typical example of Bugliosi leading Stearns to underline a point.

"You didn't feel you could tell him the real reason, is that correct?" (p. 438)

Enoki should have objected to the above question forcing Bugliosi to restate the question in a non-leading manner. However the harm was already done once the question has been proffered. An objection does not diminish the effect the leading question has upon the witness and the jury, the objecting attorney cannot unring the bell. However an objection to a leading question can remind an alert juror that it is the attorney who is testifying and not the witness. A point that can be later be brought up in final argument. (p. 438)

Bugliosi follows up with more leading questions:

"That you were trying to protect Buck?"

"Yes"

"And you never told them that Roy Allen was Buck Walker?"

"No"

Further down the page, Bugliosi continues to lead:

"You felt the authorities would be able to check and ascertain that you were really with a Buck Walker at the correct time and place?"

Testimony from Bugliosi, put in ostensible question form, requiring nothing more than the witness than a word in agreement.

Stearns responds: *"Yes"*. (p. 438)

With no objections from Enoki, Bugliosi continues testifying:

"Did you tell Mr. Shishido that you and Buck rationalized Mac's statement (realizing his error, Bugliosi corrects himself) — *Mac's alleged statement — to Buck to 'make yourselves at home' to mean that Grahams would have wanted you and Buck to take possession of the boat if anything happened to them? Did you tell Mr. Shishido that?*

381

Stearns agrees:

"I'm sure I said something to that effect." (p. 438)

(Admittedly a jury wants to hear the case presented by each side without undue interruption from the opposition, however there is a point when opposing counsel crosses the line and proper objections must be raised if for no other reason than to preserve the record on appeal.)

"Was this a truthful statement on your part?", inquires Bugliosi.

Stearns admits to lying in an effort to avoid an arrest for theft of the Sea Wind stating: *"No."*

Shortly thereafter Bugliosi goes off in a different direction.

What I Did, I Did For Love

Bugliosi had many hurdles to overcome in his race to the finish line. One of the biggest was the fact that Stearns is a compulsive liar. She weaves endless lies for self gain whenever the occasion calls for it. However, lying for self gain does not sit well with most juries, lying to protect a loved one can be more easily overlooked or excused.

Desiring to minimize the sting of chronic, selfish, self serving, sociopathic lies marking Stearns testimony, whenever possible Bugliosi shifts blame for lying to protect herself to the supposed selfless lie issued to protect Walker. We see this new tack of "what I did, I did for love" theme when she repudiates a truthful statement she made to Shishido informing him she did not report the disappearance of the Grahams because she feared losing the Sea Wind. (pp. 437-38)

Bugliosi leads:

"Did you tell Mr. Shishido that the reason you never notified the authorities about the Grahams' disappearance was that you were afraid they would take the boat away from you?" (p. 437)

Stearns replies with another lie using her default answer:

"I probably said something like that. I don't remember."

"Was this the truth?" asks Bugliosi.

"No."

Stearns told the truth to Shishido when she told him that the reason she did not inform the authorities the Grahams were missing was because she feared they would take the boat away from her. However, during trial this truthful statement does not fit into her cover for lying.   With her new approach it is necessary to re-label her truthful statement to Shishido a lie.

"Why did you tell him this then?" Inquires Bugliosi.

"Well, he asked me why I was on the boat, and why I hadn't turned the boat in and I couldn't tell him the truth. I couldn't tell him it was because of "Buck's fugitive status". So I guess ....that was just what popped out of my mouth."

What does *"Buck's fugitive status"* have to do with not turning the boat in?   The authorities were looking for Roy Allen not Buck Walker.   The reason she did not mention the disappearance of the Grahams to authorities was because she feared they would take the boat away.   This fear was well founded for that is exactly what happened. As soon as the Coast Guard discovered the Sea Wind was back in Hawaii with Stearns and Allen aboard they seized it and began hunting for Roy Allen not knowing he was Buck Walker.

Bugliosi, putting words in Stearns' mouth, presses on with his love story theme:

"You didn't feel you could tell him the real reason, is that correct?"

Following his lead Stearns replies: *"Right."*

Bugliosi, continues to lead: *"That you were trying to protect Buck."*

"Yes", agrees Stearns.

Bugliosi acknowledges the importance of this new theme stating:

"Since Jennifer's effort to protect Buck was so central to my summation, I presented further evidence of her effort." (p. 438)

"In answer to my question, Jennifer testified that during the FBI interrogation she found out for the first time whom they were looking for. They kept talking about Roy Allen." (p. 438)

This comment by Bugliosi is misleading. Stearns knew the FBI was looking for her and her companion be it Roy Allen or Buck Walker. She was informed of this fact by a fellow boater. At the time she was scurrying over the breakwater and dashing off to the hotel to escape Walker was evading his pursuers by hiding in the water under the docks at the marina. (p. 438)

"And you never told them that Roy Allen was Buck Walker."

She replies, *"No".*

Bugliosi forges ahead with his love story smoke-screen attempting to provide cover for her next lie and at the same time reinforce her newly found role of protector.

"Jennifer, Mr. Shishido testified that you told him you first joined Roy Allen on the Iola in late April of 1974 while the Iola was moored in the Keehi Lagoon on the Island of Oahu. You testified earlier that you and Buck moved to the island of Maui in 1973, and Buck bought the Iola there the same month. And the boat you and

384

Buck lived on, was moored in the Maalaea Harbor in Maui. Do you recall that?"

"Yes".

"Why did you change the date and location to Mr, Shishido?" (i.e., Why did you lie about these two facts?)

"I was afraid that otherwise they would find out that Roy Allen was really Buck Walker." (p. 438)

The theme of protecting Walker served as cover for Stearns lying, however it does not stand up under scrutiny. Since the authorities did not know that Roy Allen was Buck Walker they would not think to ask Stearns what the true name of Roy Allen was. There was nothing to cause them to focus on this issue. In the minds of the authorities Buck Walker and Roy Allen were different entities. The only way they could discover the two were one and the same was if they came face to face with Walker and could compare fingerprints, or an investigator who knew Walker was to see a photo.

Bugliosi, leading:

"You felt the authorities would be able to check and ascertain that you were really with a Buck Walker at the correct time and place."

(Exactly how the authorities could check on the identity of Roy Allen is never explained.)

"Yes," she said. (p. 438)

The authorities on first questioning Stearns had only a passing interest in what they thought was a crime on high seas. The FBI was not looking for Walker, they were looking for Roy Allen. How does lying about meeting Roy Allen in Oahu rather than Maui protect Walker? The question, answer, and implication, make no sense whatsoever. The Roy Allen/Buck Walker issue

385

was nothing but a smokescreen employed by Bugliosi to distract and confuse the jury, which it did.

Heir Apparent

Bugliosi waxes poetic during final argument when addressing the relationship between Stearns and Walker. He excuses her theft and just about every conceivable lie Stearns uttered because she was ardently in love with Walker and was trying to protect him. In keeping with this pretense she claimed to be is his common-law wife. Bugliosi hammers away at the concept somehow these two maniacal killers were star crossed lovers. He goes so far as to drag in Eva Braun, the wife of Adolph Hitler, who chose to die with Hitler rather than flee and save herself. (p. 496)

There are several problems with this analogy aside from the despicable character of Hitler and his lover Eva Braun. However much Bugliosi attempts to portray Stearns as a person who is caring and committed, no sooner is Walker back in the slammer than she commences a relationship with another violent lover, Joe Buffalo, a convicted killer, who was inadvertently released from prison. (p. 460)

There is little contact with Walker once he is back in jail. We do find one letter Walker wrote to Stearns from McNeil penitentiary. There is no mention Stearns ever replied to Walker's letter. The disinterest must have been mutual because Walker began a relationship with another woman, Ruth Thomas, while he was in federal prison at McNeil Island. (Thomas was so taken by Walker she left her family and became an outlaw eventually spending time in jail herself.) The Walker/Stearns relationship was not exactly the stuff of Abelard and Heloise. (pp. 170-1)

Her love story theme rings hollow when observed from a viewpoint of Stearns' history. She uses people and discards them at will, Walker was the fall guy. Stearns defined the role he was to play in her little drama from the very start. When pressure was on and the authorities closing in she sends Walker forward to skirmish with the oncoming forces, watching as he gets chewed up and learns from his mistakes.   Stearns did act to protect the one she loved but it was not Buck Walker....it was herself.   A shallow, manipulative, self-obsessed sociopath, always looking out for herself in the style of Bernie Madoff, the Melendez brothers, or Karla Homolka. Prevailing in trial she sleeps the sociopath's untroubled sleep.

Home Coming...Another Version

Frank Mehaffy and his wife spent two years in Hawaii living aboard their small sailboat, Juno. On October 12, 1974 they were at anchor in Nawiliwili Harbor, Kauai when defendants aboard the Sea Wind dropped anchor nearby.   The following day in late afternoon defendants came by with a bottle of wine and were invited aboard. Mehaffy recalled they stayed for about three hours.   During this time Stearns, who did most of the talking,   mentioned a trip to Palmyra Island.   Mehaffy testified that they were *"led to believe"* the visit to Palmyra occurred in 1973.

In discussing the return trip from Palmyra Island, Schroeder queried:

"Did Stephanie or Roy give you any indication of the time frame when they were at Palmyra?"

"We had — We were led to believe it was the year before."

Judge King pipes up: *"Which would be what?"*

Mehaffy replies: " 73".

Schroeder continues: *"Now, when you were talking to them about the trip from Palmyra, did Stephanie tell you where they had just come from when they sailed into Nawiliwili?"*

"Yes. We talked about....going around the various places on the island. And Stephanie said they had had a really nice anchorage on the big island just before they left and — before they left the big island to come to Kauai." (The "big island" references the island of Hawaii.)

"And I — I got out a chart, because they talked about this anchorage being such a nice private place. So I got out chart, and Roy and Stephanie showed us where the anchorage was just below Hanamalo Point on the big island."

"And did she tell you how long it had taken them to sail from Hanamalo to Nawiliwili?"

"Yes. It took five days to sail from Hanamalo to the island of Kauai." (Vol. 5, p. 857)

Many of Stearns' lies often appear to have little or no purpose, merely lying for the sake of lying. Why did Stearns claim on return to first sail to Oahu when speaking to Wollen and a few days later tell the Mehaffys they first visited the big island of Hawaii? (p. 357) Normally a liar has purpose in telling a lie, however in the case of Stearns it is a mode of behavior not necessarily with a specific purpose in mind. On return to Hawaii did Stearns sail from Palmyra to Nawiliwili, Kauai, or did she sail from Palmyra to Hanamalo Point on the big island and later proceed to Nawiliwili, Kauai? Does it make a difference? Not really, Stearns lies for no apparent reason, she is a habitual liar and that is what she does.

Bugliosi on cross-examination wisely declined to challenge Mehaffy's recollection of events, but did use Mehaffy's expertise to discuss the concept of sailing to weather and tacking. (p. 356)

LOKAHI

Of One Mind

Bugliosi elicits the following testimony from Stearns as she describes her thoughts and actions shortly before her apprehension by the Coast guard:

"What was your state of mind at the point where they were barreling down at high speed directly toward your boat?"

"I was scared. I rowed really fast."

Bugliosi, leading: *"Was it your state of mind to get away from them because you felt you had done something wrong?"*

"Yes."

"And what did you feel you had done wrong?"

"Well...I was with Buck, and Buck was on the run. And as far as I knew being with Buck made me a criminal too."

Bugliosi observes: *"Then she added these crucially important words."*

"What you have to understand is that Buck's state of mind became my state of mind. Buck was a fugitive on the run, and I was running with him."

"So his reality became your reality." Leads, Bugliosi.

"Right." (pp. 336-7)

Following the above testimony Bugliosi pens an aside to the reader:

"It must have been on the sixth or seventh time that Jennifer and I were going over why she had said and done so many incriminating things that she uttered these words for the first time: 'What you have to realize is that Buck's reality became my reality. He was a fugitive on the run and I was running with him. That was the state of my consciousness.' Sometimes a spontaneous remark perfectly distills the essence of a situation. This one went to the very heart of Jennifer's discreditable actions, and I felt how it would help the jury to see how an innocent person who is traveling with, and emotionally bound to a guilty person may talk and act towards others the same way the guilty person does. I wrote the words down verbatim and told Jennifer I wanted her to use them on the witness stand. Alongside the remark, on her copy of our tentative Q and A, I jotted a reminder: 'Extremely important. Remember verbatim.' She had come close enough." (p. 437)

Of note is the fact that Bugliosi throughly prepped Stearns for direct testimony by furnishing her with a written memorandum of proposed questions and answers for her to study and memorize. Moreover, he admits that Stearns had *"said and done so many incriminating things"* indicating he does not believe in the innocence of his client.

Going back to her testimony Bugliosi continues:

"Is there anything else that you thought you had done wrong that caused you to try and get away from the Coast Guard cutter?"

Stearns replies: *"Yes...I knew that...we should have reported what had happened to Mac and Muff to the authorities, and also we were on a boat that wasn't ours."* (p.437)

Reading the above commentary one can observe that Bugliosi is of the opinion defendants were of one mind when it came to their actions and lies. I could not agree more. The fusion of the two personalities into one is reflected in the choice of the new name for the Sea Wind — Lokahi, a name defendants believed meant "of one mind". (pp. 436-7)

Stearns claimed Walker's reality became her reality. Walker wanted to go sailing and evade punishment for his crimes. His world became her world. In like process, her need for blood and violence became his. Her constant goading and prodding, her secret hatred and need for revenge against all society was brought to life through her manipulation of Walker.

Walker's "reality became her reality," but that is only half the equation. The strongest mind would control the relationship — that belonged to Stearns. Thus her reality became Walker's reality. The theft of the Sea Wind was Walker's reality; the torture, murder and dismemberment of Muff was Stearns' reality.

Throughout the book Bugliosi hammers away at every opportunity to depict Walker as the aggressive, powerful, bad guy. In fact, he was a light-weight. He could not go back to San Quentin and survive in the general population — to avoid this prospect he feigned mental illness.

It was Stearns who made the decision to take the chance of being found out by not sending Muff to the abyss along with Mac. It was Stearns who engineered the murder plot not Walker. Muff is only released from her death agonies when Walker intervenes in Stearns "fun" stepping forward and shooting her in the head because her screams are too much for him to bear. With Muff dead on the tidal sands they both chop and hack away at her remains. The acts of two very disturbed killers high on alcohol drugs and revenge. It was probably Walker, satiated, who merciful kills Muff with a gun shot to the head not Stearns.

391

It was Stearns who hated Muff not Walker. (Even Bugliosi puzzles over the ferocity of the attack on Muff.) (p. 505) This is a case of a perfect storm of madness wherein two highly disturbed sociopaths feeding off each others lifetime of imagined wrongs spur one another on to commit a horrible crime. Walker and has childhood fantasies of sailing and piracy meeting a sociopathic "Lady Macbeth" in Stearns — together engaging in a barbarous acts — Lokahi! (p. 156) (Detectives often refer to this type of criminal as a "debt collector." His wrong doing is the fault of society and not his criminal choices — no matter how grievous the offense, someone else is always to blame.)

The combination of Walker's strength and Stearns twisted mind proved to be a lethal cocktail resulting in the death of the Grahams and merciless torture of Muff. It was Walker who was acting out Stearns' phantasies and not vice versa. Walker wanted to steal a sailboat and sail off in the South Pacific sunset. Ironically, it is Stearns' need for a "blood bath" that causes the crime to be discovered. As one would expect it is Walker "the chump", who paid the price. Had Stearns told Walker to forget about the rape of Muff instructing him to shoot her in the head and put her body aboard the Iola alongside her husband...that would have been it: Walker would have done as he was told.

Were it not for their capture in Hawaii one suspects they would continue to kill as they sailed the South Pacific. Once tasting blood they may have become serial killers of the South Pacific.

If one carefully examines nearly all the decisions in the lives of the two defendants after they met almost every important decision was made by Stearns with Walker's acquiescence. There is nothing in Walker's past that portends violence on a level Muff suffered.

Before voyaging to Palmyra, Stearns encouraged Walker as he labored on the Iola. Neither reacts with outrage or hostility when the Iola falls off her trailer and suffers severe damage as her hull is impaled by the steel cradle supports. Surprisingly, Walker walks away without verbally or physically assaulting the trailer or crane operator.

Upon launch of the Iola it is Stearns who takes the leadership role. She claims to assume the duties of the helmsman. Defendants had several months to learn the rudiments of sailing before departing for Palmyra. It is during this time they became fully aware of Iola's short-comings and decided to risk sailing to Palmyra under jib sail alone. Given the fact Stearns claims the role of helmsman and leader it must have been Stearns who opined they could complete the voyage. Walker, for the most part, was seasick on the voyage to Palmyra and of little help. Contrary to his aspirations he did not adapt well at sea.

On arrival at Palmyra Stearns stayed aboard the Iola while Walker, finding a tent, moves ashore. Stearns retained control of the dinghy. She immediately begins advancing the murder plot by circulating rumors about the Musick brothers coming down with food and supplies. She furthers the plot by making inquiries about Fanning Island. She prepares her log knowing it will play an important role in her deliverance. She engages in the gardening charade. Meanwhile Walker plays a minor role cutting down palm trees and acting in a threatening manner to chase away the Pollocks.

One sees Walker in a supporting role to Stearns, but the plot is clearly of her making. It was far too subtle for Walker to create. For the most part he seems unengaged and a distant figure....almost a hermit given the distance he places his camp from the Iola. Not on the edge of the airstrip, not on the beach near the Iola, but more or less in the middle of the jungle three or four hundred yards distant from the Iola.

It is through the constant contact with the Grahams and other sailors that Stearns advances the storyline of the plot. She observes Mac and engages him at every opportunity. She sells the generator to Mac for a pittance and then borrows it back to insure he keeps his appointment with death aboard the Iola. Stearns scurries about speaking with all who will listen concerning her purported plans to sail to Fanning. It is Stearns who borrows the chart of Fanning for copying to reinforce in the mind of Mac they truly intend to leave for Fanning Island. On the morning of the Grahams execution, it is Stearns who rows over to the Sea Wind announcing defendants are ready to sail, informing Mac he can collect his precious generator. While Mac motors off to his death it is Stearns who distracts Muff until Walker can arrive and overpower her. It is Stearns who assaults Muff as she dives below to obtain her derringer. Walker is a convenient bogeyman for Bugliosi to trot out anytime he needs a foil, but it is Stearns we see constantly in movement engaging in "overt actions" to forward the death plot.

Chumped Again

Stearns was in a difficult spot with Walker. She could not treat him too roughly because he had information that could put her in jail for the rest of her life, possibly resulting in a death sentence. After Walker's conviction for murder of Muff she knew the Feds would be offering him a deal if he cooperated and assisted in her conviction. (p. 271)

His choice not to co-operate was motivated by something more than the con's code of not "ratting out" a crime partner. In his limited way he had an emotional bond with Stearns which was not requited. It was one of the factors keeping him from going to the authorities to cut a deal seeking to ease his sentence and conditions in prison. (In one of his prison missives he bitterly complains about not being permitted time out of doors and of the miserable conditions of being in a crowded cell.)

His letter to Stearns from McNeil Island penitentiary is an interesting study. It reveals much about his character and the nature of their relationship. A man who could participate in a grotesque butchery of an innocent woman and her husband and still manifest tender feelings towards the object of his desire. Strange contrasts — a person who could kill so casually, yet while incarcerated write a rough love letter contemplating beauty. (p. 169-70)

Had Walker never met Stearns the likelihood of his murdering to obtain a boat would have been extremely remote. His approach would have been much more direct. There are hundreds of boats in Hawaii unattended; simply select the desired vessel and sail off.

Both sociopathic personalities such as one sees every day in the news seeking immediate gratification — I'm the only one that counts. It's all about "me". Hollywood, politics, and the world of finance, is full of these types. It is estimated that 1 out of every 100 people manifest sociopathic behavior, fortunately while exploitive, few sociopaths are violent.

So long as Stearns kept her silence and did not publicly condemn Walker, he would not turn on her, he would keep his silence. She was well aware of this unspoken pact and was careful not to transgress its strictures.

Throughout ATSWT the reader is constantly reassured Stearns would never suggest Walker was a killer or to blame him in any manner for the death of the Grahams. Stearns' pseudo fidelity buys Walker's silence. It is not necessary for her to shift blame, she knows Bugliosi will do the job for her. With Bugliosi doing her "dirty work" she appears to remain true to her code all the while her representative is trashing Walker the chump.

There is another over-riding interest Walker had in not turning on Stearns and securing his freedom. No father, who cares for his children, wants to go down in history as a blood-thirsty murderer. Although condemned by the jury as a killer, he asserted to his dying day he did not murder the Grahams. He asserts he was a man wrongly convicted. If he testified against Stearns to buy his freedom he would have to tell the truth about the murders and what happened on Palmyra. He could no longer play the role of the wrongly accused. His actions would be known to the world for all to see and judge. He feared this judgment, not so much from the public, but from his daughter. What man would want his child to know he acted in such a cruel and sadistic manner? When Walker got involved with Stearns he was over his head. Walker had a sense of guilt and shame. He did not sleep the untroubled sleep of the true sociopath. Later in life confined to prison he spent much of his time writing a long rambling book about Palmyra in an effort to re-write history and absolve himself of his crimes and the role he played in the grisly murders of the Grahams.

THE PRINCE OF TIDES

Tidal flow, the time of ebb and flood tide, the height of high-high tide and low-high tide became critical issues during trial. Enoki did not trouble to research tidal data. On the other hand Bugliosi spent considerable time researching tidal flow on the alleged day of the Graham's disappearance and the purported day of the discovery of the Zodiac.   Once he had established the height and time of the tides, not understanding the damning nature of the implications, he offered to include this information in trial by way of stipulation. Suspecting a trick, Enoki foolishly refused to agree to the proposal. Bugliosi, failing to comprehend   the tidal data impeached the testimony of Stearns, requested King take judicial notice of the phenomena.   Protecting Stearns, Judge King refused Bugliosi's request and in so doing deprived the jury access to information proving Stearns was lying about the supposed discovery of the Zodiac dinghy on Cooper Island thus exposing her as a liar and murderess.

Slackwater and the Rule of Twelfths

Bugliosi discovered there were four tides in any twenty-four hour period at Palmyra Island. There was a high-high tide on Friday, August 30, 1974, at 4:26 p.m. just 14 minutes before 4:40 p.m. The high-high tide had a height of 2.6 feet above the reference line. (An imaginary line of the mean lower-low tide.)

He also discovered there was a low-high tide the following morning, August 31, 1974 at 5:35 a.m. (Approximately 12 minutes after the time Stearns alleged she and Walker discovered the overturned dinghy.)   This tide had a height of 1.8 feet above the reference line. (pp. 275, 564)

Bugliosi speculated Walker dumped the bodies of Mac and Muff in the lagoon at 4:30 p.m. on August 30, 1974.   At 4:40 p.m. the same afternoon he argued Walker pulled the Zodiac ashore and turned it upside down on the beach on Cooper Island where it was purportedly found the next morning by defendants. (pp. 272, 531)

397

Stearns testified the morning of August 31, 1974 she and Walker discovered Mac's Zodiac overturned about a foot and one half to two feet above the water line on Cooper Island. (p. 273)   (This is the supposed   linear distance the stern of the Zodiac was from the water's edge).   She designated the location of discovery on *Cooper Island* by placing an X on the chart. (p. 531)   She claimed discovery of the Zodiac occurred at 5:23 a.m. approximately 12 minutes *before* the low-high tide reached its zenith at 5:35 a.m.   (This meant the tide would still be rising slowly at the time the   Zodiac was allegedly discovered.) (pp. 275-6)

Concerned about the meaning and danger inherent in the tidal data Bugliosi makes the following comment:

"I knew, of course, that if a tidal record existed somewhere, and if it showed there was a high tide between 4:40 p.m. on August 30 and dawn on August 31, 1974, that would probably mean Jennifer made up the whole story about finding the Zodiac overturned on the beach. And if she had invented this story, she was probably guilty of murdering Mac and Muff."   (p. 273)

Bugliosi, during his study of tidal flow on Palmyra, failed to take into account two commonly known phenomena pertaining to tidal ebb and flood. One of these, slackwater, is a tidal circumstance occurring between tidal changes wherein the movement of the water is suspended and the tide does not flood or ebb.   Normally it has relatively short duration — twenty minutes to an hour, depending on the location and other factors.

Had he understood the manner in which tides ebb and flood he would have known the water height at 4:26 p.m. and 4:40 p.m. on the 30th of August would have been the same.   Because of the phenomenon of slackwater, there was, in effect, a high-high tide at 4:40 p.m. on the 30th.

398

The Rule of Twelfths is another commonly known tidal phenomenon. Tides are said to ebb and flood according to the Rule of Twelfths. Whether ebb or flood, as a rule of thumb, semi-diurnal mixed tides in any six hour period generally ebb or flood in sequence. The first hour is one-twelfth of the range of the tide for that six hour period, the second hour two-twelfths, and the third hour three-twelfths, in a sequence of 1:2:3:3:2:1. Thus in any six hour period of tidal movement, whether flood or ebb, during the first and last hours there is relatively a small rise or lowering of the tide. The second and fifth hours considerable more movement of water, and the third and fourth hours maximum movement. This phenomenon is commonly known to sailors, surfers, beachcombers, scuba divers, and those who have a passing knowledge of the sea.

During summation we find Bugliosi, now the (unofficial) expert witness on tidal flow lecturing the jury.

"As you know, there are two high tides and two low tides every day. However, of the two high tides, one is a high high tide, and the other is a low high tide. Likewise, there is a high low tide and a low low tide. There is only one high high tide every twenty-four hours." (p. 509)

Bugliosi argues prosecution witness John Bryden *"testified that at high tide there would not be any beach in the area where Jennifer testified that she found the dinghy. But there was no attempt to distinguish between high-high tide and low-high tide where the water would not go up as far"* (p. 509)

True, Bryden did not distinguish between high-high tide and low-high tide. He stated *at high tide the location where Stearns says she found the dinghy on Cooper Island, would be under eighteen inches of water. (p. 370)*

399

After considerable time spent studying tides, suspecting the tidal data might torpedo his case, we find Bugliosi in full retreat:

"Because I felt the jury might feel that Stearns and perhaps even I were involved in fabricated defense, I decided against introducing the report into evidence, despite Jennifer's and Len urging that I do. My reasoning was that if the jury concluded that Jennifer's testimony was fabricated, the ball game would be over for all of us. But if there was no evidence one way or another on the issue, I could at least fashion an argument that would render the whole matter inconclusive in the jury's eyes." (p. 276)

(Rather than explain the riddle of the tides and risk jury discovery of the flaws in his argument, Bugliosi admits embarking on a campaign to confuse the jury.)

Failing to understand his case Enoki refused to stipulate to the tidal data and lost a chance to expose the fabrications of Stearns. Inundated with confusing and conflicting commentary the jury was deprived of crucial information demonstrating Stearns was lying about supposed discovery of Mac's Zodiac the morning of August 31, 1974. (pp. 276-7) Moreover, the same tidal information indicated that Walker could not have possibly over-turned the dinghy on Cooper Island at 4:00 p.m. on the 30th because the location would have been under 18 inches of water and the dinghy would have floated away.

During summation Bugliosi rubs it in, scolding Enoki for failing to introduce data relating to the tides on the days in question:

"What evidence did Mr. Enoki offer that between 4:30 P.M. on August 30th, when Jennifer heard the Zodiac, and shortly after dawn, when she found it overturned, that there was a high-high tide? If tides are going to be an issue at this trial, as he is making them, why didn't he secure tidal data for this region of the Pacific and

present it to you? Doesn't the prosecution have the burden of proof?"
(p. 509)

A point well taken.

John Bryden

In 1979, five years after the murder of the Grahams,   John
Bryden   (Bryden) was employed to start a coconut plantation on
Palmyra Island. He brought with him 16 Gilbertese as laborers. He
spent fourteen months on the island finally concluding that it was not
a profitable commercial venture. (pp. 369-70)

He was called by the prosecution as a witness. He *"confirmed
that he was familiar with the lagoon shoreline in the area where
Jennifer claimed she and Buck found the overturned Zodiac."*

On direct Enoki queried;

"How big is the beach in that area?"

Bryden responds;

*" There really isn't much beach. At low tide it's dry. At high
tide it's covered with about eighteen inches of water at the most. The
sandy area is just a little strip along the water's edge at high tide. It
would be about a foot wide."*

Enoki: *"After that foot or so, you would hit the brush line?"*

*"*Bryden: *Well, you would hit the jungle before that in some
spots. The bushes grow out into the water in some places there."* (p.
370)

Bryden's testimony was extremely damaging to Stearns. Her
defense team wisely declined to underscore its importance by
engaging him in cross-examination. Instead, Bugliosi launched a
smoke-screen to confuse the jury arguing in summation:

"John Bryden testified that at high tide there would not be any beach in the area where Jennifer testified she found the dinghy. But there was no attempt to distinguish between high-high tide and low-high tide, where the water would not go up the beach as far." (p. 509)

The foregoing comment calculated to baffle the jury no doubt it hit it's mark. In truth, there was no need to distinguish between the two different tide levels. Bryden stated that at high tide the location where Stearns claimed to have found the dinghy would have been under 18 inches of water. While there was no need for Enoki to distinguish between tides, it was necessary for the jury to be informed that there was a high-high tide at 4:26 p.m. on the afternoon of August 30th, This being so, the beach where Walker allegedly overturned the Zodiac would have been under water and the dinghy would have floated away.

If Enoki had permitted the introduction of Bugliosi's tidal date Bryden's testimony would have destroyed Stearns' narrative regarding her alleged activities of August 30th and 31st. Unfortunately all this went unnoticed by Enoki. He had another opportunity to prevail in this contest, but once again snatched defeat from the jaws of victory in not permitting the jury to be informed of the time of the tidal flow on the 30th and 31st of August 1974, on Palmyra Island.

Bugliosi Sounds Retreat

Weinglass cross-examining former prosecutor William Eggers during the murder trial of Stearns, in an attempt to define the beach where Mac's Zodiac was purportedly discovered the morning of August 31, 1974 queries:

"The beach at Strawn Island — there are parts of it where the land comes close to the water's edge and other places where the land is set back, creating small bays?"

"Yes." Answers Eggers.

"There are parts of that beach that are six and eight feet above the high-water mark?" Weinglass continues.

"There are parts that are dry, yes." Responds Eggers. (p. 348)

As the reader can observe, Eggers did *not* "flatly" contradict Bryden as Bugliosi later argued during summation. Moreover, contrary to Bugliosi's assertion, Weinglass' question is general in nature and not specific. Worse, he is completely confused about the purported location of the Zodiac. Weinglass mistakenly inquires about Strawn Island and not Cooper Island where Stearns eventually claimed to have discover the Zodiac overturned on the beach. Eggers simply agrees with Weinglass observing there were parts of Strawn Island that were dry. (He did *not* state there were parts of Strawn Island that were six to eight feet above the high water mark.) (p. 348, 531)

"I next cited the testimony of our strongest witness on this issue, former Assistant U.S. Attorney William Eggers."

"Mr Eggers was on Palmyra within months of the Grahams' disappearance, and therefore was in a much better position than Bryden to observe the effect of the tides on the area of beach in question on August 30 and 31, 1974."

"By his own admission, " I argued, *'the sand shifts on the beach. And if the sand shifts, the configuration and the dimensions of the beach change.'* I reminded the jury that Eggers had flatly contradicted Bryden, testifying there were parts of the beach that*

were dry some six to eight feet above the high-water-line-leaving
room for the beached Zodiac to have remained out of the water
between 4:30 p.m. on August 30 and dawn on August 31." (pp.
509-10)

Incredibly Bugliosi has the chutzpah to characterize the
testimony of Eggers as that of his *strongest witness* regarding the
issue of the whether or not the Zodiac was overturned in a location
that at the time in question would have been underwater.
Astonishingly, Bugliosi is talking about a feature of *Cooper Island*
while Weinglass and Eggers were talking about a feature of *Strawn
Island.*

The rout continues with Bugliosi in full retreat:

"With the beach in the area in question as irregular as it is,
and without knowing precisely where on this area of the beach
Jennifer saw the dinghy, and without even knowing whether there
was a high high or low high tide during the hours in question, we're
into a never-never land of speculation and conjecture. Nothing more,
nothing less." (p. 510)

Wisely Bugliosi decided not to offer a tide expert of his own.
Had he established during trial as he did in his book, that there was a
high-high tide on the 30th of August at 4:26 p.m., and a low-high
tide at 5:35 a.m, the following morning and that there was less than a
vertical foot of difference between these two tides, he would have
torpedoed Stearns' defense. (p. 564) Both tides inundated the
supposed location wherein Stearns claimed to have found the
overturned Zodiac on the 31st.

There is an interesting footnote to this skirmish. During trial,
Bugliosi made a request of Judge King that he take judicial notice of
the tidal data he had assembled. Normally it is the custom of most
courts to take judicial notice of commonly accepted facts. Certainly,

tidal data comes within this ambit.   However, Judge King refused Bugliosi's request — an action that greatly benefitted Stearns. Again, at a critical juncture, King put his thumb on the scale of justice and interceded on Stearns behalf.

Enoki in failing to establish tidal data pertaining to the dates in question lost an opportunity to destroy the fictional story Stearns had constructed surrounding the events of the 30th and 31st of August. He also failed to notice the specious argument of Bugliosi and did not address the issue in final argument.

JUDGE SAMUEL P. KING

Judge King Has Questions

After Enoki finished his cross examination of Stearns, Judge King, attempting to assist Stearns, dives in:

"I have a couple more. Then you folks can get in on the act. I lost the timing. When Buck said to you on August 30th —" (Vol. 12, pp. 1918.)

Stearns, not allowing King to finish, nervously interrupts:

"Yes."

The court continues:

"When did he first bring up this business about having dinner with —"

Stearns, not waiting until he finishes his question,   again interrupts:

"He came by about 9:00 a.m. and first said that he had been over at Mac's that morning and that he and Mac had played some chess and that Mac had invited us to dinner that evening."

405

"Did he say what time?" , demands the court desiring to know what time the defendants were to show up for dinner that evening.

Stearns responds:

"I'm not absolutely positive at this point whether he told me that we were supposed to go over there at 6:30, then at 9:00 o'clock, but possibly."

(Stearns suggests it was possible during the 9:00 a.m. discussion with Walker that Mac allegedly mentioned the expected time of arrival for the bon voyage dinner.)

Picking up on the implication of Stearns' response, King inquires further:

"If not then, when might he have told you?"

Stearns, wanting to please the court, guesses: *"He could have done it at 1:00 o'clock — maybe at 1:00 o'clock. Maybe then."*

King: *"Or later?"*

Stearns: *"Yeah, I just — ".*

"You don't remember?".

Stearns, fearful of a trap accepts King's lead and backs away claiming loss of memory:

"Sorry, I just can't remember if he actually mentioned 6:30 tonight' at nine o'clock in the morning or not."

Accepting Stearns excuse, changing direction, King continues:

"You didn't find any log on the Sea Wind?"

Getting jumpy, Stearns goes into full weasel mode:

"I don't have — I don't remember at this point either finding one or not finding one. I could have found a log of the Sea Wind, and it probably wouldn't have meant much to me."

406

"You don't recall?" Telegraphs the judge.

"Right." Agrees, Stearns.

"At any rate, you didn't keep a log of the Sea Wind?"

"I did not personally, no."

"Do you know if Buck did?"

"I don't believe Buck did either."

King, again changes his point of inquiry wanting more information about her activities on August 28, 1974:

"I wasn't clear about this alleged event or whether you said it did happen or didn't happen on the 28th. When you went over.....somebody said you came over with a cake or, you might have come over with a cake. Did that happen or didn't it happen?"

Not knowing which direction to turn Stearns ambiguously agrees with what she sees as the court's position and responds to King's question admitting that she did appear at the Sea Wind the night of August 28th with a cake.

"Right. It could have easily happened and I didn't put it in my log. Mac had loaned me a Fanning chart and I could have ...." (Vol. 12, pp.1918-19.)

Under pressure from King, Stearns admits she approached the Sea Wind the evening of August 28, 1974, with a cake as Shoemaker had asserted in his testimony. However, she attempts to distance the presentation of the cake from the bon voyage dinner — it was a gesture of thanks for loaning her the chart of Fanning Island for the purpose of copying it.

(If one were to bake a cake as a token of appreciation for Mac bringing over a chart of Fanning Island the only reasonable time for delivery of the gift would be during the daylight hours. The fact that the appearance of Stearns and Walker occurred during the night a few minutes before eight, is persuasive evidence they were not simply making a spur of the moment social call but were attending a bon voyage dinner party celebrating their supposed departure for Fanning Island the next morning.)

Thumb on the Scale

As much as   court rulings favored the prosecution in the murder trial of Walker wherein King treated defense counsel with sarcasm, disdain, and disrespect in the presence of the jury; in a change-up he favored the defense making many gifts to Stearns such as egregiously denying the jury knowledge of Stearns' conviction for the theft of the Sea Wind.

(The jury probably gleaned there had been a trial of Stearns for theft, but the outcome was obscure. Time and again during her murder trial Stearns was permitted by Judge King to deny stealing the Sea Wind.)

King's ruling blew a large gap in the prosecution's case that was difficult to bridge. Depriving the jury of knowledge of her theft conviction permitted Stearns to pretend she was innocent of this crime.   Had the jury known for certain she was convicted of the crime of theft of the Sea Wind it would follow she was also involved in the murder of the Grahams.   It would be difficult for a jury to believe Stearns benefitted from the death of the Grahams, stole their boat, stole their money, ate their food and was not involved in their murders.

Stearns, practiced in the art of deceit, using her "Little Miss Puffer" routine, completely seduced Judge King. King did not understand the mind of the sociopath and completely bought into her charade of an innocent, star-crossed gal who was just trying to protect her man.   Years before he presided over the theft trial of Walker.   During that trial he decided Walker was the heavy and in 1985 he assisted Enoki in obtaining a conviction of murder against Walker. As much as he vented his spleen on Walker and his attorneys during the murder trial of Walker, during the trial murder of Stearns he vented his feelings on the prosecution leaving Enoki and the jury confused and disoriented.

King's bias on behalf of the defense was a major factor in the jury's finding of not guilty: He took sides and unfairly chastised and humiliated the Pollocks: He prohibited the jury from knowledge of the guilty verdict of Stearns in the boat theft case: He unfairly denied Enoki the right to pursue a felony/murder charge against Stearns, (a classic case of felony/murder if there ever was one) and permitted Bugliosi to ignore the Evidence Code during the examination of Stearns supposed character witnesses.

So open and obvious was Judge King's partiality that half way through Stearns' trial Bugliosi filed an unusual motion to dismiss the jury and place the sole responsibility of deciding the case in the hands of judge. (Vol. 8, p. 1317)   Enoki well aware that he had lost all support from the court, vigorously opposed the motion. King not wanting sole responsibility re finding of guilt, knowing should a guilty verdict come back he could attenuate it by doling out a light sentence to Stearns,   refused to take the bait and denied Bugliosi's motion.

ENOKI SUMMATION

The Uncertain Trumpet

Enoki's summation commences with vague references to the crime of First Degree Murder. If a lawyer quotes the law in argument, as Bugliosi points out, it is best to quote the exact jury instructions he anticipates the court will charge the jury. Nothing causes a jury to focus on the issues like hearing the law that governs the case as it relates to the facts. Moreover, when the court gives a jury instruction previously used in summation by counsel it adds weight to his position. After informing the jury about the law that applies to the case it is incumbent on the trial attorney to explain with specificity exactly how the law applies to the facts. Any lawyer who shirks this responsibility is asking for defeat.

Why not commence argument using a direct quote from the jury instruction the court intends to give at the close of the trial defining murder in the first degree? After all the messing about during trial the charge to the jury is defined in no uncertain terms:

USC, Title 18, part 1, chapter 51,

§ 1111, (a) Murder is the unlawful killing of a human being with malice aforethought. Every murder perpetrated by poison, lying in wait, or any other kind of willful, deliberate, malicious, and premeditated killing; or committed in the perpetration of, or attempt to perpetrate any arson, escape, murder, kidnapping, treason, espionage, sabotage, aggravated sexual abuse or sexual abuse, child abuse, burglary, or robbery; or perpetrated as part of a pattern or practice of assault or torture against a child or children; or perpetrated from a premeditated design unlawfully and maliciously to effect the death of any human being ....is murder in the first degree.

In the opening moments of his summation Enoki argues it was Walker who killed Muff suggesting Stearns planned and assisted in the murder. Having taken this position, he fails to follow it up by describing the role each of the accused played. (p. 468)

Enoki attempts to educate the jurors on the law, but fails to quote the law of accomplices delivered by the court at the close of the case and then fails to apply the law to the facts.

The daily transcript of trial testimony permits the jury to have the testimony read back during deliberations should questions arise. When citing crucial testimony Enoki could have been more effective if he quoted the exact words of the witness with reference to the trial transcript rather than generalizing about their testimony.

Enoki weakens his prosecution by suggesting different theories concerning Stearns role in the killing of Muff. He argues Stearns might have been directly involved in the murder, but if the jury did not agree, then perhaps she might be considered an accomplice. This is an ineffective tactic. It is best for a lawyer to go with his strongest suit rather then split the jurors attention by presenting several possibilities. It creates the appearance that Enoki did not believe in his own prosecution. (p. 468)

Enoki continues to undermine his position by arguing Stearns must be guilty because there was no one else present but herself and Walker at the time of the murders. He follows by suggesting she is guilty because she associated with Walker who was a wanted and known criminal which she helped avoid capture. Both weak arguments that diminished the prosecution's case. (pp. 468-9)

It is difficult to know if Enoki's address to the jury was as fractured as it appears to be in Bugliosi's presentation. As presented in the book he wanders about trying one argument after another without settling on one vision of Stearns role in the killing of the Grahams. In reviewing the murder trial transcript one has the same impression.

He argues Stearns was attracted to the violent side of Walker and was adventurous. True she was attracted to violent men with

411

criminal backgrounds but does this equate to murder? If that is the conclusion he wants the jury to draw, then he should state Stearns is a murderess because she is attracted to violent men with criminal backgrounds and seeks them out to enable her to participate vicariously in the violence they perpetrate. Admittedly it is not a convincing argument, but it carries more persuasive weight than not making the argument and somehow hoping the jury will pick up on the issue and pursue it themselves. (p. 469)

It is irritating to note what Bugliosi terms Enoki's "ellipsistic" approach to argument. He omits final conclusions hoping the jury will arrive at a guilty verdict by reference to the context. It is a weak persuasive tool and does little but confuse the jury.

He points out Walker was attracted to Stearns who could turn him in at any time, yet she went off with him to Palmyra. Apparently, he wants the jury to infer that because Stearns was willing to accept defendant's companionship and does not turn him in she is guilty of murder. (p. 469)

He ill defines the relationship between defendants and the Grahams. While there can be little doubt there was deep seated hatred and resentment on the part of the defendants towards the Grahams, it is also easy to comprehend the attitudes the Grahams had towards defendants.

Muff writes about her attitude toward defendants in letters home. (p.96) Mac does as well. Muff is fearful of the defendants, Mac is wary. (p. 103) There are numerous passages throughout ATSWT characterizing the Graham's attitude toward defendants. (p. 118) It is safe to say by the date of the execution of the Grahams the morning of August 29th, 1974 defendants hated both the Grahams. This hatred fueled the torture and dismemberment of Muff at the hands of Stearns and Walker.

After denying the existence of the bon voyage dinner invitation and attendance by defendants throughout the trial, in summation Enoki quixotically argues defendants did attend the bon voyage dinner and implies it was during the dinner the Grahams were murdered. (pp. 470-1)

Several times during final argument he comes close to stating the Grahams were murdered the evening of August 28th, aboard the Sea Wind. However, not once does he actually state this is his interpretation of the evidence. It is as if he does not know what to make of the evidence but hopes the jury will somehow muddle through and figure it out. (pp. 485-6)

Ambuscade

George Gordon met Stearns in a bar one night shortly *after* her theft trial in 1975. The meeting was discovered by the FBI shortly before the trial of Stearns when Gordon informed them he spent an evening talking with Stearns. According to Gordon during this conversation she made several damning statements and among other things told Gordon:

"Stearns was afraid the Iola wouldn't make it away from Palmyra and the craft would sink; The two couples did not get along well; and if Buck Walker spilled his guts, she would be in a lot of trouble." (pp. 446-7)

Stearns' defense received a boost when the court sided with Bugliosi prohibiting the testimony of George Gordon. Admittedly, various jurisdictions, including the federal bench, discourage what is termed "trial by ambush" wherein one side "sandbags" the other by introducing a surprise witness at the eleventh hour. Using an unannounced witness allows advantage because of the element of

413

surprise which catches the opposing party off guard and unprepared. However, testimony from such a witness is, at times, permitted after the party on whom the surprise is launched has an opportunity, out of the presence of the jury, to examine the witness and prepare a response.

The gravity of the harm varies, depending if the witness is called as part of the case in chief or the rebuttal, as it was in this instance. The prosecution is at a disadvantage in that, until Stearns takes the stand, it does not know what her testimony might encompass. Nor, for that matter do they know whether or not the defendant will take the stand and testify on her own behalf.

The prosecution has a duty to declare itself to the defense and supply the defense with documents and a list of witnesses it intends to call. The defense is not mandated to reveal it's defensive position with the precision and clarity of the prosecution. The prosecution is mandated to reveal all pertinent documents to the defense — the police investigation, experts opinions, statements of witnesses and etc.

After the defendant presents his defense the prosecution is entitled to rebut the testimony offered by the defendant and call other witnesses. The failure of the prosecution to list Gordon as a witness was not grievous. He was a person known personally to Stearns. She could have advised Bugliosi of this fact and preparation made for his potential damaging testimony, but she did do so claiming to have forgotten the incident.

Trial work is a bit of a cat and mouse game. The prosecution had a duty to show its hand, but there is no corresponding duty for the defendant. Thus we find Bugliosi discovering Benson's October 30th interview of Pollock and making the decision to keep it quiet not calling it to Enoki's attention. In the case of Gordon it would have been a simple matter for the court to grant a recess and hear Gordon's proposed testimony out of the presence of the jury. Having heard the testimony, Stearns could have been granted extra time if she needed to prepare. Truth is, there was little preparation needed, a half-hour discussion with her attorney would have sufficed. Gordon is not offering "expert testimony" in need of rebuttal from another expert. He was a bystander who by chance possessed relevant evidence which the jury was entitled to hear. Rebuttal would come from Stearns if there was any.

Why Enoki failed to list Gordon as a witness is not known. The reader is informed the conversation occurred 1975. There is some confusion as to when the prosecution discovered Gordon. Weinglass alleges that Gordon was found in December of 1985, and his statement was taken on January 6, 1986, a month before commencement of Stearns' trial. (p. 446)

(Since Stearns had met Gordon *after* her theft trial her remarks to Gordon did not pertain to the theft of the Sea Wind, but to the disappearance of the Grahams as Bugliosi notes.) (p. 446)

Had Stearns been honest with her counsel she could have alerted him to the possibility of Gordon's appearance. However, in her usual deceptive and secretive approach to the facts, she did not inform Bugliosi. Not successful in hiding the existence of Gordon, her devious behavior in failing to inform Bugliosi about Gordon succeeded in eliminating relevant testimony when the court decreed Enoki could not call Gordon as a witness. (pp. 446-7)

Leaving Well Enough Alone

Enoki cross-examining Stearns:

415

"Now, you do admit — you testified about telling a previous jury, at your...at a theft trial where you were the defendant — that the Iola ran aground in the channel. Is that correct?"

"Yes."

"And you said it while you were on the witness stand like you are today. Is that correct?"

"Yes."

"And that means you took the oath before you testified?"

"Yes."

"So, when you told the jury while towing the Iola out of the channel it had hung up on the rocks, you knew you were lying and committed perjury?"

"Yes."

Enoki has scored a point with Stearns admitting she committed perjury, he also cleverly referenced Stearns' theft trial. He should have stopped having made it perfectly clear Stearns, by her own admission, is a liar and perjurer. Unfortunately he stumbles on in his game of "soft-ball" and gives Stearns a way out:

"Now as I understand your testimony, the reason you did this was because Mr. Walker told you on Palmyra not to tell the truth. Is that correct?" (Another one of Enoki's pseudo questions with little purpose, wherein he suggests the answer thus permitting his quarry to escape.)

"Yes, he said that I should say the Iola had gone aground, and that's why we had to go back and get the Sea Wind."

"Yet, when you got to Hawaii, Mr. Walker told people he had won the Sea Wind in a chess game. Is that right?" Inquires Enoki.

"Yes", responds Stearns.

"Isn't that totally inconsistent with even the rehearsed version of what happened?" Queries, Enoki.

Granted Stearns change in testimony is inconsistent with her earlier rehearsed statement to Shishido. So what? Enoki's question is ambiguous and argumentative and pointless. Stearns seeing an opening capitalizes:

"No", Jennifer said, "he was only talking about if the authorities asked us."

Stearns, allegedly is instructed by Walker to tell others the Iola ran aground. Later in Hawaii, Walker told others he won the Sea Wind in a chess game. Enoki wants her opinion as to whether or not the lie about the Iola running aground is inconsistent with the lie about winning the Sea Wind in a chess game. What is the point of the question? What does the lie about the Iola running aground in the channel have to do with Walker's lie about how he obtained the Sea Wind? They are both lies. If Enoki desires to argue this proposition to the jury in final argument so be it, he does not need Stearns' consent to do so.

The two stories about acquiring the Sea Wind are inconsistent. Enoki scores a point when Stearns admits she is a perjurer. He then blows his small victory with a non-relevant question that has little purpose other than to distract the jury from the impact of her admission to perjury.

With a needless opaque question by Enoki followed by an equally opaque answer by Stearns, the water is muddied and the original impact of her admission of perjury is blunted and lost. (pp. 450-1)

Ignorance Prevails

Enoki attempted to cross examine Stearns re navigation:

"So, you're saying it didn't matter to your method of navigation....the speed of the current?"

"That's correct." (A completely incorrect statement, current if present, is always a concern to a skipper. Current can impede or accelerate progress; if lateral it can throw the vessel off course.)

Enoki lurches onward:

"Doesn't there come a time when the current is so strong that you are unable to make progress tacking? "

Stearns replies; *"I never experienced that."*

This statement is probably true — her sailing experience is limited to the single voyage to Palmyra from Hawaii and back. She later admits to the jury the presence of a current would effect the time it took to get to Fanning. (p. 449)

Given the ignorance of both sides about sailing and the sea one would expect the prosecution to call expert witnesses who could opine on sailing techniques and difficulties one would expect to encounter in sailing to Fanning Island from Palmyra. Any number of experts were available; the Pollocks, Curt Shoemaker, Jack Wheeler and etc. Various sailors gave their opinions pertaining to questions about sailing and the sea during trial, but none were designated as "experts" by the prosecution. The recognition of their expertise would have given their testimony greater weight.

Missing was a navigation expert who could explain to the jury the complexities of blue water navigation by use of a sextant. Stearns should have been put to the test and her lying and navigation insufficiencies exposed when she was on the stand testifying.

For a neophyte such as Stearns to proclaim with certainty she is 120 miles way from Palmyra employing a $25.00 plastic sextant, a cheap am/fm radio and little else after a voyage of nearly a thousand miles, is patently absurd. Before the days of the GPS, navigation was a difficult, black art. A properly qualified navigator could easily have exposed Stearns' lies. Stearns presenting herself as a competent navigator is one the great hoaxes of the trial.

A shipwright's testimony would have illuminated the problems and harm caused to the Iola when she sank was salvaged and later sat on the hard exposed to tropical rain and heat for two years. He could have advised the prosecution about the repairs made to the Sea Wind after the plank in her hull penetrated by bullets from Muff's derringer was partially or completely replaced.

It would have been extremely helpful to call a designated expert who could explain to the jury the various techniques of sailing. The meaning of such words and concepts such as leeway, windward, tacking, close hauled, reaching, broad reaching, beam reach, jibs, genoa, mainsails, out haul, down haul, main, jib, genoa sheet, hull speed, speed over ground, line of position, longitude, latitude, prime meridians, center of effort, center of lateral resistance, Greenwich Mean Time, Greenwich Hour Angle, and a hundred other sailing terms and their application to the facts of the case.

It is strange a matter as serious as a double homicide where the underlying facts are intimately intertwined with sailing an old rotted wooden boat with neither side relying upon expert witnesses possessing knowledge in these areas. Both lawyers were ignorant of the skill and knowledge necessary to safely sail and navigate the South Pacific. As a result, the jury is forced to rely upon Stearns, a liar and sailing ignoramus, with no knowledge of navigation, the oceans, or wooden boat construction as their expert.

This tactic worked well for the defense as there was no one to properly impeach Stearns, a perjurious neophyte who often testified unchallenged as an expert. At the same time it reflected poorly on the prosecution which was forced, due to lack of knowledge, to accept many of the absurdities pertaining to sailing and the sea advanced by Stearns.

Inexperience

Enoki exposes his cross-examination ineptitude in the following dialogue. Cross-examining Stearns he elicits information the witness has already furnished on direct examination and in so doing undermines his prosecution:

"Ms. Jenkins.... as I understand it, you deny stealing the Sea Wind after the disappearance of the Grahams?" (A point she must have made a dozen times throughout the trial, so why ask it? Why support Stearns' fabricated position?)

Predictably, Stearns replies:

"I never planned to steal the boat," she answered *"and I had no intention of keeping her."*

Duh! Another blow is landed to the mid-section of Enoki's case. What did he expect the answer would be? *"Oh, yes, now that you mention it, I did intend to steal the Sea Wind, and I had no intent to ever return her.* (p. 442)

Not satisfied with getting his nose bloodied, he follows up leading with his chin, as he fumbles on:

"Okay. At the prior theft proceedings that Mr. Bugliosi asked you about, you steadfastly denied to that jury the stealing of the Sea Wind. Is that correct?"

(By asking this question, Enoki underlines and reinforces Stearns' testimony that, she did not *"steal"* the Sea Wind, and worse, she is "steadfast" in her denial.)

Telegraphed the expected answer, Stearns agrees:

"Yes."

Now the jury knows she was *"steadfast "* in her denial of guilt at her earlier theft trial, and by order of the court, cannot informed that she was convicted of theft.

Bugliosi observes Enoki's cross-examination ineptitude:

"Enoki was already struggling with a subject I had covered matter-of-factly during my questioning."

Aimless repetition of points already made in previous questioning serve little purpose other than to buttress the opposing case. It is also the mark of a rank amateur.

An experienced trial lawyer could easily have had Stearns on the stand for at least five days, perhaps more, depending on her skill in dodging detailed questions directed at areas pertaining to guilt. An effective trial lawyer does not through his questioning reinforce evidence that weighs against his client or cause. There should be a purpose in asking every question on cross-examination, just as there must be a purpose for asking every question on direct. There is nothing wrong with going over prior testimony where it buttresses one's position or the examiner is setting the witness up for impeachment, but aimless regurgitation of testimony is amateurish and serves no purpose.

Cross-examining counsel should, in keeping with his game plan inquire where clarification is necessary or weakness can be exposed. Not every witness must be cross-examined. If there is purpose, by all means proceed, but if there is nothing to be gained, it

421

is better to pass on cross examination.   There can be no profit in building a case against himself as Enoki stumbles blindly about the courtroom.

Enoki's Conundrum

(Enoki had several opportunities to delineate Stearns' role in the planning and murder of the Grahams.   During final argument he erroneously speculates there may have been an exterior force that caused a hole in the hull of the Sea Wind and, if that force was a bullet, there should have been some indication of damage *within* the interior of the boat.)

Enoki puzzles:

"How is it that there could be a bullet hole in the hull of the Sea Wind, from a bullet fired outside the boat, but no corresponding damage inside the vessel?" (Vol. 14, pp. 2276-7)

He errs in assuming the only approach to the issue is that the hole was caused by an external force moving from the exterior into the interior of the vessel.   His erroneous assumption is based on the testimony of Stearns who alleged the hole was created by the intrusion of the bill of a swordfish.

Enoki muses about the problem that there was no damage from the swordfish intrusion inside the boat:

"....relevance to this case that (the bullet) had no entry — no entry on the inside of the cabin?   I mean this hole was from the outside of the hull — by her own testimony through the hull and into the bilge area. Not into the interior of the boat."

Ignoring the overwhelming weight of evidence, Enoki specifically rejects the idea that the hole in the hull was caused by the discharge of Muff's derringer as the bullet exited the hull.

"I'm not arguing that this was a bullet hole."   (Vol. 14,   p. 2276)

Enoki thought the hole, if it existed, was caused by a force penetrating the hull from the outside. He expected to find   some indicia of damage within the interior of the vessel.

We find this exchange between Stearns and Enoki:

"Okay. Now the swordfish struck the boat at some area below that floor."   (Enoki, referring to the cabin sole.)

Stearns, corrects:

"No. No.   The swordfish struck the boat — I don't believe it was below the floor.   It was between the floorboard and just above, to some degree.   I'm almost positive."

(Stearns is telling Enoki that the bullet holes were above the floorboards, yet below the waterline.)

Attempting to alleviate Enoki's confusion about the intrusion of the supposed swordfish, Stearns volunteers information inadvertently describing Walker's actions as he plugged the bullet holes in the hull:

"Buck had to pull off — there was some type of covering to the wood, (on the hull of the boat) like — wall covering, but I think it was — rug — I 'm not exactly — I don't exactly remember what was covering it."

(Stearns testifies there was something covering the interior hull prohibiting Walker immediate access to the holes caused by the bullets from Muff's derringer.)

"But he had to pull out those planks, and some kind of insulate, to get to the swordfish bill."

423

"We had heard water running, and he started...pulling pieces of wood out and looking for it. And it was under table there. Not below what you would consider the floor."

(It is common in wooden sailboats where the cabin sole (floor) meets the frames, to have the exposed frames covered with a thin veneer of plywood, This prevents debris from the floor slipping down into the bilge.)

Enoki, confused by the concept the bullet holes were above the floorboards, yet below the waterline, fails to understand what Stearns said about the location and worse, does not recognize Stearns is actually describing Walker's actions on the morning of August 29, 1974 as he attempted to gain access to the location where the bullets from Muff's derringer penetrated the hull on exiting. Tearing away the superficial barriers, described by Stearns, permitted him to plug the holes and stop the water. (It also removed any interior evidence of the path of the bullets as they exited the hull of the Sea Wind.)

Enoki plods along:

"Okay. And just so I get it straight. Obviously the bill was not sticking right into the room where you guys — where you people were —"

(Enoki could not be more wrong — if one were to believe Stearns, the bill of the swordfish was protruding directly into the cabin because it was above the floorboards — it would have plainly been visible in the galley area.)

Stearns after telling him she was *positive* the hole was located below the waterline, but *above* the floorboards , where it would easily observable, seeing no advantage in explaining further, surrenders in agreement.

"No."

424

Enoki finishes his question/comment: "— *eating or whatever?"*

Stearns explains:

"No. Buck had to pull off whatever this decorative paneling was so that you didn't actually see the ribs of the boat, and the studs, or whatever they call that."

Here we find Stearns once again telling Enoki that Walker had to rip off the decorative panelling covering the frames to allow access to the bullet holes in the hull.

Stearns claims:

"We heard water running, and he started...pulling pieces of wood out and looking for it. (The location where the bullet ripped through the wooden hull.) *And it was under the table there. Not below the what you consider the*

floor. More on the side of the boat, but under the waterline."   (Vol. 11, p. 1696)

Her testimony describing Walker's actions after he had subdued Muff explains why there were no obvious indications where the bullets penetrated the hull — Walker tore out the paneling and discarded it.   Later in the yard on dry dock, a shipwright placed another piece of panelling over the new section of the hull plank.

His confusion on this issue is apparent as Enoki argues to the jury:

"But the reason the prosecution is interested in disputing the swordfish version of what happened here is that it's very skeptical that it conveniently, the swordfish that is, explains the repainting that Ms. Stearns claims was never to disguise the boat. A lie, by the way; disproven by other evidence. That she told — she told the first jury in the theft trial that the boat needed repainting. You recall Mr. and

425

Mrs. Wollen did not notice anything about the boat needing repainting."

"So I submit to you that it is a very convenient thing to have happen. Because it explains why they would dry dock the boat and repaint it. And, of course you've got to remember that back in 1975 we're talking about theft. That's what the charge was then."

Enoki rejected the idea there was a hole in the Sea Wind caused by any force. He foolishly believes the swordfish story was contrived by Stearns to cover the defendants attempt to disguise the Sea Wind by repainting her.

Clueless in San Francisco

Reviewing the transcripts of the murder trial of Stearns one is constantly shocked at Enoki's lack of insight into the events on Palmyra Island the summer of 1974. A sterling example of his state of confusion is found in his forlorn final argument where he addresses the issue of the hole in the hull of the Sea Wind. We can see the internal working of his thought process as he attempts to comprehend Stearns' testimony about the hole in the hull supposedly caused by a swordfish.

He has everything backwards speculating that the force creating the hole in the hull of the Sea Wind came from outside of the boat and not the errant discharge of Muff's derringer as she fought for her life in the cabin of the Sea Wind. At one point he argues the hole never existed and was a figment of Stearns' imagination. He specifically rejects the obvious explanation that it was created by the discharge of the derringer as Muff struggled for her life with Stearns and Walker. The relevant factor in his mind was that if the hole existed from the (external) discharge of Muff's pistol there would be internal damage caused by the bullets once they penetrated the hull and entered the vessel.

His confusion is showcased as he argues:

"....relevance to this case that had no entry — no entry on the inside of the cabin? "

(He posits there was no evidence of destruction caused by the bullets after the penetrated the hull and entered the cabin of the Saw Wind.)

I mean this hole was from the outside of the hull — by her own testimony through the hull and into the bilge area.

(Enoki believes and argues that the hole was caused by a force from the outside penetrating the hull, indicating he has bought into Stearns swordfish routine.)

Getting the facts backwards he blunders on:

"I'm not arguing that this was a bullet hole."

He specifically rejects the idea the hole was caused by the discharge of Muff's derringer and attempts to explain his reasoning:

"But the reason the prosecution is interested in disputing the swordfish version of what happened here is that it's very skeptical that it conveniently, the swordfish that is, explains the repainting M. Stearns claims was never to disguise the boat. A lie by the way; disproven by other evidence. That she told
— she told the first jury in the theft trial that the boat needed repainting. You recall Mr. and Mrs. Wollen did not notice anything about the boat needing repainting."

More befuddlement on the part of Enoki's over-burdened brain is demonstrated as he argues the purpose of repainting the Sea Wind was to disguise her, which it was to a limited degree. (In his mind the hole in the hull of the Sea Wind did not exist; it was a figment of Stearns' mind, created to furnish an excuse for the repainting of the Sea Wind. A repainting that was not necessary in the opinion of the Wollen.)

Enoki continues:

"So, I submit to you that it is a very convenient thing to have happen. Because it explains why they would dry dock the boat and repaint it. And, of course, you've got to remember that back in 1975 we're talking about theft. That's what the charge was back then. It's a very conveniently placed hole; it's below the water line, far enough so that it would cause a leak, meaning they would have to have — repaired it. But it was close enough to the waterline so that Mr. Walker could reach it with his hands down to fix it, but it wasn't far enough so that his head would be underwater."

"Well, maybe — maybe it was that way. Very convenient, I leave you to decide the credibility of that description of Mr. Walker dangling by is feet, the boat pitching in deep seas, for twenty minutes, fixing that hole."

With arguments such as the above it is no wonder the jury threw in the towel and surrendered. (Vol. 14, pp. 2276-7.)

Too Late — Too Little

During final argument Enoki reverses himself arguing defendants appeared at the Sea Wind the evening of August 28th for a bon voyage dinner as he discusses the implications of the "cake/ truce" incident. In so doing he implies during the evening of the 28th of August 1974 the Grahams were murdered. This is the same ground he had relinquished earlier in the trial when he consented to the Benson Stipulation. It was too late to trot out this argument; the

Benson Stipulation had already decimated the testimony of his witnesses. (pp. 470-1)

Enoki completely misses the major points in Mac's final conversation with Shoemaker and becomes embroiled in Bugliosi's "cake-truce incident" diversion. (p. 470) He fails to glean from Mac's final conversation with Shoemaker that Mac believed the departure date of the Iola for Fanning Island the next day; Thursday, the 29th of August. Or, that the approach of the defendants to the Sea Wind the evening of the 28th signaled the commencement of the bon voyage dinner the Grahams were giving for defendants. The Grahams were completely taken in by Stearns' assurances the Iola would be departing the next morning. Mac was happy because Muff would be relieved by their absence and he would have possession of his near new portable generator.

Bugliosi makes an interesting comment exposing his fears and the fragile nature of his defense.

"Enoki.....had just told the jury he believed that Mac and Muff Graham had been murdered on August 28th, 1974. If this was true, then inferentially my client was a murderer." (p. 471)

In other words if Enoki could demonstrate Stearns was lying about the date the Grahams disappeared, Bugliosi concedes she was involved directly in the murder of the Grahams. This is a logical inference, unfortunately Enoki was ill prepared and had not read the transcript of the hearing wherein Stearns admitted she was *"stranded"*. Moreover, he had not read Benson's article in the October 30, 1974 Honolulu Advertiser wherein Pollock speaks of Shoemaker's report of the bon voyage dinner and Mac's expectation the Iola was sailing for Fanning the next day. , August 29th. (p. 397) He also must have been snoozing when Bugliosi was cross-examining Shoemaker concerning his testimony given at the theft trial of Stearns in June of 1975 which clearly impeaches Stearns murder trial testimony.

Enoki flirts with the truth in discussing the cake/truce incident. He calls the cake a *"truce offering"* and in a sense he is correct. He properly equates it to a Trojan Horse in that it is a bribe to cause the Grahams to lower their guard, thus facilitating their murder. (p. 471)

Mea Culpa
(My Fault)

No words from Enoki more clearly demonstrate the mismatch between attorneys than the manner he opened his rebuttal argument after Bugliosi finished his summation.

Enoki apologizes to the jury for his lack of preparation:

"I'm going to apologize in advance. Obviously, I didn't know everything that Mr. Bugliosi was going to argue. As a result of that I obviously have not been able to prepare a rebuttal in some logical format." (p. 537)

(Never, in my years of trial work and countless criminal trials have I ever heard a prosecutor, or any other trial lawyer, commence his rebuttal argument stating he was not prepared to perform his duties!) Enoki should have been taking notes as Bugliosi spoke, preparing to answer the important issues and at the same time allowing lesser issues to fall by the wayside. If the jury had doubts about Enoki's argument and presentation nothing could have been more damaging than his admission he was not prepared to argue his case.)

BUGLIOSI -- SUMMATION

Bugliosi posits: *"summation is the most important part of the trial for the lawyer".* (p. 477)   The key to a successful defense or prosecution is found in the summation of the attorneys. Summation gives the skilled trial lawyer the stage in which to enact the drama of the case and apply the facts to the law. It is odd how all the clues can be on full display before a jury and yet, it is unable to interpret the evidence before their eyes.

The experienced   trial lawyer sets traps during the trial waiting for final argument and then sprung on the unwitting opposition when no further excuses or spin can be presented. With the opportunity to present further evidence prohibited, any chance for rebuttal or sneaking out the back door is foreclosed — no further explanation is allowed.

Bugliosi Suborns Perjury

Bugliosi's pushing the ethics envelope is most apparent in his manufacturing the Benson Stipulation.   It was a daring piece of tomfoolery inducing Enoki to enter into a stipulation based upon an admittedly non-existent conversation between reporter Benson and Stearns, wherein she purportedly uttered certain statements supporting her trial testimony shortly after her arrest for theft of the Sea Wind.

However, scoring a major victory by inducing Enoki to enter into the Benson Stipulation is not enough for Bugliosi. He attempts to back up his coup and underline it with testimony from Stearns about her non-existent conversation with Benson, and in so doing suborns perjury. (pp. 396-8)

Bugliosi: *"Stephanie while at the Halawa jail...you were interviewed over the phone by Bruce Benson; is that correct? A reporter from the Honolulu Advertiser?"*

Stearns: *"Yes."*

"And why did you grant the interview?"

Stearns replies: *"He said he wanted to talk to me. So I talked to him."*

"Did anyone else seek to interview you?"

"No."

"When you spoke to Mr. Benson, did you tell him the same untruth you told Shishido about the Iola going aground on the reef?"

Stearns: *"Yes."*

Bugliosi follows the above question by asking a leading question about an aspect of Benson's interview that he admits never occurred.

"But you also told him that the dinghy was found...on the beach about a half a mile west of the Sea Wind; is the correct?"

(Although the Benson Stipulation contains this assertion both Bugliosi and Enoki admit this subject was never mentioned by Stearns to Benson during his jailhouse phone conversation with her.)

Stearns commits perjury at the behest of Bugliosi when she dutifully replies: *"Yes."*

Bugliosi continues seeking another perjured statement from Stearns by use of a leading question:

"And you also told him that you had assumed that the dinghy had flipped over near Paradise Island and floated to where you found it." (Vol. 11, pages 1725-6, transcript from the murder trial of Stearns)

Finally, our somnambulant prosecutor discovering he has been hoodwinked, wakes up and engages his foe:

Enoki: *"Well, your honor, I'm going to object to — "*

Not allowing Enoki to finish his objection Bugliosi attempting to justify his questioning of Stearns interrupts:

" Well, there's already a stipulation on it."

(One can infer that Bugliosi thinks it is permissible for Stearns to perjure herself by testifying to a non-existent conversation because there was a stipulation that incorporated her fictitious testimony already before the jury.)

Judge King apparently unaware that there was no factual justification for the stipulation jumps in siding with Bugliosi — unbelievably he rebukes Enoki:

"I thought there was a stipulation on that."

Enoki does not inform the court that the Benson Stipulation is a hoax, nor does he argue that Bugliosi is asking Stearns to lie.

Enoki, hesitant and confused:

"Well, there is...but I mean -- "

Bugliosi knowing he has exceeded the law by suborning perjury starts to worry and throws in the towel:

"Okay."

King, presumably not privy to the facts underlying the Benson Stipulation, picks up on Enoki's hesitancy and the possibility that Stearns has once again engaged in perjury at the behest of Bugliosi, begins to wonder: *Well.....*

Bugliosi continues: *"How long were—"*, knowing he has crossed the line and having time to reflect withdraws from this line of questioning: *"I'll withdraw the question."* (Vol. 11, p. 1726)

433

(Having won the skirmish, Enoki fails to move the court to strike the questions and answers.)

Bugliosi Erroneously Waives Hearsay Objection

Eager to ensnare Shoemaker Bugliosi was confident, so much so, that he waived the *"usual hearsay"* objections to Shoemaker's prior testimony from Stearns' theft trial of June 1975.

Bugliosi writes:

"I knew Schroeder would elicit basically the same testimony Shoemaker had given at the Walker trial: the conversation between himself and Mac on the 28th, including the suggestive stories of the cake and truce. Technically, his line of questions would be calling for hearsay."

"Even so, I planned to waive all hearsay objections......" (p. 350)

Unknowingly, Bugliosi makes a colossal error and introduces the final missing piece of the puzzle. He foolishly reads into evidence the following colloquy between Shoemaker and prosecutor William Eggers from the June
1975 theft trial transcript of Stearns and in so doing, exposes his client as a liar and murderess.

Bugliosi:

"Mr. Shoemaker, on June 25th 1975, you testified at a theft trial in Honolulu. The clerk will hand you a photostatic copy of your testimony at the proceeding. At that trial, to these questions did you give the following answers?"

With this introduction Bugliosi reads from the transcript wherein Eggers examined Shoemaker on direct-examination:

"Question: What was the nature of that last radio contact with Mac Graham on August 28th?"

"Answer: Like all the other contacts. He (Mac) related his experiences on the island. What he was doing, what he found. We talked about what fish were poisonous. I was trying to help him out as much as I could. Also, there were other boats on the island, I was relaying messages from some of these other boats to their parents, I was handling, in other words, third-party traffic."

Following the above testimony from Shoemaker, Eggers repeats his non-specific, general question as Bugliosi reads on:

"Question: What was the nature of your conversation with Mac Graham? What was the nature of that communication with you?"

"Answer: Well, he had spoken about this prior to this. I think one of the dogs of the other two people on the island had attacked his wife. So there seemed to be a problem. It was a boat that had gone down there that was —according to him he said it was unseaworthy and was leaking badly, and the people on the boat were having a hard time, apparently, running out of food, and these were the ones with the dogs. There were several dogs, but I think there was only one that was causing trouble."

"Question: That conversation was on the 28th of August?"

"Answer: That was on the 28th, the last time I heard from them."

"Question: Did you have another contact with them after that?"

"Answer: <u>No. That was the last time I heard from him and he said that the other boat was leaving the next day.</u>" (pp. 352-3)

Thanks to Bugliosi the prosecutorial puzzle is complete! During his final conversation of August 28, 1974, Mac told Shoemaker the Iola was *"leaving the next day"*. The next day was Thursday, the 29th of August 1974. Mac's statement to Shoemaker indicates he thought the defendants were leaving for Fanning Island, Thursday, August 29th, and not Saturday, August 31st, as Stearns alleged during her murder trial. Significantly, Shoemaker testified to this conversation with Mac during the theft trial of Stearns in 1975, less than a year after the murder of the Grahams and eleven years before Stearns trial for murder.

Bugliosi totally engrossed stalking Shoemaker, fails to comprehend the import of Shoemaker's testimony. Nor did Shoemaker have the slightest notion of it's implications. So too, Enoki did not understand the meaning of Mac's last conversation with Shoemaker. And, as one might expect, all this flew over the heads of our somnambulant jurors in the thrall of "Little Miss Puffer".

Shoemaker's testimony from Stearns 1975 theft trial is further supported by his discussion with Pollock, reported by Benson in the Honolulu Advertiser, October 30, 1974:

".......Shoemaker was told during their last radio transmission from the Grahams that they had invited Allen and Jenkins to dinner, presumably as a going away party, since the man and woman were to depart from Palmyra aboard the Iola the next day." (p. 397)

The last words of Mac Graham establish the date of the alleged departure of the Iola was August 29, 1974. The above conversation between Pollock and Shoemaker, took place just a few months after the murder of the Grahams on October 30, 1974 — long before any attorney had the opportunity to "spin" the facts.

436

Ironically and incompetently, this damning evidence was introduced into Stearns' murder trial by Bugliosi himself! Cake or no cake, truce or no truce, the final conversation between Mac and Shoemaker proved beyond a reasonable doubt the alleged date of the departure of the Iola for Fanning Island was Thursday, August 29th 1974, and not Saturday, August 31st as asserted by Stearns.

With this indisputable fact established by Bugliosi the entire defense of Stearns is exposed as a fraud and sham. All the bilge water about the alleged events of the 30th and 31st...so many lies. Not only is Stearns once again exposed as the liar we know her to be, (this time by her own counsel) but her so called log is revealed as a work of fiction whose only function was to confound and flummox her pursuers.

Mass confusion during the trial was rampant in all corners: the court conned by Stearns years before the murder trial commenced; incomprehensible rulings hamstrung the prosecution; witness after witness bullied and intimidated by Bugliosi; total confusion by attorneys representing the prosecution (and the defense); the jury buried in an ocean of Stearns' lies and deceptions and a timid prosecutor refusing to protect his witnesses. Confusion reigned supreme to the point no one noticed what Shoemaker had just said. Unknowingly, Bugliosi handed victory over to Enoki who ignores the gift and once again snatches defeat from the jaws of victory.

Half Truth Lie Re Seaworthiness of Iola

Employing the lie of the half truth as a persuasive device, Bugliosi argued Don Stevens, a naval architect sailing aboard the vessel Shearwater, thought the Iola was seaworthy:

437

"Stevens, who testified he had actually boarded the Iola, repeated his testimony at Buck's trial that although he would never have purchased the Iola, he felt the boat was "seaworthy". (p. 333)

Reviewing Steven's testimony from the court reporter's transcript of Walker's murder trial, *contrary* to Bugliosi's claim, Stevens opined the Iola had a deficiency that *precluded* applying the term *seaworthy* to the Iola.

Stevens, under cross-examination queried by Walker's defense lawyer Findlay:

"And with respect to the background that you have, your discipline, your scientific discipline and your experience and so on, taking that into account, and the fact that you had the opportunity to view the Iola during the time when you were at Palmyra Island in 1974, do you have an opinion with respect to the seaworthiness of the vessel Iola at that time?"

Stevens replied:

"I would say it was seaworthy with the exception of the pumping system."

Stevens states there was a problem with the bilge pump and because of this problem the Iola was "not seaworthy".

"Do you know what kind of pumping system, bilge and pumping system that the Iola was equipped with at that time from your own knowledge?" Inquires defense attorney, Findlay.

"I know of at least one of the pumps."

"They had one pump that you know of?"

"Yes, one pump that Stephanie told us about."

"Do you have any knowledge as to any other pumps that they might have had aboard?"

"No, I don't."

438

(Volume 2, pages 91-2, Walker murder trial transcript.)

This exchange established that the Iola had only one bilge pump, contrary to Stearns' testimony. For reasons not stated, Stevens, either from his own observations, or from information Stearns gave him, *withholds* his seal of approval because of problems with the bilge pump. The faulty condition of the only identified bilge pump aboard the Iola caused him the believe the Iola was *not* seaworthy. Wisely, the defense ignored Steven's answer. Unfortunately the prosecution did not clarify this issue on direct examination which would have been easy since they were in possession of Walker's original trial transcript.

Half Truth Lie Supports Stearns Testimony

Bugliosi attempts to bolster Stearns' testimony arguing:

"In fact, within minutes prior to Jennifer talking to Shishido, when Mr. Pollock was rowing Jennifer to the Coast Guard cutter, we have his testimony that she also told him they found the dinghy over turned on the beach."

"So, we have Jennifer's testimony. we have Bruce Benson's stipulated testimony, and we have Edwin Pollock's testimony that Jennifer said it was on the beach." (p. 513)

No doubt this argument had substantial impact on the jury. The problem is Bugliosi's statement is not complete. Pollock's testimony was not as Bugliosi stated. Pollock testified Stearns told him they *found Mac's Zodiac capsized on the beach over at Paradise Island* and not merely *"on the beach"*. (footnote, p. 322) Bugliosi's argument omits reference to Paradise Island.

439

Omitting this fact is a misrepresentation of Pollock's testimony by employing a half truth lie. Lying by half-truth is routinely employed by Bugliosi during his summation to the jury, also it is found through out ATSWT as he presents his positions to the reader. Alert opposing counsel should seize on this specious technique and in so doing undermine the impact of Bugliosi's argument calling into question his ethical standards. Failure to address the issue scores a point for Stearns in that it sounds as if Pollock is agreeing with Stearns on the location of the discovery of the Zodiac.

A misstatement of this magnitude warrants an objection for misquoting the testimony. Usually a row occurs, but there is no point in allowing your opponent to run over you without protest.

Stevens Testimony Misconstrued

Attempting to minimize the impact of Captain Wheeler's testimony that the Iola was not fit to sail to Fanning Island, Bugliosi asks Stevens if his boat could have sailed against wind and current to Fanning Island had he chosen to do so.

Bugliosi: *"You could have dropped down into Fanning while under sail?"*

Stevens: *"Yes, we could have."*

"So in your opinion it would be possible to sail from Palmyra to Fanning?"

"Yes." Replies Stevens. (p. 333)

Later, Bugliosi playing off this exchange argues to the jury;

" Wheeler, himself conceded that he himself had never attempted to sail to Fanning. Don Stevens did,.....and he testified it was possible to sail from Palmyra to Fanning." (p. 490)

In making this argument Bugliosi misrepresents Stevens testimony. Stevens stated he sailed east from Palmyra until he reached a point north of Fanning Island and then headed north returning to Hawaii. He said it would be possible to "drop down" to Fanning Island. At no time did he state he had sailed to Fanning Island.

Weinglass cross-examining Wheeler during the murder trial of Stearns:

"Now it's true, is it not, Mr. Wheeler, that you told Stephanie that the trip would be — the trip from Palmyra to Fanning would be difficult."

"Very difficult."

"Very difficult. But you didn't tell her it would be impossible."

"I would be trying to indicate it's impossible."

"But you told her only that it would be very difficult."

"I think I was trying to tell her she could not make it."

"Right. But you just told her it was very difficult. As you told us yesterday.

"You can let it go at that if you want, but...." Responds Wheeler.

The court:

"Well, he is asking you if you used the word "impossible".

Wheeler: "I would like to use the word impossible."

Weinglass:

"But when you talked to Stephanie, you can't tell us that is the word you used?"

"I couldn't say." (Vol. 2, p. 210)

Wheeler thought the Iola was so deficient it would "very difficult" for the Iola to sail to Fanning Island, against wind and current, although he is not sure he used those exact words. More importantly, Wheeler confided that he had sailed aboard the Iola in her earlier days when she was known as the "Margaret". Thus he would have a superior understanding of the vessel and her sailing characteristics.

Stevens was never asked if he thought it was possible for *the Iola* to complete the voyage given her lack of seaworthiness. In couching his argument in the manner he did Bugliosi infers that Stevens opined that the Iola could complete the voyage. To the contrary, Stevens was merely asserting that it was possible to sail to Fanning from Palmyra....a proposition that no sailor would deny, providing the vessel was seaworthy and properly equipped.

Bugliosi Impeaches Client

The jury, at the urging of Bugliosi, was invited to hear a portion of Walker's 1975 theft trial testimony regarding the supposed events of August 30, 1974. Surprisingly, it directly contradicts Stearns murder trial testimony re the events of the 30th. (Bugliosi does not identify the party questioning Walker.... presumably it is Walker's defense attorney.)

After receiving permission from Judge King, Bugliosi reads the following excerpts to the jury from Walker's 1975 theft trial:

"He (Walker) gave this answer to a question about the dinner invitation. He said":

"I saw Mac early in the morning, I guess eight or nine o'clock, and we passed the time of day. We smoked a cigarette or something like that. I went aboard his boat and we played a game of chess, a couple games of chess. And he said he was going to help tow us out of the lagoon with his dinghy. So he invited us over for

dinner that night. It was sort of a bon voyage thing. Then I went back over to our boat and Stephanie and I continued getting our boat ready to go the next day."

Unidentified attorney: " Okay. *Did you see him later in the day?*"

Walker: *"I saw him about one or two o'clock in the afternoon. He said that he was going fishing that afternoon and if he wasn't back at the appointed hour, 6:30 to go ahead and board the boat and help ourselves to a drink. And he had some pupus p-u-p-u-s laid out. Some cookies and some other things. And that's the last time I talked to him."* (Vol. 12, pp. 1922-3)

During his 1975 theft trial Walker testified he saw Mac between the hours of 8:00 and 9:00 a.m. the morning of August 30th. He mentions nothing about receiving a stash of coffee and tobacco referenced by Stearns in her log note of the 30th.

Walker stated the next time he saw Mac was between the hours of 1:00 p.m. and 2:00 p.m. He claims it was at this time Mac mentioned he was going fishing that afternoon and if he wasn't back by 6:30 p.m. they could board the Sea Wind and make themselves at home. Notably, Walker testified it was the *last time* he talked with Mac.

Walker, unlike Stearns, makes no reference to Muff accompanying Mac on his fishing expedition. Moreover, Walker did not testify that he had a late morning discussion with Stearns when she was aboard the Iola.

Stearns version of the early afternoon events are in direct conflict with Walker's testimony: She testified Walker came by between one and two in the afternoon, they spoke but she does not remember what if anything, was said:

443

Bugliosi: *"After 10:30 or 11:00 in the morning when is the next time that you recall seeing Buck that day?"*

Stearns: *"Two or three hours later. Sometime in the early afternoon."*

Bugliosi: *"Okay. Do you recall what took place at that time?"*

Stearns: *"No, not really. He just — I remember him coming by...and saying something."*

Bugliosi: *"Okay. Coming by — you were still on the Iola?"*

Stearns: *"Yes."*

"I take it you can't recall every time you saw Buck that day?" leads Bugliosi.

"No." Replies Stearns, following Bugliosi's lead. (Vol. 11, p. 1646)

Stearns' testified it was only later in the afternoon, around 4:00 p.m., that Walker came by and mentioned he had just run into Mac. She claimed it was at this time Walker informed her the Grahams might be late for their dinner engagement because they were delayed working around camp, and had not yet gone fishing. (Vol. 11, pp. 1646-7)

Walker's 1975 version of his conversation with Mac, on the 30th of August is inconsistent with the account offered by Stearns. Walker testified he met with Mac between 1:00 p.m. and 2:00 p.m.: This was the *"last time"* he spoke with Mac. There is no mention he went to the Iola and spoke with Stearns at that time. Nor does Walker mention a meeting with Mac around four in the afternoon as he supposedly was going to bathe. Walker specifically stated his "last" conversation with Mac occurred between one and two p.m. On

444

the other hand, Stearns claimed that Walker, on his way to bathe around 4:00 p.m., met Mac and had a discussion.

On modest examination Stearns testimony makes little sense. Walker popping out of the jungle on his way to bathe at various times during the day; the notion Muff would be out in the lagoon at night fishing, or that Muff would be so discourteous as to invite defendants to a bon voyage dinner and not be present to welcome them aboard; that defendants were to go aboard the Sea Wind and help themselves to alcohol and food when the Grahams were not present; that Muff would permit Walker to come aboard the Sea Wind to play chess; that Mac would expect Muff in his absence to entertain defendants, and etc.

State of Mind Ruse

Bugliosi comes up with a ploy to explain away the numerous times Stearns takes positions during the trial defying common sense. The manner in which Bugliosi handles the issue of seaworthiness of the Iola is typical.   The issue he argues, is not the actual seaworthiness of the Iola since any half-wit would know she was a derelict, and being so, a persuasive indicator defendants sailed down to Palmyra with murder and piracy in mind: But did Stearns *believe* the Iola was seaworthy. (p. 490) If she was foolish enough to believe the Iola was seaworthy then it could be argued her intent on coming to Palmyra was grow pot and get rich. Conversely, if Stearns knew the Iola was a derelict incapable of a return trip to Hawaii why would defendants sail to a deserted island with little food no money and no prospect of getting off the island if they did not have boat theft, mayhem and murder in mind on arrival?

445

One observes this same stratagem come into play concerning the alleged invitation from Mac for defendants to come aboard the Sea Wind and in his absence make themselves at home. (No one their right mind would believe Mac Graham would invite the hungry, destitute defendants, in his absence, to come aboard the Sea Wind where there was nearly $5,000.00 in cash, a rifle, a .38 derringer, a full larder, and a well stocked liquor cabinet.)

Bugliosi argues the question is not if the invitation was made, but did Stearns *believe* the invitation had been made? Using this dodge the jury is no longer directed to examine the facts as to the existence or non-existence of the invitation, but whether or not Stearns thought the invitation had been made. Changing the focus to Stearns' state of mind diverts the jury's attention from ferreting out another obvious lie to speculating on the amorphous nether regions of Stearns' sociopathic state on mind. Did she truly believe Mac had invited them aboard the Sea Wind and were to "*make themselves at home*" in the event the Grahams did not return by 6:30 p.m.?

In both instances the jury is asked to believe the defendant, often described as intelligent, is suddenly ignorant and not capable of drawing logical conclusions about social or factual circumstances even a simpleton might understand. The state of mind ruse offers an easy method to avoid being caught in a lie or series of lies. The Iola was not seaworthy — but Stearns did not know it; the invitation had not been made — but Stearns thought it had been proffered; and etc.

Sufficiency of the Evidence

In the case at bar there was more than sufficient evidence presented for a jury finding of guilty. It does not take an expert to see something is wrong when a highly manipulative defendant, desperately in need of money, sells a valuable portable gas generator, in good condition, (with unlimited free fuel left over from military stocks) for a mere $50.00. It does not add up — something else is going on.

Bugliosi concedes:

"Whatever happened to Mac and Muff Graham must have involved force and violence." (p. 138)

He overlooks the suspicious physical evidence found in the burn pit ashes near Mac's camp site as he argues:

"There was not one shred of evidence that the Grahams were still on the island, dead or alive, nor had anyone found any physical evidence of any kind that even vaguely suggested foul play." (p. 140)

Bugliosi ignores Wheeler's testimony about the pair of earrings found *"sitting"* in the rubble of the fire pit when he was on Palmyra with the search team. He overlooks Wheeler's testimony about observing a pile of women's clothing found in the fire pit near the anchorage, the glasses, burned pill vials, and etc. (Vol. 1, p. 128)

He cavalierly dismisses the implications of the hatch cover found near the location where Iola was tied up to the dolphins in the lagoon. Wheeler was *"sure it belonged to the Iola."* (This was the same hatch cover that leaked badly during the voyage to Palmyra from Hawaii and was allegedly repaired on August 30th.) (Contrary to the information set forth in the log of the Iola and testimony of Stearns, the hatch was never repaired. Defendants were in such a rush the morning of August 29th to scuttle the Iola they did not stop to place the hatch in position or secure it below.) (p. 140)

The fact the hatch of the Iola was found on the beach in the lagoon by Egger's search party raises the irrefutable inference, contrary to the testimony of Stearns, defendants did not take any

447

steps to insure the seaworthiness of the Iola in preparation for the purported voyage to Fanning; an unsecured forward hatch would spell certain disaster for the Iola sailing to windward.

Remains of prescription glasses and sunglasses, a fragment of material, glass prescription bottles, the "fright wig" found in the ashes, the ashes of the fire itself located near Mac's shop and the debris found in the ashes of a fire was *physical evidence* raising the suspicion of foul play and murder. (p. 139)   One thing is certain we know that Mac did not set the fire and there was no evidence others had visited Palmyra between the departure of the Sea Wind and the arrival of the investigators.   Logically, there only two others that could have set the fire.   Why bother to burn the items found in the fire pit if they are not connected to the murders? Obviously it was an effort on the part of defendants to dispose of incriminating evidence. (p. 139)   The salt-free nine horse out board motor used to propel Mac's Zodiac is evidence defendants engaged in foul play.

The fact there was no evidence of the outboard motor being exposed to salt water is   persuasive evidence Stearns was lying to Shishido.   The bullet holes in the hull of the Sea Wind were persuasive evidence of the   life/death struggle that went on in the Sea Wind as Muff fought for her existence with Stearns and Walker. Stearns, herself, admitted the hole existed, attempting to explain it away by alleging it was caused by a one chance in a million swordfish attack.

There is evidence of foul play in the false log of the Iola; in the changes made to the Sea Wind prior to her departure and immediately upon her return to Hawaii;   in defendants efforts to escape and evade the authorities upon their return;   in Stearns constant stream of lies to Shishido; in the silly concocted fabrication by Stearns surrounding the supposed August 30th "disappearance" of the Grahams, and etc.

The statements of the Pollocks and Shoemaker are damning evidence Stearns was lying about her activities of August 29 — 31 and had been involved in the murder the Grahams.

The changes in the appearance of the Sea Wind upon her arrival in Hawaii are evidence of defendant's attempt to disguise the Sea Wind in an effort to escape detection for the theft of the Sea Wind and the murder of the Grahams.   The behavior of Stearns shortly before her arrest and upon her arrest; the repeated flushing in the bathroom as she disposed of funds from Mac's cruising kitty, all evidence of her culpability.

Most importantly it is Stearns testimony that links her to the murder of the Grahams. One preposterous admission after another; they were *"leisure sailors"*, meaning didn't sail at night; they were lost for several days once Palmyra Island had allegedly been located; her statement to Pollock that she would not return to Hawaii aboard the Iola; and her admission the Iola could not make better than two knots under sail.

Both defendants in the letter to Kit Graham of March 11, 1975, inform her a bon voyage dinner invitation was made by the Grahams. In this same letter the defendants agree the day following the bon voyage dinner the Iola was allegedly departing for Fanning Island. (pp. 154-7, 439)

It is significant the letter to Kit Graham from defendants was prepared *before* either defendant heard the testimony of Curtis Shoemaker at their respective theft trials.   Both the letter from defendants and Shoemaker's testimony state the bon voyage dinner took place on the 28th and the purported voyage to Fanning Island was to commence the following day. Until Shoemaker testified at

449

Stearns' trial for theft of the Sea Wind in June 1975 she did not know he was conversing with Mac as they approached the Sea Wind for the bon voyage dinner on the 28th. Moreover, Shoemaker at the time he testified during Stearns' theft trial had no knowledge of the existence of defendant's letter to Kit Graham

Defendants in their letter to Kit Graham of March 1975 stated they were invited to a bon voyage dinner *the night before their scheduled departure.* This is exactly the same information Shoemaker told the jury throughout his testimony in four different trials. The fact that these two separate versions of the same event are in complete agreement and could not be a result of mere chance. Obviously defendants and Shoemaker did not collude. There is no other reasonable explanation for this congruence except to conclude Shoemaker was telling the truth about the conversation he had with Mac the evening of the 28th. (pp. 155, 439)

Stearns' admission to Pollock that during the voyage to Palmyra, they were "knee-deep" in water because the boat leaked excessively is evidence that the Iola was a derelict and Stearns was well aware of it's substandard condition.

Evidence of the death struggle by Muff and the discharge of her derringer could have been found by examining the hull of the Sea Wind in the galley area where the shipwright replaced the portion of the plank .

The most persuasive evidence present on Palmyra was the forlorn derelict vessel, the Iola. A dismal wreck that with the unwitting assistance of a few well-meaning sailors managed to convey the sociopathic defendants to Palmyra Island.

The afore-mentioned items are just a few of the hundreds of evidentiary facts pointing to the guilt of Stearns.

Cause of Death

In summation Bugliosi proclaimed, *"there's no substantive evidence of a gun being used".* What is or is not substantive is a question of interpretation. Enoki cannot interrupt, *"objection your honor counsel misstates the evidence"* for it is not as if Bugliosi said there was no evidence that a gun was used, he merely argues that the evidence was weak and not persuasive—in other words a matter of opinion. (p. 504)

Fearing that the sound of a gunshot might cast doubt on Stearns' testimony, Bugliosi went to great lengths to convince the jury a gun was not used in the murder of the Grahams; reviewing the testimony of Uberlaker and Stephens.

Uberlaker thought the hole above the left ear was the result of *"erosion not trauma or projectile"* urges Bugliosi. (pp. 504-5)

Apparently Bugliosi is basing his comment on Uberlaker's written report and not his courtroom testimony. In his report he opined:

" the hole in the left temporal area appears to have been made by erosion, not trauma or projectile." (p. 342)

Later, Uberlaker supported this conclusion during direct examination when queried by Enoki stating:

"It's a part of the skull that's very thin and is one of the most easily damaged areas."

"There are natural phenomena, such as abrasion, that can produce a hole in the skull..." (pp. 244-50)

Defense attorney during the Walker murder trial, Earl Partington, cross-examining Dr. Stephens asked if he found any lead around the hole in Muff's skull. Stephens responded he had not although he did *not rule out the possibility* the hole could have been caused by a bullet. (pp. 244-246)

A few months later during the murder trial of Stearns, Dr. Stephens was again called as an expert witness. Bugliosi observes this time Enoki *"explored the possibility that Muff had been shot to death, and in more depth than he had at the Walker trial."*

Questioned by Enoki, Stephens said the hole above the left ear in Muff Graham's skull had a *"very roughened margin"* associated with *"coning"* which he explained by using the example of a BB shot hitting a plate-glass window. The force of impact causes a concentric expansion of the hole in the direction of travel; i.e. the hole gets larger as the force pushes inward. But since the hole in the skull in this case was larger on the outermost surface of the skull, the prosecutor asked for an explanation.

"In a 'contact gunshot' wound, in which the muzzle of the gun is touching or very close to the body, the gas pressure generated by the burning of the gun powder in the closed confines of the skull would cause reverse coning, said Dr. Stephens. 'In other words, the coning would be in the opposite direction of travel — the hole would be largest at the point of entry and get smaller as it proceeded inward. "

"If this hole is a gun shot wound, it's a contact wound," Stephens concluded.

Enoki inquires:

"Is there anything about this pistol or the caliber of this pistol that would preclude it from being the source of that hole in exhibit 24, the skull?"

Stephens replies:

"No, there is not. A 22-caliber has all the capabilities necessary to make such a wound, both in penetrating the skull and producing the reverse coning." (pp. 344-5)

Surely the above testimony regarding a gun shot to the head of Muff is more than sufficient to refute Bugliosi's assertion that there is *"no substantive evidence of a gun being used"* during the torture and murder of Muff Graham. It is likely Walker shot Muff because her screams of agony and pain were more than he could bear, but the evidence is not conclusive on this point. (pp. 344-45)

Truth is the means in which Muff met her final end is relatively unimportant. The prosecution should concede there was too much background noise from the wind in the trees, birds screeching and sound of the surf to enable Stearns to hear the sound of a small .22 caliber round being fired. The reason it is relatively unimportant is because Stearns formulated the plot to kill the Grahams and was *present* at the time of Muff's death and was an active participant the entire time including torture and dismemberment of her body as well as the supervision of her burial. Either of the defendants could have administered the coup de grace with a gun shot to the head of Muff for no other reason than they had to get on with their plan to dismember and bury her remains — another sailboat could wander by creating a big problem.

Conceding that Stearns could not hear the sound of Walker's pistol would position Enoki to argue her allegation that she heard the motor of the Zodiac on the afternoon of the 30th would be impossible because of the background noise.

Then again perhaps Bugliosi is right — defendants did not shoot Muff and may have sadistically decided not to dispatch her after their orgy of sex, blood and gore. Perhaps they dragged her semi-conscious body over to the Zodiac dumped it in and motored off to the shallows for butchery while she was yet alive. Whatever her final moments they had to be horrible beyond imagination.

Forensics On Sea Wind

When defendants returned to Hawaii it was seven years before murder charges were lodged against them in connection with the disappearance of the Grahams. Seven years had passed and no one had thought to examine the Sea Wind for evidence of the murder of the Grahams. Had they performed every known test on the Sea Wind they would have discovered little evidence of murder because neither of the Grahams were executed on board the boat: The plank evidencing Muff's derringer discharging into the hull was long gone. Defendants, no doubt, were quick to destroy the plank penetrated by the errant bullets from Muff's derringer immediately upon their return to Hawaii for fear someone might notice them and draw logical conclusions. Charts that would have proved Stearn's ineptitude as a navigator had long since disappeared, if they ever existed.

There would be one item of evidence any experienced mariner would look for and expect to find. If Stearns was capable of navigating by use of a sextant (a highly dubious claim) and plotting a Line of Position the chart so employed would speak volumes about her return voyage to Hawaii, the route they took and the speed travelled. It would reveal when defendants departed Palmyra and when they arrived in Hawaii. There is no comment about Stearns' navigational chart outlining her return to Hawaii. In all probability she did not chart her daily position because she did not have the necessary skills — this too would be obvious on viewing the chart.

The fact Enoki did not submit testimony from an expert to inform the jury there was no evidence of a murder taking place on board the Sea Wind does not *"redound to the detriment of the prosecution"* as argued by Bugliosi, for the simple reason that Muff was murdered on Cooper Island near Walker's camp site.

If the authorities were to examine in detail any object that might shed light on the murder of Muff they should have focused on the Zodiac. It is likely it was used to transport Muff's bloody corpse from place of execution to the site of dismemberment. One can be certain defendants attempted to clean the dinghy as best they could, however older inflatables have seams that wear with age and these may have been a repository for small quantities of Muff's blood and DNA. Careful inspection of these seams and other small crevices of the Zodiac may have revealed the presence of Muff's DNA had someone thought to look.

Hitching a Ride

Bugliosi attempts to minimize the problem Stearns faced because of the woeful condition of the Iola. He argues if worse came to worse defendants could always bum a ride with another vessel. This suggestion is not credible.   No sailor with a wit of common sense would trust either of these inexperienced and menacing people aboard his boat (to say nothing of their three damp, smelly dogs).

Small sailing vessels go to sea prepared for long voyages and the occasional emergency.   With limited room on board few carry food and supplies for unanticipated crew. Moreover, is there a single juror or reader that would take either of the defendants aboard their own vessel for a long voyage?   Walker as a shipmate?   He is inexperienced, moody, lazy, mean-spirited and has jail-house tattoos.

455

His dog is vicious. Not only does he have woefully little experience at sea, but when he finally does act he is a total clutz. He bangs his head on a stanchion, jams a fish hook through his thumb, does not perform his duties, and runs aground attempting to enter the lagoon. Hitching a ride on another vessel for these two nut-cases would out of the question.

While not overtly dangerous as Walker who would accept a scruffy, foul mouthed, inexperienced sailor, the likes of Stearns as a ship mate? Is she to be trusted? One would worry once asleep after a long watch she might beat your brains out, toss your corpse overboard, go back to Palmyra collect Walker and be off on another murderous adventure.

Perhaps the only solution would be for Stearns to contact her family and make arrangements to be picked up by a vessel with sufficient crew forewarned of the potential danger. Defendants together are a very dangerous mix. Only a fool would consider transporting the both of them without restraints of one sort or another. The only safe mode of transport for Walker is in the brig of a Coast Guard ship. Once the two were separated Stearns could be controlled if there were sufficient crew to keep her under surveillance twenty-four hours a day.

Perhaps Walker could contact one of his friends like the Musicks to come down to Palmyra and pick him up. This might be a possibility providing they trust sharing the same small boat with him. In truth no one in his right mind would want either of these deranged would be sailors on board their vessel. Suggesting defendants could hitch a ride with a passing vessel is patently absurd. Sailing a small boat on an ever dangerous sea is not the equivalent of driving a motor vehicle the same distance on land. With limited room and constant proximity, shipmates must be carefully chosen, personal frictions arise and incompetence puts all at risk. (p. 499)

Disposal of Muff's Remains

An aggressive and perceptive prosecutor would have understood the facts concerning the disposal of Muff's body pointed to the obvious conclusion the defendants dug Muff's grave in the sand, stuffed her butchered remains into an aluminum container, attempted to wire it shut and buried them where they were discovered by Sharon Jordan in 1981. In the seven years following Muff's death the sands obscuring Muff's remains were subject to tide and wave action, over time the coffin was exposed .

For Bugliosi's tenuous defense to succeed it was necessary Muff's remains be dumped into the lagoon and not buried in the sand. The juror is to imagine seven years after Muff's murder, contrary to the laws of physics, the container holding her bones floated to the surface and washed ashore where it was discovered by Sharon Jordan. To peddle Stearns' defense Bugiosi had no choice but to convince the jury Muff's remains (and Mac's) had been dumped in the lagoon by Walker in the late afternoon of August 30, 1974.

Bugliosi puzzles over the presence of ant exoskeletons found in the bone marrow of Muff by the coroner:

"In a second reading of the coroner's report on the postmortem examination conducted on Muff's remains in April of 1985, I noticed something potentially explosive that the prosecution had not brought out in the Walker trial. 'in the marrow of the long bones there is deposited coral and sandy-like material which is layered in a fashion indicative of water exposure,' the coroner wrote.

457

'From this, recognizable portions of insect exoskeletons (outer shells) are removed. These are portions of ants. The ants show anatomic features of a small, dark-colored ant, approximately 4-5 millimeters in length.'" (p. 267)

Bugliosi wonders when they crept into the bone marrow. One thing is certain the ants had years in which to find the remains of Muff and enter her bones. (p. 267)

Why everyone associated with the trial of Stearns appears to accept the nonsense about dumping the remains of both Mac and Muff in the lagoon when there is not a shred of evidence to indicate this happened is difficult to understand. Even witnesses for the prosecution mindlessly bought into the defense position Muff's remains were dumped into the lagoon. Dr. Stephens, the coroner, examining Muff's remains, told Stearns' co-counsel Weinglass:

"...that the ants would have crawled into the marrow only while the body had flesh on it and was freshly deceased, not if the bones were dry of oil..." which, I assumed, they would have been when they were washed ashore in the container in 1981. (p. 267)

With fame and fortune awaiting a successful outcome, believing the ant issue if mishandled could weigh heavily against his client, Bugliosi phoned his partner Weinglass and requested the right to handle the matter if it came up in trial. Bugliosi contacted Roy Snelling (Snelling) an entomologist at the Los Angeles Museum of Natural History. Snelling disagreed with Stephens and believed ants would have been attracted to bones even though there was no flesh on the bones. Snelling also agreed to testify as an expert on behalf of Stearns if need be. (pp. 268-70)

Snelling, an expert on ant behavior, believed without fractured bones ants would *not* be able to penetrate the surface of a bone. It is unlikely in the few minutes between the death of Muff and her dismemberment there would be sufficient time for ants to work their way into her bones. Since ants cannot survive under water they could not have gained entrance to her bones while her remains lay on the tidal sands. The only occasion the ants would have to enter her bones was when they were enclosed in the aluminum container and buried in a shallow grave in the sand of Strawn Island. (p. 269) Later, because of wave and tide action, the shallow grave was uncovered and casket of Muff became exposed.

It is common knowledge ants live in the ground and burrow extensive holes. No doubt they dug into the grave of Muff and consumed a portion of her body. They had seven years to do it. After employing an expert on ants Bugliosi decided to forego his testimony hoping the subject of the finding of ants in the bone marrow would not come up.

This issue was shamefully overlooked by the prosecution. Enoki saw no inconsistency in ants discovered deep within the bones of Muff and shared Bugliosi's belief Muff's remains were discarded into the lagoon. Any school boy would want an explanation as to how long dead ants could be found in bones that had been under water for several years in the depths of the lagoon. Or how it could be that a container holding the bones of Muff might surface years after being deposited in the depths of the lagoon and magically float ashore where it was discovered by Jordan. (pp. 267-70)

Ballast

There is another major problem with Bugliosi's conjecture that Muff's aluminum coffin was jettisoned into the lagoon by Walker. If her remains were dumped into the lagoon the container would need a heavy weight to hold it down.

459

There are several possibilities as to the manner in which it could have been weighted down. A substantial weight might have included inside the coffin, or a heavy anchor chain wrapped around the coffin.

The first possibility can be dismissed immediately. There was not enough room inside the makeshift coffin for Muff remains let alone additional space taken up by bricks or other weights. This leaves only an exterior method such as a heavy length of anchor chain wrapped around the coffin, secured in some manner. The only problem is nothing that could have served as ballast was found near the aluminum container and yet we know that the wire which secured the lid of the container was discovered along with Muff;s remains. If discarded in the depths of the lagoon one hundred and forty feet below, there is no reason the waters would be disturbed causing the aluminum coffin to surface. Any gases created by the decomposition process would dissipate through the gap left by the unclosed lid.

Without a heavy weight attached to the aluminum coffin there is no way her decaying remains would have stayed on the bottom. Decomposition gases and fatty tissue would cause it to rise. The search team sent to Palmyra in early November 1974 would have discovered Muff's remains on the beach.

There was no explanation by Bugliosi how the coffin bearing Muff's remains would sink to the bottom and stay there during the decomposition process. The obvious reason there was no explanation is because neither body of Mac or Muff was dumped in the lagoon.

Enoki went along with defendant's version of the disposal of Muff's remains even though there was no credible evidence indicating this happened. The only credible evidence pertaining to the disposal of Muff's remains indicate the coffin was buried in the sand in the area where it was found. Her watch and some of her bones were discovered inside the coffin. (pp. 237-8)   The ant exoskeletons discovered in the marrow of the bones of decedent strongly support the supposition that Muff's coffin was buried in the sand and not jettisoned into the lagoon.

Inferentially Bugliosi assigns the same treatment Mac's remains suffered to those of Muff.   When one considers this scenario Bugliosi's speculations become even more implausible. He suggests Mac's remains were interred in the same kind of aluminum coffin assigned to Muff.   Mac was considerably larger than Muff. Dismembering his body would be a challenge. Getting it into a small container that would scarcely hold Muff's butchered remains would have been impossible.

When building a house of cards   there is always the possibility of the smallest factual breeze blowing it to smithereens. Here the fact the coffin was buried in the sand rather than dumped in the lagoon causes the entire structure to collapse.   It destroys the timeline as well as the story line. Not only does Walker have to kill two people in a very short time, dig two graves, chop up two bodies making a bloody mess of the remains and himself, clean up the mess, clean up himself; do everything else to cover the crime; turn the Zodiac over on the beach out of the high tide zone;   prepare the dinner table aboard the Sea Wind; and when Stearns arrives, act as if noting had happened.

We Are All Liars

Websters dictionary defines a "lie" as a "willful mis-statement". Uttering a falsehood without knowledge of its falsity is not lying. Lying requires knowledge the utterance is false and a willful intent to deceive the recipient.

461

During final argument, pulling out all the stops, Bugliosi attempts to excuse the compulsive lying of his client by suggesting everyone in the court room is a liar:

"In other words, once a liar, always a liar. The only problem with that type of reasoning is that I don't believe any human being always tells the truth......they may say that they always tell the truth, but they don't. And if we were to accept the notion that once a liar always a liar, then we could never believe anyone."

"But I guess the position of the prosecution is that since Jennifer lied once under oath before another jury she should never be believed again on the witness stand as long as she lives." (p. 515)

Bugliosi overlooks the fact Stearns perjured herself hundreds of times during both her trials. She was found guilty by a jury in her theft trial and sentenced to prison. (Meaning the jury believed she lied about nearly every fact in the trial.) Also, in her headlong effort to escape punishment for the murder of the Grahams, she consistently lied about the facts during trial.

From time to time one tells a lie in normal social discourse, but most do not consistently lie. Very few lie under oath; few commit the felonious act of perjury. Lying under oath is a far cry from stating your spouse looks trim when he/she does not. It is an entirely different matter to be sworn in as a witness during a jury trial and commit perjury or to swear to facts under oath as true, knowing them false. Fortunately for society very few of us are willing to bear false witness. Few witnesses sworn under oath to testify truthfully in a criminal matter knowingly testify falsely. Few concoct lies causing another to be wrongfully convicted of a crime.

Bugliosi argues every prosecution witness is mis-recollecting confused or an outright liar. He labels Curtis Shoemaker a liar mockingly calling him *"Mr. Storymaker"*. The Pollocks are liars

462

"inventing incidents" to convict Stearns. FBI Special Agent Hilton Lui's testimony is in question (i.e., he is a liar) because he does not mention the words *"cake"* or *"truce"* in the summary of his interview of Shoemaker in October 30, 1974. Words that had little relevance at the time of the interview and even at trial were of only passing relevance. (pp. 370-1)

Bugliosi argues FBI agent Shishido's 302 report which recorded Stearns' lies about the discovery of the overturned Zodiac in the lagoon is frailty and in error. (pp. 485, 486, 513.) Amid all these accusations of lying Bugliosi has the gall to rely heavily on the Benson Stipulation which he admits was a compilation of lies and misrepresentations agreed upon between himself and Enoki prior to trial.   Only in the world of the trial court do we get such nonsense. (pp. 396-8)   Often during summation Bugliosi himself lies misquoting Pollock's testimony and the testimony of other witnesses without objection from Enoki.

Bugliosi is not offended if the purpose of a lie is to cover a previous lie.   At a Motion to Suppress hearing in Honolulu January 24, 1975 prior to her trial for theft of the Sea Wind, Stearns swore under oath the reason defendants took the Sea Wind was *"because they were stranded on Palmyra ."* (p. 442)

Bugliosi characterizes her testimony at this hearing as *"devastating."*   When quizzed   about her admission she was "stranded" on Palmyra, Stearns, realizing her remark was tantamount to admitting the Iola was not seaworthy, quickly takes steps to avoid being abandoned by her attorney and engages in another lie.   She informs Bugliosi her *"stranded"* testimony was *"a lie to go along with the lie that the Iola had run aground in the channel".*   (p. 442)

Bugliosi observes:

"This appeared to be a highly damaging piece of evidence that confirmed exactly what the prosecution was saying, and I was greatly relieved that Jennifer had a satisfactory explanation." (p. 442)

It is curious how quickly Bugliosi accepts the word of an admitted perjurer, yet how exercised he becomes with Shoemaker, the Pollocks, and Shishido as they testify truthfully.

Enoki questions Stearns:

"You told agent Shishido that the Grahams would have wanted you to have the Sea Wind, is that correct?"

Stearns replies:

"The problem with that conversation is that he was asking me questions that I could not answer honestly without placing Buck in jeopardy, so I came out with certain responses." (i.e. lies.) (p. 444)

Once again, the reader is treated to Stearns, seemingly unable to control what she says her words just *"came out"* of her mouth as if her brain is not engaged.

Waxing Eloquent

Bugliosi attempts to respond to each and every lie Stearns told various witnesses, investigators and the jury, offering excuses for nearly all of them. Why none of the jurors saw through these excuses which included references to H.L. Mencken, Mother Teresa and romantic themes " the man she loved" (at least for that month), is difficult understand.

He continues to wander far afield in the final hours of his summation inveighing the likes of the Puritans, Aristotle, or old will which had nothing to do with Stearns. All in an effort to obscure

Stearns' lies and the role she played in the murders of the Grahams. Hyperbole in bloom, Bugliosi excuses her "moral lapses" because *"only someone who is adept at walking between raindrops could have gone through Jennifer's incredible odyssey and ordeal unblemished and unsullied."* (p. 511)

By this logic one supposes it is ok to brutally murder a couple and evade responsibility for one's actions because it was all an incredible odyssey. An odyssey of her own choosing, one might observe.

Sleight of Hand

During questioning by Shishido concerning Stearns' statement about why they were using the Sea Wind the evening of August 30th, Stearns stated:

".......since the Grahams had invited them to dinner and said 'to make yourselves at home,' she rationalized that to mean that if anything should happen to the Grahams, she and Roy could take possession of the Sea Wind." (p. 359)

The above testimony presented a stumbling block for Bugliosi. His trial plan required Stearns to distance herself from any direct contact with the Grahams on the purported day of their disappearance.   To effect this strategy Bugliosi must convince the jury that Stearns did not have direct contact with the Grahams on August 30, 1974.   This new approach runs *contrary* to the above statement she made to Shishido while on the Coast Guard cutter, October 29, 1974.

She told Shishido the Grahams "had invited *them* to dinner" and they were *"to make yourselves at home".* (p. 359) Two straight forward clauses patently unbelievable, but not ambiguous. To avoid implication in the murder of the Grahams, Stearns must retract her statement to Shishido and convince the jury she was not present during this purported conversation. Her defense posture was that the Grahams spoke only to Walker even though she never mentioned this fact to Shishido when she told him of the conversation.

Observe Bugliosi's solution to the problem during direction examination of   Stearns wherein he employs a leading question which repudiates her prior statement to Shishido.

Bugliosi quizzes:

"Did you tell Mr. Shishido that you and Buck rationalized Mac's statement—Mac's alleged statement— to Buck to 'make yourselves at home' to mean that the Grahams would have wanted you and Buck to take possession of the boat if anything happened to them? Did you tell Mr. Shishido that?"

In the above leading question we find Bugliosi misquoting Stearns statement to Shishido subtly changing it by the addition of two words; *"to Buck"*. With the addition of these two words he banishes Stearns and has Mac speaking directly to Walker contrary to Stearns comments recorded in Shishido's 302 report.

Having laid the groundwork Stearns follows up securing her advantage:

"I'm sure I said something to that effect."

"Was this a truthful statement on your part?"

"No."

" Why did you tell him this?"

"....he was questioning me as to why we hadn't turned the boat in. And I couldn't tell him the real reason, so....I don't know why

I chose those words, except that was...as I knew it, the last words that
Mac had told to Buck. *And they just came out."* (p. 438)

Stearns reinforces Bugliosi's leading question replying:

"I don't know why I chose those words, except that was....as I
knew it, the last words that Mac had told Buck..."

She supposedly doesn't know why she made the statement to
Shishido, but they were the *"last words that Mac had told to Buck.*
And they just came out". Again we find Stearns following Bugliosi's
lead as she rewrites her testimony by including Bugliosi's new
rendition of the conversation in her response to his question.

Driving the change home, Bugliosi underlines her new
testimony by reiterating her statement:

"The last words that Buck told you that Mac had said?"

Stearns agrees: *"Yes."* (p. 438)

Presto! We no longer have Stearns in a conversation with the
Grahams on the 30th of October only Walker. Easy as pie — a little
pretrial rehearsal, a series of leading questions by an experienced trial
lawyer, a clever lying witness, and, voila, up is down and black is
white.

The Bookie

The bilge water gets a bit deep when Bugliosi resorts to
mathematical probabilities in an effort to enhance his argument in
defense of Stearns and convince the jury the so called "cake/truce"
incident could not possibly be true.

"I must say that Shoemaker's timing is quite convenient, to
say the least. He testified that in the month of August he called Mac
Graham on the 7th, 14th, 21st and 28th. That's only once a week.

467

On the 28th he spoke to Mac for forty minutes. So that's forty minutes out of the entire week. I computed this. There are ten thousand eighty minutes every week. You divide forty into ten thousand eighty and you get two hundred and fifty-two." (p. 486)

Bugliosi, desperate for support from any quarter, in a bid to destroy the immense harm of Shoemaker's testimony, launches into a flight of fancy and argues:

"That means that if the cake-truce incident took place between the Grahams and Buck and Jennifer (Stearns) the mathematical probability that it would have taken place while Curt Shoemaker was talking to the Grahams would be one out of two hundred and fifty-two. Not the best odds. One out of two hundred and fifty-two."

The fact that Bugliosi launches into such an absurd analysis proves several things. First and foremost he knows little of the sea and the voyaging customs of sailors. The traditional time in which to throw a bon voyage party is shortly before the day of departure. Since Stearns informed the Grahams they were leaving on the 29th of August, the evening of the 28th is the time most suitable for such an event.

If one wants to discuss odds, what are the odds Mac would choose Palmyra as his year long destination at the same time the killers chose it as a destination to perpetrate their murderous acts? What are the possibilities Mac would have the ideal boat the killers sought? What are the odds the Grahams intended to stay for prolonged period of time? What are the odds the Grahams would come to Palmyra with a larder comparable to a well-stocked grocery store or be carrying five thousand dollars in small bills? What are the odds a swordfish, unprovoked, might make a suicidal attack

468

against the Sea Wind on the return to Hawaii?   Odds making is best left to the bookies.

Endless Changes

The question of who had possession of the dinghy of the Iola on the 30th of August 1974, allegedly the day the Grahams disappeared, became an issue in Stearns defense.

In one of his first interview sessions Stearns told Bugliosi, Walker had the dinghy *"all day"* on the 30th of August. (p. 188)

In the transcript of her testimony given at the 1975 theft trial, Stearns stated:

"......she had the dinghy the 30th of August and nothing was said about going back and forth." (p. 188)

Bugliosi on reading Stearns' transcript of her 1975 theft trial observes:

"Now I learned that, contrary to what she had told me, she had testified that she, not Buck, had the dinghy on August 30th."

Her sworn testimony during the theft trial was at odds with Bugliosi's defense narrative.   When confronted with Bugliosi's concern, Stearns quickly changed her story telling him Walker had the dinghy that day:

"As I remember, Buck had the dinghy that day." (pp. 188-9)

Later, Bugliosi realizes it was necessary that each had occasion to use the dinghy on the 30th of August. Comprehending a need to change her testimony a third time to coincide with Bugliosi's defense Stearns pretends confusion and concludes each could have had the dinghy at different times during the day. Thus we find three different versions of the alleged facts.   Stearns, a facile liar,

469

perceives what is required to achieve freedom and immediately changes her testimony accordingly. (pp. 188-9) Bugliosi, frustrated with the constantly changing facts, fumes:

"I was to have more problems preparing Jennifer (Stearns) for trial than with any other witness I could remember......but with her, the changes were endless.   Often, entire pages of questions became useless because she would add a different twist to an incident we had already covered in detail..."

Bugliosi ponders:

"Why was there was always yet another layer of truth to be revealed? Another shadow in this hall of mirrors?" (p. 191)

"With respect to the all-important day in question — August 30, 1974, supposedly, the day Mac and Muff disappeared — I found two major discrepancies." (p. 188)

Curiously, in the introduction leading up to the discussion of Stearns constantly changing facts, we find a shadow crossing Bugliosi's brow — one would not expect *"supposedly"* a tentative adverb doubting the truth of the assertion employed by Bugliosi. (Does he doubt his client's defensive version of the facts?)

Of the three different versions of who had possession of the dinghy on the 30th of August, which is the most probable or in Stearns vernacular which was *"more close"* to the truth ? The answer can found in her first recounting during her theft trial in June of 1975. At her first trial the primary focus was the theft of the Sea Wind not murder.   There was no need for a defense attorney to extensively coach Stearns one way or another: Only nine months had passed since the murders of the Grahams.   If Stearns were capable of telling the truth her recollection of who controlled the dinghy on the 30th of August would be found in her theft trial testimony. Years later, during murder trial preparation, once Stearns knew the drift of her defense, she gave Bugliosi two other versions finally settling on the one that best suited her defensive posture for her murder trial.

Baffle 'em With Bullshit

Bugliosi injects uncertainty and confusion into his summation, arguing the location where Stearns purportedly discovered Mac's Zodiac the morning of August 31st was Strawn Island and not Cooper Island as Stearns had testified.

"It is not clear from the chart of Palmyra where Cooper Island ends and Strawn Island begins, Although Jennifer told Shishido she and Buck found the overturned dinghy on Cooper Island, the X she placed on the chart to designate the dinghy's location is closer to the words "Strawn Island" on the chart than the words "Cooper Island." (p. 422)

We are not informed what chart Bugliosi references, it is probably the same chart found on page 531 of ATSWT. Observing this chart it is easy to see where his observation is correct, but his underlying premise is wrong. One can plainly observe Stearns placed the X on Cooper Island to locate the place where defendants allegedly discovered the dinghy.

The mere fact that words designating Strawn Island are a bit closer to Stearns' X than those designating Cooper Island is probative of nothing. Neither island name is placed on the island itself. The fact that a cartographer placed the name of the islands in one place on the chart as opposed to another was mere chance. He could have placed the names in many different places. Stearns' X designating the supposed location of her discovery of the Zodiac the

471

morning of the 30th is controlling and it is clearly found on Cooper Island and not Strawn. (p. 531) Bugliosi's mislabelling the island where the dinghy was found could have been mere confusion on his part. However, there could be another purpose in Bugliosi's confusing Strawn and Cooper Islands. In the discussion of the Benson Stipulation, Bugliosi erroneously references Strawn Island as the alleged location of the discovery of the Zodiac. (p. 398) Is he attempting to cover his own error?

There may be a third motive for to Bugliosi to intentionally confuse the issue; perhaps it is an effort to support the cross-examination of Eggers by
co-counsel Weinglass who erroneously and repeatedly referenced Strawn Island as the place of discovery of the Zodiac. (p. 348) Weinglass, by incorrectly identifying the purported location of the discovery of the overturned Zodiac, vitiates any possible damage his cross-examination of Eggers might have inflicted and to some extent undermined Bugliosi's defense of Stearns. (Apparently all this went unnoticed by Enoki.)

Bugliosi Concedes A Point

Bugliosi attempts to minimize the importance of the bon voyage dinner of August 28th, arguing that it was unimportant because it does not present any evidence of murder.

During summation he harangues:

"The point I want to italicize and underline in your mind is even if the cake-truce incident took place, all it would show was that on the evening of August 28th, the Grahams and Buck and Jennifer were in each other's presence. Since we already know that there was considerable social interaction between the Grahams and Buck and

472

Jennifer, how can this presence constitute any evidence of murder?" (p. 487)

The above argument demonstrates how little insight Bugliosi had into the murder of the Grahams. He concedes, at least for purposes of argument, Stearns and Walker rowed over to the Sea Wind in the pitch-black darkness of an equatorial night the evening of August 28, 1974 to attend a bon voyage dinner, bringing with them a cake. He submits defendant's attendance is innocent and does not constitute any evidence of murder, completely ignoring the inferences that arise from this seemingly inconsequential act. (p. 487)

It implies the Grahams invited defendants over to the Sea Wind for a bon voyage dinner the evening of August 28, 1974. The appearance of the defendants at the Sea Wind with cake in hand the evening of August 28th caused Mac to interrupt his radio conversation with Shoemaker. The fact the bon voyage dinner took place aboard the Sea Wind on the 28th indicates the Grahams had dropped their guard and were no longer fearful of defendants, thus setting them up for an easy kill the next morning. It is also indicative the Grahams thought defendants were departing for Fanning Island the next day — a fact that Mac specifically mentioned to Shoemaker during their last conversation.

Tattletale

Reading " AND THE SEA WILL TELL" one encounters an insecure braggart and semi-competent trial lawyer in the persona of Vincent Bugliosi. Throughout ATSWT he incessantly demeans witnesses and lawyers, all the while overlooking his own deficiencies. Many hardcore trial types take a dim view of these

473

"kiss and tell" books wherein a lawyer, prevailing in a contest, caps his victory with a detailed written account of his exploits. All too often these self-congratulatory tomes cause harm exposing the subject to further prosecution and obloquy.

ATSWT is a trove of legal advice coming from an experienced, but erratic trial lawyer: Some is useful and some utter nonsense: i.e. In closing he delivers a five hour brain numbing summation wherein one encounters everything but the kitchen sink. His numerous argumentative cliches include the likes of Mother Teresa, Sarah Bernhardt, H.L. Mencken, and Hitler. He foolishly advises employing the "why" question; frequently introduces evidence that undermines his client's position; disregards the Rules of Evidence; directs Stearns testimony through his incessant use of leading questions, and etc.

Contrary to Bugliosi's public image, the trial transcript reveals an easily confused and distracted attorney. He breaks down in court needing assistance of Judge King to recover and is taken to the wood shed by witness Edwin Pollock. Later, he becomes lost and confused in his imagined masterful cross-examination of Curtis Shoemaker. He loses self control during the cross-examination of Marilyn Pollock yelling at her to "cough up" a document that she turned over to the prosecution.

"And The Sea Will Tell" is an example of overreach by Bugliosi. Having prevailed in trial, he subjects Stearns to further prosecution for the murder of Mac Graham because of data he includes in his book. So obvious is her guilt that I spoke with U.S. Attorney, Elliott Enoki, about the prospect of prosecuting Stearns for his murder, going so far as to suggest he appoint me special counsel to prosecute the case. The U.S. Attorneys office declined my offer even though Stearns' guilt beyond a reasonable doubt is inadvertently laid out by Bugliosi in his best selling account of the trial. Had the U.S. Attorneys office not have been distracted with jihad and the middle east she could have been facing a second trial for the murder of Mac Graham, with the prospect of the death penalty in the event of loss which would most certainly occur.

In the early 1960's Bugliosi entertained the notion of running for the office of District Attorney for the County of Los Angeles. However his enthusiasm was dampened by the fact that he had broken into the apartment of an ex-girlfriend that had misspent $500.00 he had given her for an abortion; and in so doing committed a serious felony for which he was never charged. Moreover, the Los Angeles Times revealed he was obsessed with the delusion that a milkman had sired one of his children. No doubt these revelations weighed heavily in his decision not to proceed with a campaign to win the office of the District Attorney of Los Angeles County.

Bugliosi commences ATSWT with a peon to his mother thanking her for all her support throughout his life. While most of us could say the same or more for the patience of our parents for the role they played in out upbringing, nonetheless viewing his erratic behavior one suspects that he was afflicted with a mild case of autism, ADD, Aspergers, or the like. He is unable to deduce logical conclusions about human behavior; is addicted to eight hour summations; prepares himself and witnesses through constant repetition and rehearsal; generates dozens of legal pads and trial stratagems prepared in advance; endlessly instructs, directs, and rehearses Stearns testimony, all with the intent of being acted out in court.

Moreover, a pall hangs over his past trial achievements with revelations of his dishonesty exposed by Stearns' murder trial transcript. The lying and misrepresentation by both Bugliosi and

475

Stearns found in his book "And The Sea Will Tell" begs the question: Were there other trials wherein he abused his power in his role as prosecutor by suggesting to critical witnesses they change their testimony to assist his pursuit of victory?

FINAL ARGUMENT

Dinner at Eight

In the spring of 1975 while Walker was in jail awaiting trial for the theft of the Sea Wind and Stearns released on bail, sent a letter to Mary (Kit) Muncey, the sister of Mac. The envelope was postmarked March 11, 1975, however, defendants attempted to convince Kit it was penned in October of 1974 by placing an October notation in the upper right hand corner of the first page. On receipt Kit turned it over to the prosecuting authorities. (We are not informed as to what role, if any, the letter played in trial.) (p. 15)

Bugliosi suggests the letter was written by Walker with minor corrections by Stearns. There are clues within the letter indicating Stearns input; it was replete with her defensive lies; i.e., the alleged disappearance of the Grahams while fishing; the discovery of the Zodiac washed up on the beach; and the lie about the Iola *"crunching up"* on the reef while purportedly exiting the lagoon.

By far and away the most damaging information in the letter was the statement referencing the alleged trip to Fanning Island and that Mac had invited them *"for a bon voyage dinner the night before their scheduled departure"*. (p. 154)

The above statement in the letter written is determinative of several crucial issues; the defendants informed the Grahams they would be departing for Fanning Island the day after the bon voyage dinner, and more importantly, that the Grahams had fallen for the ruse of the defendants believing they intended to sail the Iola to Fanning Island the following day, August 29, 1974.

There is a sentence in the letter concerning a problem Stearns had to contend with as she formulated her plan to murder the Grahams:

"There is the fear of serious injury because outside help is days away..." . (p. 155)

This is not a typical concern Walker would entertain, but it was a major concern of Stearns as she plotted the death of the Grahams. Moreover, the letter contains a segment of child-talk used by Stearns' alter ego, "Little Miss Puffer", language Walker would not employ. In the letter Stearns reiterated her lie about the attempted exit of the Iola while under tow stating:

"But on the narrow passage out of the Palmyra lagoon, 'the Iola 'crunched up' on the coral head." (p. 155)

The defendant's statements in the letter combined with the comments of Shoemaker regarding his last conversation with Mac Graham on the 28th of August establish beyond a reasonable doubt the date set for the purported sailing of the Iola was Thursday, August 29th, 1974 and not the date suggested by Stearns, that of Saturday, August 31, 1974.

The letter to Kit Graham is an important evidentiary document. It was prepared at a time when neither defendant thought they would face a murder charge so there would be no need in carelessly mixing fact and fiction. (pp. 154-5)

The letter to Kit Graham also yields other interesting bits of relevant information, defendants were aware that without proper documentation it would be virtually impossible to sail about the South Pacific on the Sea Wind.

"After awhile we decided that going to Fanning wasn't a good plan because we'd be in a foreign jurisdiction and there was a question of whether the Sea Wind would be confiscated leaving us homeless and stranded." (pp. 155-6)

The letter proves there was a bon voyage dinner invitation extended by the Grahams to defendants for the 28th of August 1974. This coincides with Shoemaker's testimony at the 1975 theft trial of Stearns establishing the date of the dinner was the 28th as he recounted his last conversation with Mac which was interrupted by the arrival of defendants and clearly establishes the putative date of the defendant's voyage to Fanning Island was the 29th of August and not the 31st.

If there was any further doubt about the precise date the Iola was allegedly sailing for Fanning Island the answer was supplied by Bugliosi during his cross examination of Shoemaker when he introduces into evidence a portion of prosecutor Egger's direct examination of Shoemaker from Stearns trial for theft, June 25, 1975.

Prosecutor Eggers questioning Shoemaker about his conversation with Mac on the 28th:

"That conversation was on the 28th of August?" Inquires Eggers.

Shoemaker: *" That was on the 28th, the last time I heard from them."*

"Did you have another contact with him after that?"

"No. That the was the last time I heard from him and he said that the other boat (the Iola) *was leaving the next day."* Responds, Shoemaker. (pp. 352-3)

Thanks to Bugliosi any ambiguity about the date of the supposed departure of the Iola for Fanning Island is clarified beyond a reasonable doubt.   From the above excerpt of Stearns theft trial occurring in June of 1975 one observes Shoemaker informing the jury that Mac thought the Iola was departing Palmyra on the 29th of August 1974 and *not* on the 31st as Stearns alleged throughout her murder trial testimony.

It follows the carefully orchestrated scenario presented by Stearns about supposed events of Friday the 30th and Saturday the 31st is a complete fiction.   All the lies about the dinner invite on the morning of the 30th; the sound of the outboard going away from the Iola; the failure of the Grahams to
appear for the dinner that evening; the concocted search for the Grahams the night of the 30th; all the bilgewater about finding the "overturned dinghy on the beach;" and etc.

Stearns Asserts Ownership

Bugliosi was aware of a salvage claim filed by Stearns demanding ownership of the Sea Wind. In the game of hide and seek from justice Bugliosi thought it wiser not to bring up Stearns' salvage claim hoping that Enoki was unaware of its existence. The claim was filed two months before Stearns theft trial on May 22, 1975. (The intent of Stearns and Walker to file a salvage claim was referenced in their letter to Kit Graham written in March of 1975.) (p. 441)

The salvage claim raises several interesting points. Had defendants boldly sailed back to Hawaii demanding the Sea Wind or fair compensation for their services in returning the vessel, they may have had a fairly strong argument to rightful possession under the law of salvage.   If they could not prevail on the salvage claim in a

479

civil suit at the least they might be entitled to fair compensation for the alleged loss of the Iola and saving the Sea Wind.

Years later, facing murder charges Bugliosi is apprehensive about the salvage claim and sees it as *"particularly damaging"* if the jury did not believe the idea came from her lawyer because *"it was completely inconsistent with her testimony that she intended to return the Sea Wind to Kit Muncey after two years."* (p. 441)

There is another issue that could swing the trial against Stearns — the salvage claim goes to the heart of this issue. Bugliosi had been careful to distance Stearns from any claim of ownership of the Sea Wind. According to his game plan ownership of the Sea Wind was Walker's interest and not hers. Walker was the one who supposedly removed the figurehead, repainted the boat and painted out the name of the vessel. With the filing of the salvage claim, it is Stearns who asserts her right to ownership of the Sea Wind. We are not informed whether Walker participated in Stearns' salvage claim although he announces his intention to do so in the March 1975 letter to Kit Graham. With knowledge of the salvage claim by Stearns the jury might surmise she was as interested in ownership of the vessel as Walker, and contrary to her testimony, had no intent of returning the Sea Wind to Mac's sister. (p. 441)

The Alchemist

On arrival at Palmyra, Stearns informed the Pollocks she only had ten dollars to her name. Defendant's letter to Kit Graham claims they *found four hundred dollars* on the Sea Wind which they spent for paint and labor when the Sea Wind was on the "hard" (dry docked) getting repaired. (p. 156)

Stearns must deal in alchemy — for she still has the magical four hundred dollars in her purse when she is arrested. How does this work? The answer is obvious — Mac had nearly five thousand dollars in small bills stashed on board the Sea Wind, funds he could use as the need arose during the year or more of anticipated travel in the South Pacific. (p. 137)

After the murder of the Grahams defendants went over the Sea Wind with a fine tooth comb looking for everything and anything they could find. They discovered the cruising stash of nearly five thousand dollars. This explains why Stearns was in such a rush to get ashore on the day of her apprehension; she wanted to hide the money before she was arrested and charged with felony grand theft.

From her prior experience with petty theft arrests she knew five hundred dollars was the dividing line between grand theft, a felony, and petty theft, a misdemeanor. Unable to secrete the money she was caught red handed with cash on her person . To avoid an additional charge of grand theft she was forced to flush the bulk of the cruising cash down the toilet at the yacht club.

The authorities, caught off guard, permitted her to go into the bathroom of the Ala Wai Yacht Club without examining the contents of her purse. After engaging in numerous flushes overheard by Pollock and the FBI agents present, she was able to dispose of the bulk of Mac's cash reserve without plugging up the toilet.

Alas there was no alchemy or new math, four hundred dollars will never mysteriously become eight hundred dollars. Stearns found several thousand dollars in small bills belonging to Mac. This explains how she could pay the yard bill, purportedly for four hundred dollars (probably substantially more) and still have four hundred dollars on her person at the time of her apprehension. The fact that she controlled the money and not Walker is another indication it was Stearns who made the decisions in the relationship. (p. 156)

For Whom the Diary Was Written

Bugliosi, discussing the log of the Iola, suggested there were two possible purposes the log could serve; one would be for private use and the other that it was written to deceive future pursuers. He argues the diary was written for the eyes of Stearns only. Bugliosi reasons that if she wrote the diary for others she would have cast herself in a better light and not dwelled on commonplace matters such as reading a book or baking a cake. (p. 520)

He ignores the most vital function of the alleged diary — to confuse the authorities by fabricating a false time line and throwing out misleading clues. It served as a skeleton outline for Stearns when and if she was confronted by the law. If Stearns had truly not expected others to read her diary why did she call Walker by the name of Allen? Why did she refer to Walker in the log as "R"? Why did she not use his true name? After all what is the harm since no one would be reading her diary but herself? Why reference marijuana by the letter "m"?

Bugliosi encouraging Stearns' web of deceit argues if the purpose of the alleged diary was to mislead the reader Stearns would have been much more dramatic about the death of the Grahams; the diary would have presented a more sympathetic persona rather than the callous, sociopathic entry of September 4, 1974, boasting how fat they became while eating the Graham's stores.

"We grow fatter and fatter on ham and cheese and pancakes and turkey and all the things we hadn't had in so long." (p. 415)

Bugliosi argues:

482

"The other characteristic we could expect from her diary entries to have if she were involved in these murders and these entries were meant for other people's eyes would be a tone of considerable sensitivity. She never in a million years would have depicted herself as somewhat insensitive, as her entry about eating the Graham's food arguably comes across as being. Never in a million years."

He follows up this observation excusing Stearns' insensitivity:

"What was Jennifer supposed to do? Not eat the Graham's food? Let it rot and live off the fish in the ocean?" (p. 521)

Bugliosi greatly underestimates his client's scheming mind. Stearns' diary/log was written to substantiate her fictitious version of the facts of the murder. Changing the date of the murders and disappearance of the Grahams from the 29th of August to the 30th August was a wise stratagem on the part of Stearns. It confused her pursuers and prevented the prosecution from constructing a narrative as to how and where the murders occurred. Stearns' ruse backed up by the so called diary/log fooled all including both prosecution and defense attorneys. Bugliosi reasons if Stearns truly was a murderess she would not have included notes that most would consider an indication of selfishness and a callous personality typical of the sociopath capable of murder.

Stearns was always a step ahead of Bugliosi. His kind of thinking was exactly what she anticipated. For the same reason she included in her false log the comments concerning a sexual encounter she had with Walker, describing it in the language of the street.

"Talked awhile, then Mac and Muff bid goodnite. (sic) After which, R and I smoked some hash and had an exquisite fuck — all and all, a very fine birthday." (p. 95)

These personal comments lend authenticity and suggest an expectation of privacy re the diary. By including them she sends a strong signal to the reader — they were meant for her eyes only and not to serve as a testament for an anticipated trial. (The above comments were not read to the jury by Stearns.)

Such is the subtlety of her duplicitous mind. Stearns enjoys playing with her captors, taunting them in a cunning and devious manner. She flaunts her criminal intent in her August 5th diary entry, wherein she and Walker spent the night *"drooling and dreaming"* over their next sailboat (and the coming execution of the Grahams.) (p. 470)

Enoki knows he is being played but does not comprehend how it all went down. He reminds the jury of the *"curious diary entry"*, but is unable to place the puzzle piece for the jury. He observed the September 4th entry in the so called diary/log reflected no grief on the part of Stearns at the disappearance of the Grahams. Most would think not only was there no showing of grief, but the entry showed a callousness and indifference on her part — a trait one would associate with sociopathy. (p. 521) Stearns, in her glory, flaunts the beginnings of her plot to murder the Grahams. (p. 470)

Bugliosi counters by pointing out that on the alleged day of disappearance August 30, 1974, Stearns had written the word, *"Tragedy"*. He contends the selection of the word demonstrated a showing of grief on the part of Stearns. Bugliosi asserts that by selecting this word to describe Stearns' view of the loss of the Grahams, *"she wouldn't be likely to be the murderer, would she?"* (One supposes by the same logic had Stearns wrote *"great tragedy"* that would be even more proof of her innocence.) (p. 521)

The obvious reason there was no outpouring of grief or distress in the diary is because defendants were elated their plan had succeeded. The Grahams with their superior social status and well found ship lost the chess game. Defendants prevailed, the Sea Wind was theirs for the taking, Mac and his .357 magnum were lying at the bottom of the ocean.   Muff the love of his life, in a drug induced frenzy, was raped and torn pieces. Why should there be any showing of grief? Defendants hated the Grahams.   They were the winners of the game of life and death that played out on Palmyra the summer of 1974.

It was only a matter of time before Stearns would succeed, Mac completely underestimated his opponent, but then this too was anticipated by Stearns the mistress of murder, lies and deception.

Consciousness of Guilt

Bugliosi touts Stearns return of Joel Peters' laundry and her coming back to the Sea Wind to put the dogs below as acts indicating a consciousness of innocence. He reasons these were not the actions of a person that had recently committed murder and had something to hide. However at the time of these acts were performed by Stearns the authorities were not in hot pursuit.   Stearns had been informed the authorities were looking for her, however there was no immediate impending sense of arrest.   She felt secure in the disposal of the bodies of the Grahams — no one was going to charge her with murder, at the worst, perhaps grand theft. (p. 523)

Returning to the Sea Wind to put the dogs below deck was done to draw attention away from the Sea Wind. Nothing would cause others to take notice of a boat at anchor than to have three yapping dogs on deck barking and disturbing every dinghy passing by. The only reasonable interpretation of this act was prevent undue attention directed to the Sea Wind for fear someone might recognize her. Putting the dogs below deck indicated a desire on the part of Stearns *not* to draw attention to the Sea Wind for fear she might have more explaining to do and, contrary to Bugliosi's argument, were actions showing a consciousness of guilt not innocence.

When the Coast Guard cutter bore down on her Stearns did what any party guilty of criminal misconduct would do, she beats it on the lam. If she were innocent she would have continued casually rowing to shore. After all what is the rush? They are probably looking for someone else? Why would she, as an innocent, think they were after her? Racing to shore to avoid apprehension she abandons her skiff without securing it and mad dashes off leaving Puffer behind, taking refuge in a nearby hotel in an effort to escape. All actions consistent with a consciousness of guilt.

However as Bugliosi notes the question is guilt as to what criminal acts? It is safe to say she had several purposes in mind as she fled the Coast Guard cutter. Most immediately she was carrying the better part of Mac's cruising funds in small bills in her purse. An experienced thief she knew if caught with nearly $5,000.00 in cash she would have faced an additional felony charge of grand theft. At the same time she did not want to give up her stolen money. (p. 137)

The second reason she was fleeing is that she feared arrest for her part in the theft of the Sea Wind. It was an open and shut case. There could be little doubt conviction lay just around the corner if apprehended. Was she fleeing because she feared prosecution for the murders of the Grahams? Probably not — Mac's body lay in the

486

cabin of the Iola at rest in the deep.   It would be years, if ever, before anyone chanced upon the remains of Muff buried in the sands of Palmyra.   Stearns had prepared her diary and memorized her story, all of which exculpated her — no need for her to worry on that score.

One Step Ahead of the Chump

Bugliosi attempts to get   mileage from the fact   Stearns refused to sign on as a co-owner of the Sea Wind when Walker re-registered the Sea Wind.   (p. 497)   He is right, Stearns had "*no compelling reason*" to be involved in the re-registration of the Sea Wind. Aside from pillage and piracy Stearns had no interest in the Sea Wind. Stearns reasoned her name on the title would be one more indication she was equally guilty of theft of the Sea Wind and murder of the Grahams.

Stearns was   more interested in the murder and mayhem aspect of her relationship with Walker rather than participating in his dream of sailing.   Had they not been stopped by the Pollocks, Shoemaker, and Shishido, who knows how many other sailors might have disappeared under mysterious circumstances as these two sociopaths cruised the South Pacific stealing and plundering, weaving a web of friendship, then murder when no observers are present. (p. 523)

Bugliosi argues Walker, in several conversations, referred to the Sea Wind as "*his*" boat.   Walker would naturally refer to the Sea Wind as "his" boat because Stearns at that point in time was not interested in ownership of the boat. She made this fact very clear to Walker when he attempted to get her to sign on as owner in the new title documents.   (p. 526)

487

Bugliosi wants the jury to infer since Stearns did not want to be on the title she had no interest in the boat and therefore was not guilty of the theft of the Sea Wind. It is precisely this argument that would have been foreclosed had King permitted the jury to know Stearns had been convicted of theft of the Sea Wind in trial by jury — the issue had already be adjudicated.

Method Acting

Bugliosi as part of his summation asserts *"guilty people do not act innocent"*. True, many criminals unschooled in crime fail to act innocent in their effort to escape the heavy hand of the law. As the criminal progresses in his education he becomes more practiced in crime; learning to put on a convincing act of innocence when caught committing a criminal act. Moreover, many who are innocent of criminal wrongdoing act guilty when they are not. Authorities misinterpreting the actions of those innocent of crime often erroneously focus on a person who has nothing to do with a criminal act.

Apparently unaware of these facts Bugliosi asserts:

"For her to have been guilty of these two hellish murders and testify the way she did on the witness stand for over two days would require the performance and acting virtuosity of Sarah Bernhardt." (p. 525)

He explains her presence before the jury charged with murder was the result of falling in love *"with the wrong man"*.

To be certain Stearns possesses great acting abilities. Well schooled in crime, combined with a lifetime of lying, she was able to shift blame at every turn. Use of her little dog Puffer a picture of which is included in ATSWT, is instructive. (p. 93) Here we see one of her alter egos, little Miss Puffer in full bloom. Stearns owes her freedom as much to Puffer as she does to the zeal and skill of her lawyers. Using the innocent Puffer as a metaphor for her character she is seldom seen without him. After all, how could a person who loves a sweet little dog be a foul-mouthed liar, thief and sociopathic killer? Stearns learned long before her participation in the murder of the Grahams that Puffer's innocence was the finest of disguises. My learned colleague mistakes the sociopath's lack of guilt and absence of conscience to be an indicia of innocence rather than depravity.

Speculations

Bugliosi speculates about the evidence of burning the experts found on the remains of Muff Graham. He suggests Walker had set her remains afire in an effort to destroy her identity in line with his defense premised upon the proposition it was only Walker that was responsible for the death of the Grahams. He speculates that her remains were not entirely destroyed by the fire because Walker was pressed for time. (p. 527)

In making this argument Bugliosi ignores the testimony of Douglas Uberlaker, the forensic anthropologist, who testified *the body was burned at a later date and not at the time of the murder.* (pp. 245, 527)

Earle Partington, defense attorney representing Walker at his murder trial, asked Uberlaker this question:

"Didn't you express the opinion to me when I spoke to you at the Smithsonian that the burning (discovered in the interior of the aluminum coffin) *which caused the black spots, as opposed to the whitening, had taken place years after death?"*

"Yes, the anthropologist answered casually just before stepping down." (p. 245)

Bugliosi speculates:

"But the implications were not casual. Was it possible that someone had set fire to Muff's remains years after she was murdered? If so who? And why?" (p. 245)

In his zeal to shift blame on Walker, Bugliosi ignores his earlier speculations suggesting the burning of Muff's body happened contemporaneously with the murder, contrary to the testimony of the expert Dr. Uberlaker. (pp. 528-9)

The fact that Muff's remains were burned *"years after her death"* is a persuasive evidence that Muff's remains were buried in the sand of Strawn Island and not deposited in the lagoon. Obviously had they been at the bottom of the lagoon in one hundred and forty feet of water it would have been impossible to retrieve and set fire to them.

Walker had doubts about the efficacy of burying Muff's remains on Strawn Island fearful they could surface in the relatively shallow grave. This fear proved well founded when in 1981 Muff's remains were discovered by Sharon Jordan. (Bugliosi suggests fear of discovery of the remains of Muff was one of the motivating factors causing Walker to escape from McNeil Island penitentiary in Washington.) (p. 168) Walker's fear may explain Musick's trips to Palmyra in 1977. It is possible one of the purposes of his voyage was to ascertain the condition of the coffin and the likelihood it would remain buried. Perhaps it was Musick who attempted to destroy her remains by setting fire to them.

Jekyll or Hyde

Bugliosi never quite comprehends the violent nature of one of Stearns' alter egos. He speaks at length about the burning of Muff's skull by torch assuming that it was Walker who was the instigator of this torture. While Walker wanted to sexually attack Muff and have his way with her, he did not harbor the pent up fury that possessed Stearns. In all likelihood it was Stearns who savagely attacked Muff with the torch not Walker. Walker, unable to tolerate the screams of Muff probably ended her life by a bullet to the head. Stearns would have continued on with her macabre sport until there was no response from Muff's bloodied and moribund corpse.

Most horrific were the findings of Uberlaker and Stephens concerning the *"calcination"* above the left eye of Muff's skull. Both experts agreed the *"calcination was a result of localized burning resulting from extreme heat being applied to the bone."* Stephens, the coroner, called it a *"localized burn of high intensity"*. Both agreed *"the acetylene torch could have been the burning agent"*. (p. 526)

One finds in these observations and conclusions a brief window into the horrendous last moments of Muff Graham. Was the torch applied solely to the skull of Muff or did Stearns commence her attack by applying the torch to the left eye of Muff and only after having inflicted unbelievable pain in the process of burning out her eye then continuing on over the skull? If maximum pain was Stearns' purpose why would she be satisfied in merely applying the white hot torch to Muff's skull? If she first applied the flame to the eye of Muff there would be no indication of this other than the calcination found *above* the eye socket as she drew the flame over and above the eye. Thus, we find the result of the attack commencing on Muff's left eye first observable as calcination over the left eye as the white hot torch moved away from the eye and onto her skull.

Bucky the Pirate Man

There is a recurring theme that surfaces in ATSWT regarding pirate fantasies emanating from Walker. Ingman, a cell-mate of Walker at McNeil Island Federal Prison recalled a story wherein Walker claimed he murdered the Grahams by forcing them to " *walk the plank"* after chumming the lagoon to attract sharks. (pp. 204-5)

Williams, another inmate pal from prison, also testified re Walker's pirate fantasies. Again, it was a walking the plank episode. However, this time Walker and Stearns *dressed as pirates,* smoking dope, forced the couple to walk the plank.

It is highly unlikely the Grahams met their end as described in either of these versions of Walker's pirate fantasy. Notably, both versions demonstrate a childish fascination that obsessed Walker linking him to the crime scene. (p. 206)

Why would any ordinary sailor burn prescription glasses, common sunglasses, prescription bottles with no names, cotton material, (probably remnants of a bloody shirt), or a pirate's mask in a burn pit located near the Sea Wind if not in an effort to hide a crime? One might reasonably suspect the so-called fright wig that survived the fire was once attached to a pirate mask. There was no showing any sailing vessel had visited Palmyra during the intervening two months that passed from the day of the murder of the Grahams …this was the height of the typhoon season in the South Pacific. Under the circumstances one might reasonably suspect the destruction and attempted destruction of these items had something to do with the murders. (Vol. 11, p.1654)

Is there proof beyond a reasonable doubt the residue found by Eggers in the ashes of the burn pit shortly after the murder of the Grahams was connected to their deaths? No, the proof does not rise to this level, but all evidence indicates the fire was intended to dispose of items of clothing and paraphernalia one might reasonably associate with the murders. Walker had a fixation with pirate phantasies. Since his childhood he read books about pirates. He thought the pirate's life was for him — departing Hawaii for Palmyra aboard the Iola offered his first real opportunity to act out these juvenile dreams. To this end he may have brought with him a pirate's mask with attached fiberglass wig.

Echoes of the pirate theme are very common among cruising sailors. Catalina Island, in Southern California has a raucous yearly celebration at Two Harbors, where sailors dressed as pirates, water balloons for cannon-shot, and plenty of rum, are mixed for a riotous weekend.

In all likelihood Walker and Stearns talked at length about the possible pirate scenario long before departing Hawaii for Palmyra. To this end, Walker probably made preparations to act out childhood phantasies with encouragement, direction and participation from Stearns.

Taxidermy

During Lorraine Wollen's visit to the Sea Wind while defendants were in Pokai Bay, on their return from Palmyra, she noticed pictures of Mac and Muff on a bulkhead and asked why they were there. Stearns told Wollen the pictures were still up was because she *"never wanted to change anything about the boat. I wanted to keep it just the way they had it."* (p. 434)

The jury did not catch the sardonic nature of this statement which was made by Stearns immediately following her testimony Walker had removed the name of the Sea Wind while they were still at Palmyra. What could be a greater change for a sailing vessel than to change it's name? Her comment about *keeping the boat as it was* is another of her many lies. If she was truly of this belief, why did they remove the name of the boat, change the color of the trim, remove the figurehead on the bow? (p. 432)

There is a much darker explanation why the pictures of Mac and Muff remained on the bulkhead. In days of old when successful combatants returned from the battle it was not unusual for them to keep the heads of their foes mounted on a stake and displayed for all to see. This was a tradition in England as late as the reign of Henry VIII. Even today a visit to a hunting lodge reveals animal heads stuffed and displayed as part of the lodge decor, animals that had lost their life to a "superior foe".

While our killers could not very well display the heads of the Grahams on a pike, they could keep the photos posted on the bulkhead to remind themselves of their glorious victory over the hated Grahams. No doubt defendants imbibing Muff's Graham's wine drank many a toast to the trophy photos obscenely boasting about how they taught the Grahams a lesson, all the while enjoying their dark secrets, reliving the slaughter of the Grahams and, in this twisted way, flaunt their foul deeds in plain sight for all to see. (pp. 433-34)

There is another instance of "trophy" presentation found in the book. Defendants took several photos of the Iola under full canvas, scuttled and sinking. The photo of the sinking Iola had dual purpose;

it commemorated the scuttling of the Iola and at the same time a mere glance at it gave defendants a tinge of pleasure knowing Mac's body was aboard. It was their dirty little secret hiding in plain sight.

(One wonders the number of times during her murder trial, Stearns smirking privately, thought herself superior — not only to judge and jury, but even her own counsel — what fools she thought....)

Another secret in capturing the stricken Iola on her way to the bottom: at the very instant the photos were taken, Muff knowing that she had lost Mac and was doomed, lay weeping on the cabin floor of the Sea Wind bound and gagged. No doubt she was bombarded by defendants's scathing remarks about Mac as the Iola went to the her watery grave. Muff knew her end was going to be a horror beyond comprehension. Every time defendants looked at the picture of the stricken Iola on her way to the bottom they secretly relieved the moment, relishing Muff's plight and their victory. (pp. 433-35)

If one were possessed of sailor's superstitions, after the brutal attack on the Grahams and the malicious destruction of the Iola, a vessel that did her all for the murderous duo, Stearns and Walker might be cursed. Walker led an extremely unhappy existence confined for many years, ejected from prison
only because he was dying of cancer and the prison system did not want to be burdened with caring for him in his final days. As for Stearns, Bugliosi suggests she went on to live a successful life working for a telecomm company owned by a relative. Others suggest her present circumstances are not all that pleasant. Though she avoided a death sentence, after her Palmyra experience, it is highly unlikely she would tempt fate and venture to sea in a small boat.

Out of His League

Enoki had numerous documents available to impeach the murder trial testimony of Stearns. Aside from the numerous interviews Stearns gave to the press another rich source were the 1975 transcripts of the theft trials of Walker and Stearns. Walker's theft trial transcript was a valuable instrument of impeachment undermining Stearns defense. An example can be found in Walker's assertion contrary to Stearns' testimony that on the 30th of August he was at work on the Iola repairing the forward hatch. (Vol. 10, p. 1455)

Walker ventured far from the agreed upon script during his 1975 theft trial. To his way of thinking the deviation from the agreed upon script was of no importance. Stearns' theft trial had preceded his by several months — she had already been found guilty. He was attempting to save himself from an additional prison time and thought little harm could come from departing from the agreed upon script. His theft trial testimony sharply conflicted with Stearns murder trial testimony wherein she recalled the supposed events of August 30, 1974 with Walker allegedly wandering about all day in pursuit of his elusive bath. Neither account was believable, regardless each witness impeached the testimony of the other. The theft transcripts were a treasure trove of conflicting testimony, yet it was Bugliosi who mistakenly introduced into Stearns murder trial testimony from Walker that refuted her account of their alleged activities on August 30th, not Enoki.

During summation Bugliosi shamelessly ridiculed Enoki:

"I can just hear Mr. Enoki now in his rebuttal. 'Mr Bugliosi has an explanation for everything Jennifer Jenkins did, and this just

isn't realistic.' He'll probably say something like that. (I knew the jury would probably be thinking the same precise thing.)"

"I turned towards the prosecution's table."

"Are you going to say that Elliot? I asked playfully. The pleasant faced prosecutor did not return my smile and, of course said nothing — 'You're not going to tell me?' I paused in a brief moment of levity." (p. 515)

(One wonders about Bugliosi's judgment in relating this incident to his readers as most would see his actions as demeaning, petty and unprofessional. Any seasoned trial lawyer would issue a strong rebuke for such a trespass! This is an example of an unprofessional "cheap shot" that earned Bugliosi the derisive moniker "the Bug" among many of his fellow trial lawyers in Los Angeles. Oddly, Bugliosi does not seem to understand that the jury might find his comment inappropriate. Nor does he appreciate the fact that most readers of ATSWT might also draw the same conclusion!)

Future Prospects

Succeeding in their first murderous act of piracy it is difficult to predict how defendant's activities might have played out in the future. If Walker and Stearns had not been stopped by Shoemaker, the Pollocks and Shishido, one wonders how many others would have died as defendants plied the South Pacific? Would they refine their technique as they meandered about preying on isolated boaters as the opportunity and need arose? Sailors from hell....a demon ship...a convincing pretense of friendship; all the while looking for vulnerabilities of the potential prey, once discovered, a quick death, followed by theft and scuttling. Any isolated trusting couple could

497

have been their next target. Under the guise of friendship defendants could assess the target, murder the crew, steal what is useful and sink the victim's boat in several thousand feet of water in an unknown location. The likelihood of arrest would be slim. Most island nations, including those in the Caribbean, have limited jurisdiction and only a modest understanding of investigative procedures. With boat and crew in a thousand fathoms who would ever know?

There is another possible scenario. Both defendants were incompetent sailors to the extreme. Sailing a boat the likes of the Sea Wind with numerous complex systems aboard requires experience and training. Neither defendant was capable of navigation. The inability to operate many of these systems or repair them when they needed maintenance would put them at risk. There is a considerable probability the Sea Wind, with defendants aboard, would end up on a reef a thousand miles from nowhere. Sooner or later supplies would run out (if they survived the destruction of the boat) and they would be at the mercy of forces of nature.

Poison

Several times in ATSWT there is the mention of substantial amounts of poison stored in one of the sheds on Palmyra. (p. 80) The poison is identified as warfarin commonly used to thin blood and control rats. It had been mixed with cornmeal and made into cubes.

During the murder trial of Walker, Tom Wolfe of the Toloa testified that the day before his departure the 17th of August the boxes of rat poison he had observed in the shed were missing. (pp. 232-3) Shortly after his testimony Bugliosi overheard various trial spectators discussing Wolfe's testimony...they were speculating

Walker had put poison in the cake which defendants gave to the Grahams during the bon voyage dinner of the 28th.

Alarmed that the jury might come to the same conclusion Bugliosi filed a Motion in Limine to prohibit the prosecution from mentioning the poison or that it was missing on the 17th of August. Judge King, the self-appointed role as protector of Stearns, granted the motion. (p. 115)

The suppression of reference to the missing rat poison unfairly prejudiced the prosecution — it may have been a reasonable inference that the disappearance of the poison was somehow related to the death of the Grahams.

However, it is unlikely that defendants employed poison as a means of doing away with the Grahams. Warfarin is slow acting, once the Grahams had been poisoned. it would not take long for Mac to conclude who was to blame. He would have hunted down defendants and executed both of them before dying himself.

The more probable explanation for the missing rat poison might be found in the defendant's fear that a disgruntled sailor, attacked by the pit bull, might seek revenge and poison their dogs. In all probability it was the defendants who did away with the poison either by burying it at a deserted place on the island or dumping it into the ocean. (pp. 115, 235-6)

The Contrivance

From time to time during trial there exists vital testimony supporting one position or the other, yet it is problematic to raise the issue on direct examination because it may appear to be contrived. Bugliosi asserts Walker's tale of being invited aboard the Sea Wind the evening of the August 30, 1974 must to have been a subterfuge

499

created by Walker because the table was supposedly set with Stearns' favorite drink, apricot brandy. Bugliosi concedes it is not a common liqueur, arguing she never informed the Grahams of this uncommon preference, leaving one to infer Stearns is telling the truth about the invitation.

The juror is faced with a question — the existence, or non-existence of the table allegedly set with apricot brandy. There is no corroborative testimony establishing this supposed fact. In all probability the apricot brandy story was a figment of Stearns imagination conjured to assist her defense and sell her "nibbles" testimony to the jury shifting blame for the murder of the Grahams to Walker. (p. 503)

Bugliosi appreciates the delicate nature of bringing up the issue during direct examination of his client. In an aside, he informs the reader (and budding trial lawyers) of the proper method to obtain maximum impact upon the jury when such situations arise.

"I purposefully didn't bring up the apricot brandy. It was evidence favorable to my prosecution of Buck, but I feared the jury might think it sounded contrived so that Jennifer could point the finger at her former lover. It was one of those two-edged swords peculiar to the trial of a lawsuit. If it somehow came out on cross-examination, of course, the suspicion of contrivance would be substantially reduced, and this is what I was hoping for." (p. 420)

The above comment presents a solution to a testimonial problem lawyers face every day in court. Anticipating cross-examination in situations such as that described above it is more strategic for counsel to refrain from asking the pertinent question of his client on direct examination allowing the unknowing opposition to broach the subject. When opposing counsel on cross-examination asks the anticipated question, the contrived response of the defendant appears to the jury to be less rehearsed and has the "ring of truth" to it. The testimony of the witness appears to be spontaneous and not a ploy planned by an adroit attorney.   After all...the testimony was brought out by the opposing attorney — how could it possible be contrived?   In the event that opposing counsel fails to trigger the testimony, counsel for the testifying witness has a second bite at the apple and can still elicit the needed information by re-opening direct examination.

One can observe Bugliosi's trap succeeds in that this is exactly what occurred when prosecutor Schroeder tumbles into the trap during cross-examination of Stearns:

"What did you do when you went on board the boat?"

Stearns, after hours of rehearsal unloads on Schroeder:

"Well, we went below and we saw this table set out with certain things and it was apricot brandy and vodka and dry roasted peanuts and olives, and a box of cookies and they had told — Buck had said that they had told him that
we could have the cookies because they didn't want them and they were going to throw them out, so I poured myself a small glass of apricot brandy and Buck poured himself a small glass of vodka and we took the box of cookies and we went up on deck."   (Vol. 8, p. 1311)

Successful though it was even so, there is a trifle amiss in her testimony. What host would serve guests food they intended to throw away, and worse, inform the guests they intended to throw the food out?   Most would not consider serving any welcomed guest stale cookies let alone tell them of their intent to throw them away. Stearns always "gilds the lily" and in so doing exposes herself as the liar she is.

Few would dispute the allegation of apricot brandy aboard the Iola, was an assist in selling Stearns fictitious defense to the jury — that Walker was the heavy and she knew nothing about his depraved acts. The alleged appearance of apricot brandy sitting on the table clues the jury that it was Walker who engineered the death of the Grahams and not Stearns because only Walker was privy to the fact that Stearns was fond of apricot brandy. (p. 503)

By introducing the spurious tale of the table set with the apricot brandy in response to questioning from the prosecution during cross-examination Stearns' testimony had much greater weight than if she introduced the information in response to a question from Bugliosi. Had she offered the testimony in response to a question by Bugliosi it would have appeared to be an obvious contrivance, which of course, it was.

Atonement and Absolution

In the defendant's letter to Kit Graham of March 1975, the reader is treated to another effort at manipulation and perhaps something more.

Walker writes:

"I know this letter must be a sensitive experience for you, and I know I've stated things badly. I seem to have great difficulty finding an end and a beginning, and in determining appropriate language for in between. I apologize for my lack, but we want and very much need your understanding." (p. 156)

What is Walker trying to say? What does he seek? We know that Walker had brutally murdered Mac Graham. It was a foul deed, but pales in comparison to the torture/murder and dismemberment of Muff. Walker, far weaker psychologically than Stearns, was conned into participating in this unspeakable, psychopathic w. Stearns led the way engaging in the most gruesome acts against Muff.

One might paraphrase the above paragraph. *"I know this letter must be a sensitive experience for you."*   (Meaning the letter is a sensitive experience for Walker.)   *"and I know I've stated things badly,"*   (and I know I've done bad things).   Walker, is tacitly admitting he killed Mac and was an accomplice to Stearns in the murder of Muff.

Then we have the understatement of the book:

"I seem to have great difficulty finding an end and a beginning, and in determining appropriate language for in between."

Since the murders Walker cannot make sense of his life. He needs help, but cannot find the words.   His life is over.... but he cannot verbalize this fact. Words fail him. Words are inadequate — since his involvement in these hellish deeds he is struck dumb.

Somehow he wants to atone, but doesn't know what it means or how it could be done.   He is unable to come to grip with his actions, the voyage to Palmyra, planning the deaths of the Grahams and the *"in between"* — the execution of Mac and torture/murder of Muff.   In the end he fears it is his fate to spend the rest of his life in jail even though murder is not presently the charge.   Sooner or later judgment will come. He knows he is cursed and, unlike Stearns, is concerned about his fate.

Words continue to fail Walker, he writes:

"I apologize for my lack, but we want and very much need an understanding."

"I apologize for my lack..." Lack of what? Candor? He can go no further.   The trauma is too great. He knows he is the fall guy, but cannot escape his fate.   It is too late.   He has been involved in

terrible acts of cruelty and witnessed far more heinous deeds on the part of Stearns as she ripped into her helpless victim with a blow torch.   He cannot rewrite his fate.   He needs to atone — he needs forgiveness, but his deeds are so demonic and bloodstained he cannot voice them.   He cannot ask for forgiveness which is conditioned on admitting his misdeeds.   He is trapped, unable to confess his crimes he cannot atone or be granted absolution.\

If one were to look for a Dostoevskian character in this drama it would be Walker, not Stearns.   Walker was haunted all his life by the horror of his deeds on Palmyra.   It was probably a factor in his death by cancer.   He was never be able to throw off the self-imposed yoke.   Unlike Stearns,   feels guilt and a terrible sense of shame which haunted him to his grave.

Walker is unable to confess his crimes for another reason, he has a child: To publicly confess he was involved in the slaying of the Grahams would alert all the world to his deeds. His daughter would know her father participated in   the monstrous murders of the Grahams. He fears her judgment. So long as he does not admit to the crime she can think he was wrongly convicted.   His acts, if confessed to the world, would bring great shame upon his offspring and his daughter would suffer accordingly.   He was concerned about not exposing her to the opprobrium that would follow.

Stearns, on the other hand, could horribly torture Muff Graham; literally bathe in her blood and a moment later   live an untroubled guilt free existence.   She is a true homicidal sociopath. She too is haunted — not by her heinous acts, but by the fear that she will be caught and punished.

(She must have been horrified to read Bugliosi's book and the account of her murder trial.   Seeing her actions laid out in ATSWT for all to study had to be the source of great distress,   fearing someday an investigator, reviewing the facts, might piece together what truly transpired.)

Her sociopathy allays all guilt. There is always a rationalization no matter how inane. It is never her fault, admitting to obvious lies only when it serves her purpose or she is backed into a corner. She leads an untroubled existence. With the true sociopath empathy, guilt, or weight of conscience does not exist.

FLOTSAM AND JETSAM

Recovering the Remains of Mac Graham

As Bugliosi and Weinglass prepared for trial they made a second trip to Palmyra Island with the intent of looking for the supposed second aluminum container holding Mac's remains. Walker allegedly informed his attorney he had no objection to their search stating:

"Go ahead and search. You'll never find him." (p. 563)

Walker makes this statement secure in the knowledge the last time he saw Mac's body it was locked in the cabin of the scuttled Iola as she settled into several thousand feet of water a few miles south, south-west of the island of Palmyra.

Defendants, seeking a souvenir of their victory over the Grahams, took several pictures of the Iola as she was on her way into the depths. In one of the photos Palmyra Island is observable in the distance. Using this photo as a point of reference it would not be too difficult to ascertain the approximate location where the Iola went down. With prevailing southeasterly winds, and the approximate distance from shore, one could narrow the search area down to a few square miles. While the bottom appears to be uneven it is possible

505

the Iola sits on an abyssal plain. Once located it may be possible to send down a deep-sea submarine to observe the wreck and explore.

Even without a photograph it would probably be fairly easy to find the location of the Iola given the limitations on time facing the defendants the morning of the executions. They had to get rid of the Iola as soon as possible....there was always the chance another vessel would wander by. No doubt they motored out of the channel with the Iola in tow heading in a southwesterly direction, A mile or two off shore Stearns cast the Iola free of the Sea Wind. Walker aboard the Iola set her sails for the last time. Having done so, he went below and opened a sea-cock. As incoming sea water flooded her bilge he drew the Zodiac abreast, lowered himself aboard and sped back to the Sea Wind, arriving in time to see the Iola, carrying the body of Mac Graham slowly disappear into the sea.

At this late date should anyone attempt to find the Iola is all probability there would be no physical remains of Mac, perhaps a baseball cap, belt or belt-buckle, an old shoe, his 357 still in it's holster, and the ill-fated portable generator still on the cabin sole.

Just Supposing

Reading ATSWT I found myself continuously rooting for Muff and chide Mac for his hubris and trust in weaponry as the answer to security. Sooner or later he would slip up. The odds are always on the side of the aggressor. One way or another Stearns and Walker would prevail. But let us suppose for a moment Muff got the drop on Stearns aboard the Sea Wind the morning of the 29th.

As Stearns and Muff tumbled down the companionway of the Sea Wind, Muff obtained her derringer hidden in the galley and brought it to bear, on Stearns. One might imagine the following scenario.

Muff, sweating with exertion and fear, levels her derringer at Stearns. She orders her to slowly clasp her hands together and rest them on the top of her head, explaining the derringer has a special hair trigger that can go off with the slightest jar. She orders Stearns to turn around and face the companionway. With Stearns ahead of her the two proceed up the companionway.

Stearns, hearing Walker board the Sea Wind, yells out *"she has a gun!"* Walker realizing there is something wrong looks down into the saloon and sizes up the situation, Having just murdered Mac he informs Muff that Mac was injured while lifting the heavy generator. According to Walker, Mac's leg is broken and he is unable to move Mac aboard the Zodiac without help.

Muff, observing the panic in Walkers demeanor, fears Mac is dead, however she is conflicted. Holding her pistol to the back of Stearns head, with Stearns between herself and Walker, she orders him off the boat demanding he jump into the water and swim ashore. Once ashore he is ordered to position himself a hundred yards to the west on the sea plane ramp where Muff can see him. When he has reached the sea plane ramp and is in sight she agrees to release Stearns. She warns Walker before he departs if she sees either of the two after the release of Stearns she will kill them with the 30.06 rifle on board the Sea Wind.

While Walker is moving to the designated position on the shore, with the pistol at the back of Stearns head Muff explains that if Stearns wishes to survive the next minute or two of her life she must move slowly and carefully follow her instructions. Explaining any sudden movement will cause her to fire the derringer. Moving in tandem up the companionway, they slowly reach the cockpit where

507

they sit, Stearns back towards Muff, hands with fingers intertwined clasped on her head, awaiting Walker's appearance on the sea plane ramp in the distance.

With Walker's appearance on the ramp Muff releases Stearns who is free to join Walker. Before release Muff once again reiterates her warning that should she see either of them along the shore she will use the rifle to kill them. With that Stearns jumps overboard swims ashore and scurries off to join Walker. Muff dashes below grabbing the rifle and a box of ammunition.

Experienced with firearms Muff knows she has a great advantage over defendants with the rifle. Firing off-hand with the rifle she can easily hit a target the size of a human being between one hundred and one hundred and fifty yards distant. Walker's twenty-two caliber pistol is no match for the 30.06 rifle. Moreover, even if Walker has Mac's .357 the likelihood of accuracy at a distance greater than twenty-five yards is remote.

With Stearns ashore she quickly starts the powerful diesel engine. Leaving it in idle, she cuts the shore lines. With hard dinghy secured, keeping a watchful eye out for defendants, she goes forward and raises the anchor. With the anchor out of the water, but not fully aboard, she dashes back to the wheel, places the transmission in gear, and slowly motors out in the lagoon to retrieve the Zodiac.

Out of effective pistol range, throttling back, she glides up to the Zodiac. With the boat hook she picks up the painter of the dinghy and ties it to the Sea Wind. With both dinghies in tow she heads for the opposite side of the lagoon and drops the anchor in twenty feet of water off Kalua Islet.

Believing her beloved Mac is dead, nonetheless she must return to the Iola to see for herself. She cannot approach the Iola while aboard the Sea Wind. It would require too much concentration

— she must keep a watchful eye out for defendants as the Iola is only fifty feet from shore secured to a dolphin. Muff picks up the rifle and cartridges, boards the hard dinghy and commences rowing to the Iola. (She selected the hard dinghy fearing the rubber dinghy is too fragile and easily sunk with a shot or two from Walker's pistol.)

One hundred yards distant from the Iola she spins the dinghy about and commences rowing facing the Iola, pushing the oars rather than pulling on them. Spotting defendants on the shore she pauses and fires a warning shot with her rifle which causes them to hastily retreat back into the jungle.

Muff securing the dinghy to the starboard bow of the Iola, places her rifle on board and clambers over the rail. Peering into the cabin through the forward hatch she sees Mac's body lying below in a pool of blood. He is obviously dead his .357 still in it's holster. In shock she lowers herself into the cabin, steps over the body of her slain husband, climbs the companionway and enters the cockpit.

She again fires several shots into the jungle to scare off defendants, thereafter hastily moves aft severing the line securing the stern of the Iola to shore. Slowly the Iola drifts away from shore in response to the current running through the lagoon. Now offshore approximately 100 feet, parallel to shore, with the bow still secured to the dolphins she opens the sea-cocks and an intake valve allowing salt water to flood the cabin. With sea water flowing into the hull she knows within a short time the vessel will be on the bottom. Using the hull as cover she climbs over the starboard rail with her rifle and enters her dinghy.

Rowing back to the Sea Wind she secures both dinghies, climbs aboard the Sea Wind and starts the diesel engine. Placing the transmission in neutral, going forward she weighs anchor.

509

Returning to the wheel she points the Sea Wind towards the channel and open sea.

Until she saw with her own eyes that Mac was dead there was always the remote possibility Walker was telling the truth about Mac's injury. If she shot Stearns to death on-board the Iola and Mac was alive and injured what would happen then?

At the time of Walker's appearance aboard the Sea Wind she did not know if he was armed with Mac's 357. If so, had she shot Stearns immediately she would have no leverage over him. By forcing Walker down the shore to appear in plain sight one hundred yards distant out of pistol range, she had time to obtain the rifle. With the extended range of the rifle and its superior accuracy she could control the situation.

Tears flowing, she decides to motor to Washington Island anchor off shore and request help. It is fairly close-by, approximately a hundred miles to the south-east.

Alas this is nothing but a flight of fancy. Muff did not prevail in her death struggle with Stearns the morning of August 29th, 1974. Had she done so her survival would still have been very precarious as the hypothetical scenario points out. All too often one finds a couple sailing about with a division of labor such as set up by the Grahams. Most of the "sailing" duties are left to the male with the first mate involved in what one might call domestic duties. This is all well and good so long as no emergency arises. If Muff was not capable of helming the Sea Wind or proficient with firearms getting the drop on Stearns would serve little purpose but to delay her doom.

Truth is that the advantage is always with the aggressor. The victim usually does not know he is the object of attention. Nor does he know exactly when an attack will occur. No matter how well armed he is whoever gets off the first accurate shot prevails.

CONCLUSION

If ever there were two bozos attempting to plan a murder, it was these two homicidal clowns resembling the "Three Stooges" in the execution of their crime. They nearly committed suicide sailing to Palmyra Island in a small derelict sailboat with three dogs, inadequate food and water with Stearns, a numbskull with no knowledge of navigation, at the helm. (How they avoided the submerged sixteen kilometer Kingman Reef guarding the northern approach to Palmyra Island was a matter of luck.)

With the departure of Wolfe and Sanders aboard the Toloa on the 17th of August the coast was clear. When her co-conspirator Richard Musick contacted Shoemaker with information advising Stearns they would not be coming to Palmyra until late fall, Stearns put her heinous scheme into action giving away her valuable portable generator to Mac for a token $50.00.

On return to Hawaii aboard the Sea Wind they hauled out at the Tuna Packers yard to replace a portion of the plank damaged by the bullets from Muff's derringer. While on the hard they repainted the hull its original white and changed the color of the trim to lavender hoping to disguise her identity. In an incredibly imbecilic move they failed to paint her new name and hailing port on the stern of the vessel. Compounding their stupidity, they sailed into the busiest harbor in Hawaii where they were almost immediately identified by Edwin Pollock, who promptly contacted the Coast Guard.

Exposing the murderous deeds of the defendants, the Pollocks had their lives threatened necessitating armed guards and

511

nearly lost their jobs as teachers merely because they performed their civic duties for in testifying at the four trials that followed.

Defendants were accompanied in this goofy, bloody, criminal enterprise, by their erstwhile lying and bumbling co-conspirators the Musick brothers and Walker's perjurious pal Larry Seibert. Add to this mise-en-scene a gullible judge, an inept prosecutorial team, a highly motivated defense attorney, and
one ends up with an obviously guilty, compulsive liar and sociopathic murderess, escaping punishment.

A writer of dime novel, crime fiction, could not make up this crap! As Bugliosi himself might exclaim had he been prosecuting...*Unfucking, believable!* (p. 547)

After Thoughts

Reading ATSWT several years ago I was struck by Stearns numerous assertions that did not ring true.   She claimed to master the art of navigation by means of a sextant despite numerous inaccuracies while describing her method; her inability to engage in simple addition demonstrated in her diary; her inability to apply her new found skill of navigation upon discovery of Palmyra, and the impossibly long return voyage to Hawaii.   The most glaring of clues provided by Bugliosi was the sale of the portable generator to Mac for the paltry sum of $50.00.

Stearns' so-called log/diary notes made no sense whatsoever; the bogus marijuana grow-op with the Musicks; the absurd notion defendants could sail the crippled Iola to Fanning Island on a mission of resupply with a few dollars in their pocket. And, even more zany, the idea the Iola, a derelict, could make a return voyage to Hawaii in her decrepit state.

I shared some of my thoughts with prosecutor Enoki, assuring him that if he appointed me special counsel I could guarantee a conviction of Stearns in the murder of Mac Graham. However, he did not wish to revisit the worst defeat in his career and rejected the offer.

The FBI had been soundly drubbed by Bugliosi and had no interest in a reprise. Many of the key witnesses have died, Judge King died a few years ago, Walker in 2010 and Curtis Shoemaker in 2012. These days there are more important fish to fry with jihad and 9/11 and Trump paralyzing the nation. As for Stearns, she probably has the trappings of success, and has moved on as well. Like her murderous counterpart, Karla Holmolka (*with three children*) now living in Quebec, Canada under an assumed name, Stearns sleeps peacefully and dreams untroubled dreams.

Walker carried the terrible burden of his role in the murder of the Grahams throughout his life. Sorry that he had made so many bad choices, even more sorry he had been caught. Suffering from a lifetime of incarceration hating every moment yet unable to finger Stearns, a prerequisite of which would require a full confession of his role in the murders of the Grahams. Not wishing to foist this burden off on his daughter he kept his mouth shut.

Most shocking is the fact that Vincent Bugliosi lied and mislead his readers about his trial skills. He had the chutzpah to fabricate his supposed devastating cross examination of the Pollocks, Shoemaker, Shishido and other witnesses, With the assistance of Judge King he disregarded the Evidence Code. Time and again he inadvertently introduced evidence that impeached Stearns. In summation employing the lie of the half truth, he intentionally misquotes witness after witness in an effort to gain advantage. Most grievously, his encouraging Stearns to fabricate false testimony regarding her conversation re Bruce Benson knowing it to be false, is inexcusable and in most jurisdictions, cause for disbarment and imprisonment.

While Bugliosi brags about his supposed performance in ATSWT much of his supposed skills exist only in his mind, however without my going to the time and expense of digging through the archives, the reader would never know the truth of these matters.

Pretty much all there is to the story.   Bugliosi cashed in by writing a New York Times best seller with the assistance of Bruce Henderson. Later his book was made into a TV movie. Walker died of cancer a few years back. As for Stearns she struggles on encased in a prison of her own making every night haunted by the prospect of prosecution for the murder of Mac Graham and living in fear of the vision of Muff Graham in her final tortured moments.

"So we beat on, boats against the current, borne ceaselessly back into the past."

"The Great Gatsby" —   F. Scott Fitzgerald

Made in the USA
Middletown, DE
13 July 2019